EUROPEAN RELIGION IN THE AGE OF GREAT CITIES 1830–1930

Nineteenth-century Europe saw a spectacular growth in the size and number of cities, and the proportion of the population living in urban areas. Metropolitan giants like London, Paris, Berlin and St Petersburg towered above the greatest cities of any earlier epoch. They also exerted an increasingly powerful cultural influence, shaping life even in remote rural areas. Many contemporaries feared (and some hoped) that this social revolution would bring about equally dramatic changes in religious life. Established churches, with deep roots in the pre-industrial era, struggled to build new churches, recruit more clergy and meet new pastoral needs. Nonconformists, Jews and secularists often saw these cities as places of freedom and opportunity.

This highly readable book, written by a team of specialists from Britain, Ireland, Germany and North America, explores every level of urban religious life in this age of great cities.

CHRISTIANITY AND SOCIETY IN THE MODERN WORLD

General editors: Hugh McLeod and Bob Scribner

EUROPEAN RELIGION IN THE AGE OF GREAT CITIES 1830–1930

Edited by Hugh McLeod

London and New York

First published 1995
by Routledge
11 New Fetter Lane, London EC4P 4EE

Simultaneously published in the USA and Canada
by Routledge
29 West 35th Street, New York NY 10001

Typeset in Garamond by
Florencetype Ltd, Stoodleigh, Devon

Printed and bound in Great Britain by
TJ Press Ltd, Padstow, Cornwall

British Library Cataloguing in Publication Data
A catalogue record for this book is available from the British Library.

Library of Congress Cataloging in Publication Data
European religion in the age of great cities, 1830–1930/edited by Hugh
McLeod.
p. cm. – (Christianity and society in the modern world)
Includes bibliographical references and index.
1. Christianity–Europe–19th century. 2. Christianity–Europe–20th
century. 3. City churches–Europe–History–19th century. 4. City
churches–Europe–History–20th century. 5. Cities and
towns–Europe–Religious aspects–Christianity.
I. McLeod, Hugh. II. Series.
BR735.E89 1994
274'.081'091732–dc20   94-9724
ISBN 0–415–09522–0

CONTENTS

CONTENTS

Part II Urban religious cultures

Part III The religious consequences of urbanization

NOTES ON CONTRIBUTORS

Clyde Binfield is a Reader in History at the University of Sheffield and was Chairman of the Editorial Board for *History of Sheffield*, 3 vols, Sheffield, 1993. Other books include *So Down to Prayers: Studies in English Nonconformity*, London, 1977.

Callum G. Brown is Senior Lecturer in History at the University of Strathclyde. His publications include *The Social History of Religion in Scotland since 1730*, London, 1987, and 'Did urbanisation secularise Britain?', *Urban History Yearbook*, 1988.

William J. Callahan is Professor of History at the University of Toronto and Fellow of Victoria College. His books include *La santa y real hermandad del refugio y piedad de Madrid, 1619–1832*, Madrid, 1980, and *Church, Politics and Society in Spain, 1750–1874*, Cambridge, Mass., 1984.

Simon Dixon is a Lecturer in Modern History at the University of Glasgow. His articles include 'The church's social role in St Petersburg, 1880–1914', in G. Hosking (ed.), *Church, Nation and State in Russia and Ukraine*, Basingstoke, 1991, and 'Reflections on modern Russian martyrdom', in Diana Wood (ed.), *Martyrs and Martyrologies*, Oxford, 1993.

David Hempton is Professor of Modern History at Queen's University, Belfast. He is author of *Methodism and Politics in British Society 1750–1850*, London, 1984, and (with Myrtle Hill), *Evangelical Protestantism in Ulster Society 1740–1890*, London, 1992.

Lucian Hölscher is Professor of Modern History at Ruhr-Universität Bochum. He is the author of *Öffentlichkeit und Geheimnis*, Stuttgart, 1979, and *Weltgericht oder Revolution*, Stuttgart, 1989.

Thomas Kselman is Associate Professor and Chair of History at the University of Notre Dame. He is the author of *Miracles and Prophecies in Nineteenth-Century France*, New Brunswick, NJ, 1983, and *Death and the Afterlife in Nineteenth-Century France*, Princeton, NJ, 1993.

Hugh McLeod is Professor of Church History at the University of Birmingham. His books include *Religion and the People of Western Europe 1789–1970*, Oxford, 1981, and *Poverty and Piety: Working Class Religion in Berlin, London and New York 1870–1914*, New York, 1994.

Hans Otte is Head of the Archives of the Lutheran Church of Hanover and part-time Lecturer in Church History at the University of Göttingen. Books include *Milde Aufklärung*, Göttingen, 1988, and *Vernünftig und christlich*, Göttingen, 1989.

Carl Strikwerda is Associate Professor of History at the University of Kansas. He edited (with Camille Guerin-Gonzales) *The Politics of Immigrant Workers: Labor Activism and Migration in the World Economy since 1830*, New York, 1993 and his articles include 'The troubled origins of European economic integration: International iron and steel and labor migration in the era of World War I', *American Historical Review*, 1993.

Sarah Williams is a theology student at Regent College, Vancouver. She was awarded an Oxford D.Phil in 1993 for her thesis, 'Religious belief and popular culture: A study of the south London borough of Southwark c. 1880–1939'.

PREFACE

The main themes of this book are the impact on religious beliefs and institutions of the urbanization of European societies in the nineteenth and early twentieth centuries, and the ways in which the churches responded to these social changes. Although many historians have studied these themes in the context of individual cities, or sometimes countries, very little attempt has been made to approach these issues in a more systematic way by comparing what happened in different countries or within different religious traditions. This book will not attempt to be in any way comprehensive, but by selecting several major themes, and then looking at them from the point of view of cities with different religious histories and different confessional composition, it could mark the first step towards a more systematic comparative history, and it ought to permit more subtle and nuanced generalizations than those current at the moment.

The four chapters in Part I examine in three contexts (Catholic, Lutheran and Orthodox) the familiar problem of the difficulties faced by the churches in responding to the very rapid growth of cities in this period. The two chapters in Part III, drawing respectively on British and on German evidence, attempt an overall assessment of the connections between urbanization and religious change, focusing especially on the debate over secularization. The theme of Part II, entitled 'Urban religious cultures', is less sharply defined. One aim is to present something of the range of possibilities inherent in the urban religious situation in this period. Another is to permit the kind of highly detailed exploration of popular religious attitudes or local church life which would be out of place in the other sections of the book. This part also offers an opportunity to consider aspects of urban religion that are largely neglected elsewhere – for instance, the city as an arena of sectarian conflict, or as a field for religious experimentation, whether by older churches or by new and often unorthodox movements.

The volume arises out of a conference on 'The church in the city', organized by CIHEC (Commission Internationale d'Histoire Ecclésiastique Comparée) and held in Madrid in August 1990 as part of the International Historical Congress. A selection of papers from the conference were subsequently edited by José Andrés-Gallego and published in *Hispania sacra*, 86, 1990, pp. 385–481. Among the contributors to the present volume, Callum Brown, William Callahan, David Hempton, Lucian Hölscher and myself all gave papers at Madrid, while Clyde Binfield chaired discussion. In reading the papers I became convinced that they provided the foundation for an innovative book. To give the volume coherence, the field would have to be defined more narrowly than at Madrid, thus excluding some contributions to the conference. On the other hand, new contributors would have to be recruited to handle additional countries or themes. In approaching potential contributors, my main concern has been to maintain a reasonable balance between the coverage of Europe's various religious traditions, between cities with different kinds of religious histories and between authors with different approaches to the writing of history. Inevitably some countries which I originally hoped to include had to be omitted because no author could be found who was willing to write about them. My biggest regret is that I had to miss out an intended chapter on Judaism, because none of the specialists approached was able to accept my invitation. The contributions by Lucian Hölscher and Hans Otte were originally written in German and the translations are mine.

Hugh McLeod
Birmingham
December 1993

INTRODUCTION

Hugh McLeod

I

The church was an integral, and in many ways a central part of urban life in eighteenth-century Europe. The very visible presence of the church, whether in Catholic Paris, Lutheran Berlin, Orthodox Moscow or Anglican and Dissenting London was vividly symbolized by the forests of church spires (or, in Moscow, onion-domes) which are so familiar from prints of eighteenth-century townscapes. As the artists correctly indicated, churches were numerous. They also tended to be well-staffed, and their clergy were often prominent public figures closely associated with the urban élite. In Catholic cities, such as Paris, Madrid or Venice, there was a massive clerical presence. In Madrid, for instance, at the end of the eighteenth century, priests and nuns made up approximately 1.5 per cent of the population.[1] A similar estimate was made for Paris in 1768.[2] In both Spain and Portugal the clerical presence was indeed considerably stronger in the towns than in the countryside, mainly because, as in most parts of Catholic Europe, religious orders were concentrated in the towns. In Russia into the middle years of the nineteenth century, the church continued to be stronger in town than in country.[3] In all parts of Europe, the church had an extensive role in many areas of public welfare, including education, poor relief and the care of orphans. For instance, Callahan notes the important part played by the church in feeding the hungry during the famine of 1768–9, and argues that a major factor in the growth of anticlericalism in the early nineteenth century was the inability of the church, in view of its depleted resources, to fulfil its traditional social role.[4] In Catholic and Orthodox cities, the processions associated with Corpus Christi, with Holy Week or with the feast-day of the local patron saint were among the most colourful and dramatic events in the annual calendar,

1

involving huge numbers of people, whether as active participants or as spectators. Confraternities, organized on the basis of occupation, or of willingness to perform particular ritual or charitable services, took a prominent part in these processions. They embraced large sections of the male population, and enabled their members to play a public religious role, even in a church apparently dominated by the clergy.[5] Protestant styles of devotion tended to be more restrained. But in Protestant cities preachers were prominent public personalities, and sermons and hymn-singing had a role as great as that of devotion to the saints in Catholic cities.[6]

In the majority of Europe's cities in the later eighteenth century, the dominant church claimed the whole population, or an overwhelming majority of the population, as members. There were some important exceptions to this rule, though the dissenting minorities generally suffered civil disabilities. In English and Dutch cities a wide range of religious groups had a conspicuous public presence, both in terms of church buildings and in personal wealth, but full political rights were restricted to members of the Church of England and Dutch Reformed Church respectively. In Dublin, the Catholic majority was by the later eighteenth century re-emerging in terms of organized religious life, while still restricted in political terms. Many Russian cities had a significant Old Believer element, but their organized religious life was limited by the fact that full toleration was not granted until 1905.[7] Most of Europe's larger cities had Jewish communities, these were generally small – the major exception being Amsterdam, where over 10 per cent of the population was Jewish in 1800. Conditions varied greatly. In Rome Jews were still confined to a ghetto, and Warsaw (until 1799) and Vienna (until 1848) denied Jews any right of residence – though some Jews did none the less live in those cities. At the other end of the spectrum was London, where Jews suffered no formal disabilities other than those imposed on all non-Anglicans. At the end of the eighteenth century the city where Jews enjoyed the greatest degree of prosperity was probably Berlin, where they were beginning to play a prominent part in intellectual as well as economic life.[8] A rare exception to the general rule was the situation in some German cities where a system of 'parity' had been instituted at some point in the sixteenth or seventeenth centuries between Catholicism and the locally prevailing form of Protestantism. In Augsburg, the most important of these cities, equality had not, however, led to integration: every aspect of life in the city had a Catholic and a Lutheran dimension, and the two communities tried so far as possible to maintain a separate existence.[9]

The later eighteenth century brought important religious changes. The most familiar aspect of the Enlightenment is the criticism of Christianity by deists like Voltaire and religious sceptics like Hume. There are signs that a significant section of the educated middle class, at least in France, was moving in this direction in the last decades of the *ancien régime*.[10] But, as Hölscher's contribution to this volume shows, more important in the short term was the changing religious mentality of many Protestants and Catholics, who rejected the 'fanatical', 'superstitious', 'irrational' and 'baroque' aspects of traditional piety, and wanted to discover the deeper spiritual realities beneath. One fundamental of the new religious thinking was the necessity for religious toleration, and in the 1780s a series of Edicts of Toleration were enacted – by Austria in 1781, Hamburg in 1785 and France in 1787. Even more significant, so far as their effects on Catholic societies were concerned, were the attacks on the religious orders. An enlightened Catholic, like Joseph II of Austria, valued the work of the parish clergy, but was hostile to the contemplative orders, which in his view made no useful contribution to society. He accordingly closed down several hundred religious houses in the 1780s, and used their income to fund parishes and schools. Similar measures were enacted in Milan and Tuscany. And the Jesuits, after being expelled from a succession of states, were dissolved by the Pope in 1773.

A second pointer to the future was the evidence that in some fast-growing towns and cities the church was failing to keep pace with urban growth. As early as 1736 and 1751 clergy in the developing industrial centres of Leeds and Sheffield were complaining that the shortage of Anglican churches was leading to a growth both in religious dissent and in non-churchgoing. The problem tended to be most acute in outlying communities on the margins of the cities. Olwen Hufton quotes the example of a suburb of Montpellier, which lost its church in the Wars of Religion, and over the centuries had developed a tradition of non-churchgoing. Church spires filled the city centres, but they were often conspicuously missing among the hovels and shacks on the outskirts.[11]

II

In some cities the old religious order remained intact until well into the nineteenth century. For instance, various studies of cities in southern France have shown how Catholicism revived after the disasters of the 1790s, and remained a central aspect of urban life, providing a crucial bond between the various sectors of the population until around the middle of the nineteenth century. In Marseille, Charpin provided a statistical test of the strength of Catholic discipline and the presumed hold of the church over the population: canon law required that a child be baptized within three days of birth. Charpin was able to show that 75 per cent of babies born in 1806 were baptized within this period, and that in 1829 the figure rose to 80 per cent. It dropped again to 71 per cent in 1841, and from then on there was a continuous decline – to 44 per cent in 1861, 34 per cent in 1881, 14 per cent in 1901 and 7 per cent in 1921. In some major cities, such as Naples or Moscow, the old order continued for much longer.[12]

But from the late eighteenth century the old religious order was under threat from three directions. Most obviously there was the French Revolution of 1789, with all its manifold ramifications, which had enormous implications for the social role of the church. Second, there was the growth in size and the changing economic character of cities. And third, there was the increasing severity of class conflict.

The economic and demographic changes were of most general significance. First, the number of cities and large towns was growing very rapidly. For instance, between 1750 and 1850, the number of European cities with populations of over 100,000 increased from twelve to forty-three, and by 1890 the number had risen to 101. In the same period the number of towns and cities with populations of over 20,000 increased from 123 to 327, to 685. Second, there was a substantial increase in the proportion of urbanites in the total population – though this is much harder to measure because of the difficulty of deciding when a large village becomes a small town. Taking a rather strict definition – the proportion of the population living in towns with populations of over 10,000 – all but one of those European countries for which figures are available registered an increase between 1800 and 1890, and in most cases the increase was substantial. According to one estimate, the proportion of Europeans living in towns of over 10,000 people rose very gradually, from 6 per cent in 1500 to 8 per cent in 1600, 9 per cent in 1700 and 10 per cent in 1800, and then leapt to 29 per cent by 1890. Of course, there were big variations. In 1800, by far the most urbanized country was the Netherlands, followed by

Britain, Belgium and Italy. In 1890, Britain was far ahead, followed by Belgium, the Netherlands, Germany, Spain, France, Denmark and Italy. Third, the nineteenth century saw the birth of the giant city. In 1800, London, Europe's greatest city, had slightly under a million inhabitants, and Paris followed with 550,000. Some authorities claim that London was already the world's greatest city, while others argue that it lagged behind Peking, Canton or Edo. By 1900 there could no longer be any question as to where the British capital stood in the history of the world's cities. London, with over 6 million people, and indeed Paris with over 3 million, were cities on a totally different scale from any the world had seen before. By now, Berlin, Vienna, St Petersburg and Moscow had also passed the million mark, while Manchester, Birmingham, Glasgow and Essen lay at the heart of huge industrial conurbations, each containing more than a million people.[13] Equally significant was the growing cultural dominance of the cities, even in countries where the majority of the population lived in the countryside. The railway, the newspaper, compulsory education and sometimes weekly or seasonal migration to work in the cities, meant that rural cultures were more and more vulnerable to urban influences.

Whatever the ideological context, the rapid growth in city populations presented the church with logistical problems that were not easily solved. These problems are vividly depicted in the chapters by Callahan, Otte and Dixon, and it is apparent that the Catholic church in Madrid and Barcelona, the Orthodox Church in St Petersburg and the Lutheran Church in Hanover faced many of the same problems; in every case the difficulties encountered in working-class parishes were particularly acute. New churches, schools, parish centres, etc., had to be built, additional clergy had to be recruited and paid. Moreover, immigrants were not always easily integrated into city parishes. Language differences were often a major problem, and even if they spoke the same language as the native population, they might well be regarded as socially alien. And, indeed, city clergy might well share the prejudices of their parishioners.[14] Urban growth was also associated with new sources of wealth, and the emergence of new economic élites. Battles for power and status with the older élites inevitably followed, and often the conflict had a religious dimension. In British cities the new élites usually included a disproportionately large number of Dissenters or (in Scotland) members of the Free Church, and many of them were active Liberals committed to attacking the privileges of the established churches. In eastern Europe a high proportion of the élites were Jewish.

The political context thus had an essential bearing on the church's ability to deal with the challenges it faced. In Protestant countries the church was already relatively poor, and subject to various legal restrictions or political controls. For instance, in England and Wales up to 1836 the formation of a new parish required an Act of Parliament; in Germany and Scotland, urban parish churches were frequently under the control of the city council, so that both the political complexion and the theological sympathies of the council could be crucially significant for the church. Otte, in his contribution to this volume, shows the importance of this factor in Hanover and also the relevance of the conflict between the religiously liberal city and the religiously conservative state, which was repeated in various other German territories.[15]

Up until the eighteenth century the church in Catholic and Orthodox countries generally enjoyed a considerable degree of independence as a result of extensive landholdings. But the Enlightenment generated a climate in which church wealth was regarded as excessive and a hindrance to economic development, and in which the degree of independence enjoyed by the church was deemed dangerous to the state. The process of nationalizing church property and introducing tighter state controls over the church was initiated in Russia and Austria before 1789. It was pursued with added ideological fervour by the revolutionary governments in France and later in the conquered territories of Germany and what was to become Belgium and by Liberal governments in such countries as Spain, Portugal and Italy in the nineteenth century. The Catholic and Orthodox Churches thus faced the demographic upheavals of the nineteenth century with diminished resources, and often with their hands tied by government controls, as in France, Belgium and Spain, where the concordats of 1801 and 1851 required government permission for the formation of a new parish.

There is also no doubt that in psychological terms the events of the 1790s in France cast a shadow over the religious history of the whole nineteenth century, even in places where the church made good the material losses of these years. In both France and Spain the memory of the revolutionary terror decisively altered the balance of power within the Catholic Church in favour of the more conservative elements, who were able to argue that compromise with the forces of reason and progress was a first step on the road which led ultimately to the horrors of the September massacres and the mass-drownings of priests in the River Loire. In the eyes of many radicals, the role of Catholicism in the Vendean counter-revolution discredited the Catholic Church, and possibly religion in general, as agents of reaction. Thus was set in train the vicious circle, which took its most tragic shape in Spain, whereby the conservatism of the church made the left more violently anticlerical, and the violent anticlericalism of the left made the church more conservative. The importance of such ideological considerations in predetermining the church's response to the challenges of urbanization is very clearly brought out in Callahan's chapter.

The significance of all this for urban religious development was that the French Revolution was predominantly an urban movement (in some of its phases it took the form of a war of town against countryside) and the heirs to the revolutionary tradition were initially found mainly in the towns, both among middle-class liberals and increasingly among lower middle-class and working-class radicals and socialists. For much of the nineteenth century there were many parts of Europe where a conservative countryside stood against the liberal and radical cities and towns.[16]

The intensification of class conflict in nineteenth-century cities was associated with the emergence of the working class as a body concentrated in distinctive quarters of the city, largely isolated from social contacts with other social groups and organized in trades unions and political parties. Situations of intensified class conflict often found the clergy performing a difficult balancing act, in which they tried to act as mediators; sometimes, however, it found them unequivocally identified with the conservative forces. An early example of the latter situation was the aftermath of the Peterloo massacre of 1819 in Manchester, when eleven demonstrators were killed by soldiers. Most of the Anglican clergy identified themselves with the authorities, and Anglican complicity in the massacre was symbolized in many people's minds by the fact that a clerical magistrate, the Rev. W.R. Hay, had called out the troops. But the Wesleyan Methodist Connexion was split down the middle. The strongly conservative superintendent of the Manchester Circuit instituted a massive purge of radicals. On the other hand, the Wesleyan leadership in Newcastle was divided on the question of disciplinary action against a preacher who had spoken at a reform meeting: calculating that three-quarters of local Methodists supported the reform cause, they feared that mass defections might ensue if the Connexion were seen to be identified with the reactionary forces. In the event the preacher was put on trial, but was acquitted.[17]

III

By the 1830s and 1840s there were many voices proclaiming that the cities were strongholds of irreligion. Most famous perhaps was Engels's study of the English working class in 1844, in which he claimed that religion had effectively died out. While most such comments concerned the working class, some observers saw the city as a whole as a religious desert. A London clergyman claimed in a sermon of 1844 that: 'The life of cities is essentially a worldly life', whereas 'the country with its pure serenity – oh, how unlike the hot thick breath of the towns, of itself inspires some feeling of religion'. Meanwhile, a Berlin clergyman was comparing his city to Sodom and Gomorrha, and suggesting that it would be a suitable site for a mission to the heathen.[18]

But at the same time there were also those who saw the cities as the most dynamic centres of religious activism. To a Scottish evangelical in the 1830s, Glasgow was 'Gospel City', leading the nation in its religiously inspired reform movements and its evangelistic enterprises. And Robert Vaughan, the English Congregational minister who published *The Age of Great Cities* in 1843, was equally optimistic about the influence these cities could exercise over the nation.[19] Of course, most of these commentators were deeply involved in the religious controversies of their time, and their commitments strongly coloured their judgements. For instance, the enthusiasm of Nonconformists for urbanization was influenced by the fact that they saw the cities as a powerful counterweight to the religious traditionalism of the countryside: their sectarian partisanship may have led them to play down the less welcome aspects of city life.

A third view, characteristic of many journalists and novelists, was to emphasize, with a mixture of fascination and revulsion, the endless complexity and variety of the urban scene. In 1846 a radical journalist, Friedrich Sass, described Berlin as 'a model example of spiritual and intellectual freedom', in which a bewildering variety of religious movements, from pietism to atheism, all flourished. And in the same year, another journalist, Ernst Dronke, enumerated in all their contradictory variety some of the contemporary images of the Prussian capital. For pietists it was a 'Babel', where all ties were broken and nothing was sacred – 'neither God, nor church, nor fatherland, not even the holiest family bonds, not marriage or the sense of duty'. For liberals, it was a citadel of reaction, swarming with police spies and arrogant aristocrats, 'where the government pampers the pietists and suppresses the free pursuit of knowledge'. Rhinelanders saw it principally as the seat of their Prussian rulers, while south Germans dismissed it as a city 'without a heart', archetypally Prussian. Some claimed that an exaggerated religiosity held sway, and that attempts were being made to introduce a sabbath of 'English severity', while others accused the city's papers of holding up believers to ridicule and alleged that the drinking-places were full of blasphemers singing irreligious songs. Dronke concluded that it was precisely this many-sidedness that was of the essence of the great city:

> It is, – it is, – it is. Yes, it is many things, it is the great city. There everyone can live as he wishes, because everything is to be found there. In the great city no-one cares what anyone else is up to.[20]

The same differences of interpretation are to be found among modern historians and sociologists writing the religious history of the nineteenth-century cities. The first two views quoted above have their counterpart in what I have termed the 'orthodox' and 'revisionist' schools of modern historiography – and the quotations from Sass and Dronke point to a third line of interpretation, which has received less attention from historians, but which I shall return to later. Among the contributors to the present volume, it is probably Callahan who comes closest to the 'orthodox' position. The majority of the others lean in a 'revisionist' direction, with Williams leaning furthest. Brown has been the leading advocate of 'revisionism' among historians of urban religion in Britain, and his contribution to this volume represents the latest refinement of a critique of 'orthodoxy' which he has been developing over several years.[21]

The 'orthodox' view is that there was an intimate relationship between urbanization and secularization in nineteenth-century Europe. Much of the pioneering work in this field was done by Christians concerned with devising more effective missionary strategies for the church. E.R. Wickham, director of the Church of England's Sheffield Industrial Mission, began his influential study of Sheffield by stating that: 'The weakness and collapse of the churches in the urbanized and industrialized areas of the country should be transparently clear to any who are not wilfully blind.' The aim of his book was to discover how and why this situation came about. Many of the historians writing in the 1960s and 1970s did not attempt to duplicate Wickham's detailed local research, but concentrated on offering more sophisticated explanations as to why the 'collapse of the churches' had taken place. Two of the major influences on these historians were 'modernization' theory, which stressed the role of impersonal forces such as the development of technology, and Marxism, which accepted the significance of the 'modernizing' forces, but placed an overriding stress on the development of working-class consciousness and organization.[22] There is a very similar tradition within the historiography of European Jewry which stresses the association between urbanization and assimilation, whether in the form of conversion to Christianity or simply of the abandonment of all Jewish religious practices, and the adoption of a way of life as nearly as possible indistinguishable from that of their gentile neighbours.[23] Unfortunately, the religious histories of Jews and Christians in modern Europe have very largely been written in isolation from one another, with little attempt to study the parallels between them.

There is general agreement that the demographic upheavals of the nineteenth century presented the churches with enormous logistical problems; that immigrants to the cities sometimes remained highly mobile and accordingly found it difficult to form close attachments to any particular clergyman or congregation; and that some gave up in the town religious practices which derived their meaning from the rural context in which they had first been learnt. Some historians would go further, and argue that giant cities of the type which developed in the nineteenth century are by their nature pluralistic, and lend themselves to the formation of numerous discrete subcultures, since the supervision of morals, beliefs and religious practices by employers, magistrates or the church was no longer practicable. This argument is sometimes extended to suggest that the pluralism of urban life leads to the development of a relativistic outlook, which breeds religious scepticism. Some historians have gone further still, positing a mental revolution in nineteenth-century cities whereby all forms of supernaturalism lost their credibility and a rationalistic and mechanistic outlook came to predominate.[24] Berlin offers a striking example of a city where the course of events in the nineteenth century appears to fit this model reasonably well.[25]

The growth of Berlin in the nineteenth century was very rapid, even by comparison with other major cities. The population rose from 450,000 in 1848 to 900,000 in 1871. In the next twenty years the population doubled again, reaching nearly 2 million by 1890, and on the eve of the First World War Berlin and its suburbs housed nearly 4 million people. The church thus faced an enormous task in responding to this growth, building churches and parish centres and paying clergy and other church workers to minister to this ever growing population. But the Protestant church in Berlin suffered from a severe shortage of churches and clergy even before the onset of rapid population growth. The kings of Prussia were patrons of most of the city parishes, which was an advantage in the later seventeenth and early eighteenth centuries when Kings Frederick I and Frederick William I took their religious responsibilities very seriously; later this royal patronage was a severe handicap. During a period of nearly a century between 1739 and 1835 not a single new Protestant church was built, as the church had as 'supreme bishop' first the antagonistic Frederick the Great and then Frederick William III, who was not hostile to the church, but was reluctant to spend money on it. Frederick William IV, who inherited the throne in 1840, gave the church a higher priority, and in the 1840s, 1850s and 1860s there was a steady trickle of new church buildings. But the slowly increasing supply was quite insufficient to meet the needs of a very rapidly increasing population. An added problem was the conflict between the theological conservatism of Kings Frederick William IV and William I and of the consistory, and the liberalism of the city council and after 1874 of the city synod, consisting of elected representatives of the parishes. Both sides wanted to ensure that when a new parish was created, a pastor of the right kind was appointed, and very frequently they would rather have no parish at all than a pastor belonging to the wrong church party. In 1700 there had been approximately one pastor for every 1,000 Protestants in the city; by 1800 the ratio was about 1:3,000, in 1850 it was about 1:4,300 and in 1890 it reached a maximum of 1:9,593. This was the age of the 'giant parishes': Holy Cross, in the working-class district of Luisenstadt, set the record with 128,000, but parishes with 60,000 and more people were quite commonplace. Only in the 1890s did the long-discussed church-building programme finally get underway, as a result of a combination of favourable factors: the new emperor, and more especially his wife, the Empress Augusta Victoria, were keen supporters of the cause, the conservative victory in the 1889 synodal elections meant that it was at last possible for the synod and consistory to co-operate, and the growing threat from social democracy persuaded many members of the upper and middle classes to give money for church-building in the hope that the church might provide a counterweight to socialism in the working-class districts.[26]

While coping with enormous organizational problems, the Protestant church also faced increasing political unpopularity. The March revolution of 1848, and its suppression by the royal *coup d'état* in November cast long shadows over the city's life for the rest of the century. A large section of the clergy – most notably the pietists – gave vocal support to the royal coup, and in the reactionary 1850s king and church worked hand in hand. The events of these years discredited the church in the eyes of many of Berlin's liberals and democrats, and, with the revival in the 1860s of a free press, the city's newspapers tended to assume a strongly anticlerical tone. In the later nineteenth century, Berlin clergymen often blamed their problems on a hostile press. The Social Democrats, who emerged as a major force in the city's political life in the later 1860s, inherited to the full the anticlericalism of their liberal political ancestors, and took it very much further. In 1878 some Social Democrats launched a *Kirchenaustrittsbewegung* (movement of mass resignation from the churches). This proved a failure, but a second, and more successful, movement was organized in the years 1906–14. Although the official policy of the party was that religion was 'a private matter', and that Social Democrats could belong to any religion or none, the prevailing tone within the party was strongly secular, and few party activists found it possible to maintain links with a church or synagogue.[27]

In 1878, the court preacher, Adolf Stoecker, who was one of the most colourful and controversial figures in the Berlin church, founded a Christian Social Workers' Party, which aimed to counter the appeal of the Social Democrats by offering a kind of 'Tory Radicalism' – combining patriotism and support for the monarchy with a rejection of *laissez-faire* economics and a programme for improvements in living and working conditions. However, the 1878 election was a fiasco for Stoecker: his party obtained 1,400 votes in Berlin, as against 60,000 for the Social Democrats, and Stoecker soon transferred his political base to Siegen, a strongly Protestant small town and rural constituency in west–central Germany, where his ideas had a resonance which they no longer possessed in the

Liberal-, and Social Democrat-dominated cities. Meanwhile, the close control over the church's affairs exercised by the Prussian kings in their role as 'supreme bishop' inhibited the development of a radical or socialist element among the clergy, who might identify themselves with the aspirations of their working-class parishioners in the way that happened to some extent in such countries as Britain, the United States and Switzerland in the later nineteenth century. But this had in fact happened in Germany in the years 1890–5, when the Evangelical Social Congress emerged as a forum for the more radical clergy. After the publication of a report that was severely critical of East Elbian landlords, the Prussian church authorities decided to clamp down on radical clergy, and the later 1890s saw a series of disciplinary actions, including the suspension from office of the small number of clergy who had gone so far as to join the Social Democrats.[28]

The fact that so many Prussian Liberals and Social Democrats had rejected the church on political grounds made them very open to new scientific or literary critiques of religion. Under Frederick the Great in the later eighteenth century the city had enjoyed a reputation as a haven for religious sceptics, but there is no evidence that at that point these ideas gained a wide hearing. However, in the course of the nineteenth century they began to influence much broader sections of the population. One strand of religious criticism was literary: in the eyes of many Liberals and Social Democrats, the German classics – Goethe, Heine and, above all, Schiller – were prophets of a new religion of freedom, focused on the rights of individual conscience and rejection of all authority. The other strand was the tradition of scientific–materialism, going back to the 1830s and 1840s, but most fully developed by Büchner and Moleschott in the 1850s, and substantially reinforced by Darwinism, which initially had a bigger impact in Germany than in the English-speaking countries.[29] Berliners saw themselves as practical, down to earth, no-nonsense people, with no inclination towards anything mystical or other-worldly. Some saw this as a limitation. But many were proud of their sober realism. For instance, a rather enthusiastic (if partly tongue-in-cheek) city guide of 1905 concluded with a section on 'Why we love Berlin', in which irreverence (*Pietätslosigkeit*) was among the qualities singled out for praise.[30]

Berlin was noted for its low levels of church attendance. In 1869 about 3 per cent of the members of the Protestant church went to services on Sunday. By 1913 this figure had dropped to 1 per cent.

Perhaps another 1 per cent attended the services of the free churches. Even making a fairly generous allowance for attendance by Catholics, it seems unlikely that more than about 5 per cent of the city's population attended the services of all Christian denominations on a Sunday.[31] The annual communion rate in the years 1891–5 of sixteen per 100 members of the Protestant *Landeskirche* in Berlin was far below the Prussian average of forty-three.[32] While Protestant church attendance was generally fairly low in the German cities in the later nineteenth century, Berlin stood out because significant numbers of Protestants and Catholics, especially in the working-class suburbs, abstained from some or all of the rites of passage. In 1910, for instance, 89 per cent of babies born to Protestant parents were baptized, but only 62 per cent of Protestants dying in that year were buried in the presence of a pastor, and only 56 per cent of Protestant couples marrying in that year had a religious ceremony. Catholic couples were more likely to follow the civil marriage ceremony with a religious ceremony (81 per cent did so), but Catholic babies were less likely to be baptized (72 per cent), and only 49 per cent of the Catholics who died in that year were buried in the presence of a priest.[33]

The Berlin Jews, who comprised about 5 per cent of the city's population at the end of the nineteenth century, were by far the largest and most important Jewish community in Germany. In spite of the presence of a minority of Yiddish-speaking Jews from the eastern provinces, many of whom lived in the impoverished Scheunenviertel near the city centre and tended to be religiously conservative, the majority of Jewish Berliners were prosperous and highly acculturated. Those who maintained their links with the synagogue were predominantly liberal. But there was also a large element who had largely or entirely given up religious observances. Before 1914, many of these joined the Protestant church in order to escape the social disadvantages which could still result from membership of the Jewish community. However, under the Weimar Republic there was less stigma attached to being *konfessionslos* (without religious affiliation) and many non-observant Jews left the Jewish community without joining another denomination.[34]

In the later nineteenth century there were signs that a whole series of 'substitute religions' (as they were often termed by contemporaries) were taking the place of Christianity and Judaism. The most obvious example was socialism, which in the eyes of many of its followers offered a complete view of the world, often synthesized with

Darwinism. This was reflected in the tendency for Socialists to replace the Protestant confirmation with their own *Jugendweihe* (youth consecration ceremony), to provide their comrades with secular funerals, where Socialist 'speakers' would take the place of the pastor at the grave-side, and to organize Socialist festivals, like May Day, in the hope of superseding the older Christian festivals.[35] While socialism appealed mainly to the working class, there were also many middle-class Berliners who were drawn towards religious alternatives of one kind or another. The best-known example is the religion of music, and especially the Wagner cult. For others it was the theatre that was seen as best fulfilling humanity's spiritual needs.[36] Particularly characteristic of Berlin was the cult of nature. This often meant a Sunday spent on the allotments, where many families had a little patch of ground and a summer-house. The delightful lakes and pine woods, placed a few miles to the east and west of the nineteenth-century city and now on the outskirts of modern Berlin, also provided ideal picnic spots. For many Berliners the open air possessed a sacramental quality. The author of a city guide published in 1905, claimed that a trip into the countryside was the 'noblest' form of Sunday pleasure, and in 1896 a liberal journalist, who felt that the recent programme of new church-building had gone too far, suggested that Berlin's real need was for more parks. Any open space that was used for a church would be better used for parks, which offered 'all the people, big and small, poor and rich, throughout the week and at every time of the day, the opportunity of relaxation amid God's own Nature, and the strengthening and revival of heart and soul'. Through the cult of nature Berliners were able to retain in a secularized form the idea of the sabbath as a day of rest.[37]

Most aspects of the Berlin situation had their parallels elsewhere, but Berlin was unusual in that so many factors unfavourable to organized religion came together in the same place. Returning to the distinction made earlier between 'orthodox' and 'revisionist' views of nineteenth-century urban religion, the 'orthodox' school would tend to see Berlin as an extreme example of a general trend, while 'revisionists' would stress the variety of religious situations, and would see the Berlin model as being one among several, rather than being 'the' characteristic pattern of urban religious development.

In two respects Berlin probably can be taken as an extreme example of a general trend: first, the severe shortage of churches and clergy, which lasted for most of the nineteenth century and, second, the low level of churchgoing by working-class adults. On the other hand, the low level of churchgoing by other social groups in Berlin probably was untypical, and the relatively low participation in the rites of passage, while certainly not unique to Berlin, was not typical either. In some other areas of religious life, European experience was so varied that no city could be regarded as typical.

The shortage of churches and clergy was paralleled in most large cities at some point in the nineteenth century, though I know of no case where the shortage was as severe as in Berlin. In 1890 the ratio of Protestant clergy to Protestant population in Berlin reached a maximum of 1:9,593. The city that came nearest to this was Hamburg, where the ratio had been 1:8,995 in 1881 and was 1:8,166 in 1891. In Lübeck and Bremen, the other German Protestant cities for which figures are available, ratios were considerably more favourable.[38] Severely deteriorating ratios of clergy to people were also common in Catholic cities during the nineteenth century, but the figures never came anywhere near to those in Berlin – for one thing, Catholic priests came cheaper as they were not expected to support a family. In Brussels the ratio changed from 1:1,675 in 1803 to 1:3,795 in 1900. In Paris in 1906, after a century of deteriorating provision, the ratios were 1:3,681 in the central *arrondissements*, 1:5,760 in the peripheral *arrondissements* and 1:4,095 in the suburbs. In Vienna, which was probably worse provided with churches and clergy than any other predominantly Catholic city, the ratio of priests to Catholics was 1:1,641 in 1783, 1:4,290 in 1842 and 1:5,949 in 1910. This average concealed considerable variations, and in some of the working-class suburbs the situation was fairly similar to that in Berlin. In 1900 the ultra-proletarian Favoriten district had a population of 102,000 and six Catholic clergy.[39] Madrid, as William Callahan's chapter shows, had a similar contrast between relatively favourable ratios in wealthy areas close to the city centre and very poor ratios in some working-class suburbs.

So the deterioration of ecclesiastical provision certainly reached extreme forms in Berlin. But the difference was perhaps of degree rather than kind. Certainly, there were many cities where the clergy believed that the lack of provision was sufficiently acute to cause many people to lose touch with the church.

In its low rates of churchgoing and of participation in communion, Berlin was fairly typical of north German Protestant cities – in Hamburg and Bremen the communion figures were in fact even lower.[40] But it probably was not typical of urban Europe in the late nineteenth and early twentieth centuries. Protestant participation seems to have been somewhat higher in southern and western Germany, and, though figures are less easily available, all the indications are that Catholic religious participation was generally considerably higher than that by Protestants in Germany.[41] Stockholm, where 10 per cent of adult males were communicants in 1880, may have stood fairly close to Berlin.[42] But Berlin's rate of weekly churchgoing was considerably below that for other large cities for which figures are available. Paris, which shared some of Berlin's reputation for irreligion had an estimated mass attendance rate of 15 per cent in the early twentieth century, London had a weekly church attendance rate of 22 per cent, and in Liverpool it was 31 per cent.[43] Generally speaking, the lowest rates of religious practice in this period were found in agricultural areas and areas of rural industry – for instance, the Limousin in central France or the sawmill districts round Sundsvall in northern Sweden.[44] The irreligious consensus in parts of the rural Limousin was the other side of the coin of the religious consensus in parts of rural Brittany: in a small community it was sometimes possible to impose a uniformity of conduct which became progressively harder to achieve with each step up the urban hierarchy. However, even the most apparently irreligious cities usually included in their populations some groups who were more devout. For example, in Berlin there were some areas of the city, like the Tiergarten with its aristocrats, state officials and army officers, which retained a reputation for piety, and some social groups, notably the 'old middle class' of shopkeepers and master craftsmen, who remained loyal to the pietist traditions which had been strong in the early nineteenth century.[45]

Berlin was also certainly not unique in the fact that many of its nominally Christian population abstained from some or all of the Christian rites of passage. Comparison is difficult, both because few other cities have such good statistics as Berlin and also because the meaning attached to the various rites of passage varied considerably within different religious cultures. Generally speaking, the importance attached to these rites was greatest in Catholic and Orthodox cultures, and lowest in those that were Reformed, with Lutheran and Anglican cultures in an intermediate position. So, for instance, in a predominantly Catholic country failure to marry in church or to baptize one's children would be regarded as an act of extreme impiety, whereas in a country where the main tradition was Reformed a much less serious view might be taken of such neglect. Thus, the high rates of civil marriage in some parts of Wales in the nineteenth century probably do not reflect widespread irreligion,[46] whereas the high rate in Limoges probably does.[47] Equally, the fact that about 40 per cent of those dying in Paris in the early twentieth century received a secular funeral probably had more significance than the similar figure in Berlin.[48] Though statistics are patchy, the general picture around the end of nineteenth century seems to be that participation in the rites of passage was still high, even in areas where churchgoing was low. For instance in 'Red Saxony', one of the greatest strongholds of German Social Democracy, 96 per cent of children with Protestant parents were baptized in the period 1896–1900, 90 per cent of couples were married in church and 99 per cent of those dying were buried with a religious ceremony. Similarly, in 1901 96 per cent of babies born in Marseille were baptized.[49]

IV

If the historians of the 'orthodox' school differ radically among themselves in matters of ideology and methodology, the same is equally true of the 'revisionists'. One factor influencing the development of the 'revisionist' school has been a realization by some Catholic historians that the 'orthodox' interpretation, with its emphasis on the failures of the nineteenth-century church, has been used by church reformers to justify sweeping changes in the church's liturgy, pastoral strategy, political orientation, etc.: the concern of these historians is to set the record straight by presenting a more nuanced picture of the nineteenth-century church, in which achievements, as well as weaknesses, are given due recognition.[50] A second kind of motivation seems to be dissatisfaction with the dogmatism and determinism both of many Marxist historians and of those influenced by 'modernization' theory. Historians who make complaints of this sort sometimes do so because they themselves regard religion as important, or because they come out of a milieu in which religion is important;[51] but they also include those like Callum Brown, who writes as an historical materialist, but also as an empiricist, who is offended by attempts to minimize the role of religious forces in situations where they are manifestly important.[52]

The first point that most of the 'revisionists' make is that Berlin and Paris are not typical, but that they lie at one end of a very wide spectrum. Most of the 'orthodox' school would probably accept this, but they would insist that Berlin and Paris were the pace-makers, and that, apart from one or two mavericks, everyone else was moving in the same direction. The 'revisionist' case is particularly strong in the field of urban politics, where it is clear that the Berlin model of a conservative church, politically isolated in an overwhelmingly Liberal and Socialist city was only one among several possibilities. In many British and Swedish cities the conservative established churches were counterbalanced by liberal free churches, and, indeed, in Britain, Nonconformists also played a significant part in the rise of socialism around the end of the nineteenth and the beginning of the twentieth centuries.[53] Second, there were cities where some form of conservatism achieved political dominance in the later nineteenth century, with important backing from the established church. Examples would include the Christian Social hegemony in Vienna, and the even longer conservative hegemony in Liverpool.[54] Third, there were cases where the central importance of national, ethnic, linguistic or sectarian identity made the classic division between conservative and liberal or socialist irrelevant, as new types of political party took the place of the older ones.

An extreme example of the latter phenomenon would be the polarization of Irish politics after 1886 between nationalists and unionists. There were also several countries where politically effective Catholic parties emerged in the later nineteenth century, the prototype being the German Centre Party, founded in 1871, which in the 1870s and 1880s succeeded in gaining the support of the majority of Catholics in many parts of Germany and became the dominant political force in many parts of the Rhine–Ruhr industrial region. In spite of significant losses of working-class support from the 1890s onwards it remained a major force until 1933. In such situations priests became popular political leaders, and loyalty to church and party were often mutually reinforcing.

The revisionists also lay much more stress on the ability of nineteenth-century church leaders to adapt and to respond creatively to social change. Rather than seeing the nineteenth century merely as a period of decline, they have traced the development of new missionary and pastoral strategies, and the appearance of a characteristic set of new institutions. One of the first needs to be generally recognized was that of funds to pay for additional churches and clergy, and in most cities it was eventually possible to mount a big church-building programme. In London and Manchester this happened as early as the 1840s, in Hamburg in the 1880s, in Brussels and Berlin in the 1890s, in Paris in the 1930s.[55] But by the later nineteenth century a whole series of new ideas were being tried out. In France, the Assumptionist Order took a special interest in journalism, and in the 1880s and 1890s, their paper, *La croix*, was one of the country's most popular and most shamelessly sensational papers. In England, a characteristic innovation of the 1880s was the Methodist Central Mission which, reflecting current thinking about the needs of the 'whole man', combined evangelism, social service, leisure facilities and political campaigns. Various initiatives from this period in Sheffield are discussed in Binfield's chapter. In several countries, the 1890s saw the beginnings of the Christian trades unions, which in some regions and industries – for instance, the mining industry on the Ruhr – attained considerable importance. In most places the churches were worried by their failure to attract young men: the usual answer to this problem was the founding of the numerous church-based sporting organizations which sprang up in the early twentieth century.[56] Pastors of well-funded parishes were alert to new social needs and the possibility that the church might help to meet them: parish-based crèches, doctors, nurses and labour exchanges multiplied during this period. And so on.[57] The popular response to these efforts varied greatly, and even where the numbers involved were impressive, the organizations may have had serious limitations, as, for instance, is shown by a recent study of the Catholic Workers' Associations in their stronghold of Cologne.[58] Strikwerda's chapter not only provides a detailed account of the Catholic social movement in this period, but also shows why it was more successful in some cities than others. What should not be in doubt is the energy and inventiveness with which many of the clergy were responding to the urban situation in the later nineteenth century. As against the overriding emphasis on the church's failures which marked much of the older historiography, the 'revisionists' present a much more positive view of organized religion in nineteenth-century cities – even to the extent of putting their main accent on success.

The 'revisionists' also lay more stress on the continuities between countryside and town. Nineteenth-century observers of city life often painted a lurid picture of the effects of 'uprooting', of loss of cultural traditions, the sense of anomie suffered by city-dwellers and the spectacular increase in anti-social behaviour. Many historians have echoed these claims.[59] However, there is an alternative historical tradition which places much more emphasis on the ties between countryside and town, on the ability of migrants from the countryside to bring much of their traditional culture with them and on the strong sense of neighbourhood and community which could develop within the city.[60]

These migrants from the villages and small towns came from very varied religious backgrounds. In the period of rapid urbanization in the second half of the nineteenth century, there were, for instance, still many parts of Catholic and Orthodox rural Europe where traditional forms of religion embraced the whole community. Protestant rural areas were usually religiously divided, but in Britain, the Scandinavian countries, the Netherlands and to a lesser extent Germany, many migrants to the cities would be Methodists, Baptists, ultra-Calvinists or adherents of other Dissenting faiths. While rejecting the established church, they had adopted a more democratic and often more dogmatic and puritanical alternative. Some rural communities were strongly affected by secularizing currents. This was especially so in France, where the role of the Catholic Church was a bitterly debated political question throughout the nineteenth century. These conflicts began with the revolutionary attempt at 'dechristianization' in 1793–4, and they reached a climax in the period from the establishment of the Third Republic in the 1870s up to the Separation of Church and State in 1905. There were also regions, mainly on the periphery of Europe, where the church had been weak for several centuries and perhaps had never had much of a presence.[61] The same regional variations could be found in rural and small-town Judaism: by the 1880s and 1890s there were some regions, such as Galicia, where the Jews remained strongly traditionalist, and others, such as Bohemia and Moravia, where reforming ideas had already made a big impact.[62]

The very considerable religious differences between European cities in the nineteenth century can partly be explained in terms of the different religious traditions that immigrants to the city brought with them. In England, for instance, the 1851 religious census showed that cities, like Bristol, Plymouth and Leicester, with above average levels of church attendance lay in regions where rural church attendance was above average. Similarly with denominational distribution: southern cities, drawing immigrants from a predominantly Anglican countryside, tended to be predominantly Anglican, while northern cities, lying close to the strongholds of rural Methodism, tended to have a Nonconformist majority.[63] A pioneering work of the 'revisionist' school was a study of religious practice in French towns and cities in the 1950s and 1960s, which showed that there was no correlation between the level of practice and either the size of the town or its economic structure, but that the best predictor of the rate of religious practice in a French town was the rate of practice in the surrounding countryside.[64] While smaller cities have tended to draw migrants mainly from their immediate hinterland, larger cities and fast-growing industrial regions, like the Ruhrgebiet, attracted migrants from further afield, including distant regions and even foreign countries. But Brepohl's pioneering research on the Ruhr showed many years ago that within that region there were concentrations of immigrants from particular countries or regions, who brought distinctive religious traditions and succeeded to a considerable degree in re-establishing them in their new home.[65] The importance of the distinctive religious inheritance of different immigrant groups is generally recognized by historians of Judaism. For instance, the prevalence of Hasidism in nineteenth-century Warsaw has been attributed to the fact that the majority of Jewish immigrants had come from central and southern Poland, where Hasidism was strong, and the growing strength of radicalism and secularism in the later nineteenth and early twentieth centuries has been linked with the major influx of Jews from Lithuania in that period. Rozenblit notes the crucial role of immigrants from Galicia and western Hungary in Viennese Jewish Orthodoxy in the later nineteenth century.[66]

Some revisionist research has called in question the extent of the mental revolution undergone in nineteenth-century cities. Admittedly evidence is hard to come by and often inconclusive. One line of argument, which was pioneered by Jörg Kniffka in a study of Berlin, has been to suggest that the widespread participation of city-dwellers in the Christian rites of passage needs to be taken much more seriously, and that it reflects an alternative form of religiosity, rather than being a matter of unthinking habit. Jeffrey Cox, in his study of south London, coined the term 'diffusive Christianity' to describe the beliefs of the many Londoners who were not regular churchgoers but retained some kind of belief in Christian doctrine, continued to observe the Christian rites of passage and were firmly committed to Christian ethics, at least as they understood them.[67] There have for long been scattered hints that various forms of 'folk belief' and 'superstition' which have often been seen as rural phenomena, alien to the rationalism of the cities, remained deeply entrenched in some of Europe's greatest cities. Sarah Williams's chapter on London confirms that this was so. There are also signs that even in the most apparently 'dechristianized' city there was often a latent religiosity that could come to the fore in certain situations of crisis. For instance, nineteenth-century epidemics frequently triggered a temporary religious revival, and this applied not only to cities known for their piety, but also to Hamburg, which in 1892 was devastated by the last of the big European cholera epidemics.[68] Wars usually evoked some kind of religious response, though of a more complex and varied kind. In August 1914 open-air services were held in Berlin parks, there was a sharp increase in the numbers of communicants and in 'red' Wedding, the most famous of the city's working-class Social Democratic strongholds, a crowd was said to have 'stormed' a church, demanding a service at a time when one was not normally scheduled. But disillusionment followed, and the years immediately following the German defeat were accompanied by an unprecedented number of resignations from the church.[69]

V

At the moment, the 'revisionists' seem to be having the better of the argument – not necessarily because their case is intrinsically stronger, but because the most interesting research at any time tends to be done by those who are challenging accepted wisdom. 'Orthodox' and 'revisionist' historians are, however, agreed on one thing: their overriding concern is with secularization.[70] This concern is fully justified, for secularization is a theme of central importance in the religious history of the nineteenth and twentieth centuries. Yet this preoccupation may lead historians to ignore other, equally fruitful, ways of looking at the period – as, in their different ways, the chapters by Kselman and Hölscher both indicate.

At this point I want to return to the third of the contemporary comments on the religious situation in the 1840s which were quoted earlier (p. 8–9). Ernst Dronke referred to Berlin as a city of contradictions, which every observer perceived in a different way, and he saw precisely in this the essence of the great city. This offers a pointer to a third way of looking at the religious development of European cities in the nineteenth and early twentieth centuries. It could be argued that the salient feature in this development was neither religious decline nor religious vitality, but religious conflict. Instead of an historical framework based on growth and decline, another, and equally revealing approach, would be to focus on the change from the relatively homogeneous religious cultures which characterized the eighteenth-century city, to the polarized religious world of the nineteenth-century city, to the relatively fragmented religious structure of cities in the later twentieth century. The high level of antagonism between rival sects, and between believers and unbelievers, was perhaps the most distinctive feature of urban religion in the nineteenth and early twentieth centuries. By comparison with the preceding era, nineteenth-century cities were much more religiously heterogeneous: rather than binding the urban community together, religion had become a major source of internal division. By comparison with the later twentieth century, religion or irreligion were far more closely bound up with the identity of social classes or ethnic groups – religious convictions were more of a collective phenomenon and less a matter of individual choice.

I am going to conclude this section by looking at the reasons for the prevalence of religious conflict in the cities of this period. This was increasing because rival religious groups were increasingly living in close proximity to one another, because the capacity for mutual toleration in such situations was diminishing, because new sources of religious division were emerging during the century and because the social significance of the resulting conflicts was increasing.

There were several reasons for the increasing religious heterogeneity of nineteenth-century cities. The most obvious point is that fast-growing cities acted as magnets for migrants from very different religious and ethnic backgrounds, and that a great mixing of populations resulted. Protestant cities, like Geneva, became predominantly Catholic; Catholic cities, like Vienna and Munich, acquired large Jewish or Protestant minorities. And even where there was a common religion, urban populations could be deeply divided on national and linguistic lines, like Marseille, with its large Italian minority or Roubaix with its Belgians. Hempton's account of Belfast describes a situation that was in many respects typical of rapidly expanding nineteenth-century cities. The assumption that the great mixing of those from different religious or ethnic backgrounds would lead to a melting-pot or to a tolerant relativism was wildly optimistic. Mixed marriages certainly led to some dilution of confessional identities, but they also provoked a great deal of hostility from neighbours, family and clergy. In general, areas where Protestants and Catholics lived together in fairly equal numbers were distinguished by high levels of participation in church organizations, a politics that was strongly influenced by sectarianism and a considerable degree of prejudice and mutual stereotyping.[71] In cities with large Jewish minorities, the prejudice, mutual stereotyping and political antagonism between Christian and Jew were even more blatant, though the degree to which either community participated in its own religious institutions varied considerably.[72]

Moreover, all nineteenth-century cities to some extent, and some to a very considerable extent, saw movements out of the national church. In Scotland in 1843 and in the Netherlands in 1886 the established church split in two, and in some cities a very considerable proportion of the population joined the seceders. In both England and Scotland the religious census of 1851 showed that in most cities the established churches attracted only a minority of worshippers, and that a huge variety of forms of religious dissent were available.[73] At the popular end of the religious market, Methodism had an unrivalled appeal and came in many different forms, ranging from Wesleyan Methodism, which appealed to many of the *nouveaux riches* of the northern industrial cities, to Primitive Methodism which had a big following among miners, nail-makers and fishermen. Among the urban élite in such cities as Liverpool, Manchester and Birmingham, there was a strong interest in Unitarianism, which attracted the kind of upper middle-class liberals who had been largely alienated from the church in many continental countries.[74] Something similar briefly flourished in Germany in the 1840s, where, in 1845, a group of liberal Catholics seceded from the Roman Church, adopting the name of German Catholics. They were protesting at what they saw as the superstitions associated with the hugely popular pilgrimages to Trier in the previous year to see what the cathedral authorities claimed was the seamless robe of Christ. They were soon followed by a group of liberal Protestants who called themselves 'Friends of Light'. The latter tried initially to reform the church from within, but eventually they were forced out by the church authorities acting in concert with the Prussian state. Both groups won considerable support from the middle and lower middle classes in the cities, and both played a significant part in the revolutions of 1848–9. But they went into decline in the years of reactionary rule that followed the failure of the revolutions, and neither fully recovered.[75] Religious sectarianism made little headway in predominantly Catholic cities, but various Protestant groups did have some success in winning converts from Orthodoxy in St Petersburg and other Russian cities in the later nineteenth and early twentieth centuries. In St Petersburg some of the first converts to Protestantism were drawn from the aristocracy in the 1870s, but later the Protestants succeeded in moving further down the social scale.[76] Within most of the Jewish communities in nineteenth-century cities there were deep divisions between, on the one hand, the various forms of Orthodoxy and, on the other, those influenced by the *Haskalah* (Jewish Enlightenment), who sought reforms in Jewish worship, tried to obtain the best possible secular education for their sons and identified themselves with much of the culture of their gentile compatriots. In Warsaw, as indeed in some other cities with large Jewish communities, Jews of different religious tendencies lived in different areas of the city: the Muranów district, where the Nazis later established their 'ghetto', was both heavily Jewish and heavily orthodox, whereas assimilated Jews were more widely scattered across the city, often living in districts where most of the population were gentiles.[77]

By the end of the century most large cities also included significant numbers of professed unbelievers in their population, but the spread of unbelief had a different time-scale in different cities. Paris and some other French cities certainly led the way, and from the 1790s onwards there was a significant element, especially of middle-class men, who were avowed 'Voltairians'.[78] At the same time a current of working-class and lower middle-class secularism established itself in London, remaining a distinct though fairly small force in the city's life throughout the nineteenth century[79] – though not until about 1880 were they joined by a substantial element of middle-class unbelievers, who tended to call themselves 'agnostics'.[80] In Berlin middle-class unbelief was reasonably well-established from about the 1830s and 1840s, and by the 1860s and 1870s there was also a large element of working-class Social Democrats, who were often more outspoken in their irreligion.[81] By about the 1860s irreligion was widespread among the Russian intelligentsia,[82] and in Spanish cities the 1870s seems to mark an important stage.[83]

Within the same city there were also enormous differences in religious practice between districts, even when the inhabitants of both were nominally members of the same church. For instance, in Paris between 1909 and 1914 regular attendance at mass ranged from 46 per cent in the aristocratic seventh *arrondissement* to 4 per cent in the proletarian and petit bourgeois eleventh. In London in 1902–3 average adult attendance at churches of all denominations varied from 37 per cent in upper middle-class areas to 12 per cent in the poorest districts.[84] In both kinds of area social pressures could play a part in influencing people's religious practices. In the working-class districts of Bremen, for instance, in 1914 it was claimed that a kind of anti-religious tyranny operated, which meant that only very determined people insisted on going to church.[85] In middle-class districts of British cities for much of the nineteenth century social pressures operated in the opposite direction to ensure that only very determined people kept away from church.[86] All the present evidence for nineteenth-century European cities suggests that both in Catholicism and in most branches of Protestantism, the level of church involvement was considerably higher among women than among men, though there were a few Protestant sects in which the level was more or less equal for the two sexes. (Unfortunately, this issue does not seem yet to have been explored by historians of Orthodoxy.)[87] In Judaism the picture was more complicated as there tended to be a sharply defined religious division of labour, with synagogue attendance being a mainly male responsibility, while women were responsible for religious observances in the home. However, there was some tendency for male religious involvement to decline, while that by women remained fairly high, so that the same contrast that was seen in some branches of Christianity between pious women and more secular men, was also sometimes seen in Judaism.[88] Class patterns of religious involvement showed considerable variations. Generally speaking, working-class church-going was lower than that by other classes within the same city – though there were enormous differences between, for instance, the high levels of working-class churchgoing in Dublin and Belfast, and the low levels in Berlin. Patterns of observance by other classes varied a good deal. In Germany, aristocratic piety tended to contrast with bourgeois scepticism. In Russia it was often precisely the reverse. In many French cities the piety of the upper middle class contrasted with the militant anticlericalism of the lower middle class, while in Germany it was usually the other way round.[89]

This religious diversity was frequently a recipe for conflict at every level from the domestic to that of national politics. One reason for this was the growing dominance of exclusivist forms of faith, often superseding more tolerant versions which had enabled rival faiths to live together in relative peace during the latter part of the eighteenth century. A striking example of this trend is Belfast, which in the later eighteenth century had been a stronghold of liberal Presbyterianism. Belfast's liberal tradition did not die out entirely but, as Hempton's chapter shows, by the later part of the nineteenth century it had become completely eclipsed by more strident versions of

Christianity. In Belfast the question of the Union with Great Britain gave a unique dimension to politics and to sectarian relationships. But the pattern of growing sectarian intolerance was repeated in many other places. In Manchester, Catholics and Unitarians, as well as Anglicans and mainstream Nonconformists, had worked together to set up a city-wide Sunday school in 1784, in a spirit of ecumenical co-operation that would have been impossible to imagine fifty years later.[90]

But the intensity of religious conflict also arose from the fact that religious differences were closely intertwined with political and class differences. One fundamental factor was the presence throughout Europe of powerful and privileged established churches. These churches lay at the centre of political debate and, in particular, differences in attitude to established religion were among the principal differences between Liberal and Conservative political parties. If there was one thing that all Conservative parties had in common it was loyalty to the established church of their country and a conviction that social stability depended on preserving the church's position of influence. Liberal parties differed greatly in religious orientation, but they were generally agreed in defending the principles of free competition between religious bodies and the right of the individual to choose any religion or none. Throughout the nineteenth century Liberal governments repeatedly found themselves in conflict with the Roman Catholic Church, and in the eyes of many Catholics the self-styled apostles of freedom and enlightenment were in fact persecutors.[91] The biggest issue was education, and in particular the role of religion and the church within the national system of elementary education. But other issues also played a part, notably the position of the religious orders, among which the most controversial were the Jesuits. In the eyes of many Liberals, the religious orders were enemies of political and spiritual freedom and any measure to restrict their freedom of action actually enhanced everyone else's. In a number of instances, including the Prussian *Kulturkampf* of the 1870s, attacks on the church by the state proved counterproductive as they led to a closing of ranks and an increased sense of loyalty to the clergy within the Catholic community.[92] This was a major reason for the depth of popular support for the church and the political dominance of the Centre Party in such Rhineland cities as Cologne and Düsseldorf in the later nineteenth century.

Furthermore, the depth and bitterness of class differences in nineteenth-century cities often had important repercussions for religion. Religious denominations became identified with the values and interests of specific social groups. Members of other social classes felt themselves forced out. For instance, Gustafsson's analysis of declining church attendance and participation in communion in Stockholm and Gothenburg in the 1880s shows that the decline was most marked among artisans. He explains this in terms of growing class consciousness, and a desire to avoid the close contact with members of higher social strata that churchgoing would involve: church marriage and baptism, which only involved the participation of social equals, remained at a high level.[93] Koditschek's study of Bradford in the first half of the nineteenth century discusses in some detail the relationship between class conflict and sectarianism. Up to about 1830 Bradford was dominated by a 'genteel' Tory Anglican élite, drawn from the landed gentry, the professions and descendants of the successful merchants and manufacturers of an earlier generation. In the 1830s and 1840s their position was increasingly challenged by younger men of relatively humble origins, mostly born outside Bradford, predominantly Nonconformist, fervently Liberal and hostile to what they saw as an effete and parasitic ruling élite. Many of this new group were Baptists or Congregationalists, and in particular Horton Lane Congregational chapel became a 'cathedral of Nonconformity', attended by the editor of the *Bradford Observer* and by four of the town's first five mayors. Up to the 1820s, Koditschek argues, many chapels were attended by a mixture of the different classes, but this became less common after the 1825 weavers' strike, which led to a sharpening of class tensions. In the 1830s and 1840s the new bourgeois élite came to dominate many Congregational and Baptist chapels, making them strongholds of Liberal politics and the gospel of self-help. The Methodists retained a relatively large working-class membership, but many workers gave up any active connection with church or chapel, while retaining their belief in a kind of Christian radicalism, which shaped much of the rhetoric of Chartism.[94]

Nineteenth-century cities contained an immense variety of types of religion, as is indicated both by Kselman's overview of the situation in French cities and by Binfield's more microscopic study of the various kinds of church and chapel community in Sheffield. In 1874–5 a famous series of volumes was published, written by an Anglican clergyman, the Rev. C.M. Davies, and entitled respectively *Orthodox London*, *Unorthodox London* and *Hereterodox London*, the first referring to Anglicanism, the second to mainstream Non-conformity and the third to the many smaller bodies which fell outside the bounds of religious respectability. The latter groups may have been small, but there were a lot of them: London offered both freedom and a large enough pool of potential converts for any heretical thinker, no matter how idiosyncratic, to gather together a body of like-minded souls. In the early twentieth century a collection of 'Metropolitan Documents', focused on the more sensational, and often the sleazier, aspects of life in Berlin and Vienna, also found room for volumes on sects and on spiritualism in Berlin. While the sects did rather better in some rural and mining areas than in the German capital, spiritualism seems to have been a characteristically urban phenomenon in this period.[95] As Kselman shows, it ranked among the more significant religious alternatives to Catholicism in French cities during the Third Republic. It had a special appeal to those who longed for contact with the supernatural, but who wished to escape from the doctrinal and ethical rigidities of orthodox religion, and who wanted scope for individual experimentation.[96]

Journalists revelled in the opportunities for good stories afforded by the numerous species of exotic belief that flourished around them. But in the eyes of many of their fellow citizens this pluralism was a source for regret. They looked at the signs of social disintegration around them, and they longed for the moral unity which a common faith had once offered. Ultramontane Catholics, evangelical Protestants and Marxist socialists were agreed on one thing: that they themselves had found the path that would lead to unity and justice, and that all other paths led to disaster.[97] Of course, similar battles were fought out with equal bitterness between Orthodox, liberal and secular Jews. In terms of the law, the nineteenth century was an oasis of toleration between the era of established church religious monoplies and the era of totalitarian states. But mentally this toleration was very limited. Occasionally it broke down altogether, as in Belfast's periodic sectarian battles, in the pogroms in Odessa and Warsaw, in the executions of priests by the Paris Commune or in Barcelona's Tragic Week, where anticlerical gangs toured the city burning down religious buildings.[98] More frequently, Catholics, Protestants and Socialists dealt with pluralism by building their own ghettos within which their own people would be protected from over-close contact with alien beliefs. The Belgian example, described by Strikwerda in his contribution to this volume, had its counterparts all over Europe in the later nineteenth and early twentieth

INTRODUCTION

centuries as Catholics, Protestants and Socialists set up their own newspapers, founded their own educational institutions, formed their own youth groups, women's organizations and football clubs. In some cities the formation of housing co-operatives even led literally to the construction of ghettos, as one block of flats would house only Social Democrats and another was available only to Protestants.[99] Nineteenth-century European cities thus combined high levels of de facto religious pluralism with low levels of mutual acceptance and understanding.

NOTES

1 Owen Chadwick, *The Popes and the European Revolution*, Oxford, 1981, p. 97; William Callahan, 'The Spanish church,' in W.J. Callahan and D. Higgs (eds), *Church and Society in Catholic Europe of the Nineteenth Century*, Cambridge, 1979, p. 36.
2 Jeffrey Kaplow, *The Names of Kings: The Parisian Laboring Poor in the Eighteenth Century*, New York, 1972, p. 112.
3 Gregory Freeze, '"Going to the intelligentsia": The church and its urban mission in post-reform Russia', in E.W. Clowes, S.D. Kassow and J.L. West (eds), *Between Tsar and People*, Princeton, NJ, 1991, p. 217; Callahan 'The Spanish church', p. 37; David Higgs, 'The Portuguese church', in Callahan and Higgs (eds), *Church and Society*, pp. 54–5.
4 Callahan, 'The Spanish church', p. 46.
5 Higgs, 'The Portuguese church', pp. 58–60; David Garrioch, *Neighbourhood and Community in Paris 1740–1790*, Cambridge, 1986, pp. 149–68.
6 Christina Rathgeber, 'The reception of the religious Aufklärung in Berlin at the end of the eighteenth century', Ph.D. thesis, University of Cambridge, 1986, pp. 219–21, 282–5; Peter Fassl, *Konfession, Wirtschaft und Politik: Von der Reichsstadt zur Industriestadt, Augsburg 1750–1850*, Sigmaringen, 1988; pp. 111–14.
7 G. Rudé, *Hanoverian London*, London, 1971, pp. 107–10, 112–13; Herman Diederiks, 'Grosstadt und Konfession: Amsterdam', in K. Elm and H.-D. Loock (eds), *Seelsorge und Diakonie in Berlin*, Berlin, 1990, pp. 33–4; P. Corish, *The Catholic Community in the Seventeenth and Eighteenth Centuries*, Dublin, 1981, pp. 82–8; Thomas C. Owen, *Capitalism and Politics in Russia: A Social History of the Moscow Merchants 1855–1905*, Cambridge, 1981, p. 11; F.C. Conybeare, *Russian Dissenters*, Cambridge, Mass., 1921, pp. 215–58.
8 Joseph Michman, 'The impact of German–Jewish modernization on Dutch Jewry', in Jacob Katz (ed.), *Towards Modernity: The European Jewish Model*, New Brunswick, NJ, 1987, p. 174; Jacob Katz, *Out of the Ghetto: The Social Background of Jewish Emancipation 1770–1870*, New York, 1978, pp. 9–13; Deborah Hertz, 'Seductive conversion

in Berlin, 1770–1809', in Todd Endelman (ed.), *Jewish Apostasy in the Modern World*, New York, 1987, p. 49.
9   Fassl, *Konfession, Wirtschaft und Politik*, pp. 107–9.
10 Ralph Gibson, *A Social History of French Catholicism 1789–1914*, London, 1987, pp. 12–13.
11 B. Greaves, 'Methodism in Yorkshire, 1740–1851', Ph.D. thesis, University of Liverpool, 1968, pp. 54, 84; Olwen Hufton, 'The French church', in Callahan and Higgs (eds), *Church and Society*, p. 29.
12 F. Charpin, *Pratique religieuse et formation d'une grande ville (Marseille 1806–1958)*, Paris, 1964; Joseph Bradley, *Muzhik and Muscovite*, Berkeley, Calif., 1985, pp. 65–6; Peter Allum, *Politics and Society in Post-War Naples*, Cambridge, 1973.
13 Statistics are taken from Adna F. Weber, *The Growth of Cities in the Nineteenth Century*, New York, 1899; P. de Vries, *European Urbanization 1500–1800*, London, 1984; Anthony Sutcliffe (ed.), *Metropolis, 1890–1940*, London, 1984.
14 Charpin, *Pratique religieuse*, pp. 281–301; Felix Escher, 'Pfarrgemeinden und Gemeinde-Organisation der katholischen Kirche in Berlin bis zur Gründung des Bistums Berlin', in Elm and Loock (eds), *Seelsorge und Diakonie*, pp. 285–6 (describing conflict between Catholic clergy and Polish immigrants).
15 For Scotland, see Callum Brown, *A Social History of Religion in Scotland since 1730*, London, 1987, p. 131.
16 See, for instance, Maurice Agulhon (ed.), *La ville de l'âge industrielle*, Paris, 1983, pp. 577–91.
17 W.R. Ward, *Religion and Society in England 1790–1850*, London, 1972, pp. 88–93.
18 Friedrich Engels, *The Condition of the Working Class in England in 1844*, English trans., Oxford, 1958, p. 141; B.I. Coleman, *The Idea of the City in Nineteenth-Century Britain*, London, 1973, p. 97; J. Boeck, 'Predigt in Berlin', in Elm and Loock (eds), *Seelsorge und Diakonie*, pp. 315–18. Very similar comments were being made some fifty years later by Russian bishops: Daniel R. Brower, *The Russian City between Tradition and Modernity 1850–1900*, Berkeley, Calif., 1990, p. 152.
19 Brown, *Social History of Religion in Scotland*, p. 141; Andrew Lees, *Cities Perceived*, Manchester, 1985, pp. 45–7.
20 Friedrich Sass, *Berlin in seiner neuesten Zeit und Entwicklung, 1846*, Berlin, 1983, pp. 111–12; Ernst Dronke, *Berlin*, 2 vols, Frankfurt-am-Main, 1846, vol. 1, pp. 9–10.
21 Callum G. Brown, 'Did urbanization secularize Britain?', *Urban History Yearbook*, 1988, pp. 1–14.
22 E.R. Wickham, *Church and People in an Industrial City*, London, 1957, p. 11. For 'modernization', Alan D. Gilbert, *Religion and Society in Industrial England: Church, Chapel and Social Change, 1740–1914*, London, 1976; and Werner K. Blessing, *Staat und Kirche in der Gesellschaft: Institutionelle Autorität und mentaler Wandel in Bayern während des 19. Jahrhunderts*, Göttingen, 1982. For the Marxist approach, various writings by Eric Hobsbawm, notably the essay

'Religion and the rise of socialism', in his collection *Worlds of Labour*, London, 1984, pp. 33–48.

23 See the discussion in Martha Rosenblit, *The Jews of Vienna, 1867–1914*, Albany, NY, 1983, pp. 1–10.

24 The clearest statement of the latter position is Bonnie Smith, *Ladies of the Leisure Class: The Bourgeoises of Lille*, Princeton, NJ, 1981. The most thorough statement of the case for a direct connection between urbanization and secularization is Gregory Singleton, *Religion in the City of Angels: American Protestant Culture and Urbanization, Los Angeles 1850–1930*, n.p., 1979.

25 This section draws on material from Hugh McLeod, *Poverty and Piety: Working Class Religion in Berlin, London and New York, 1870–1914*, New York, 1994.

26 F.G. Lisco, *Zur Kirchengeschichte Berlins*, Berlin, 1857, pp. 113–14; Lucian Hölscher, *Weltgericht oder Revolution*, Stuttgart, 1989, p. 158; Wolfgang Ribbe, 'Zur Entwicklung und Funktion der Pfarrgemeinden in der evangelischen Kirche Berlins bis zum Ende der Monarchie', in Elm and Loock (eds), *Seelsorge und Diakonie*, pp. 233–63.

27 Walter Wendland, *Siebenhundert Jahre Kirchengeschichte Berlins*, Berlin, 1930; Günter Wirth (ed.), *Beiträge zur Berliner Kirchengeschichte*, Berlin, 1987; Jochen-Christoph Kaiser, 'Sozialdemokratie und "praktische" Religionskritik. Das Beispiel der Kirchenaustrittsbewegung, 1878–1914', *Archiv für Sozialgeschichte*, 22, 1982, pp. 263–98.

28 Günter Brakelmann, Martin Greschat and Werner Jochmann, *Protestantismus und Politik, Werk und Wirkung Adolf Stoeckers*, Hamburg, 1982; K.E. Pollman, *Landesherrliches Kirchenregiment und Sozialfrage*, Berlin, 1973; Hugh McLeod, 'Religion in the British and German labour movements c.1890–1914: A comparison', *Bulletin of the Society for the Study of Labour History*, 50, 1986, p. 27.

29 Rathgeber, 'The Aufklärung in Berlin', pp. 17–18, 75–80; Alfred Kelly, *The Descent of Darwin: The Popularisation of Darwin in Germany 1860–1914*, Chapel Hill, NC, 1981; Thomas Nipperdey, *Religion im Umbruch: Deutschland 1870–1918*, Munich, 1988, pp. 124–53 provides an overview of the currents of religious unbelief in Germany – unfortunately there is no detailed study of Berlin.

30 *Berlin und die Berliner: Leute, Dinge, Sitten, Winke*, Karlsruhe, 1905, p. 508.

31 For fuller discussion of figures, see McLeod, *Poverty and Piety*.

32 P. Pieper, *Kirchliche Statistik Deutschlands*, Freiburg, 1899, p. 232.

33 *Statistisches Jahrbuch der Stadt Berlin*, 32, 1908–11, pp. 873–4.

34 Burkhard Asmuss and Andreas Nachama, 'Zur Geschichte der Juden in Berlin und das Jüdische Gemeindezentrum in Charlottenburg', in Wolfgang Ribbe (ed.), *Von der Residenz zur City: 275 Jahre Charlottenburg*, Berlin, 1980, pp. 165–228; Peter Hönigmann, *Die Austritte aus der Jüdischen Gemeinde Berlin 1873–1941*, Frankfurt-am-Main, 1988.

35 Brigitte Emig, *Die Veredelung des Arbeiters*, Frankfurt-am-Main, 1980,

HUGH MCLEOD

pp. 94–103; Vernon L. Lidtke, *The Alternative Culture*, New York, 1985.

36 Jim Obelkevich, 'Music and religion in the nineteenth century', in Jim Obelkevich, Lyndal Roper and Raphael Samuel (eds), *Disciplines of Faith*, London, 1987, pp. 561–3; Nipperdey, *Religion im Umbruch*, pp. 140–3.

37 McLeod, *Poverty and Piety*, ch. 4; Dietrich Mühlberg (ed.), *Arbeiterleben um 1900*, Berlin, 1983, pp. 155–9.

38 Pieper, *Kirchliche Statistik*, pp. 150–4.

39 F. Houtart, *Les paroisses de Bruxelles*, Brussels, 1955, p. 34; Y. Daniel, *L'équipement paroissiale d'un diocèse urbain (Paris 1802–1956)*, Paris, 1957, p. 110; J. Weissensteiner, 'Die Erzdiozese Wien', in Erwin Gatz (ed.), *Pfarr- und Gemeindeorganisation: Studien zu ihrer Entwicklung in Deutschland, Österreich und der Schweiz seit dem Ende des 18.Jahrhunderts*, Paderborn, 1987, p. 44; J. Weissensteiner, 'Grossstadtseelsorge in Wien', in Elm and Loock (eds), *Seelsorge und Diakonie*, p. 118.

40 Lucien Hölscher, 'Die Religion des Bürgers. Bürgerliche Frömmigkeit und Protestantische Kirche im 19. Jahrhundert', *Historische Zeitschrift*, 256, 1990, pp. 629–30.

41 Pieper, *Kirchliche Statistik*, p. 232; Blessing, *Staat und Kirche*, pp. 240–5; H.J. Brandt, 'Kirchliches Vereinswesen und Freizeitgestaltung in einer Arbeitergemeinde 1872–1933', in G. Huck (ed.) *Sozialgeschichte der Freizeit*, Hamburg, 1980, pp. 207–22.

42 B. Gustafsson, *Socialdemokratien och kyrkan, 1881–90*, Stockholm, 1953, p. 145.

43 G. Cholvy and Y.-M. Hilaire, *Histoire religieuse de la France contemporaine*, 3 vols, Toulouse, 1985–8, vol. 2, p. 198; Hugh McLeod, 'White collar values and the role of religion', in Geoffrey Crossick (ed.), *The Lower Middle Class in Britain 1870–1914*, London, 1977, p. 87.

44 Gibson, *Social History of French Catholicism*, p. 178; Gustafsson, *Socialdemokratien*, pp. 181–3.

45 For the social profile of Berlin Protestantism in the early nineteenth century, see Rathgeber, 'The Aufklärung in Berlin', and for the later part of the century, McLeod, *Poverty and Piety*.

46 Olive Anderson, 'The incidence of civil marriage in Victorian England and Wales', *Past and Present*, 69, 1975, p. 77.

47 Cholvy and Hilaire, *Histoire religieuse*, vol. 2, p. 204.

48 G. Jacquemet, 'Déchristianisation, structures familiales et anticléricalisme; Belleville au XIXe siècle', *Archives des sciences sociales de la religion*, 57, 1984, pp. 69–82; E. Hülle, *Die kirchliche Statistik in Berlin*, Berlin, 1876, p. 32.

49 Paul Drews, *Das kirchliche Leben der evangelisch-lutherischen Landeskirche des Königreichs Sachsen*, Tübingen, 1902, pp. 80–2; Gibson, *Social History of French Catholicism*, p. 164.

50 Cf. the critical comments by Cholvy and Hilaire in *Histoire religieuse*, vol. 1, p. 333, on the 'culpabilization' of French Catholics, and Claude Langlois's stress in his contribution ('Permanence, renouveau et affrontements (1830–1880)') to F. Lebrun (ed.), *Histoire des*

34

catholiques en France, Toulouse, 1980, p. 291, on the achievements of the nineteenth-century church.

51 Cf. Jeffrey Cox's comments on the myopia of American intellectuals in matters to do with religion in *English Churches in a Secular Society: Lambeth 1870–1930*, Oxford, 1982, p. 276.

52 For a brief declaration of historical faith by Callum Brown see the introduction to his *The People in the Pews: Religion and Society in Scotland since 1780*, Glasgow, 1993, and for an impassioned critique of the secularization thesis on the grounds that it is 'insufficiently "bedded down" in the empirical evidence' see his essay, 'A revisionist approach to religious change', in Steve Bruce (ed.), *Religion and Modernization: Sociologists and Historians debate the Secularization Thesis*, Oxford, 1992, p. 31–58.

53 A statistical study that emphasizes the influence of religion on voting in pre-1914 Britain is Kenneth D. Wald, *Crosses on the Ballot*, Princeton, NJ, 1983. Numerous local studies have illuminated the religious dimension of Liberal/Conservative conflict: see, for instance, Patrick Joyce, *Work, Society and Politics*, Brighton, 1980. There is also a considerable literature on the religious dimensions of the rise of Labour, though historians remain fundamentally divided on this subject. See, for instance, A. Ainsworth, 'Religion in the working class community, and the evolution of socialism in late Victorian Lancashire: A case of working class consciousness', *Histoire sociale*, 10, 1977, pp. 354–80; W. Knox, 'Religion and the Scottish labour movement 1900–1939', *Journal of Contemporary History*, 23, 1988, pp. 609–30.

54 See John W. Boyer, *Political Radicalism in Late Imperial Vienna*, Chicago, Ill., 1981; P.J. Waller, *Democracy and Sectarianism: A Social and Political History of Liverpool 1868–1939*, Liverpool, 1981.

55 B.I. Coleman, 'The church extension movement in London c.1800–1860', Ph.D. thesis, University of Cambridge, 1968; W.R. Ward, 'The cost of establishment: Some reflections on church building in Manchester', *Studies in Church History*, 3, 1966, pp. 273–87; Richard J. Evans, *Death in Hamburg*, Harmondsworth, 1990, p. 102; Houtart, *Les paroisses de Bruxelles*, pp. 36–7; Daniel, *L'équipment paroissiale*, pp. 42–3.

56 Judson Mather, 'The Assumptionist response to secularization 1870–1900', in Robert Bezucha (ed.), *Modern European Social History*, Lexington, Mass., 1972, pp. 59–89; Alan Bartlett, 'Churches in Bermondsey, 1880–1939', Ph.D. thesis, University of Birmingham, 1987, pp. 261–85; Michael Schneider, *Die christlichen Gewerkschaften 1894–1933*, Bonn 1982; Willi Schwank, *Kirche und Sport in Deutschland von 1848 bis 1920*, Hochheim-am-Rhein, 1979; Gerard Cholvy (ed.), *Le Patronage: ghetto ou vivier?*, Paris, 1989.

57 Cox, *English Churches*, pp. 48–89; Bartlett, 'Churches in Bermondsey', pp. 135–69.

58 R.C. Sun, '"Before the enemy is within our walls": A social, cultural and political history of the Catholic workers in Cologne, 1885–1912', Ph.D. thesis, Johns Hopkins University, 1991.

59 The classic statement of this interpretation is Louis Chevalier, *Classes laborieuses et classes dangereuses à Paris pendant la première moitié du XIXe siècle*, Paris, 1958. Among histories of nineteenth-century religion, the one who comes closet to this approach is Charpin, *Pratique religieuse*.

60 Paul M. Hohenberg and Lynn Hollen Lees, *The Making of Urban Europe 1000–1950*, Cambridge, Mass., 1985, pp. 263–5; Lynn Hollen Lees, *Exiles of Erin*, Manchester, 1979. Two of my own works are very much in this tradition: Hugh McLeod, 'Class, community and region: The religious geography of nineteenth-century England', in Michael Hill (ed.), *A Sociological Yearbook of Religion in Britain*, vol. 6, London, 1973, pp. 29–73, and *Class and Religion in the Late Victorian City*, London, 1974.

61 For example, many rural areas of southern Spain and Portugal. See Higgs, 'The Portuguese church', pp. 54–5; Frances Lannon, *Privilege, Persecution and Prophecy: The Catholic Church in Spain 1875–1975*, Oxford, 1987, pp. 13–14. For a detailed account of an isolated area of eastern France, where the church had little presence before the mid-nineteenth century, see S. Bonnet, 'Verriers et bûcherons d'Agronne', in F. Bédarida and J. Maitron (eds), *Christianisme et monde ouvrier*, Paris, 1975.

62 Marsha Rosenblit, 'Jewish assimilation in Habsburg Vienna', in Jonathan Frankel and Steven Zipperstein (eds), *Assimilation and Community: The Jews in Nineteenth Century Europe*, Cambridge, 1992, pp. 231–2.

63 McLeod, 'Class, community and region'.

64 F. Boulard and J. Remy, *Pratique religieuse urbaine et régions culturelles*, Paris, 1968.

65 W. Brepohl, *Industrievolk im Wandel von der agraren zur industriellen Daseinsform dargestellt am Ruhrgebiet*, Tübingen, 1957, pp. 70–90.

66 W. Bartoszewski and A. Polonsky (eds), *Jews in Warsaw: A History*, Oxford, 1991, pp. 11, 21; Rozenblit, 'Jewish assimilation', pp. 232–4, and *Jews of Vienna*, pp. 150–3.

67 Jörg Kniffka, *Das kirchliche Leben in Berlin-Ost in der Mitte der zwanziger Jahre*, Münster, 1971; Cox, *English Churches*, p. 193.

68 Hugh McLeod, *Religion and the People of Western Europe, 1789–1970*, Oxford, 1981, pp. 81–3; Evans, *Death in Hamburg*, pp. 356–63.

69 J. Rohde, 'Streiflichter aus der Berliner Kirchengeschichte von 1900 bis 1918', in Wirth (ed.), *Beiträge zur Berliner Kirchengeschichte*, pp. 228–37.

70 Bruce (ed.), *Religion and Modernization*, contains some of the latest ideas on secularization. Several contributors focus on the relationship between secularization and urbanization, with Callum Brown and Steve Bruce arguing from opposite standpoints.

71 The fullest discussion of this theme is A. Wahl, 'Confession et comportement dans les campagnes d'Alsace et de Bade, 1871–1939', doctoral thesis, University of Metz, 1980, 2 vols. See also Hugh McLeod, 'Building the "Catholic ghetto": Catholic organisations 1870–1914', in W.J. Sheils and Diana Wood (eds), *Voluntary Religion*,

Studies in Church History, vol. 23, Oxford, 1986, pp. 411–44.

72 Rozenblit, *Jews of Vienna*, pp. 8–10 and *passim*; Stephen D. Corssin, 'Warsaw: Poles and Jews in a conquered city', in Michael F. Hamm (ed.), *The City in Late Imperial Russia*, Bloomington, Ind., 1986, pp. 123–50.

73 K.S. Inglis, 'Patterns of religious worship in 1851', *Journal of Ecclesiastical History*, 11, 1960, pp. 74–86; Brown, *Social History of Religion in Scotland*, p. 61.

74 For patterns of middle-class religious affiliation in English cities in the nineteenth century, see E.P. Hennock, *Fit and Proper Persons*, London, 1973; L. Davidoff and C. Hall, *Family Fortunes*, London, 1987; Theodore Koditschek, *Class Formation in Urban–Industrial Society: Bradford 1750–1850*, Cambridge, 1990. For patterns of working-class affiliation, see Wickham, *Church and People*; Bartlett, 'Churches in Bermondsey'. The most thorough statistical studies of church membership records are P.T. Phillips, *The Sectarian Spirit*, Toronto, 1982; Rosemary Chadwick, 'Church and people in Bradford and district, 1880–1914', D.Phil. thesis, University of Oxford, 1986; Mark Smith, 'Religion in industrial society: Oldham and Saddleworth, 1780–1865', D.Phil. thesis, University of Oxford, 1987. For Scotland, see A.A. MacLaren, *Religious and Social Class: The Disruption Years in Aberdeen*, London, 1974; P. Hillis, 'Presbyterianism and social class in mid-nineteenth century Glasgow: A study of nine churches', *Journal of Ecclesiastical History*, 32, 1981, pp. 47–64; Brown, *Social History of Religion in Scotland*.

75 R.M. Bigler, *The Politics of German Protestantism*, Los Angeles, Calif., 1972; Catherine M. Prelinger, *Charity, Challenge and Change: Religious Dimensions of the Mid-Nineteenth Century Women's Movement in Germany*, New York, 1987; Sylvia Paletschek, *Frauen und Dissens: Frauen im Deutschkatholizismus und in den Freien Gemeinden*, Göttingen, 1990.

76 Andrew Blane, 'Protestant sects in late Imperial Russia', in Andrew Blane (ed.), *The Religious World of Russian Culture*, 2 vols, The Hague, 1975, pp. 267–304; S.M. Dixon, 'Church, state and society in late imperial Russia: The Diocese of St Petersburg, 1880–1914', Ph.D. thesis, University of London, 1993, pp. 247–56.

77 Peter Martyn, 'The undefined town within a town', in Bartoszewski and Polonsky (eds) *Jews in Warsaw*, pp. 55–83; Stefan Kieniwicz, 'Assimilated Jews in nineteenth-century Warsaw', in ibid., pp. 171–80.

78 Jean-Pierre Chaline, *Les bourgeois de Rouen: Une élite urbaine au XIXe siècle*, Paris, 1982, pp. 261–3; Colin Heywood, 'The Catholic Church and the business community in nineteenth-century France', in Frank Tallett and Nicholas Atkin (eds), *Religion, Society and Politics in France since 1789*, London, 1991, pp. 83–4.

79 Iain McCalman, *Radical Underworld: Prophets, Revolutionaries and Pornographers in London, 1795–1840*, Cambridge, 1988.

80 McLeod, *Class and Religion*, pp. 231–9.

81 Wendland, *Siebenhundert Jahre Kirchengeschichte Berlins*, pp. 287–91, 317.

82 Christopher Read, *Religion, Revolution and the Russian Intelligentsia*, London, 1979, p. 13.
83 William J. Callahan, *Church, Politics and Society in Spain, 1750–1874*, Cambridge, Mass., 1984.
84 Cholvy and Hilaire, *Histoire religieuse*, vol. 2, p. 198; McLeod, *Class and Religion*, p. 304.
85 E. Rolffs, *Das kirchliche Leben der evangelischen kirchen in Niedersachsen*, Tübingen, 1917, p. 447.
86 McLeod, *Religion and the People*, p. 107.
87 Hugh McLeod, 'Weibliche Frömmigkeit, männlicher Unglaube?', in Ute Frevert (ed.), *Bürgerinnen und Bürger*, Göttingen, 1988, pp. 134–56; Clive Field, 'Adam and Eve: Gender and the English Free Church constituency', *Journal of Ecclesiastical History*, 44, 1993, pp. 63–79.
88 Rickie Burman, '"She looketh well to the Ways of her Household": The changing role of Jewish women in religious life, c.1880–1930', in Gail Malmgreen (ed.), *Religion in the Lives of English Women, 1760–1930*, London, 1986, pp. 234–57; Marion A. Kaplan, *The Making of the Jewish Middle Class: Women, Family and Identity in Imperial Germany*, New York, 1991, pp. 69–70, 78–9.
89 For an overview of the patterns of working-class religious adherence, see Hugh McLeod, 'The dechristianization of the working class in western Europe, c.1850–1900', *Social Compass*, 27, 1980, pp. 191–214; and for Belfast, see David Hempton and Myrtle Hill, *Evangelical Protestantism and Ulster Society 1740–1890*, London, 1992, pp. 115–21. For the overall social profile of religion in various countries, see Gibson, *Social History of French Catholicism*, pp. 193–226; for Germany, Lucian Hölscher's contribution to this volume; for Spain, José Andrés-Gallego, 'Sobre las formas de pensar y de ser: La Iglesia', *Historia general de España y América*, 16: 1, Madrid, 1983, pp. 287–303; for Russia, Freeze, '"Going to the intelligentsia"', pp. 219–20. For comments on the piety of Moscow merchants, Owen, *Capitalism and Politics*, pp. 11–12, 83, 148–50.
90 Ward, *Religion and Society*, p. 13.
91 Jonathan Sperber, *Popular Catholicism in Nineteenth-Century Germany*, Princeton, NJ, 1984, pp. 216–7.
92 Gottfried Korff, 'Kulturkampf und Volksfrömmigkeit', in Wolfgang Schieder (ed.), *Volksreligiosität in der modernen Sozialgeschichte*, Göttingen, 1986, pp. 137–51.
93 Gustafsson, *Socialdemokratien*, English summary.
94 Koditschek, *Class Formation*.
95 Eberhard Büchner, *Sekten und Sektierer in Berlin*, Berlin, 1905; H. Freimark, *Moderne Geisterbeschwörer und Wahrheitssücher*, Berlin, n.d.
96 See Logie Barrow, *Independent Spirits: Spiritualism and English Plebeians 1850–1910*, London, 1986.
97 McLeod, *Religion and the People*, p. 36.
98 J.C. Ullman, *The Tragic Week*, Cambridge, Mass., 1968; Frederick Skinner, 'Odessa and the problem of urban modernization', in Hamm (ed.), *City in Late Imperial Russia*, pp. 209–48.

99 For some discussion of this phenomenon in the case of Berlin, see
    McLeod, *Poverty and Piety*, ch. 1. There is a brief mention of it in
    Leiden in Manuela du Bois Reymond and Agnes E.M. Jonker, 'The
    city's public space and urban childhood', in Lex Heerma van Voss and
    Frits van Holthoon (eds), *Working Class and Popular Culture*,
    Amsterdam, 1988, p. 50.

Part I

RESPONSES OF THE CHURCHES TO URBANIZATION

1

AN ORGANIZATIONAL AND PASTORAL FAILURE

Urbanization, industrialization and religion in Spain, 1850–1930

William J. Callahan

On 2 July 1855, the first general strike in Spanish history took place in Barcelona and nearby industrial towns. In the absence of the city's bishop, the prelate of the neighbouring diocese of Vich, Antonio Palau, urged workers to return to work with a spirit of Christian resignation. By 1858, after becoming bishop of the country's manufacturing capital, Palau viewed growing social tensions in a more pessimistic light. He warned the rich of his diocese: 'Your pride will cause the disbelieving masses to rise up; your banquets will irritate the appetite of the naked and hungry crowds, and neither laws, courts, gallows nor armies will be sufficient to contain the outburst of the unbridled multitude.'[1] The bishop's fear of an imminent explosion of violence proved unfounded, but Palau foresaw in some measure the religious implications of incipient urbanization and industrialization: 'Who can doubt that people from all parts of the world, of all religions . . . flow to the great centres of manufacturing and commerce, and communicate . . . their religious indifference.' In his own diocese, the prelate believed that 'faith has grown languid, charity has become cold [and] religious sentiment has grown weak'.[2]

Palau was not alone in perceiving that capitalist economic change and its social effects posed a new and troubling challenge for the church. Neither the bishop nor other ecclesiastical commentators of the time suggested an institutional response other than to lament the excesses of liberal economic policy and to urge workers to reject the utopian socialism that had already made an appearance in Catalonia. Palau's predecessor in Barcelona, Bishop Costa y Borràs, was sufficiently alarmed, however, by the progress of what he saw as radical social ideas to promote an ambitious campaign of urban missions directed to workers, although results were disappointing. Costa y Borràs also encouraged the initiatives of a Carmelite friar, Francesc Palau, whose Escola de Virtut, established in 1851, attempted to reach the city's working class through an innovative programme of pastoral instruction. The success of the Escola aroused the suspicions of the civil authorities who unjustly accused it of fomenting social unrest. Indeed, the Progressive government in power during the labour agitation of 1854–5 ordered Palau's arrest and the Escola's dissolution.

More than other ecclesiastical figures of the time, Palau recognized that the church required new methods to communicate its message to industrial workers, many of whom were living in impoverished industrial districts without parish churches. 'The common and ordinary methods' employed by the clergy in its pastoral work, he argued, were no longer adequate to halt the spread of religious indifference among a population living in economic and social conditions radically different from those existing in a traditional agrarian society.[3] The Escola's method of 2-hour weekly sessions, open to both sexes and all social classes, was based on the 'free examination' of doctrinal and philosophical questions. Although innovative from a pastoral perspective, the discussions were general in character and presented no challenge to the existing political order. The hostile reaction of a government obsessed with the danger of social revolution arose less from the message delivered by Palau than from the suspicion that a conspiracy was in the making when 2,000 workers gathered weekly to hear the Carmelite preacher.

With the exception of the Escola and the foundation in 1865 of a Workers' Circle at Manresa by a young Jesuit, Antonio Vicent, the church's response to the pastoral problems created by industrialization and urbanization scarcely existed prior to the revolution of 1868. The reasons for this neglect were several. The episodic capitalist revolution of mid-nineteenth-century Spain remained highly localized. Barcelona and its environs had emerged as the centre of cotton manufacturing by the 1840s, while banking and speculation in property and railway shares expanded Madrid's bureaucratic and artisan economy in new directions. Valencia continued to maintain, although with difficulty, a traditional silk industry based on small enterprises. The capitalist surge that later would convert Bilbao into the centre of a regional economy based on mining and metallurgy had only just begun. Beyond these and a few other industrial pockets, Spain remained an agricultural country. Indeed, as late as 1900, two-thirds of the active labour force continued to work the land. As a result, few bishops and priests came into direct contact with the pastoral problems created by economic change. A late nineteenth-century bishop of Segovia thus felt no scruples about delaying publication of Leo XIII's encyclical, *Rerum Novarum* (1891), on the grounds that 'neither workers nor factories, nor, by the mercy of God, the errors combatted by the encyclical, abound in the city'.[4]

Between the final triumph of liberalism over absolute monarchy in 1834 and the establishment of the First Republic in 1873, the church's energies were consumed by the necessity of coming to terms with a political system which virtually destroyed a centuries-old ecclesiastical superstructure. In 1836, the ministry of Juan Alvarez Mendizábal suppressed the male religious orders, while successive liberal governments between 1835 and 1860 sold off the vast properties of the secular and regular clergy. During the regency of General Espartero (1840–3), there loomed the possibility that the government would succeed in implementing a revolutionary scheme for a national church tied to the papacy only by loose ceremonial ties. This radical plan, identified with the Progressive Party, was partially implemented until it was set aside by the other great party of mid-nineteenth–century Spain, the Moderates, who seized power after the revolution of 1843.

The Moderate triumph began a decade of rule by the most conservative sectors of liberalism. As a result, the church was able to escape in some measure from the crucible of institutional change imposed by earlier liberal governments. Determined to create a highly centralized state designed to exclude the vaguely populist Progressives from power, the Moderates began to see the church as a possible source of support. Their attempt to solidify a narrow, oligarchic liberalism opposed to political radicalism and to undo the most extreme ecclesiastical reforms of the Espartero regency was welcomed by the church with a sigh of relief, although years passed before agreement was reached between the papacy and the Moderate government. The concordat of 1851 finally sealed a new, if uneasy, accommodation between the church and the conservative version of liberalism, although the agreement did not by any means resolve the chronic and divisive issue of the church's place within liberal Spain. Following the revolution of 1854, which brought the Progressives to power, the sale of ecclesiastical property was resumed.

Even during periods of Moderate rule, relations between church and state were rarely smooth, while the clergy always viewed the Progressives with suspicion. In these circumstances, the church saw liberalism as its principal enemy, although at a practical level, the hierarchy and the papacy reluctantly recognized the necessity of coming to terms with the new order as best they could. Some Catholic thinkers, notably Donoso Cortes, began to perceive socialism as more dangerous than liberalism around mid-century, but, in general, the church saw the fragmented diffusion of communitarian ideas and the tentative beginnings of trades unionism, especially in Barcelona during the 1850s, as less an immediate threat to ecclesiastical interests than as one of the many dangerous currents loosed on the country as a result of liberalism's triumph. Still moved by a traditional organic view of mutual rights and responsibilities on the part of all social classes, the church regarded the free-wheeling economic development of liberal Spain as an example of egoistical excess. Denunciations of the rich and exhortations to the obligation of charity became the stock-in-trade of clerical commentaries on the social question.

Despite the ambiguity of clerical attitudes towards liberalism and the capitalism associated with it, a church that had been victimized by outbursts of violent anticlericalism in 1834 and 1835 feared popular revolution as an ever present danger capable of exploding at any time to sweep away religion, order and property.[5] This general fear of revolution provided the bridge to a stronger accommodation with liberalism that developed between 1866 and 1868 when the hierarchy supported a semi-dictatorial Moderate government led by General Ramón Narváez. The regime's determination to crush social unrest and its willingness to grant financial and educational concessions to the church did not give the clergy all it wanted, but the government's social and ecclesiastical policies offered more than any previous liberal ministry had provided.

This satisfactory state of affairs from a clerical perspective came to an abrupt end with the revolution of 1868. Dominated by Progressives and some disgruntled Moderates, the new government quickly alienated the church. Enactment of a broad programme of civil liberties, including freedom of the press, and proclamation of religious toleration in 1869 angered the clergy. The church also feared that sporadic disorders in town and country threatened the social upheaval it had long feared. The appearance of the First International in the country intensified clerical apprehensions. The International, declared Bishop Lluch y Garriga of Salamanca in 1872, represented nothing less than 'a frightening despotism' intent on placing Spain 'beneath the yoke of communism'.[6] Although there was no prospect that the country would be engulfed by social revolution, clerical fears of impending disaster deepened when the unstable constitutional monarchy established in the wake of the 1868 revolution gave way to the equally shaky First Republic.

The church welcomed, therefore, the social and political stability promised by a former Moderate, Antonio Cánovas del Castillo, who became prime minister in 1874 after a military rising against the transitional regime that had succeeded the failed republic. The new minister's grand design envisaged the creation of a political system based on a constitutional monarchy and a political accommodation between the two great liberal factions, eventually realigned into the Liberal–Conservative Party dominated by Cánovas and the Liberal Party of Práxedes Sagasta. The nature of the Restoration state designed by Cánovas during the 1870s has generated considerable controversy. On the one hand, it rested on liberal parliamentary institutions and allowed, to a greater or lesser degree depending on circumstances, freedom of the press and a measure of cultural pluralism. On the other, it depended for its survival on electoral manipulation in the interests of the social élites controlling the governing parties.

Clerical attitudes towards the Restoration system were ambiguous in many respects. The church recovered its religious monopoly through the 1876 constitution, received increased official funding and won a valuable concession when the government authorized the re-establishment of the male religious orders during the late 1870s. At a practical level, the hierarchy appreciated the advantages secured from the church's constitutional position as the country's established church. But many bishops and priests held serious reservations about the liberal political philosophy on which, however imperfectly, the regime was based. They were also disgruntled by the refusal of successive governments to accept without question wide-ranging ecclesiastical demands for further changes in official policy. But on the other side of the coin, the church looked with favour upon the Restoration's commitment to defend society against the danger of political and social revolution. This shared concern provided the ideological glue cementing relations between church and state.

Although there was never a formal agreement between the civil and ecclesiastical powers in this respect, there is little doubt that an informal 'pact' existed between the church and the bourgeois, conservative élites of the Restoration.[7] For all practical purposes, the hierarchy accepted a tacit alliance with the Restoration system that converted the church into one of the regime's most influential interest groups. The historic ambiguity with which the clergy viewed liberalism and capitalism did not by any means disappear. But by 1900 it was considerably diminished in the name of what Catholic commentators euphemistically called 'social defence'.

After the turn of the century, the growing strength of anarchism in the southern countryside, Marxist socialism in Madrid and Bilbao and a fiercely anticlerical populist republicanism in Barcelona and Valencia moved the hierarchy to identify even more closely with the Restoration's governing élites, especially those gathered in the Conservative party which moved in a pro-clerical direction following the assassination of Cánovas in 1897. The masses, declared Cardinal C.M. Sancha y Hervas of Valencia, had become 'ungovernable' because they had been taught that 'there is no God, no supernatural order, ... nor punishments to be feared' as they moved to destroy the foundations of society.[8] Increasing awareness of growing radicalism among workers, as well as renewed interest in the social question produced by *Rerum Novarum*, led to intense discussion, beginning in the 1890s, about the urgency of devising a more effective strategy to meet these dangerous challenges to religion and the social order. The debate among Catholics concerned with social unrest was conducted by university professors, aristocrats and politicians. Workers contributed nothing to the discussion which focused on the need to defend society against 'the eruption of the ideas of utopian socialism and fierce anarchism'.[9]

The church's identification with the bourgeois society created by nineteenth-century liberalism in the common cause of defending society against radical assault did not occur overnight. It is significant that it developed during a period of intense demographic expansion in the country's most important cities. Between 1857 and 1900, the population of Barcelona grew from 178,625 to 533,000; Madrid, from 281,170 to 539,835; Valencia from 106,435 to 213,550 and Bilbao, from 17,649 to 83,306.

In itself, urban growth posed immense problems of pastoral organization for which the church was unprepared. Although the dynamism of the male religious orders had weakened before their suppression, the regulars were concentrated in the cities where they played an important pastoral role. The disappearance of the male orders shifted the burden of ministering to urban populations entirely to parish priests whose training and largely rural backgrounds provided little guidance as they confronted the enormous pastoral difficulties created by urban expansion. Indeed, as late as 1934, most parish priests in the highly industrialized ecclesiastical provinces of Tarragona and Valencia were still drawn from the ranks of the peasantry. The rural composition of the hierarchy was no less marked until 1878, although after this date, more prelates of urban, bourgeois origins became bishops.

The inflexible organization of the parochial clergy also raised obstacles to the development of an effective pastoral response in urban areas. As a result of the 1851 concordat, parish priests received salaries from the government through a specific appropriation (*Culto y Clero*) in the national budget. For all practical purposes, this constituted an ecclesiastical list which could be expanded only with official permission. Although bishops recognized the need to increase the number of urban parishes, no government, Liberal or Conservative, proved willing to provide funding for more than a token parochial expansion. Madrid's population rose dramatically, for example, to 750,896 by 1920, but the number of parishes remained at thirty. By the first decade of the twentieth century, Barcelona and Madrid possessed parishes that were among the largest in Europe. In Valencia, not a single new parish was created in the city between 1902 and 1944, while the ratio of priests to people was the worst of any diocese in the country.[10]

The church's inability to increase the number of urban parishes in a time of demographic growth was accompanied by severe imbalances in the distribution of clergy, especially in Madrid, Barcelona and Valencia. Canon law and the self-interest of sitting parish priests prevented bishops from carrying out the redistribution of personnel from already well-staffed parishes in urban cores to those located in rapidly expanding industrial suburbs. This problem was aggravated by the male regulars, again abundant in cities by the turn of the century, who preferred choice urban sites close to the upper-class and bourgeois clienteles who attended their churches. As a result of these imbalances, older, well-established parishes and the regular clergy's churches in central Madrid were incomparably better staffed than the few new parishes created in jerry-built suburbs inhabited by thousands of immigrants to the

WILLIAM J. CALLAHAN

capital. The parish of Santa Barbara, located near the fashionable Castellana Avenue, possessed sixteen priests to serve a population of 16,000; the parish of San Ramón in working-class Vallecas only five for its 80,000 residents.[11]

The situation was not improved by career patterns prevailing among parish priests. Work in densely packed, squalid working-class *barrios* held little appeal for many clergy according to Father Hilario Herranz Estáblés, a former seminary professor who became *cura* of such a Madrid parish (Carabanchel Bajo) in 1911. Young priests, he believed, preferred to seek positions as military chaplains, teachers in church schools and employees of cathedral chapters rather than accept difficult and poorly remunerated pastoral charges among the poor. His experience in a parish of 16,000 inhabitants living in ramshackle, congested housing within a maze of unpaved streets convinced him that the church had failed to develop an effective pastoral strategy for the uneducated masses flowing into the capital. His published account of his years in Carabanchel Bajo provides a scathing indictment of the church's failure to develop an urban apostolate. He criticized bishops for their lack of energy in pressing for the creation of more parishes in working-class districts. He censured cathedral canons for enjoying their comfortable positions while ignoring immense pastoral problems close to their doors. He took Madrid's smug Catholic bourgeoisie to task for regarding priests who dared to provide social and medical services to their parishioners as revolutionaries. The Spanish church, he argued, had got its priorities wrong by failing to accord priority to serving 'the humble, [and] the dispossessed'. The priests of working-class parishes, he observed, were 'left alone and without direction in the line of battle' as they struggled in adverse conditions to fulfill their pastoral responsibilities.[12]

The extent to which religious alienation progressed during the second half of the nineteenth century in the country's large cities is difficult to determine. The topic has received little serious study for the nineteenth and early twentieth centuries, but the limited evidence available suggests that the dechristianization lamented by Bishop Palau during the 1850s represented more than an example of the typically catastrophic clerical rhetoric of the times. During the late 1850s, for example, a Barcelona parish priest observed that only one-third of his parishioners were fulfilling the Easter communion obligation, while another noted another early sign of a crisis in observance, the heavy predominance of women meeting this ecclesiastical precept.[13] A map of religious practice cannot be drawn for the nineteenth century, but statistics on fulfilment of the Easter duty in the city of Logroño, which experienced modest economic development between 1860 and 1900, are revealing. The percentage of individuals failing to meet the church's obligation moved from 6.68 per cent in 1860 to 57.8 by 1890, with the greatest decline occurring after 1872.[14]

By the early twentieth century, the clergy viewed the religious condition of Madrid and Barcelona in the bleakest light. On the eve of the Civil War of the 1930s, only 7 per cent of the 80,000 residents of the Madrid working-class parish of San Ramón were attending Sunday mass, 6 per cent fulfilled the Easter communion obligation, 20 per cent chose to be married in civil rather than religious ceremonies. Of those marrying in church, 40 per cent did not know the words of the 'Our Father'. In Madrid, Barcelona, Seville and Bilbao, declared the clerical compiler of these statistics, 'great contingents of the population living in complete paganism can be found'.[15]

Whether the dechristianization lamented by the clergy represented simple non-observance or indicated the existence of a deep crisis of belief among sectors of the population cannot be definitively answered given the present state of research. Fragmentary evidence suggests that the church had ample cause for concern. Less than 50 per cent of the dying in the parish of San José in the Catalan industrial town of Mataró received the last rites in 1900, a proportion that had fallen even lower by the mid-1930s when only one-third did so. In Málaga between 1900 and 1920, the percentage of the dying receiving extreme unction oscillated between 20–30 per cent, in contrast to the strongly observant region of the Tierra de Campos in Old Castile where 90 per cent received the sacrament. The statistics gathered for the parish of San Ramón also show that during the early 1930s one-quarter of its children were unbaptized.[16] Given the transcendent importance attached to the last rites and baptism by the clergy, there seems little doubt that the church faced a religious crisis that went well beyond simple non-observance, although the scale, chronology and social causes of this phenomenon remain to be explored.

The church failed to develop an effective means of reaching out to those who had abandoned religious observance. The clergy relied heavily on the practices of a highly individualistic and often picturesque 'ultramontane piety' in which private devotions predominated over any sense of the liturgy as a community rite. The luxuriant world of popular devotions promoted by the nineteenth-century church held little appeal for those who had given up religious practice. Indeed, it appeared remote and inexplicable to an urban working class desperately seeking to survive in adverse economic conditions. It was scarcely surprising that Father Herranz Establés encountered massive religious absenteeism among his parishioners, for they were

> people carried along as in a flood, atomized socially, without any structure, social, civil or religious. . . . The struggle for life absorbs them. . . . If you ask any of them if there is a God, they reply with a shrug of the shoulders that they have heard nothing of this.[17]

The church's message was also coloured by political and social considerations more likely to provoke than appeal to the religiously alienated. Avidly promoted by the clergy during the nineteenth and early twentieth centuries, the cult of the Sacred Heart provides an example of how closely devotion and conservative ideology became intertwined. Indeed, no cult in Spain was more closely identified with opposition to what the church perceived as the dangerous, secularizing currents of the time. The imposing statue of the Sacred Heart raised on Barcelona's Tibidabo Hill during the 1880s by the city's wealthy Catholic bourgeoisie loomed less as a symbol of divine love than as a threatening presence for the thousands of workers who had already abandoned religious practice and for whom the church was an object of suspicion because of its identification with the upper- and middle-class élites controlling the Restoration state. This identification reached its apotheosis in 1919 when a ceremony dedicating a statue and the nation to the Sacred Heart was attended by King Alfonso XIII and the Conservative prime minister, Antonio Maura. Although by this time the Restoration system was staggering under the weight of accumulated problems, those assembled, 'having closed their ears to tenacious campaigns, terrible strikes and revolutionary threats', heard the sovereign refer to the country's 'strength and constancy in its love for Religion and Monarchy'.[18] Moreover, throughout the Restoration, clerical attacks on Protestantism, rationalism, freemasonry, socialism, anarchism and liberal political philosophy were unceasing. The faithful were exhorted to erect a spiritual redoubt against a corrupt and decadent Spain 'in which the most repugnant scenes of brazen immorality seek to break . . . the barriers imposed by reason and religion'.[19] Religious practice was seen less as a road to salvation than as a sign of a faith of testimony within a church believing itself surrounded by a host of sinister and dangerous forces.

It is likely that the drift away from religious practice and belief preceded by several decades the development of a virulent anti-clerical republicanism, first in Valencia beginning in the 1890s under the leadership of the novelist, Vicente Blasco Ibáñez, and later, between 1900 and 1909, in Barcelona where the Radical Republican Party of Alejandro Lerroux made aggressive hostility towards the church an essential part of its strategy. In Valencia, the stones and cat-calls hurled by resentful crowds against Catholic workers boarding ships for an 1894 pilgrimage to Rome and the violent street riots directed against Archbishop Guisasola in 1907 testify to the depths of anticlerical sentiment among the city's lower classes. In Barcelona, years of demagogic propaganda by Lerroux and his followers contributed directly to the wave of church burnings occurring during the Tragic Week of 1909. By 1910, populist republicanism began to lose adherents in Catalonia and, to a lesser extent, in Valencia to anarcho-syndicalism in the form of the Confederación Nacional de Trabajo (CNT). During the first decade of the century, the Marxist socialism of the Partido Socialista de Obreros Españoles (PSOE) led by Pablo Iglesias also began to expand its ranks significantly in Madrid and Bilbao through its trades union, the Unión General de Trabajadores (UGT). Although hostility towards the church because of its alliance with the existing social and political order was more central to anarchist than socialist concerns, the rank-and-file of the CNT and the UGT viewed the church as a co-conspirator with state and capitalism against the interests of the working class.

For a church historically preoccupied with the danger of popular upheaval, the emergence of these organizations strengthened the clergy's fear of imminent revolution. The acute social tensions gripping the country between 1916 and 1921 further hardened clerical determination to resist at any price what the church saw as dangerous social movements. Indeed, the country was seen as being on the verge of a life or death struggle between Christian civilization and revolutionary hordes bent on its destruction. On one side stood a 'Christian, Catholic society, faithful to Holy Mother the church'; on the other, 'a revolutionary society, the servant of a malignant spirit, moved by its true originator and chief, Satan'.[20]

Belatedly and fitfully, fear of social revolution moved the church to action on a broader front through a series of initiatives identified with the movement known as Social Catholicism. Clerical and lay activists looked to organizational models employed in France, Germany and Belgium as they promoted a variety of working-class associations designed to win back the urban masses of the industrial towns. The new social apostolate was dominated by the male religious orders, especially the Jesuits and Dominicans. The regulars' international character made them more aware of Catholic social action elsewhere in Europe than was the case with a culturally isolated parochial clergy which scarcely participated in the campaign 'to reconquer' the urban masses, although parish priests did play a role in Social Catholicism's efforts to organize co-operatives, credit unions and agrarian syndicates in the countryside.[21]

Between 1890 and 1912, Father Antonio Vicent, a Jesuit long concerned with the social problem, promoted the organization of Workers' Circles modelled on those established in France by Count Albert de Mun.[22] From his base in the order's college in Valencia, Vicent first organized circles in the city and surrounding region before extending his efforts to the country as a whole. Although by the early twentieth century, 258 circles with 180,000 members were in operation, they were concentrated in Valencia, Madrid, Old Castile and the northern coast. They penetrated Catalonia, Aragón, New Castile and Andalucía less successfully. In Madrid and Valencia, the circles attracted workers from the artisan trades and the service sector. But in Barcelona and its manufacturing suburbs, the existence of an industrial working-class and acute social tensions between capital and labour produced a less hospitable recruiting environment.

Assessments of the Workers' Circles and their underlying principles have been harsh even among scholars recognizing the pioneering contribution of Vicent to Spanish Social Catholicism. In his own time and later, critics argued that the circles were incapable by their very nature of effectively organizing workers under Catholic auspices. Vicent's insistence that the circles should be 'mixed' organizations of employers and employees made them suspect in the eyes of many workers. Indeed, the prominent role played by members of the Restoration's élites in the organization of the circles exposed them to the charge that they were little more than devices to prevent the radicalization of the working class. The board of directors of a Madrid circle included, for example, two noblemen, a general, an admiral and a prominent establishment politician. Employers, declared one former disgruntled member, 'have come to believe that they have found the secret of suppressing strikes and workers'.[23] At Vicent's insistence the circles were also ruthlessly confessional to the point of requiring members to meet in a body for compulsory religious services. Imposition of these religious obligations reflected the clergy's desire 'to reconquer' alienated workers, but in practical terms, this was a strategy certain to exclude those who had already abandoned religious practice.

The negative purpose of the circles also undermined their appeal. Although Vicent lamented the damaging social effects of the liberal economic system, his emphasis on the circles' mixed character within an idealistic model of class harmony based on admiration for the medieval guild system did not correspond to the harsh reality of class antagonisms in turn of the century Spain. Vicent saw the circles less as a means to improve the economic plight of workers than as an instrument for saving them from the clutches of socialism. This negative message, often delivered in aggressive tones by the Jesuit and his followers, ensured that neither the circles nor the ideas that lay behind them could win broad support among a working class increasingly attracted by the promise of social and economic transformation offered by the church's ideological competitors.

By the early twentieth century, even Vicent realized that his idealistic vision of class harmony as embodied in the circles was out of touch with reality. The growing strength of the UGT troubled Vicent, who increasingly feared socialism's powerful appeal among urban workers. 'Where have all the workers gone?', he once plaintively asked a member of a circle, only to receive the discouraging reply: 'Father, they have all gone off with the socialists.'[24] The model of a 'mixed' organization also came to be questioned by clerical and lay activists who argued for 'pure' labour unions without employer participation as the only course to follow if the church expected to make any progress in its social apostolate. Even Vicent accepted this change of direction. In 1906 he gave a series of lectures in Barcelona in which he finally abandoned the idea of 'mixed' associations in favour of straightforward labour syndicates.

By this time, however, Vicent was being displaced as the leading figure in Social Catholicism by a fellow Jesuit, Gabriel Palau, who chose the country's industrial capital to launch an ambitious campaign to organize Catholic unions within the framework of a broader movement, the Acción Social Popular, which took the

German Catholic Volksverein as its model. Palau recognized that the unions of the ASP ran the same risk as Vicent's circles of being rejected by workers. To allay their apprehensions, Palau's new labour organizations were allowed to function with a degree of independence, although the ASP, dominated by the city's Catholic bourgeoisie, remained the power behind the scenes.[25]

Palau developed a more sophisticated view of the social question than Vicent, but he was unable to avoid the weaknesses that had undermined the effectiveness of the Workers' Circles. The trades unions of the ASP also emphasized religious practice as a condition of membership in a region where alienation from the church had reached massive proportions. Further, the anti-socialist rhetoric of the ASP as well as its unwillingness to take any action that might provoke employers deprived them of credibility among the workers of Barcelona and its industrial hinterland. The success of Palau's unions was, therefore, minimal. Membership never exceeded 7,000 in a region with more than 200,000 persons employed in manufacturing.[26]

'Pure' labour syndicates also appeared in Madrid, sponsored in many cases by members of the Restoration élites prominent in the direction of Workers' Circles. The first appeared in 1907; others soon followed. The new unions remained under the thumb of the employers, military men and politicians who had once controlled the circles. The grey eminence of Spanish Catholicism, a wealthy industrialist, the marqués de Comillas, saw to it that no breath of independence stirred within the capital's Catholic unions. Over the country as a whole, the success of these 'pure' labour syndicates was unimpressive. It has been estimated that between 1910 and 1913 they enlisted between 15,000 and 20,000 members.[27] By contrast, the UGT contained twice this number by 1910.

Isolated efforts to establish Catholic labour organizations untainted by the epithet of being 'yellow unions' dominated by employers were undertaken. Canon Maximiliano Arboleya of Oviedo promoted the establishment of *sindicatos independientes* in the coalmining districts of Asturias beginning in 1911, an initiative soon frustrated by Comillas, himself a mine-owner in the region. Around the same time, Pedro Gerard, a Dominican influenced by Belgian Social Catholicism, subjected the Workers' Circles and employer-dominated 'pure' syndicates to withering criticism. The history of Catholic social action, he argued, 'has not produced until now any benefits worth mentioning'.[28]

Gerard founded *sindicatos libres* in several cities, but his harsh dismissal of the efforts of conservative Social Catholics gathered around the marqués de Comillas aroused their bitter hostility. Comillas and his clerical allies, especially the Jesuit organizer of the Valladolid railway workers, Sisinio Nevares, and even the ASP of Palau accused the Dominican of advocating a class struggle based on social hatred. No shrinking violet, Gerard replied in kind. He accused his opponents of undermining the effectiveness of the Catholic labour movement by promoting 'yellow unions' controlled by employers.

The struggle between the two camps of Spanish Social Catholicism raged for years. Although in 1919 a compromise of sorts emerged with the formation of a national Catholic labour federation (Consejo Nacional de las Corporaciones Católicas Obreras), it was far too late to recover lost ground. By 1919, the CNT and the UGT had recruited nearly a million members in contrast to the 60,000 in Catholic trades unions. The new federation quickly fell under the domination of the Comillas–Nevares faction that left little room for unions free of employer influence. Arboleya's *sindicatos independientes* soon disappeared, while Gerard's *sindicatos libres* moved in a direction only tangentially related to their origins in Social Catholicism. A handful of effective and independent unions managed to survive, notably the Solidaridad de Trabajadores Vascos, founded at Bilbao in 1911, although it provided little real competition, in this case, to the UGT.

The failure of the church's social apostolate among urban workers between 1880 and 1920 had many causes. Chronic organizational weaknesses, excessive internal factionalism and the lack of any positive theory of social action were contributing factors. The theoretical basis of Social Catholicism rested on a curious intellectual mix based on admiration for the medieval guild system and a neothomistic restatement of the need for class harmony to which its more advanced figures, like the Dominicans Gerard and his successor, José Gafo, added a dash of Social Darwinism and the idea, derived from Georges Sorel, of the centrality of strike action. The factions of Spanish Social Catholicism shared, however, the essentially negative concept that the primary purpose of the movement was not to improve the economic condition of workers but to reconquer them for the faith. 'Social reform and Christian reconquest or the 'rechristianization' of a 'people lost' through liberal and social propaganda' were but two sides of the same coin.[29] In many respects, Social Catholicism represented 'a prolongation of the struggle against liberalism' and, as such, attached priority to combating radical social movements rather than to developing a positive plan of action capable of appealing to the working class. In the worst of cases, Social Catholicism was used as a blunt instrument to destroy competing labour organizations. During 1917, a year of rising social tensions, for example, labour syndicates under the influence of Comillas and his Jesuit ally, Father Nevares, worked actively to frustrate the revolutionary general strike begun in August by the Socialist party and the UGT.[30]

The railway workers' union promoted by Comillas and Nevares represented a rare, though limited, success of Catholic labour activity among a modern industrial proletariat. The vast majority of Catholic syndicates, even those organized by Gerard, developed in large measure from the initiatives of priests and bourgeois lay activists. Few Catholic unions succeeded in attracting recruits from the country's growing industrial working class. Indeed, membership in the Workers' Circles, the 'mixed' and 'pure' syndicates drew heavily upon the artisan, semi-artisan trades and the service sector. The labour organizations developed by Spanish Social Catholicism were, on the whole, artificial creations unable to compete with the worker-directed CNT and UGT.

The church's failure at the pastoral and organizational levels to devise an effective response to the challenges presented by urban, industrial growth proved catastrophic over the long term. The wave of church burnings that swept Madrid and southern cities in April 1931, the assassinations of clergy carried out in Oviedo and the mining districts of Asturias in October 1934 and, finally, the execution of nearly 7,000 priests during the Civil War (1936–9) shows how completely the clergy and lay activists had lost the battle to reconquer the alienated masses who saw 'the malign trilogy of church, state and capitalism' as entrenched enemies of social change.[31]

NOTES

1 Pastoral Letter, 30 January 1858, *La revista católica*, 1858, pp. 401–2.
2 ibid., pp. 393, 397.
3 Quoted in H.J. Pastor Miralles, 'La obra socio-religiosa del P. Francisco Palau en Barcelona, 1851–1854', in *Una figura carismática*

del siglo XIX: El P. Francisco Palau y Quer, O.C.D., apóstol y fundador,
Burgos, 1973, p. 515.

4 Quoted in Feliciano Montero García, *El primero catolicismo social y la
'Rerum Novarum' en España,* Madrid, 1983, p. 166.

5 Although some anticlerical violence occurred during the later stages
of the liberal revolution of 1820–3, it took place sporadically, often
in the countryside where it was linked to military operations. The
assassination of monks and friars carried out in the summers of 1834
and 1835 in Madrid and Barcelona represented something new as
urban mobs egged on by political radicals turned against the regulars
with a ferocity unknown in Spanish anticlericalism's earlier manifestations.

6 Quoted in Casimir Martí, 'Datos sobre la sensibilidad social de la Iglesia
durante los primeros 30 años del movimiento obrero en España', in M.
Andrés, V. Cacho Viu, J.M. Cuenca *et al., Aproximación a la historia
social de la Iglesia española contemporánea,* El Escorial, 1978, p. 135.

7 Fernando García de Cortazar, 'La Iglesia española y la nueva sociedad
burguesa de la Restauración, 1876–1923', *Revista de fomento
social,*128, 1977, p. 167.

8 C.M. Sancha y Hervas, *Carta pastoral del Emmo. Señor Cardenal,
Arzobispo de Valencia sobre los medios de efectuar la reforma moral de la
sociedad,* Valencia, 1897, pp. 9, 21.

9 'Nuestros propósitos', *Revista católica de las cuestiones sociales,* 1895,
p. 4.

10 Between 1900 and 1920, the average size of Barcelona's thirty-two
parishes stood at 18,800, that of Madrid's thirty parishes at 20,830.
Munich, Paris and Vienna exceeded this average marginally, but other
European cities, Milan, Brussels, Cologne, Oporto and Turin,
possessed parishes with considerably smaller populations. E. Swoboda,
La cura de almas en las grandes ciudades, trans. J. Moragués, Barcelona,
1921, p. 173. As late as 1931, five of Madrid's parishes served
populations in excess of 50,000 persons: *Almanaque popular de cultura
religiosa,* Madrid, 1931, pp. 88–9. The ratio of priests to population
in the archdiocese of Valencia in 1927, 1:2,501, contrasted with that
of Vitoria, where Bilbao was located, 1:271, Madrid, 1:1,626 and
Barcelona, 1:1,125: *Anuario estadístico de España, 1927,* Madrid,
1929, p. 604; *Ecclesia,* 166, 16 September 1944, p. 11.

11 Francisco Peiró, *El problema religioso-social en España,* 2nd edn,
Madrid, 1936, pp. 604–5.

12 Hilario Herranz Establés, *El párroco y la parroquia en los tiempos
presentes,* Barcelona, 1925, pp. 344–6.

13 Casimir Martí, *L'Esglèsia de Barcelona. 1850–1857,* 2 vols, Barcelona,
1984, vol. 2, p. 336.

14 M. Sáez de Ocariz y Ruiz de Azcua, 'El cumplimiento pascual en la
ciudad de Logroño a lo largo del siglo XIX', *Berceo,* 76, 1965,
pp. 275–9.

15 Peiró, *El problema religioso-social,* p. 14.

16 Rogelio Duocastella, *Mataró: estudio de sociología religiosa sobre una
ciudad industrial española,* Barcelona, 1971, p. 290; Rogelio

Duocastella, *El fenómeno religioso y sus condicionamientos socio-culturales: estudio socio-religioso de la diócesis de Málaga*, Malaga, 1972, p. 172; Rogelio Duocastella, *Religiosidad y subdesarrollo: estudio sociológico sobre Tierra de Campos*, Madrid and Barcelona, 1971, section 6, part 21.

17 Herranz Establés, *El párroco*, pp. 318–19.
18 *La ciencia tomista*, 1919, p. 78; *Ilustración del clero*, 1919, p. 12.
19 *Crónica del sínodo diócesano celebrado en Jaca los días 23, 24 y 25 de agosto de 1899*, Madrid, 1899, pp. 17–18.
20 E.A. Villeloa Rodríguez, 'Inevitable disyuntiva', *Revista eclesiástica*, 1920, p. 92.
21 For the important and controversial role played by the religious orders in education and charitable assistance, see, Frances Lannon, *Privilege, Persecution and Prophecy: The Catholic Church in Spain, 1875–1975*, Oxford, 1987, pp. 68–77.
22 Some Workers' Circles appeared before 1890, but the organizational surge taking place after this date owed a considerable debt to Vicent who made the social apostolate his life's work beginning in 1889.
23 Quoted in Florentino del Valle, *El P. Antonio Vicent, S.J. y la acción católica española*, Madrid, 1947, p. 261.
24 Quoted in Domingo Benavides Gómez, *Democracia y cristianismo en la España de la Restauración*, 1875–1931, Madrid, 1978, p. 251.
25 Colin M. Winston, *Workers and the Right in Spain, 1900–1936*, Princeton, NJ, 1985, p. 49.
26 ibid., p. 51
27 Benavides Gómez, *Democracia y cristianismo*, p. 313.
28 Quoted in José Andrés-Gallego, *Pensamiento y acción social de la Iglesia de España*, Madrid, 1984, p. 320.
29 Feliciano Montero García, 'Los católicos españoles y los origenes de la politica social', *Studia histórica*, 4, 1984, p. 58.
30 The Sindicato Católico de los Ferroviarios Españoles was founded at Valladolid in 1913. By 1915, it had recruited a modest membership of 5,000, largely concentrated in Old Castile and León.
31 Quoted in José Alvarez Junco, *La ideología política del anarquismo español, 1868–1910*, 2nd edn, Madrid, 1991, p. 211.

2

A RESURGENT RELIGION
The rise of Catholic social movements in nineteenth-century Belgian cities
Carl Strikwerda

INTRODUCTION: THE DECLINE OF RELIGION?

The nineteenth century witnessed one of the great transformations of western history: the loss of a privileged place for religion in almost all European countries. Christian churches had their state subsidies, control over education and charity and legal powers severely curtailed. Simultaneously, large sections of society, especially many in the urban lower classes and the cultural élite, effectively disassociated themselves from religious faith and practice. Even religious groups which had survived earlier persecution – Jews, Protestant Dissenters and Catholic minorities – were weakened by the forces of secularization.[1]

Yet, in contrast to this general picture, Belgian Catholicism demonstrated a striking ability to withstand some of the tide against religion sweeping the western world. Already early in the nineteenth century, Belgium was one of the most highly urbanized and industrialized societies in the world. Vehement anticlericalism, supported by powerful Liberal and Socialist movements, challenged the power of the Catholic Church. None the less, well into the twentieth century, religious practice and the hold of Catholicism on significant parts of both the urban and upper-class populations remained strong. Why Belgium should have followed this rather distinctive path has only rarely been explored, yet investigating it can suggest ways in which the decline of religion in the face of urbanization and secularization was not necessarily inevitable. The nineteenth century saw creeds such as socialism and nationalism provide many people with a sense of community and stability in societies which were rapidly changing and fragmenting. Many continental European countries, especially, saw the rise of what the French sometimes call 'spiritual families' or what the Germans, referring to the Socialists, called a 'state within the state'. Belgian Catholicism, this chapter will argue, should probably be seen as perhaps the most successful example of a revitalized religion providing this sense of community and stability.[2]

Several factors help to explain the relative vitality of Belgian Catholicism by the early twentieth century. These include pre-existing strengths of the church before the nineteenth century, the church's early acceptance of constitutional government and, most important, the support given during the late nineteenth century to emancipatory movements of farmers, the lower middle class, workers and Flemish nationalists by key Catholic leaders. Willingness to back emancipatory movements, I would argue, was the most critical element in preserving Catholicism's place in Belgian society. Middle- and upper-class Catholic leaders decided to broaden their focus and take bold steps to hold on to the lower classes within the Catholic camp. These leaders and members of the lower class succeeded in large measure in building mass organizations which could challenge Catholicism's largest rival, socialism.

This essay will first introduce the economic, linguistic and demographic situation of nineteenth-century Belgium, then examine the two earlier factors which contributed to the vitality of Belgian Catholicism: the pre-existing strength of Counter-Reformation Catholicism and the acceptance of constitutional government. Both of these, it will be argued, were advantages, but by themselves could not account for the later strength of Catholicism. Most of the argument of the chapter will consequently be devoted to comparing how Catholicism embraced new social movements in three cities – Ghent, Brussels and Liège.

BELGIUM: INDUSTRY, LANGUAGE AND URBAN GEOGRAPHY

Despite encompassing only a twentieth the area of Germany or France, Belgium possessed an unusual amount of diversity. In its reliance on coal, metallurgy and textile industries it resembled Britain and Germany, while its overwhelmingly Catholic population and Francophone culture made it similar to France. At the same time, in Flanders, the northern, more agricultural half of the country, the middle and lower classes spoke Flemish dialects of Dutch, the same language as that of the Netherlands. The country only owed its existence as a state to several accidents of history. The Belgian provinces belonged to the region of the Low Countries which the Spanish reconquered in the sixteenth century after the northern, largely Protestant ones broke away. Ruled by Austria in the eighteenth century and by France during the revolution, the provinces were joined to the northern Netherlands after Napoleon's defeat in 1815. Unhappiness with the autocratic and Protestant aspects of Dutch rule led to the successful Belgian revolution of 1830. The new state only survived, however, when the great powers agreed not to compel its annexation to either France or the Netherlands.[3]

Late nineteenth-century Belgium possessed characteristics of both the most industrialized of European societies and the more undeveloped; England and Ireland squeezed into a tiny state as it were. Belgium was the second nation in the world to industrialize, but its economy rested on longer working days, more women's and children's work and a lower standard of living than other industrialized countries.[4] One reason why organizing consumer co-operatives and offering social insurance became such important tactics for the socialist and Catholic social movements in Belgium was because so many working women and their families lived very precariously.

As a bilingual country, Belgium has often resisted study by outsiders. Dutch or dialects of Dutch are spoken in the northern part of the country called Flanders, and French is spoken in the south, which has come to be referred to as Wallonia.[5] Flanders has always been smaller in geographical area but more densely populated than Wallonia, so that for most of modern history Flemish speakers have outnumbered French-speakers by approximately 55 to 45 per cent. After stating this, very little is simple. Two issues particularly complicate matters – the role of bilingualism in Flanders and the position of Brussels, the largest city and capital of Belgium.[6]

In the nineteenth century, the linguistic struggle in Belgium was not primarily between regions, but between different classes. The major conflict was within the region of Flanders itself, between the upper class which used French and the middle and lower classes which spoke only Dutch. Since the Middle Ages, French had gradually taken hold among the upper class, the church and the government in Flanders, although Dutch, or rather varieties of Dutch dialects known as Flemish, continued to be the spoken language for the vast majority of people in Flanders. The demands of the Industrial Revolution, the expansion of education and, most of all, mass politics challenged the dominance of French. The number of educated middle-class people grew too quickly for the process of 'Frenchification' to absorb them. Many of these middle-class Dutch-speakers, along with some farmers, workers and artisans, resented the privileged place of French-speakers in Flanders. The movement for Flemish language rights – 'Flamingantism' – tapped this discontent.[7] For decades, however, Flemish language demands had little success because the Flamingant movement failed to appeal to the lower classes and to address the divisions between Catholics and Liberals. It was the introduction of universal male suffrage in 1894, and the need for politicians to appeal to lower-class Flemings in Dutch for the first time, which transformed the Flemish question.[8] From 1894 on, the major question was how much the two traditional parties, Liberals and Catholics, and the new Socialists, would be able to draw in lower-class Flemings as voters.

Although Flanders gradually began to become a truly Dutch-language region, the existence of Brussels prevented the linguistic situation from developing into a simple regional confrontation. Geographically, Brussels lies within Flanders. During the nineteenth century, however, the French-speaking and bilingual population grew until it became larger than that of any Francophone city in Belgium.[9] Yet Brussels remained the economic and political heart of the country for Flemish and French-speakers alike. Thousands of Flemings commuted to the city to work, and the Flemish rights advocates almost always had to lobby the national government to achieve some of their aims.[10]

THE COUNTER-REFORMATION AND CONSTITUTIONALISM

The original basis of Belgian Catholicism was laid in the Catholic or Counter-Reformation of the late sixteenth and seventeenth centuries. During the sixteenth century, when all of the Low Countries passed from Burgundian to Spanish Hapsburg rule, many people in both the southern and northern Netherlands converted to Protestantism and rose in revolt. When the armies of Philip II reconquered the southern provinces, however, the Spanish government and the church began a systematic process of reimposing Catholicism to ensure that Protestantism would never emerge again.

RESURGENT RELIGION

Protestantism was banned, and thousands of Protestant Flemings and Walloons fled north to what became the independent United Provinces.[11] In a vigorous application of the Counter-Reformation reforms, church authorities, often aided by the Hapsburg government, improved Catholic ritual, diocesan discipline and organization and the recruitment of priests. Over the next century, the Jesuits and other Catholic orders created numerous schools to educate the upper and middle classes of the southern Netherlands, many convents were established to provide primary schoolteachers and nurses and a large number of churches were rebuilt or expanded. Since, within the southern Netherlands, Protestantism had been more successful in Flanders than in Wallonia, it was Flanders which was most deeply affected by the Counter-Reformation. Flanders became almost 100 per cent Catholic, while a few small pockets of Protestantism survived in Wallonia.[12]

Despite the effect of the Counter-Reformation, from the eighteenth century into the early nineteenth, the church suffered severe blows of the kind which weakened its position in many other continental European countries. From the 1770s through 1830, the governments ruling the southern Netherlands – the Austrian Hapsburgs, the French and finally King William of the United Kingdom of the Netherlands – dismantled important pieces of the institutional foundation of the Counter-Reformation church. The Jesuits were expelled in 1774, monasteries were dissolved, church lands expropriated and state-controlled schools set up as potential rivals to Catholic schools. Most of the population, especially the lower classes, remained practising Catholics, but for the first time an anticlerical élite emerged and the church found itself unable to rely on the guarantee of state help. Although the level of Catholic practice, especially in Flanders, remained higher than in some other areas of Europe, it is still possible that without a revival, Belgian Catholicism would have eventually been little different than that of other countries. The city of Ghent, for example, was the fastest growing city of Belgium in this period. A flood of immigrants from rural areas rushed to the newly-mechanized textile industry between 1800 and the 1840s. The church, still stung by the losses of the revolutionary and Dutch periods, proved unable to provide new parishes or priests for the new urban population. After the 1840s, when Ghent's textile industry stagnated, the city's population preserved some of the character of the first decades for the rest of the century. Not coincidentally, Ghent was the most anticlerical

65

city of Belgium, 'Red Ghent' as it was known. The Counter-Reformation heritage, in other words, was important but did not by itself guarantee Catholic strength.

The second factor favouring Catholicism in the nineteenth century was the remarkable decisions of the bishops and leading Catholic laity to ally with liberals, to support independence from the Dutch and to establish a constitutional monarchy in 1830. The Belgians, in effect, adopted the solution advocated by Lamennais in France: Catholicism should compete within modern liberal society rather than rely on particularist privilege to defend itself. The alliance of Catholics and liberals, however, was a marriage of convenience; there was never any sense that the Belgian church would change its fundamental theological orthodoxy or give up its desire to play a dominant role in social welfare and education. Under the Liberals, the constitution limited the new Belgian monarch to the role of head of state and guaranteed freedom of the press, assembly and religion. Even though many, if not most Liberals were at least nominally Catholic, they opposed an established state church which had a monopoly on religious practice. They tried to limit the subsidies and privileges accorded to the Catholic Church to the minimum level necessary for Catholic support of a constitutional state. In contrast to most of the rest of Europe, Belgian Catholics accepted freedom of religion because the constitution still provided for government subsidies to religious groups – Catholic, Protestant or Jewish. Shrewdly, and, as later events proved, correctly, they gambled that with its long history of institutional strength and with the large number of nominal Catholics in Belgium, the church could use government subsidies and constitutional freedoms to acquire a position virtually as strong as if it had been an established state church. Despite disapproval by the Pope and the opposition of some conservative Catholics, the Belgian bishops succeeded in working with a liberal, constitutional government and, at the same time, recooping from some of the losses which the church had suffered under the French and Dutch regimes.[13]

Until the 1880s, Belgian politics remained remarkably stable because Catholics and Liberals shared an essentially *laissez-faire* policy towards regulating the economy.[14] The parties united, too, in fundamental constitutionalism. Catholics' love of the past and their view of the Liberals as dangerously secular never led them to desire a true monarchy. The Belgians had never known a native, divine-right king, with the possible exception of Charles V in the sixteenth century. The more vivid memory of the secularizing monarchs Joseph II of Austria and Napoleon and the Protestant William I of the Netherlands ensured that an alliance of 'throne and altar' did not rally conservative Belgian Catholics. The unusual early acceptance by Belgian Catholics of constitutional government and freedom of religion meant that there did not develop the estrangement between conservative Catholics and the state which Italy, France and Germany experienced.[15]

Urban politics provide an excellent example of how Belgian Catholics utilized constitutional government to their advantage, even though this constitutional arrangement could not by itself guarantee religious stability. Under the Belgian constitution, local governments (*communes* or *gemeenten*), with the approval of provincial authorities and the Ministry of Interior, had primary responsibility for funding education, approving new churches or adding priests to existing churches. In most Belgian cities, Catholics succeeded in persuading the government to pay for new parishes or additional priests as the population grew. In Britain and France, a number of scholars suggest, the established church failed to adapt to changing population patterns so that eventually large parts of the urban population became effectively lost to Christianity. Whereas the number of people per parish in many industrial cities in Britain and France more than doubled, for example, in Belgium even industrial cities like Ghent, Liège and Seraing managed to increase the number of parishes so that the number of people per parish stayed roughly the same.[16]

Until Belgian politics became more polarized in the 1880s, Catholics in large cities tried several different strategies to deal with opposition from the Liberals who controlled municipal governments. In Ghent, for example, the Catholics concentrated on creating a kind of counterculture or smaller city within the city. Led on by arch conservative lay people, they built up a network of workmen's clubs, confraternities and charitable organizations. Later, more militant Catholic leaders like Arthur Verhaegen criticized these groups as essentially defensive and paternalist. Verhaegen believed they often attracted only the more passive and needy of the workers, while the more energetic went over to the Socialists.[17] While it is true that these groups only succeeded in recruiting a small portion of the city's working class, they none the less maintained the church's influence where it otherwise might have been lost. Even anticlerical workers recognized that these Catholic organizations could occasionally have an impact. The Socialist Pol DeWitte remembered that as a boy he saw a heavy-drinking worker change his life and become a responsible provider after joining a Catholic club.[18] In Brussels, the Catholics virtually gave up fighting the Liberals' dominance of charity and local government in the city itself, but they concentrated on trying to retain some influence in the many suburban and urbanizing *communes* which surrounded the city of Brussels itself. (Brussels grew as an urban area without the city of Brussels annexing the areas around it.) As in Ghent, the political strength of the Catholics was buttressed by the rural areas of the province which voted Catholic. The provincial government overseeing Brussels could sometimes check the anticlericalism of the Liberal municipal council.

THE 1880s CRISIS AND THE ORIGINS OF CHRISTIAN DEMOCRACY

The stability of Belgian politics abruptly changed in the early 1880s when the governing Liberals tried to curtail the teaching of religion in publicly supported primary schools. The Catholics mobilized to create a network of independent schools and to defeat the Liberals in the elections of 1884. The victory of the Catholics in the 1884 elections, however, was a narrow one, and, along with the intellectual and economic changes going on at the same time, marked a profound transformation in Belgian history. The Liberals' school policy shattered the complacency of the Catholic élite. By trying to create a government-run educational system and demote church schools to second-class status, the Liberals appeared to be upsetting the foundations of the Belgian constitution. This called into question the moderate policies of the Catholic Party which appeared to have played into the Liberals' hands. In trying to reform their programme and oppose the Liberals, Catholic leaders opened up the party both to more conservative, reactionary influences and to those who wished to reach out to workers, farmers and the lower middle class.

Ultramontanists, supporters of direct obedience to the pope, acquired a share of power for the first time from the chagrined leaders of the established Catholic Party. Whereas the traditional Catholic leadership had eschewed demonstrations of religious enthusiasm, the ultramontanists often advocated new forms of religious piety, lay confraternities and public manifestations of spirituality such as pilgrimages to Lourdes.[19]

Also undermining the complacency of traditional Catholic leaders were the collapse of agricultural prices in the face of new imports from overseas and the accompanying industrial recession of the 1880s. Thousands of impoverished Flemish Belgians migrated to France, while unemployment drove Walloon coalminers to riot and strike in a huge wave of violence in 1886.[20] Agrarian discontent in Flanders threatened the rural base of the Catholic Party while the industrial crisis soon made the new Socialist Party a major threat – one much more extreme than the Liberals had been.[21]

The first Christian Democrats were a group of young lawyers, professionals and priests who had actively opposed the Liberal government's school policy in the mid-1880s. The campaign to build a separate school system and to defeat the Liberals in the 1884 elections, combined with the shock of the Walloon strikes of 1886, gave these young activists a deeper perception of how many people, especially workers, had lost contact with the church. After the election victory, these leaders turned their attention to how the Catholic community could prevent further secularization. They organized a series of large congresses of Catholics concerned about social problems. These congresses, held in Liège in 1886, 1887 and 1890, included German, Swiss and French representatives. As an immediate result of the congresses, almost every diocese in Belgium formed new secretariats for social works and expanded their workmen's clubs, farmers' leagues and mutual insurance societies.[22] An intellectual shift towards new interpretations of Thomist theology supported the movement. The so-called neo-Thomist revival had been going on for some years in Catholic Europe, with the University of Louvain outside Brussels as one of its centres. Increasingly, some theologians, such as Victor Brants at Louvain, wedded Thomist notions of justice to measures such as lower-class representation in politics and working-class associations. Many of the later Christian Democrats leaders studied at Louvain with Brants.[23]

Fear that the Catholic Party might need the Christian Democrats' ties to the lower classes prevented conservative upper-class Catholics from simply ignoring or repressing the new movement. By the late 1880s it had become increasingly clear that the narrow suffrage would be extended; the only question was how quickly and whether it would be extended to all males or some restricted group. Only a few Catholics favoured universal male suffrage or even a large extension, but all Socialists and many Liberals did. Catholic politicians feared that without an alternative, they might eventually be outflanked by their political opponents. Once the suffrage was extended, the conservative Catholic Party might desperately need the ties of the Christian Democrats to the lower classes.

Although questions of suffrage and politics were not always of central concern for the new Catholic movement, its leaders soon used the movement's political potential to their advantage. As the network of local Christian Democratic groups proliferated, the new movement's leaders in 1891 created a national umbrella organization: the Belgisch Volksbond/Ligue démocratique belge which included clubs, mutual insurance societies, political associations and charitable groups begun by or influenced by Christian Democrats. Georges Helleputte, an ultramontanist professor at the University of Louvain, helped found the Volksbond/Ligue as well as a similar organization of Catholic farmers' associations, the Belgisch Boerenbond.[24]

The real story of Christian Democracy in Belgium unfolded on the local level, where activists had to bring lower-class people into permanent organizations, to wrest places on electoral slates from conservative Catholics and to match the appeal of Liberals and Socialists. A close comparison of Christian Democracy's successes and failures in three different cities – Ghent, Brussels and Liège – reveals that there was nothing inevitable about Catholicism's ability to survive in the era of mass politics. In the Flemish textile and harbour town of Ghent, Christian Democrats quickly challenged the Socialists and went on to foster other organizations of lower-class Catholics all over Belgium. In the bilingual capital of Brussels, upper-class Christian Democrats took several decades to learn how to transcend their paternalist heritage. Once they did, with the help of Christian Democrats from Ghent, they too competed well with the Socialists. By contrast, Christian Democrats in the French-speaking coal and steel city of Liège suffered so much opposition both from conservative Catholics and from Liberals and Socialists that they never succeeded in creating a viable lower-class Catholic movement.

What factors explain these varying successes? Alongside the heritage of the Counter-Reformation and constitutional rule were several key factors: the role of lay – as well as clerical or episcopal – leaders, the extension of social welfare and the mobilization of groups of lower-class people whom the Socialists and Liberals neglected – Flemish migrants, women and commuting and suburban workers.

LAY AND CLERICAL LEADERSHIP AND
CHRISTIAN DEMOCRACY

In order for Christian Democracy to succeed, lay leaders and supportive priests had to form a strong enough alliance that they could withstand the opposition of conservative lay Catholics. In Ghent, the wealthy young architect Arthur Verhaegen spearheaded this alliance. An ardent ultramontanist, Verhaegen had helped call the first Catholic social congress in Liège in 1886 and served as its secretary. In 1891, Verhaegen convinced a number of independent, that is non-Socialist, unions in Ghent to join with a group of Catholic workmen's clubs and form an 'Anti-Socialist Workers League', AntiSocialistische Werkliedenbond. Although ostensibly non-partisan, the Werkliedenbond recognized 'Religion, the Family, and Property as the necessary bases of society', and Verhaegen managed to have a priest, a teacher at the episcopal seminary, named as 'spiritual counsellor' of the organization.[25] Verhaegen recruited Catholic schoolteachers as organizers for the Werkliedenbond and convinced the Bishop of Ghent, Bishop Antoine Stillemans, to bless the new organizations. Stillemans's protection was vital for the workers groups when upper-class, conservative Catholics attacked Verhaegen as a 'Red' and saw labour unions as a violation of everything Catholicism stood for.[26] Just as important, however, was Verhaegen's skill in convincing a crucial segment of both the clergy and middle- and lower middle-class Catholic laity that stopping the Socialists required the creation of a genuine Catholic worker movement such as the Werkliedenbond. With his allies, Verhaegen was able to force the conservative upper-class leaders who dominated the local Catholic Party to – grudgingly – give places on Catholic election slates to candidates of the Werkliedenbond.

By holding off the conservatives and by keeping the clergy on their side, Verhaegen's Anti-Socialists created genuine worker-run institutions – mutual insurance societies, a daily newspaper and consumer co-operative which were both named *Het Volk* (*The People*), as well as a range of new Catholic labour unions. While the Socialists in Ghent had organized some 10,000 union members, the Catholics soon had a respectable 4,000, with about 10,000 families enrolled in Catholic pension plans.[27] At the same time as they tried to match the Socialists by organizing workers, Verhaegen and his followers insisted that theirs was a genuinely Catholic movement. As a counter to May Day, the Anti-Socialists had huge celebrations on 15 May, the anniversary of *Rerum Novarum*, Pope Leo XIII's encyclical on workers' issues. The celebrations featured speeches, parades and a blessing of labour union banners at the cathedral. By 1900, the Anti-Socialists in Ghent had created one of the most successful religious movements of workers of any city in the world.

By contrast, the Christian Democrats in Liège, led by abbé Antoine Pottier, a professor at the episcopal seminary, were never able to create a successful movement despite many early advantages. The Liégeois Christian Democrats had the support of Bishop Victor Doutreloux of Liége, enjoyed enormous intellectual authority and created innovative workers' organizations. In the late 1880s and early 1890s, Pottier first set up Catholic consumer and producers co-operatives then founded a weekly Christian Democratic newspaper, *Le bien du peuple*, and finally helped to organize unions of bakers, tailors, armaments workers and painters, as well as a federation of Catholic miners' unions.[28] In the late 1880s and 1890s, Doutreloux, Pottier and other Christian Democrats in Liège influenced social Catholics and Christian Democrats all over Francophone Europe and even Europe as a whole. Doutreloux was surprisingly receptive to Pottier's call for state intervention to protect workers' health and safety at a time when most Catholics still preferred private charity. Another impressive voice in the so-called 'Liège school' was that of Godefroid Kurth, a medievalist at the University of Liège who had left Germany in the *Kulturkampf* and become Henri Pirenne's teacher.[29]

Despite their intellectual prominence and Pottier's activism, the Liégeois Christian Democrats fell victim to the opposition of conservative upper-class Catholics. These conservatives never saw anything in Pottier's movement but socialism masquerading as religion. In Ghent, upper-class conservatives disliked Verhaegen's creation of a separate Catholic workers organization, but they settled for trying to curtail its influence rather than sabotaging it completely. The Liégeois conservatives knew no such restraint. Catholic employers sometimes fired workers who marched in Christian Democratic demonstrations or who belonged to Pottier's Union démocratique chrétienne. In 1895, conservatives brought all the Catholic workmen's clubs which the Christian Democrats did not yet control into a docile Fédération ouvrière catholique. By putting up candidates from the Fédération for local elections, the conservatives could claim that they had opened up their ranks to the lower classes when in fact they prevented any workers from having real power. The publications of the Fédération were all published by the conservatives' own organization, the Union catholique. In the published proceedings of a Fédération meeting, Henri Francotte, the wealthy arms manufacturer who was president of the Union catholique, did almost all the talking while the worker candidates said virtually nothing.[30] Conservatives also betrayed the Christian Democrats several times in elections. They agreed to field a joint list of candidates but, while the Christian Democratic supporters dutifully voted for conservative and Christian Democratic candidates alike, many conservatives voted only for their own leaders.[31] By the late 1890s, conservatives dropped even the pretence of co-operation. In a number of provincial and local elections, they allied with anticlerical, upper-class Liberals against the Christian Democrats.[32]

As a result of the conservatives' attacks, Christian Democracy had only a small impact in Liège. Most of the labour unions and producers and consumers co-operatives begun by Pottier and his followers had little success.[33] With additional pressure from King Leopold II, conservatives managed to get the Vatican first to silence Pottier and then to transfer him to Rome. Once Bishop Doutreloux had died and been replaced in 1902 by the much more conservative Monsignor Rutten, Christian Democrats in Liège were extremely isolated.[34]

Observers and later historians have sometimes suggested that it was almost inevitable that the Christian Democrats in Ghent would succeed where those in Liège would fail. Flanders had higher levels of religious practice than Walloon areas, and the church recruited more priests in Flanders from the lower classes than it did in Wallonia.[35] But as pointed out earlier, in the course of the nineteenth century Ghent had become much more secularized than the surrounding areas of Flanders and indeed much of the rest of Belgium. Even Seraing, the suburb of the city of Liège which was the most industrialized city in Belgium, had a parish for every 3,000 people when those in Ghent had 11,000.[36] Nor did Pottier fail because of lack of support from the clergy. In 1898, seven of twenty-three leaders of Liégeois Christian Democratic local groups had priests as their officers.[37]

The strength of Flemish Catholicism does not explain Christian Democracy's varying fortunes in Ghent and Liège. Instead, Verhaegen's leadership and the viciousness of the Liègeois conservative Catholics seem to be the key factors. Verhaegen had impeccable ultramontanist credentials, and he constantly portrayed the groups of Christian Democratic workers as organizations which were as much religious as economic or political. Pottier, although orthodox, had not been an ultramontanist, and he paid less attention to assuring other Catholics that his Christian Democratic movement would help keep workers within the church.[38] Verhaegen was also cautious in his public pronouncements and in print, while the Werkliedenbond in practice was bolder. Until the mid-1890s, Verhaegen still called for 'mixed unions' of workers and employers, while the Anti-Socialists had already formed genuine labour unions.[39] At times, Verhaegen bordered on deception: the strike funds of the Anti-Socialist unions, he implied, were not intended to encourage strikes. They only served to support Catholic workers during Socialist-led strikes so that the workers would not come to depend on the Socialists. In fact, in industries in Ghent where Anti-Socialist unions had a strong following, the Socialists often contacted these unions about directing the strikes and negotiating with employers. Some strikes only succeeded because of de facto alliances between Socialist and Anti-Socialist unions.[40]

SOCIAL WELFARE AND THE RECRUITMENT OF NEGLECTED GROUPS

Catholics' provision of economic assistance to workers and their own base of strength in the countryside also shaped the success of Christian Democracy. In Ghent, as opposed to Liège, Christian Democrats tried to outflank their rivals by using social welfare and their ties to rural areas. Christian Democracy in Brussels, which was initially as weak as in Liège, eventually became as strong as in Ghent by using these tactics as well.

Soon after it was established in the early 1890s, Christian Democrats in Ghent gained a large share of influence over the diocesan Secretariat of Social Work. The Secretariat encouraged local parishes and priests to create workmen's clubs and mutual insurance societies, and supported charitable efforts within the diocese by religious orders such as the Society of Saint Vincent de Paul and the Xaverians. It also furthered new social work efforts, such as aid associations for Flemish migratory workers in France and vocational schools.[41] Verhaegen himself set up a Comité des oeuvres sociales in 1888 which was the forerunner of the Secretariat, and his past experience with Catholic charity made it natural for Bishop Stillemans to depend on him for advice. Verhaegen had been president of the Society of Saint Vincent de Paul in the diocese and honorary president of several workmen's clubs.[42] Gradually, over the 1890s, Verhaegen and his sympathizers persuaded more and more priests that Catholic social work should be aimed not only at helping the lower classes but at mobilizing them for the Christian Democratic movement as well. By 1910, the diocese routinely asked priests whether they encouraged activities designed to stop the spread of socialism such as Catholic labour unions or work-men's clubs.[43] After 1900, Christian Democrats also succeeded in having all the economic and social welfare efforts in the diocese run by the Werkliedenbond, the Catholic farmers' leagues and the organizations for the lower middle class brought under the sponsorship of the Secretariat.[44] To the chagrin of Catholic conservatives and the outrage of Liberals and Socialists, the Christian Democrats used much of the church's own network of parishes and charity as a recruiting tool for the Catholic unions and for the Werkliedenbond's electoral slates.[45]

By contrast, in Liège, the conservatives kept a firm grip on the diocesan Secretariat of Social Work. The Secretariat ran a labour exchange, published three newspapers, loaned workers money for housing, sponsored libraries and gymnastic teams and, by 1910, administered mutual insurance societies with over 9,000 members.[46] But it gave no help whatsoever to the labour unions, insurance societies and consumer co-operatives created by the Christian Democrats. Pottier's followers complained bitterly that the conservatives in Ghent had, however reluctantly, allowed Verhaegen and the Werkliedenbond to use Catholic institutions for the Christian Democrat movement while the conservatives in Liège shut them out. The response of the Liégeois conservatives was to blame the Christian Democrats in Liège for creating a controversy. Henri Francotte, president of the conservative Union catholique, in an open letter published in 1897, declared,

> Christian democracy in Liège often takes the liberty to invoke the examples of Ghent and elsewhere. To me it differs entirely. It differs in that its preoccupation has been to penetrate into institutions [oeuvres] which are not affiliated to it, and when it does not succeed, to hamper, thwart, and make war on them.[47]

While observers and historians sometimes portray Catholicism as inevitably weaker than socialism in Liège, it is clear that workers were open to the efforts by Liégeois Catholics to offer social welfare.

CARL STRIKWERDA

After accident insurance was enacted, the Socialists dragged their feet in assisting workers who wanted to get help under the new law. Activists within the Socialist miners' and metallurgists' unions urged the unions to assist workers in order to prevent them from turning to the Catholic Social Work Secretariat for legal advice.[48] Unfortunately for the Catholics, the divisions between conservatives and Christian Democrats, and the conservatives' own lack of initiative, prevented them from exploiting this opportunity. As a result, neither the Christian Democrats nor the conservatives posed a credible challenge to the Socialists in Liège.

In Brussels, social welfare institutions and the diocesan Secretariat of Social Work proved all-important in encouraging a real Christian Democratic movement to grow in the last years before the First World War. Intellectually, the Christian Democrats in Brussels were always an impressive group, boasting several later prime ministers in their ranks – Léon de Lantsheere, Jules Renkin and Henry Carton de Wiart. They also won four seats in parliament as early as 1894, when a coalition of Christian Democrats, renegade Liberals, Flemish rights activists and conservatives emerged victorious on the Catholic ticket.[49] The Christian Democrats, however, found it difficult to organize grass-roots worker organizations. Initially, in the 1880s and 1890s, conservatives and Christian Democrats in Brussels often co-operated in setting up paternalist worker clubs, some of which were intended to revive the guilds. In these revived guilds, workers organized in 'corporations' would share the leadership with employers. The Maison des ouvriers, the largest of these clubs, had over a thousand members at its height. But joining workers and employers in these clubs proved impractical. Until after 1900, the Catholic worker groups consequently posed little threat to the Socialists.[50]

Only when the Bruxellois Christian Democrats worked with the diocesan officials to create a Secrétariat des oeuvres sociales and, together with this Secretariat, created mutual insurance societies and consumer co-operatives did the Catholic workers' movement pose a real challenge to the Socialists. In 1900, a federation of mutual insurance societies which the Christian Democrats created with the help of the Secretariat had about 3,200 members; by 1911, it had over 11,000.[51] Since the Christian Democrats in Brussels had not earlier formed an autonomous worker federation like the Werkliedenbond in Ghent, the Secretariat of Social Work played a crucial role in linking the growth of mutual insurance to unions and

76

co-operatives. A labour newspaper, *Het Syndikaat/Le Syndicat*, and an almanac published by the Secretariat proclaimed, 'Housewives! only buy bread from the *Bon Pain Bruxellois*', the Christian Democratic consumer co-operative.[52] The Catholic experience with insurance meant that Catholic labour unions grew steadily along with Socialist ones when municipally subsidized unemployment insurance suddenly attracted workers after 1909. While the Socialist unions grew from 8,000 to 18,000 members between 1909 and 1913, the Catholic ones grew even faster, from 1,900 to over 5,000.[53] From a much later start, the Christian Democratic labour movement in Brussels eventually competed almost as well against the Socialists as did that in Ghent. Clearly, Catholic social welfare proved a tremendous advantage for Christian Democrats in Brussels and Ghent just as its absence proved a great disadvantage in Liège. It was no coincidence, furthermore, that Christian Democratic workers groups were weaker in Liège than in other coal and iron areas in southern, French-speaking Belgium. These areas in Hainaut lay in the diocese of Tournai, where the bishops allowed the Secretariat of Social Work to aid the movement.[54]

By comparison with Ghent and Liège, Brussels also demonstrates that organizing groups of workers whom the Socialists neglected played an important role in building Christian Democratic movements. Because Ghent had few migrants or commuting workers in its labour force, there were only a few identifiable groups in the city which the Socialists overlooked and the Catholics recruited. Catholics in Ghent did try to attract construction workers who often came from outside the city. They also worked with the Catholic farmers' leagues organized in the Boerenbond to reach small town and rural workers in towns outside of Ghent.[55] By contrast, Liège actually had many immigrant and commuting workers. Increasingly, workmen's trains meant that many Flemish workers travelled weekly from rural Limburg in the north to work in and around Liège.[56] By 1910, in Seraing, the largest and most industrialized suburb of the city of Liège, 37 per cent of the industrial workforce came from outside Seraing.[57] For decades, the Socialists did little to organize these workers. Indeed, there was a close connection between the high number of commuting and immigrant workers in Liège whom the Socialists failed to organize and the fact that Liège had the weakest union movement of any city or industrial region in Belgium.[58] The Catholic conservatives and Christian Democrats in Liège organized rival efforts to reach the

Flemish, but neither pursued these efforts systematically. Once the Socialists created a strong union movement just before the First World War, they made a deliberate effort to reach commuting workers. They never succeeded in recruiting the Flemish, but the Catholics did not take advantage of this.[59]

In contrast, Christian Democrats in Brussels, with the help of priests and organizers from Ghent, recruited not only Flemings who commuted to the capital, but workers in the newly industrializing suburbs and small towns around Brussels whom the Socialist leaders in Brussels failed to reach. In elections to the Labour Courts (*Conseils des Prud'hommes/Werkrechtersraaden*) in 1912 and 1913, Socialists won almost three times as many votes as the Catholics inside Brussels, but only narrowly edged them out in the suburban and small towns around the capital.[60] This difference was ominous for the Socialists since industry was more rapidly growing in the areas just outside the city than in the capital itself. The initiative for many of these efforts came from Ghent, where in 1904 the Belgisch Volksbond/Ligue démocratique belge established the national Confederation of Christian Unions, with the Dominican Georges-Celas Rutten as secretary-general. Rutten, with the help of able assistants such as René Debruyne, the former president of the Catholic bakers' union in Ghent, tirelessly criss-crossed Flanders to set up new Catholic union locals.[61] Perhaps nowhere did Rutten's leadership have a greater impact than Brussels and its hinterland. The archbishopric of Mechelen (Malines) which oversaw Brussels allowed Catholic union propagandists to mobilize priests, parish councils and Catholic charity for the labour movement.

The contrast between Brussels and Liège is especially clear in the case of women workers. After 1900, Victoire Cappe, a young Catholic activist who had been inspired by Pottier, Kurth and the 'Liège school', began organizing women workers in Liège into co-operatives and associations. The opposition from conservatives, however, made her work difficult. With the sponsorship of Father Rutten and Cardinal Mercier, Archbishop of Mechelen, she moved her work to Brussels where she set up a secretariat for Catholic women's unions. Like so many other Christian Democrats, Cappe was influenced by Professor Victor Brants, neo-Thomist professor at Leuven. By 1913, all over Belgium, she and her assistants had organized women's labour unions and encouraged working-class women to join Catholic insurance societies and co-operatives.[62]

Flemish consciousness also proved to be an important building block for social Catholic or Christian Democratic movements. The close association of Flemish grievances with Catholicism is so ingrained in Belgian history that, once again, one has to emphasize that it was not inevitable.[63] The original Flemish rights movement of the mid-nineteenth century was led by Liberals. The Catholic Flemish cultural league, the Davidsfonds, was smaller, newer, and for a long time less influential than the Liberal Willemsfonds. The church hierarchy in Flanders tended to be overwhelmingly Francophone, and, for both historical and pragmatic reasons, supportive of the Belgian state and opposed to demands for autonomy. Cardinal Mercier, Archbishop of Mechelen, for example, was actively opposed to Flemish demands. Meanwhile, Bishop Rutten of Liège was strongly pro-Flemish, but, as mentioned above, opposed to Christian Democracy. Indeed, he was pro-Flemish because he saw the Flemish as more traditionally religious, while Walloons appeared to him as fatally infected by French anticlericalism. Meanwhile, Socialists in Antwerp, unlike their counterparts in Ghent or Brussels, claimed that the oppression of the Flemish as a linguistic group was similar to that of the workers as a class.[64]

The association of Flemish consciousness with Christian Democracy came about, I would argue, because certain Christian Democratic leaders consciously brought together language and politics when their rivals failed to do so. Although universal male suffrage came in 1894, the Liberals never mobilized the lower classes, Flemish or Walloon. Socialists frequently opposed Flemish rights. The majority of the workers in Brussels until the twentieth century spoke Dutch, but the Socialists depended on the support of a handful of craft unions in the centre of the city who were largely Francophone.[65] They ignored commuting workers and workers in the newly industrializing suburbs, who were predominantly Flemish. Meanwhile, the powerful Flemish Socialist movement in Ghent opposed the 'petty bourgeois' nationalism of the Flemish movement in the name of internationalism, and the Ghent Socialists had far more influence than the more Flemish-minded Antwerpers. Outside the few Flemish leaders who could speak French easily, the Socialist Party was run by Francophones. Yet as August DeWinne, a Socialist leader from Brussels, said in 1902, with only slight hyperbole, 'Flanders is as unknown to most French-speaking Belgians as Australia.'[66]

Christian Democrats in Brussels and Flanders did not begin as strongly Flamingant. Verhaegen, raised in an upper-class Bruxellois family, actually had to learn Dutch in Ghent while trying to create a Catholic workers' movement. Indeed, being strongly pro-Flemish and Catholic was made more difficult in the late 1890s. A dissident Christian Democrat, Father Adolf Daens, set up a radical 'Christian People's Party' (Christelijke Volkspartij) which was strongly Flamingant. Daens's closeness to the Socialists not only made him a heretic to both conservatives and Christian Democrats, but also risked tarring Catholic Flamingantism with the brush of radicalism.[67] None the less, after 1900, Christian Democratic organizers consciously sought out Flemish workers and portrayed Catholic working-class groups as defenders both of economic and linguistic grievances. In 1914, *De Metaalarbeider*, the newspaper of the Flemish Catholic metalworkers' unions, attacked both Catholic Flamingants who were not in favour of workers' demands and socially conscious Catholics who were not in favour of Flemish demands. The only people who deserved to be called friends, the newspaper declared, were those who were 'Catholic, Democratic, and Flamingant'.[68] Christian Democrats' use of '*volk*' meaning people, neatly captured how they joined Flemish patriotism with support for lower-class demands. Because the upper class in Flanders used French, Christian Democrats used '*ons volk*', 'our people', to mean simultaneously the lower classes and Flemish speakers. Consequently, to be truly '*volksgezind*', democratic or popular-minded, one had to support the cause of Flemish linguistic rights.[69]

A natural hypothesis on the part of social historians has been to assume that religious social movements grow up where more secular ones fail to develop. Or, put differently, where more secular movements arise, there is less likelihood that religious ones will grow. Was this true in the case of Christian Democrats and Socialists in Belgium? In fact, the achievement of the Christian Democrats in Ghent is even more astonishing in that the Socialists in Ghent had a tremendous organization, with some 11,000 union members and a mutual insurance society which insured almost a third of the city's population. Yet the Catholic Anti-Socialists managed to grow in the face of this Socialist success, and with little help and indeed some opposition from the Catholic community itself. By contrast, socialism in Liège had many weaknesses even at the same time that Christian Democracy could hardly get off the ground in the region. The Socialists did well in elections from the 1890s on, but Socialist labour unions, consumer co-operatives and insurance societies were all weaker in Liège than most other urban areas in Belgium.[70]

There may have even been a kind of symbiosis between Socialist and Catholic worker movements. Just because, already in the 1880s, the Socialists in Ghent were so precocious in organizing, Verhaegen was able more easily to convince Catholics there to accept radical measures which Catholics elsewhere would still resist. There was no question that the Christian Democrats in Ghent borrowed the model of an integrated community with labour unions, insurance societies, political leagues, a daily newspaper and consumer co-operative. As Verhaegen put it at the founding of the Werkliedenbond: 'We have to borrow something from the Socialists, the power they get from a well-disciplined army.'[71] The Werkliedenbond – although the Socialists would rarely admit it – also provided a model for its rivals. The Anti-Socialists had a union federation secretary, René Debruyne, before the Socialists did, and the Anti-Socialists were pioneers in hiring labour organizers and advocating the innovative idea of municipal unemployment insurance.[72]

In Brussels, too, Socialists re-created their movement at the same time the Christian Democrats got theirs off the ground after 1904. When the union leader, Louis Vandersmissen, in 1904 urged the Socialists in Brussels to build up the unions, the danger, he pointed out, was that the increasing numbers of commuting workers who were not unionized would be lost to the Socialists: 'Everywhere in the countryside, the *dompers* [duped ones, i.e., Catholics] are forming mutual insurance societies and savings and pension funds, principally for workers who are employed in the city.'[73] Thus, by 1913, organized Catholic workers formed a significant and growing group within the working-class community in Belgium. While Socialist union members numbered some 127,000, Catholic unionists totalled 87,000.[74] In addition, Christian Democrats had far out-organized the Socialists in the area of mutual insurance. By the First World War, while the Socialists had recruited approximately 150,000 workers' families into Socialist societies, the Catholics had over 250,000 members.[75] In no other country in Europe had Catholics organized such a serious rival to the dominant Socialist or secular labour movement.

CONCLUSION: SOCIAL MOVEMENTS AND SECULARIZATION

Belgian Catholicism provides an excellent example of a resurgent religious community in western Europe, one which depended less on traditionalism and more on innovation and a sense of mission. The Christian Democratic movement, where it succeeded in cities like Ghent and Brussels, provided a strong competitor to socialism. Whereas in cities like Liège and in cities in many other countries, workers recruited by socialism or another anticlerical movement would most often be lost to the church, the Catholic unions and other organizations provided an avenue for workers to advance their economic interests and become more, rather than less, religious. Concerned members of other classes, too, found the Christian Democratic movement a place to join their social action and their religious practice. Belgian Catholicism demonstrated its dynamism in attracting or winning over individuals whose family background might just as easily have led them to liberalism or even socialism. A striking number of prominent Christian Democrats had older relatives who were Liberals or freemasons or both. Arthur Verhaegen's grandfather was the founder of the liberal Université libre de Bruxelles, established in opposition to the Catholic University of Leuven, while Father Rutten's uncle was the architect Baron Horta who designed the Socialist Maison du peuple of Brussels and Victoire Cappe's own father was a freemason.[76]

It seems clear, furthermore, that the success and failure of Christian Democracy at the end of the nineteenth century made a profound difference to later developments. Abbé Cardijn, one of the most active Christian Democratic supporters in Brussels on the eve of the First World War, went on in the interwar period to found the Young Christian Workers (Jeunesse Ouvrière Chretienne/ Katholieke Arbeiders Jeugd) which played a tremendous role in Catholic circles in many European countries in the twentieth century.[77] In Belgium itself, the strength of the Christian Democratic movement was one reason why authoritarianism and fascism, in the form of the Rex Party, did not have the success that it did among many Catholics in Austria, Spain, Italy and France.[78] During the interwar and post-Second World War era, the Belgian Catholic unions built on the foundation of the pre-1914 years so that, since 1960, the Catholic union federation has been larger in Belgium than the Socialist one. Indeed, the contrast during the late nineteenth century between Ghent and Brussels, on the one hand, and Liège, on the other, could be seen decades later. The famous 'worker–priest' movement after the Second World War, in which priests laboured alongside workers, spread through France and, in Belgium, to Liège but not to Flanders or Brussels.[79] As in France, so in Liège, bringing priests into the predominantly Socialist or Communist working class was a radical step, whereas in the rest of Belgium, Catholic unions had made encounters with priests a much more common event.

Like certain other areas in the western world – Quebec, the Rhineland, the Netherlands, the Nord in France – Belgium, and especially Flanders, demonstrates the potential of Catholicism to rejuvenate itself and maintain strong support from certain groups in society in the face of secularization. The persistence of a strong Catholicism in these areas has often been attributed to the alleged religiosity of backward areas or to the accidental convergence of nationalism and religion. Yet some of these areas are hardly backward, and there are numerous, more backward areas in Spain, Italy and central and eastern Europe where Catholicism had a much weaker hold. Nor can nationalism alone explain the strength of Catholicism. The map of Catholicism's weaknesses and strengths has still to be fully drawn and explained. There may, in fact, have been a distinctive kind of northern European Catholicism, or Catholicism may have been stronger where it was challenged most by Protestantism or by industrialization.[80] Belgium at least, I would argue, shows that Catholicism could survive by taking the initiative in the midst of a competitive situation. The Catholic community rejuvenated itself by embracing many of the methods employed by its anti-religious rivals, particularly the Socialists. The Belgian case, in other words, suggests the need to re-examine the decline and the survival of religious communities in various societies in the modern world. Rather than a story of inevitable trends, we may more accurately see a tale of struggle and unanticipated consequences.

NOTES

1 Hugh McLeod, *Religion and the People of Western Europe, 1789–1970*, Oxford, 1981; David Martin, *A General Theory of Secularization*, New York, 1979, pp. 18–94.
2 The importance of these subcultures as a European phenomenon is still beginning to be realized by many scholars: Kenneth McRae (ed.), *Consociational Democracy: Political Accommodation in Segmented Societies*, Toronto, 1974; Staf Hellemans, *Strijd om de Moderniteit*, Leuven, 1990; Jaak Billiet (ed.), *Tussen Bescherming en Verovering: Sociologen en Historici over Zuilvorming*, Leuven, 1988.
3 E.H. Kossmann, *The Low Countries 1780–1940*, Oxford, 1978, pp. 37–159.
4 Hervé Hasquin (ed.), *La Wallonie, le pays, les hommes*, Brussels, 1976;

Joel Mokyr, *Industrialization in the Low Countries, 1795–1850*, New Haven, Conn., 1976.

5 A tiny minority of German-speakers exists on the far eastern border, but it was only after the First World War with annexations from Germany that this community reached even 1 per cent of the country's population.

6 For an excellent overview, Kenneth D. McRae, *Conflict and Compromise in Multilingual Societies*, vol. 2, *Belgium*, Waterloo, Canada, 1986.

7 Theo Hermans (ed.), *The Flemish Movement: A Documentary History 1780–1990*, London, 1992; H.J. Elias, *Geschiedenis van de Vlaamse Gedachte, 1780–1914*, 4 vols, Antwerp, 1963–5; Shepherd B. Clough, *A History of the Flemish Movement in Belgium*, New York, 1968 (originally published New York, 1930).

8 Harry Van Velthoven, *De Vlaamse Kwestie 1830–1914*, Kortrijk, 1982; Carl Strikwerda, 'Language and class consciousness: Netherlandic culture and the Flemish working class', in William Fletcher (ed.), *Papers from the First Interdisciplinary Conference on Netherlandic Studies*, Lanham, Md. and London, 1985.

9 Roger Mols, 'Le problème bruxellois: son aspect démographique', *Le revue nouvelle*, 39, 1964, pp. 140–55; Louis Verniers, *Bruxelles et son agglomeration, de 1830 à nos jours*, Brussels, 1958; Aristide Zolberg, 'The making of Flemings and Walloons: Belgium, 1830–1914', *Journal of Interdisciplinary History*, 5, 1974.

10 Jan Stengers (ed.), *Bruxelles, croissance d'une capitale*, Brussels, 1976; Karel van Isacker, *Mijn Land in de Kering, 1830–1980*, vol. 1: *En ouderwetsewereld 1830–1914*, Antwerp, 1976.

11 Geoffrey Parker, *The Dutch Revolt*, rev. edn, London, 1985.

12 J.-F. Gilmont 'Les structures ecclésiastiques de la Wallonie: XVIe–XVIIIe siècles', in Jean-E. Humblet and Tony Dhanis (eds), *Eglise-Wallonie: Chances et risques pour un peuple*, Brussels, 1983.

13 The Belgian church acted as boldly as it did because it had already evolved a custom of de facto independence from the Vatican and because it was desperate to secure a more favourable political regime, even one which tolerated freedom of religion. One has to remember that by 1830, the Belgian church had known an almost continuous period of fifty years during which the state, in the church's view, had been unfavourable: Joseph II, the last Hapsburg emperor, undertook a series of controversial reforms in the 1780s, followed by the French revolutionary and Napoleonic regimes and Dutch rule. In a sense, what the Belgian Catholics adopted was the policy of Lammenais, rejected in France and most other Catholic countries. See Norman Ravitch, *Catholicism and the French Nation*, London, 1991, pp. 66–78; Alois Simon, *L'Eglise catholique et les débuts de la Belgique indépendante*, Wetteren, 1949.

14 B.S. Chlepner, *Cent ans d'histoire sociale en Belgique*, Brussels, 1958, pp. 55–64.

15 Alois Simon, *Le parti catholique belge 1830–1945*, Brussels, 1958; Roger Aubert, 'L'église et l'état en Belgique au XIXe siècle', *Res Publica*, 10, 1968.

16 François Houtart, 'Les paroisses de Bruxelles, 1803–1951', *Bulletin de l'institut des recherches économiques et sociales*, 19: 7, 1953, pp. 710–13; Jan Art, *Kerkelijke Structuur en Pastorale Werking in het Bisdom Gent*, Kortrijk, 1977, pp. 370–1. McLeod, *Religion and the People*, pp. 86–8. As McLeod points out, Brussels is an exception to the Belgian pattern: the number of people per parish grew only slightly less than it did in Paris in the nineteenth century.

17 Arthur Verhaegen, *Vingt-cinq anneés d'action sociale*, Brussels, 1911, pp. 17–19.

18 Pol De Witte, *Alles is Omgekeerd*, (eds) Helmut Gaus and Guy Vanschoenbeek, Leuven, 1986, p. 74.

19 Jacques Lory, 'La résistance des catholiques belges à la "loi de malheur", 1879–1884', *Revue du nord*, 67: 266, 1985, pp. 729–47; Els Witte and Jan Craeybeckx, *Politieke Geschiedenis van Belgie sinds 1830*, Antwerp, 1983, pp. 92–9; Simon, *Le parti catholique belge*, pp. 82–9. Another group came into the Catholic Party in 1884 which cannot be dealt with here, the so-called 'Independents', practising Catholics who had previously voted Liberal but reacted against the Liberals' anticlericalism in the 1880s. Massia Gruman, 'Origines et naissance du parti indépendant (1879–1884)', *Cahiers bruxellois*, 9, 1964, pp. 89–171.

20 Carl Strikwerda, 'France and the Belgian immigration of the nineteenth century', in Camille Guerin-Gonzales and Carl Strikwerda (eds), *The Politics of Immigrant Workers: Labor Activism and Migration in the World Economy since 1830*, New York, 1993; *Wallonie Né d'une grève?*, Brussels, 1989.

21 On agriculture, Leen van Molle, *Ieder voor Allen: De Belgische Boerenbond 1890–1990*, Leuven, 1990, pp. 28–45; Jan Craeybeckx, 'De Agrarische Depressie van het einde der XIXe eeuw en de politieke strijd om de boeren', *Belgisch Tijdschrift voor Nieuwste Geschiedenis/ Revue belge d'histoire contemporaine* (hereafter *BTNG/RBHC*), 1973, pp. 191–230; and 1974, pp. 181–225. On socialism, Andre Mommen, *De Belgische Werkliedenpartij 1880–1914*, Ghent, 1980; Marcel Liebman, *Les socialistes belges 1885–1914*, Brussels, 1979.

22 Emiel Lamberts, 'Van Kerk naar zuil: de ontwikkeling van het katholiek organisatiewezen in Belgie in de 19e eeuw', in Billiet, *Tussen Bescherming en Verovering*, pp. 119–27.

23 Kristin Meerts, 'De Leuvense hoogleraar Victor Brants: Een brugfiguur in het sociaal-katholicisme (1856–1891)', *Bijdragen tot Geschiedenis*, 65, 1982.

24 Rudolph Rezsohazy, *Origines et formation du catholicisme social en Belgique, 1842–1909*, Louvain, 1959; Van Molle, *Ieder voor Allen*, pp. 47–65.

25 Verhaegen, *Vingt-cinq*, p. 225.

26 Jan De Maeyer, 'Op zoek naar de wortels van de christelijke arbeidersbeweging. De Antisocialistische Werkliedenbond van Gent vóór 1914', in Emmanuel Gerard and Jozef Mampuys (eds), *Voor Kerk en Werk: Opstellen over de geschiedenis van de christelijke arbeidersbeweging 1886–1986*, Leuven, 1986, p. 60; Chanoine van den Gheyn, *Le diocese de Gand, 1830–1930*, Brussels, 1930, pp. 55–65.

27 De Maeyer, 'Op zoek naar de wortels', p. 91.
28 A. Pottier, *La coopération et les sociétés ouvrières*, Liège, 1889; Rezsohazy, *Origines*, pp. 130–4; Paul Gérin, *Les débuts de la démocratie chrétiennes à Liège*, Brussels, 1958, pp. 204–8; *Le bien du peuple*, 5 March 1893.
29 Robert Kothen, *La pensée et l'action sociale des catholiques 1789–1944*, Louvain, 1945, pp. 292–307; Emile Poulat, *Catholicisme, démocratie et socialisme*, Tournai, 1977, pp. 80, 151. Kurth later served from 1907 to 1916 as director of the Institut historique belge à Rome.
30 *Appel aux ouvriers*, Liège, 1897.
31 Rezsohazy, *Origines*, pp. 220–2. Under Belgian election law, parties fielded slates of candidates and voters could vote for whole slates or for individual candidates.
32 Gérin, *Les débuts*, pp. 388–9, 458.
33 Rezsohazy, *Origines*, p. 326; Victor Serwy, *La coopération en Belgique*, Brussels, 1942, vol. 2, pp. 251–2.
34 Paul Gérin, 'Antonie-Denis Pottier', *Biographie nationale*, 30, pp. 726–30. Although they won no seats in local government, Christian Democrats did win one parliamentary seat in 1900 after the national Catholic Party forced Liégeois conservatives to open up their slate for national elections. Rezsohazy, *Origines*, pp. 299–300. The conservative Bishop Rutten of Liège should not be confused with the Dominican labour organizer Father George-Celas Rutten discussed below.
35 Pierre Joye and Rosine Lewin, *L'église et classe ouvrière en Belgique*, Brussels, 1967, pp. 114–245; Val Lorwin, 'Belgium: religion, class and language in national politics', in Robert Dahl (ed.), *Political Oppositions in Western Democracies*, New Haven, Conn., 1966, p. 159.
36 Léon de Saint Moulin, 'Contribution à l'histoire de la déchristianisation. La pratique religieuse à Seraing depuis 1830', *Annuaire d'histoire liégeoise*, 10, 1967; Art, *Kerkelijke*, pp. 370–1.
37 Calculated from Belgisch Volksbond/Ligue démocratique belge, *Jaarboek/Annuaire*, Brussels, 1898.
38 Gérin, 'Pottier'.
39 Arthur Verhaegen, *De Vakvereenigingen*, Ghent, 1895, pp. 23–4.
40 ibid., pp. 20–4; Louis Varlez, 'Quelques pages d'histoire synidcale belge', *Le musée social*, 3, March 1902, pp. 119, 131–2; 'Les grèves', *Journal des correspondances*, April 1910, p. 25.
41 Rezsohazy, *Origines*, pp. 50–61; van den Gheyn, *Le diocese*, pp. 64–73.
42 Verhaegen, *Vingt-cinq*, pp. 58–62.
43 Art, *Kerkelijke*, pp. 100–11.
44 *Verslag der Katholieken Maatschappelijke Werken*, Ghent, 1905; *Congres der Katholieken werken van het arrondissement Gent-Eekloo, 1911*, Ghent, 1911.
45 Art, *Kerkelijke*, pp. 110–11; Georges Barnich, *Le régime clerical en Belgique*, Brussels, 1911.
46 Fédération ouvrière catholique, *Almanach du pays de Liège*, Liège, 1910.

47 *Appel aux ouvriers*, Liège, 1897, p. 4.

48 *L'ouvrier mineur*, April 1906, pp. 76–7.

49 Van Velthoven, *De Vlaamse Kwestie*, p. 52. The former Liberals were known as 'Independents', see note 19.

50 *La voix de l'ouvrier*, 11 May 1889, p. 1, and 22 June 1890, p. 2; Verheagen, *Vingt-cinq*, pp. 117–19; Karel van Isacker, *Averechtse Demokratie*, Antwerp, 1959, pp. 86–9.

51 *De Christelijke Arbeid*, March 1900, p. 157; Rudolph Rezsohazy, *Histoire du mouvement mutualiste chrétien en Belgique*, Paris, 1956, pp. 216, 295.

52 *1911. Almanach Vade-Mecum de la Grande Boulangerie Le Bon Pain Bruxellois et les Syndicats Chrétiens affiliées au Secretariat des Ouevres Sociales*, Brussels, 1911, cover; *Het Syndikaat/Le syndicat*, 6 October 1912, p. 1.

53 Fédération Bruxelloise, Parti Ouvrier Belge, *Rapports, exercise, 1912–13*, Brussels, 1913, p. 172. The unemployment subsidies were first pioneered in Ghent, where the Catholic and Socialist unions co-operated in setting them up. This so-called 'Ghent system' then spread throughout Belgium and to many other countries. Guy Vanthemsche, 'Unemployment insurance in interwar Belgium', *International Review of Social History*, 35, 1990.

54 Barnich, *Le regime clerical*, pp. 217–18; Jozef Mampuys, 'Aan de oorsprong van het Algemeen Christelijk Vakverbond', in Gerard and Mampuys (eds), *Voor Kerk en Werk*, pp. 171–5.

55 Carl Strikwerda, 'Urban structure, religion, and language: Belgian workers, 1880–1914', Ph.D. diss., University of Michigan, 1983, pp. 244, 322. Catholics probably also recruited what few immigrants did come to the city in the 1890s, many of whom came from the western part of the province of East Flanders – Waarschoot, Nazaret and Zomergem – from one of the most deeply Catholic areas of Belgium: Art, *Kerkelijke*, pp. 325–6.

56 E. Mahaim, *Les abonnements d'ouvriers*, Brussels, 1910.

57 Calculated from Office du travail, *Recensement industrielle et commerciale, 1910*, Brussels, 1913, in Strikwerda, 'Urban structure', p. 387.

58 Carl Strikwerda 'Interest-group politics and the international economy: Mass politics and big business corporations in the Liège coal basin, 1870–1914', *Journal of Social History*, 25: 2, 1991.

59 J. Bondas, *Histoire anecdotique du mouvement ouvrier au pays de Liège*, Liège, 1955, pp. 297–9; Isidor Delvigne, *Au Terrain du combat*, Liège, 1918, pp. 111 and endmaps.

60 Results from Brussels: Socialists 31,047, Catholics 10,904; results from suburbs and small towns: Socialists 6,291, Catholics 4,563: Fédération Bruxelloise, *Rapports*, p. 175.

61 Jozef Mampuys, 'De propaganda van pater Rutten voor de christelijk vakbeweging 1900–1914', in Gerrard and Mampuys (eds) *Voor Kerk en Werk*; Jules Verstraelen, 'Twee bouwmeesters van het christelijk syndicalisme: Rutten and Arendt', in S.H. Scholl (ed.) *Zij Bouwden voor Morgen: Figuren uit de Christelijke Arbeidersbeweging*, Brussels, 1966.

62 Maria Jacues, 'De K.A.V. en de vrouwenemancipatie: Baers, Cappe, and VandePutte', Scholl (ed.), *Zij Bouwden voor Morgen*.

63 Lode Wils has passionately argued for decades that Christian Democracy and the Flemish movement are inextricably tied, but I find the arguments of Jan Craeybeckx, Karel van Isacker, Harry van Velthoven more persuasive. Lode Wils, *Het Daenisme*, Leuven, 1969 and *Honderd Jaar Vlaamse Beweging*, Leuven, 1977; Jan Craeybeckx, *Arbeidersbeweging en Vlaamsgezindheid voor de Eerste Wereldoorlog*, Brussels, 1978; Karel Van Isacker, *Het Daenisme 1893–1914*, Antwerp, 1965.

64 Strikwerda, 'Language and class consciousness'; Craeybeckx, *Arbeidersbeweging*; van Velthoven, *De Vlaamse Kwestie*, pp. 95–133.

65 Carl Strikwerda, 'The divided class: Catholics vs. Socialists in Belgium, 1880–1914', *Comparative Studies in Society and History*, 30: 2, 1988, pp. 344–58.

66 *A travers les Flandres*, Ghent, 1902, p. 122.

67 De Maeyer, 'Op zoek naar de wortels', 70–2; Van Isacker, *Het Daenisme*.

68 'Guido Gezelle en 't Ontwakken van Vlaanderen', *De Metaalarbeider*, 5 June 1914, p. 43.

69 'Guido Gezelle'; *Zesde Vlaamsche Sociale Week, 1913*, Ghent, 1914, p. 146.

70 Of course, it is also true that the Liégeois Socialists chose to avoid taking on the tough job of building up labour unions, co-operatives and mutual insurance societies in the face of employers' opposition, and concentrated on elections and participation in local and provincial government which was easier: Strikwerda, 'Interest-group politics'.

71 Verhaegen, *Vingt-cinq*, pp. 93–4.

72 Rezsohazy, *Origines*, p. 324.

73 L. Vandersmissen, 'Les syndicats et les campagnards', *Journal des correspondances*, December 1904, pp. 71–2; Strikwerda, 'Urban structure', pp. 440–58.

74 Commission syndicale, *Rapports présentés au congres syndicale, juillet, 1914*, Brussels, 1914, pp. 56–7; S.H. Scholl, *150 Jaar Katholiek Arbeidersbeweging in Belgie*, 3 vols, Brussels, 1965, vol. 2, appendix.

75 Total membership in the pre-First World War era is difficult to determine because many societies were not affiliated into national federations. See J. Dockx, 'De "Prévoyance Social" als typevoorbeeld van een socialistische verzekerscooperatie', *BTNG/RBHC*, 22: 1–2, 1991; Reszohazy, *Histoire du mouvement*, tables.

76 Robert Rock, 'Vlaamse pioniers: Bruggeman, Eylenbosch, en Verhaegen', in Scholl (ed.), *Zij Bouwden voor Morgen*, p. 24; Verstraelen, 'Twee bouwmeesters', p. 61; Jacues, 'De K.A.V.', p. 112.

77 Françoise Peemans, 'Joseph-Léon Cardijn', *Biographie nationale*, 41, pp. 156–64; Joseph Delbes, *Naissance de l'action ouvrière catholique*, Paris, 1982, pp. 26–33; Gianfranco Poggi, *Catholic Action in Italy*, Stanford, Calif., 1967, pp. 111–29.

78 Jean Stengers, 'Belgium', in Hans Rogger and Eugen Weber (eds), *The

European Right, Berkeley, Calif., 1966; Carl Strikwerda, 'Corporatism and the lower middle classes: Interwar Belgium', *Splintered Classes: Politics and the Lower Middle Classes in Interwar Europe*, Rudy Koshar (ed.), New York, 1990, pp. 218–25.

79 Oscar L. Arnal, *Priests in Working-Class Blue: The History of the Worker-Priests (1943–1954)*, Mahwah, NJ, 1986.

80 Yves-Marie Hilaire, 'Les ouvriers du Nord devant l'église catholique (XIX–XXe siècles)', *Le mouvement social*, 57, 1966; Michael Fogarty, *Christian Democracy in Western Europe, 1820–1953*, Notre Dame, Ind., 1957, pp. 7–9; Carl Strikwerda, 'Catholic working class movements in western Europe', *International Labor and Working Class History*, Autumn 1988, pp. 81–5.

3

'MORE CHURCHES – MORE CHURCHGOERS'

The Lutheran Church in Hanover between 1850 and 1914

Hans Otte

INTRODUCTION: THE CITY OF HANOVER

Around 1850, agrarian conditions of life were still predominant in Germany, except in a few industrial districts. Two generations later, at the start of the twentieth century, Germany had risen to become the leading industrial power on the European continent. Now the large and medium-sized cities placed their stamp on the countryside and on the thinking of the rural population. The concentrated social relations in the cities changed the character of organized religion, and especially the relationship between church members and clergy. It is especially from the point of view of the latter that the process of change, as illustrated by Hanover, will be portrayed. This city is a good choice for such an analysis because in Hanover the transition from town to city, proceeding first gradually and then rapidly, was complete within a mere sixty years between 1850 and 1914. By the beginning of the First World War, Hanover was counted among Germany's greatest cities. Starting in 1850 with 53,800 inhabitants, Hanover reached 100,000 by 1874 and in 1914 it had a population of 324,700.

Since the Middle Ages, Hanover had been an urban centre in the middle of Lower Saxony, but up to 1850 it preserved the character of a medium-sized court town.[1] Up to the end of Hanoverian independence (1866), the town lacked large-scale industry, as the king wanted no noisy or smelly factories in his capital. So only small- and medium-sized businesses were established, and they settled close to the town boundaries on the south and north-east sides of

Hanover. These were thinly populated areas, though development was much more rapid after the railway reached the town in 1843.

The first large-scale industry was established on the west of the town, in the village of Linden, which only became part of Hanover in 1921. In Linden population growth was even more rapid than in Hanover.[2] With 4,993 inhabitants in 1852, Linden grew to 28,095 in 1890 and 86,500 in 1913. Even in 1850 the place had an industrial character. In 1833 the first steam engine in central Lower Saxony had been put into operation there, and in 1845 came the first machine-building firm, with 678 workers. Textile factories soon followed.

Hanover's time as a capital ended in 1866 when King George V was driven out by the Prussian troops and the Kingdom of Hanover was annexed by Prussia. From this point on, the character of the town changed fast. Admittedly it remained an important administrative centre, but the liberal economic legislation of the North German Confederation facilitated industrial development, as well as the free movement of workers. This was the background to the *Gründerzeit*, after the defeat of France, when numerous industrial establishments were founded. The Great Depression, which set in from 1873, had a severe effect on the Linden machine-building industry. However, in the north-eastern section of the city, the rising unemployment was partly held in check by the establishment of new chemical, rubber and electrical industries. Several of the businesses set up at that time developed in the decades before the First World War into big industrial complexes of international importance.

The rise in population affected the different quarters of the town in varying degrees. Working-class and middle-class districts came to be ever more sharply separated. Except for a few streets with large middle-class houses, Linden became a town of densely populated proletarian districts, inhabited by industrial workers and their families. In Hanover the better-off citizens deserted the narrow inner-city streets and moved to the former garden areas to the south-east, where a strongly middle-class district developed. This area was sharply distinguished from the working-class districts in the north, where houses rapidly sprang up around the factories. Commercial and administrative offices remained in the old city,[3] but many of the old bourgeois houses with their courts and their picturesque nooks were turned into cheap and crowded dwelling-houses: in the area beside the River Leine several streets took on the character of a slum.

Since the time of the Reformation Lutheranism was the established religion in Hanover. There were only small Catholic, Reformed and Jewish minorities. In 1850 just under 91 per cent of the population were Lutherans, and in 1910 it was 86.5 per cent. The relative decline was mainly due to the immigration of Catholic industrial workers.[4] Since the number of people leaving the church was small, [5] and since the other religious minorities could scarcely make much impression on the city, established Lutheranism was the determining factor in religious discussion. Up to the beginning of the First World War, Hanover was, in the minds of its bourgeois representatives, a Lutheran city. This chapter will concentrate upon that church.

CHURCH ORGANIZATION

The parochial structure of the church in the city of Hanover had changed little since the Reformation. In the area of the *Altstadt* and *Neustadt* there were four Lutheran churches, with two pastorates each; there were also two personal parishes, namely the Palace Church for court and state officials and the Garrison Church for the military. Those living outside the gates had several possibilities: in the south there was the Garden Church, in the north the Hainholz village church (4 kilometres from the city) and Linden had its own little church with one pastorate. This parochial system now had to deal with Hanover's growth into a city. There were already differences in parish size and, in particular, some parishes had already entered into rapid growth. In 1826 there was on average one pastor for 2,046 parishioners, and none had to care for more than 3,000 souls; [6] by 1855 the average had risen to 1:2,350, but the pastor of Hainholz had 7,500 parishioners and, in 1856, the pastor of the Garden Church had as many as 8,205.

The pastorates were attached to ecclesiastical parishes, each of which was a financial unit. In 1848, following the revolution, and under the influence of liberal demands, each church with at least one pastorate was made an autonomous parish. Each ecclesiastical parish was independent of the civil parish and had a church council whose members were laymen. They were responsible for the financial administration, and in conjunction with the pastor they provided more general leadership for the parish.

The right to vote for the church council was restricted to those who could vote for the city council, namely those possessing property[7] and paying a certain sum in taxes. A proposal that the franchise be extended was rejected by the city authorities, who argued that those living on low incomes 'change houses frequently, living in this parish today, and in that one tomorrow, and as a result they seldom have a real interest in parish affairs'.[8] Similar arguments were advanced with regard to the franchise in city elections, where the electorate was divided into tax classes. This ensured a bourgeois majority on the city council: from 1887 onwards the Social Democrats had the most votes in Hanover in Reichstag elections, but they had no chance on the city council until 1918. So far as church elections were concerned, this system meant that the number of those entitled to vote remained small – never more than 10 per cent of church members. As a result, only members of certain occupational groups were elected to parish councils. Most of them came from the middle class (rentiers, merchants, state officials), and especially from the lower middle class (artisans, foremen). Committed Social Democrats never stood for parish councils in Hanover.[9]

The financial administration of the inner-city parishes was controlled by the city council. Since the city council was also the patron of these parishes, it had considerable influence on questions of church politics. In this respect there was potential conflict with the two central church bodies, the Consistory and the Provincial Consistory. These were made up predominantly of followers of the former Hanoverian king, George V; in theological terms, they were adherents of Lutheran confessionalism. By contrast, the city authorities and other spokesmen for the urban bourgeoisie, tended to be National Liberal in politics, welcoming the union of Hanover with Prussia, and in church politics supporters of the liberal clergy, who relativized the Reformation Confessions and saw the purpose of their work as lying in the development of the free moral personality. This difference of standpoint between city council and Consistory led to long-drawn out legal proceedings concerning patronage rights in respect of newly founded pastorates. The city council wanted to retain the patronage of new pastorates, as they hoped to retain a means of exercising pressure in church–political conflicts. The city authorities could use their position as patrons to put forward liberal clergy for vacant pastorates. Given the church–political orientation of the Consistory, such clergy otherwise had very little chance. If they came from churches in other parts of Prussia, they were generally rejected by the Consistory;[10] the city council thus had good reason to fear that no liberal clergymen would be selected in suburban parishes, unless they themselves were able to retain an influence over the appointments. Since, however, the legal proceedings ended in the defeat of the city council, only confessional Lutherans were appointed by church councils and the Consistory to pastorates in these newly-founded parishes. Only after the turn of the century were a few liberals chosen as pastors in the suburban churches.

Up until 1918 the traditional organs of church leadership were able to retain their power. The establishment of church councils, elected by parishioners, changed nothing. Equally, the Lutheran Church remained closely entwined with the state and with the city government. From a legal point of view the church parish and the civil parish remained entirely separate. But this separation was not maintained in reality, and in the older inner-city parishes the city authorities retained their rights in church matters. This was particularly evident at the time of celebrations, such as the church service which marked the beginning of the period during which the city council sat, the anniversaries of great events in the city's history[11] or such church festivals as the Luther jubilee in 1883: on such occasions city officials and pastors appeared side by side, and the relationship between them was made visible to everyone.

CHURCH–POLITICAL OPTIONS

The beginnings of the industrial age in the Kingdom of Hanover were accompanied by severe church–political struggles. These were sparked off by the reforms proposed by representatives of the Lutheran *Erweckungsbewegung* (revival movement). The confessional Lutherans were labelled by their opponents 'confessionalists', because they turned against the modifications in preaching, hymn-books and catechism which were introduced at the time of the Enlightenment. In Hanover they had it much easier than in other parts of Germany. As political conservatives, they were supported by King George V (1851–66), and gradually they took over the key positions in the church. In theological terms, they defended the Reformation Confessions as valid for all time, they emphasized the central role of the pastorate in the transmission of Christianity and in their understanding of the church they wanted to drive a middle path between Catholicism on the one side and anti-institutionalism on the other. At the same time they advocated such reforms as the return to a richly developed liturgy (named 'high church' by their opponents) and they sought to re-establish the sixteenth-century

Confessions as official orthodoxy. They called for the reintroduction of visitations, for the pastor to go with the coffin to the cemetery and for the use of the old forms in the administration of the sacraments.[12] They also supported certain branches of the Inner Mission, such as the *Henriettenstift*, founded in 1860 and staffed by deaconesses.

The liberal bourgeoisie's suspicion of the king's political conservatism and of the official church orthodoxy reached a peak in 1862, when the king introduced and declared compulsory a new orthodox catechism. After a storm of protests the compulsion was dropped, but the deep-seated alienation between laity and confessional clergy remained, and it continued to have a determining influence on the church–political conflicts of the following years, including those which followed the overthrow of the Welf king. After the Prussian annexation of 1866, the Lutheran Church of Hanover did not become part of the Prussian Evangelical Church. This was because, in Hanover, unlike Prussia, there had been no union of Lutherans and Reformed, and thus there was a confessional difference between the former and the latter. For the laity and also for the city authorities this difference within Protestantism was of marginal significance. They allied themselves with the liberal clergy, who denied the juridical validity of the Confessions and rejected the church reform programme of the confessional Lutherans. Thus in Hanover the city authorities obstructed the introduction of visitations in the inner-city churches, and in none of these was the catechism officially used. In this respect the bourgeoisie and its liberal representatives were in church matters defenders of tradition. They were less interested in the church as an institution, and so devoted less energy to attempts at reform. They were quite different from those clergy and lay people who had been influenced by the *Erweckungsbewegung* and who had a vital interest in the church, not least because they believed they had a divine calling to act as its representatives.

In parallel with the reforming ideas of the confessional clergy there was also discussion of the proposals developed by church people in Berlin and Hamburg under the title of 'Inner Mission'. The parochial system had proved inadequate to deal with the problems of pastoral care in cities and to respond to the social evils associated with industrialization. J.H. Wichern from Hamburg therefore suggested new measures, based on Anglo-Saxon models. In order to deal in an effective way with the miseries of the proletariat, he wanted to combine missionary and charitable work. As a man strongly influenced by the *Erweckungsbewegung*, Wichern recognized that material need was the result of social injustice, but what concerned him even more was the spiritual estrangement of the masses from Christianity. In order to bring about the 'Christian rebirth of social relationships in the life of the people'[13] he called for house visits by missionaries, Bible studies and the distribution of Christian literature, as well as charitable assistance. Work of this kind should not only be carried out by pastors, but trained lay people should also be involved. From 1848 the Central Committee for Inner Mission made this model its own. This Central Committee had been formed in 1848 after the first successes of the (bourgeois) revolution in order to resist the church reforms proposed by the democrats, and in particular their demand for the separation of church and state. It saw the Inner Mission as the best means of fighting against the turning away from God which had shown itself in the revolution.

Although Hanover's confessional clergy shared entirely the conservative critique of contemporary events put forward by members of the Central Committee, they did not accept their proposals for the future shaping of church work. They were critical of the fact that most members of the Central Committee belonged to Prussia's United Church, and even more they argued that the organization of religious work through free associations would be damaging to the church.[14] They accepted that such societies could occasionally be useful in particular areas of church work, but argued that they should never supersede the pastor. The latter 'provides in the parish the natural society [*Verein*] for all areas of work, with himself as the born president, and each parishioner as a born member'.[15] From this point of view, the development of the existing parish system had to take priority over all other kinds of church work. Furthermore, the Inner Mission was a competitor within the parish:

> Under the guise of friendliness to the church, it [the Inner Mission] is in fact its ruin; it is a parasitic growth which threatens to cover the whole trunk and branches of the church tree, and to suck out all its life; the way things stand, one of the two, either the church or the Inner Mission, will have to quit the field.[16]

This assessment of the Inner Mission did not take account of the alarming reports of the situation in Berlin and Frankfurt: for the

Hanovarian Church and its pastors still had a chance. Maybe Hanover had not developed so far as the industrial districts on the Ruhr or the 'old' cities like Berlin and Hamburg. That, at least, was the view of the Göttingen Professor Friedrich Ehrenfeuchter when he explained to the Central Committee in Berlin in 1850 why the Inner Mission won no support in the Kingdom of Hanover:

> It seems to me that the crisis conditions that require the work of the Inner Mission are not present on the same scale. . . . The density of population, except in a few districts, is not very high, there are no great cities, and for this reason there is also no real proletariat.[17]

First attempts at a solution

This assessment is only partly valid for the city of Hanover. Linden was growing so fast, as were the incorporated suburbs on the northern and southern sides of the city, that the continuation of the old forms of church care through the pastors could not be assured. In 1854 the pastors of Hainholz and of the Garden Church each had more than 7,000 parishioners to look after. Both of them therefore asked to be transferred to another parish. They felt themselves overworked.[18] However, the Consistory's plans for dividing these big parishes and erecting new churches soon proved impracticable. The cost was too great, as the new parishes would need not only to build a church, but also to pay the future pastor.

In order to bring about some improvement in the care of the new districts, further consideration was concentrated on the Hainholz parish. However, the pastor of that parish now became an obstacle. He was afraid that the division of the parish would lead to the loss of a large part of his income, notably the fees received for presiding at baptisms, weddings and burials. After hard negotiations, lasting four years, a solution was finally found: the parish, which by now had grown to 17,077, was divided, and the pastor was transferred to another, equally well-endowed, parish. From those parts of the parish which lay right next to the city gates a new parish was formed with its own church and pastor. The king contributed 3,000 *Talers* towards the costs of building the new Christ Church, and the remaining costs were to be met by a collection in all churches of the consistorial district. However, the collection was a failure. Only about 2,000 *Talers* were collected. Since the planned church was going to cost 74,000 *Talers*, it again looked as if the scheme might have to be dropped. But then it proved possible to interest the king again. Since a part of the summer palace area lay within the new parish, the king declared that he would be willing to provide all the money needed, so long as a sufficiently impressive building was erected. This solution to all the problems permitted the building of a large church, with three aisles and a powerful tower-façade, which was consecrated in 1862.

The example of Christ Church indicates the problems which continued to determine the relationship between urban growth and the church. Incumbent pastors were not ready simply to give up their rights, and they had to be compensated. It was difficult to obtain the funds for the extension of the church organization as it did not prove possible to interest the rural parishes in the church problems of the towns. Collections for the building of new urban churches brought in very little money in rural parishes. The solution which was then found was typical of this early phase. The king took responsibility for the cost of the building and justified this in terms of his monarchical self-understanding:

> We are conscious all the time that we have been placed by the will of God not only to further the temporal peace and earthly well-being of Our subjects, but also to promote the right knowledge and true worship of God.[19]

Still fully caught up in a romantic conception of monarchy by God's grace, the king felt himself responsible for the spiritual health of his subjects, and so financed the building.

The same point can also be made about the building of the church in Linden. For several centuries, Linden only possessed a small village church, and as a result of a fire it did not even have a tower. It was only when Linden grew to be a large industrial village that the pastor dared to suggest the building of a tower. Here, too, the king contributed a large sum from the privy purse. Even more important was the biggest employer in Linden, the owner of the machine-building factory who contributed all the building materials for the tower. The spirit of the times was also reflected in the rivalry between donors. The factory-owner did not wish to remain an anonymous benefactor and he wanted his contribution to receive due recognition. He selected the winning design, and the procession of maidens of honour to the consecration of the now suitably imposing church began at his house.[20]

None the less it was soon apparent that the church building was not big enough: on the great festivals the congregation spilled out on to the street.[21] In 1864 the church council decided to build a second church in Linden. This project was also supported by the king, and it was intended that the Linden factory-owners should contribute. The parish council, still dominated by farmers, held them responsible for the great growth of population in Linden.[22] In 1864, the same architect who had designed Christ Church presented an elegant but economical building plan – an imposing church was not considered necessary for this village. While the war with Prussia was actually in progress (1866), the king donated a site for the church in the southern part of Linden. But then other rules came into force. After the Prussian annexation, the factory-owners consistently refused any contribution to the church building, arguing that it was a task for the parish. As a result of this, the disheartened church council gave up its right to the building site, and the building of the church was delayed for years.

These two examples show how much the Hanoverian church depended on its king. Since there were no central church funds to turn to in cases of need, the king, in his role of protector of the church, provided the money which could not be obtained from collections. This intimate relationship between church and throne was broken when Hanover was annexed by Prussia in 1866. It is understandable, therefore, that the confessional clergy remained loyal to the Welfish royal house for long after its downfall.

The City Mission

In the 1860s the rigid rejection of the Inner Mission in Hanover was gradually modified. Younger clergy from the confessional camp saw the successes of the 'City Mission' in Berlin and Hamburg and, together with several young legal officials, took the first steps towards organizing a Hanover City Mission. Their model was the Berlin City Mission, which tried to create islands of belief within the densely populated mass parishes. Missionaries visited from house to house in the poorest quarters, committed Christians who wanted to be involved in social action had their energies canalized in a meaningful way through special charitable organizations.[23] On this pattern a City Mission was founded in 1865. However, the name 'mission' was avoided in order not to revive the old controversies.

As well as the establishment of a hostel for itinerant craftsmen (the *Herberge zur Heimat*), the Evangelical Association engaged in a combination of charitable assistance with missionary activity, supported by apologetic lectures. This very soon proved successful. In particular middle-class women, who did not need to earn an income and who otherwise had no opportunities for independent work,[24] quickly organized various charitable efforts, such as a society for providing clothing for the sick.[25] The Association's work enabled, for example, a bricklayer who was unemployed during the winter to work as a *colporteur*, selling religious books.

The committee of the Evangelical Association recognized the potential conflict between lay activity and the self-understanding of the pastors, and after two years they decided to appoint a chaplain. Financially, he would have to be supported by donations, because, since the fall of the Hanoverian monarchy, there was no possibility of obtaining the money from state or church funds. In the appeal for contributions, the committee stressed the success of their social projects, but only referred indirectly to the missionary activities of the future pastor:

> With parishes growing to the size of many thousands, and being in a state of constant flux because of the movement here and there of their members, the pastoral office has for long been insufficient, and the new church councils are in the best circumstances no more than a hope.

But in order to allay pastors' fears about unwanted competition, it was declared that the chaplain

> would act not by virtue of his office as a public servant of the church but for the sake of love, as a brother, and moreover this appointment in no sense means the establishment of a public post, and in particular the church order of the city will remain completely undisturbed.[26]

This statement reflects the anxieties of the city pastors. At the same time it shows that the church situation was not yet regarded as being so critical that changes in the existing order could be demanded of the clergy.

Thus, in the practical work of the Association's chaplain, social–charitable work, such as a mission to domestic servants with an employment agency, stood on an equal footing with missionary initiatives – in the long run, the social–charitable work would even take first place. The first chaplain concentrated on implementing the Lutheran confessional reform programme, beginning with an increase in the number of church services. He brought in evening services (1866), started a Sunday school (1872), introduced Christmas trees in a Christmas service and held the first watch-night service.[27] Unlike the City Missions in Berlin and Hamburg, however, there were for many years no specially trained missionaries or deacons employed to make house visits in poorer districts. From this one can deduce that the activities of the Association chaplain in Hanover reached not so much those who were totally estranged from the church, as those whose involvement with the church might be intensified.

This work was crowned in 1874–5 by the building of a club house which offered meeting rooms for the various sub-branches[28] of the Evangelical Association. At the dedication of the club house, the President of the Association declared:

> It is one of the hallmarks of our time that the old, secure patterns of human society as we . . . inherited them from our fathers, crumble and dissolve. . . . There has scarcely been another time in which the people was so far reduced to a broken up mass, or in which each one stood at the side of the next one, equal and separate, and then again there has scarcely been another time in which there were so many associations, co-operative societies and clubs, founded for every kind of purpose. . . . The church cannot escape from these signs of the times, it cannot, and even if it could, it must not. . . . So may we now in our Club House offer a place of unity, where people can come together from every parish, standing on one common ground, that of the gospel and the confession of our dear church, and working for one goal, namely the building of the Kingdom of God among our people, in order to find one another, get to know one another, learn from one another and strengthen one another. . . .[29]

These words make clear how the perception of the Inner Mission and its associated organizations changed. It was now (1875) seen as a part of modernity and (perhaps quite realistically) its function as an aspect of the church's internal organization was accepted. Here too the confessional basis was taken for granted – there was no place for a liberal understanding of Christianity.

There is only one example of the Evangelical Association trying to go outside the circle of those 'faithful to the church', and this was the publication of a weekly newspaper. The catalyst was again a financial problem. Since the Association's chaplain could not in the long run live upon continually fluctuating donations, he took the initiative in publishing, and in 1868 the first *Hannoversche Sonntagsblatt* appeared. The chaplain was allowed to keep the profits from this paper, and soon more than half his income came from this source. As a result, Hanover and the surrounding area had a Christian–Conservative newspaper that was relatively successful. In 1880 it already had 22,000 subscribers,[30] though admittedly it was mainly distributed in the surrounding rural areas, so that its influence on readers in Hanover was rather limited.[31] The paper had few intellectual pretensions and was clearly directed at the 'lower classes'; it combined religious articles with entertainment, politics and information. The problems of city life did not play a very prominent role in the paper and, later, with comments on cattle markets and weather news, the interests of the rural population were even explicitly catered for.

Between the young pastors who, together with the Consistory, supported the Inner Mission and the liberal bourgeoisie, who rejected the revivalist association of missionary and charitable work,[32] there stood the pastors of the inner city. Their equivocal stance in this situation of tension was described by a supporter of the Berlin City Mission after a visit to Hanover:

> The clergy of the city of Hanover are through their ministry entrenched opponents of action. It is a wonderful conservative principle that generally rules these city clergy. In their eyes it is a dangerous novelty when the opponents of the orthodox catechism want to get rid of it, and an equally dangerous novelty when the church authorities want to present the old orthodoxy in new forms in order to breathe new life into forms that have gradually been emptied of their content. . . . They do not welcome the appointment of a genuinely liberal clergyman to a city parish, but neither will they allow the Consistory to choose for a city parish a man whom it trusts, a man of fresh, warm faith, and witnessing love.[33]

Even if there is an element of stylization in the portrait of the innovative activist on the Consistory, standing against the immobile pastors, it certainly indicates the difficulties that the reformers faced. The pastors of the inner-city churches were less affected by the changes that were being carried through outside the gates of the old city. They also refused fully to commit themselves to the scepticism with which many of the bourgeoisie regarded the attempts at renewal by the confessional clergy.

More churches

The function of the Evangelical Association as a field of action for those lay people who were interested in the church and its rejection of the use of special missionaries, excluded the possibility that it might become the basis for some kind of major missionary strategy. If the church was going to reach the people who lived in the suburbs, other ways of doing this would have to be adopted. After 1870, this realization led to the debate about improving involvement in the church, which had been broken off after 1866, being taken up again. The decline in religious practice which in these years was made shockingly clear through falling attendance at church services and reduced participation in communion,[34] had in the eyes of Gerhard Uhlhorn,[35] the leading theologian among the Hanover clergy, only one cause:

> that the number of clergy and the number of churches is far short of what is needed. Mass parishes exist, and therefore the evil will progressively grow. . . . What's the use of any inner or outer mission, when the first and most essential thing is missing, namely the orderly and sufficient provision of each member of our own church with Word and Sacrament?[36]

As a reflection of his confessional orientation Uhlhorn pleaded for the strengthening of the pastoral office and ties to the parish church. Two alternatives to this programme were favoured in other places: in Berlin, they contented themselves with the introduction of the City Mission and of cheap assistant pastors;[37] in Hamburg they dropped the requirement that church members use the services of their own parish church, and gave them a free choice of pastor.[38] The latter solution, which corresponded to the liberal ideal, whereby the pastor should form the religious personality of his hearers, was for Uhlhorn a programme of despair:

> Perhaps it would be possible by these means to draw from a parish numbering thousands a small group numbering hundreds of those attracted by the personality of the individual

preacher, but only at the price of completely giving up the thousands.[39]

The first alternative, the employment of additional assistant pastors at the old churches, was for him no more than an emergency measure that could be used only until enough money was available to endow more pastorates. He remained committed to the establishment of manageable parishes with their own pastorates and churches. His programme was clear: 'The more churches, the more churchgoers, the more altars, the more people there are who take communion.'[40]

As superintendent of the suburban parishes, which had been strongly affected by the new church building, Gerhard Uhlhorn struggled for his programme, even when the large-scale help, that the King of Hanover had earlier guaranteed, was lacking. In Linden and in the northern parts of the city, whose inhabitants almost entirely depended on the economic situation, it became particularly problematic after the onset of the Great Depression in 1873 to collect money for building projects. Thus the chances of achieving a church-building programme varied from parish to parish. Progress was fastest in the area of the Garden Church parish, because the bourgeois character of the southern residential district and its high tax base meant that new building plans were greatly facilitated. Already in 1870 a chapel had been built behind the station, and in 1873 a further chapel was added in the Kleefeld district. Characteristically the parish council was always responsible for these building developments, whereas in Hamburg such chapels could only be erected through the private initiatives of awakened Christians.[41] When the chapel behind the station became too small, the addition of a further pastorate was delayed by a conflict between the city authorities and the Consistory concerning patronage. Only after the city council had lost the legal case, and the pastor was in retirement, could the Consistory, in 1878, introduce a second pastorate at the Garden Church.

From then on the ice was broken; it was only the financial problems that made the establishment of new pastorates and the building of new churches difficult. None the less a place for an assistant pastor was established in 1878 for Kleefeld, and then in 1883 the foundation stone was laid for a third parish church in the same part of the town, which was consecrated in 1886 with the name of St Paul's. Meanwhile, permanent church taxes, raised as a supplement to the state property tax, had been introduced in the area of the Garden

Church. Since the tax base of the parish was, in the view of the church council, sufficient, a magnificent new building was provided in 1888–91 which reflected the self-image of the upper middle-class Garden parish. The church buildings that followed were an easier task for the parish: in 1898–1902 it undertook a fourth church, which was built in the *Jugendstil* and situated in Kleefeld, and only a little later plans were started for the building of a fifth church, which was consecrated in 1907. Since, in addition to the churches, houses for the clergy also had to be erected, the parishioners sometimes had to pay 18 per cent of the state tax in church taxes.[42] At least in the Garden Church it was possible to find this money, but other poorer parishes had much bigger problems.

Thus, at first it was impossible to carry through a similar church-building programme in the Christ Church parish in the impoverished north of the city, although the population was growing even faster than in the Garden Church district. In 1870 the provincial Consistory gave a sum of 3,000 *Talers* to pay for a site for a chapel, but the church council of this very poor parish insisted on an impressive church building, so at first nothing was done at all. Finally in 1876 they had collected enough money to be able to buy a site, and then it was a further four years before they had collected together enough promises of support to be able to pay completely for the site and for the architect's design. It also proved possible in this working-class parish to activate the women. They formed a church association whose members undertook to contribute a small weekly sum towards the building of the church.[43] After four years of building, the second church (the Apostles' Church) was finally consecrated in 1884. Since only half the cost of the building was initially financed, the parishioners also had to pay an 18 per cent church tax, although it brought in relatively little as most parishioners had such low incomes. The difficulty can be indicated by a comparison of church taxes: Trinity parish with 17,900 parishioners raised 20,173 marks through an 8 per cent church tax, whereas the Apostles' Church district with 30,575 parishioners raised 15,900 marks through an 18 per cent church tax.[44] There were similar problems in the Linden parish when they finally built their second church (Zion) in 1878.[45]

State support for the church-building programme

Between 1866 and 1890 there were two chapels and five new churches built in the suburban parishes of Hanover and Linden.

Hanoverians were proud of this: 'Hanover has the reputation of being the first city in Germany to increase the number of its churches.'[46] However, the efforts that had been made up to this point were not enough: Uhlhorn and his colleagues immediately pressed for the building of further churches. Their objective was still the ideal of pastoral work in a manageable parish, even if in the urban parish this ideal no longer had much connection with reality. There the pastor had become an overworked official, whose primary concern was with the conduct of baptisms, confirmations, weddings and funerals.[47] In this unclear situation the stage that they had reached could only be a temporary base. None the less the pride of the Hanoverians is worth noting, and at first it had a symbolic cause. The Empress Auguste Victoria took an interest in the Hanoverian church-building programme and indicated her support through a high-profile visit to the new churches. Thus church-building was seen as having political significance – it was part of the 'New Course' in social policy, pursued by the Emperor Wilhelm II since his ascent to the throne, in relation to the workers and especially to Social Democracy. The young empress then also took up ideas from the circle of the Christian Social Court Preacher, Stoecker, as she tried to find her own independent sphere of public social activity. Her aim was to provide 'Help to these lower social classes' which she otherwise did not reach.[48] At first she wanted to support the work carried out by the Berlin City Mission, but then she decided that she wanted to promote work in other places. Uhlhorn, as an expert on urban church life, was asked what he thought of the idea of an *Evangelisch-Kirchlicher Hilfsverein*[49] which would support the work of City Missions. He was against the idea: the only way to remedy the insufficient pastoral provision in the cities was through the division of parishes, the building of churches and the supply of additional clergy. The City Mission

> can never achieve that which is the function of the orderly preaching of the Word and administration of the sacraments. ... On Protestant ground the aim can only always be to bring about a healthy parish life, and to integrate the individual, with his personal Christianity into it.

The work of City Missionaries carries

> within it the great danger, the more it goes beyond the sphere of caring for the poor, of producing a highly subjective, and

in many respects unhealthy form of Christianity, that all too easily creates dangers for the properly ordained church [*geordnete Kirche*] because of its separatist tendencies.[50]

Uhlhorn therefore recommended that the proposed association would be better advised to support the building of new churches. Uhlhorn's suggestion was at first ignored at the imperial court. But already in 1890 a church-building association, which supported church-building in the Kingdom of Prussia, arose out of the *Evangelisch-Kirchlicher Hilfsverein*. Meanwhile, the high-profile backing given by the empress meant that church-building received more support from the state and from local authorities than hitherto. For instance, the Ministry of Education and Church Affairs authorized the coming together of Lutheran parishes to form a joint organization that would support church-building through regular grants. But local authorities were especially active in this field. They provided free building sites and often made supplementary grants, though they expected by doing this to have a decisive voice in the selection of the site and design of the building. Thus in the building of the Luther Church (1898), St Peter's in Kleefeld (1902) and St Mark's (1906), the original plans were even changed to accommodate the wishes of the city government for buildings that would make worthy contributions to the townscape.

The political perception of the meaning of church buildings had changed – and Uhlhorn's tireless efforts also played a role in this. Until the 1880s, a church building had merely been seen as a matter for the parish concerned, existing for the purpose of facilitating church attendance by the parishioners. But now the political dimension began to be stressed. Since the methods employed up to this time to suppress Social Democracy had failed, new ways of enlisting Christianity had to be found. One possibility was the erection of new churches – the church had to come nearer to those members who had become estranged. This task required political support.

The building up of real parishes

By the outbreak of the First World War the building programme had gobbled up several million marks. Yet it had not proved possible to reconstruct really small, manageable parishes as they had been understood in Hanover before 1850. As soon as this was recognized, yet more ways had to be suggested for integrating churches into the neighbourhood. In Hanover, as a Lutheran city, the church-building programme had admittedly been in the forefront, because places for the holding of church services were required in order to 'nourish' the parish with preaching and with the Eucharist. It followed from this that by the time the building was completed, pastors, organists and sextons were appointed. However, these did not remain for long the only parish officials: first of all, in the working-class parishes in the north and in Linden, deaconesses were quickly introduced to fulfil two tasks. They looked after the children in a nursery school and they could be asked to care for the sick. They were financed partly from church and city funds, but also to a considerable extent by the owners of neighbouring factories because the sisters' work 'is valued by the workers and helps to make them more attached to the factory and increases their love of their job'.[51] Thus, here was a field of church work that relatively quickly won general recognition, and was made use of even by church members who otherwise hardly ever came to church services and whose 'religious practice' thus did not measure up to the norms of the clergy.[52] Because there was no problem in obtaining the finance, this form of work developed rapidly and by 1900 every parish in Hanover had deaconesses.

Beside these facilities there were at first no other means of strengthening the parishioners' ties to their church. Only gradually did people realize that the work of City Missions also had a relevance for the work of individual parishes. The branch organizations of the Evangelical Association, such as the Young Men's Club and the Clothing Society, already provided an indication of the ways in which parishioners might be won for a Christian-influenced way of life, especially in respect of their use of their free time. Thus one could have a stronger Christian influence on the life of parishioners. The facilities offered by the Evangelical Association had a disadvantage, which was that participants in their activities and members of the Association came from all parts of the city but that only small groups were reached by these activities. None of the branches had more than 200 members, so only a fraction of the city's Lutherans were reached in this way. Thus, the next step was to organize this kind of work on a parochial basis.

Around 1890 there began in Hanover the new form of so-called parish work. Beside the holding of church services, parishes now began to organize parochial societies for limited purposes, for example, brass bands, or for specific social groups, for instance, women workers or fathers of families. Within a decade parochial societies of this kind were established in every one of the city's parishes. At the same time, pastors began to hold evening meetings on particular themes. These mainly social occasions, known as 'Family Evenings' or later 'Parish Evenings', were innovations, for the first generation of confessional clergy had only known, beside the ordinary church services, Bible studies, which were mainly held in the church.[53] These parish societies had, so far as membership figures are available,[54] numbers ranging up to 100. So far as the big working-class parishes were concerned, this meant that these societies only reached approximately 0.5–2 per cent of parishioners, though they broadened the social base of the parish and together they reached more people than the branches of the Evangelical Association had done. In so far as they addressed themselves to the workers, they did so by explicitly attacking Social Democracy, aiming, as the Linden Protestant Workers' Association put it, 'to awaken the Protestant consciousness of their members . . . [and] to strengthen loyalty to the Emperor and the nation'.[55]

This form of 'new' parish work changed the pastors' field of work. No longer was it limited to teaching and holding services. But since in the large parishes the burden of the numerous christenings, confirmations, weddings and funerals remained great, there was a fairly speedy introduction after about 1900 of so-called Parish Helpers. These were laymen who, after a two- or three-year training as 'deacons', were taken on to help the pastor in teaching, in the supervision of church groups and in parish administration. These new forms of parish work also meant that the central club house was superseded by parish halls. Admittedly in Hanover only the Trinity parish was sufficiently well-off to have built its own parish hall before 1914, whereas the other parishes met the financial problem by using part of the parsonage as a parish hall. All these forms of church work came into operation after 1890, by which time the first generation of confessional clergy had retired. Hanover was thus taking part in a development which had already been promoted by some clergy in other places at an earlier date.[56]

THE RESULTS

This overview shows what kinds of efforts were undertaken to maintain and develop church life during the changes in the urban environment between 1850 and 1914. Were the clergy successful?

If one looks at the comments made by the clergy at meetings of the District Synod it is clear that they were not satisfied, even if they were able to report a relative degree of success. Did this sense of failure correspond with reality?

If one starts with the ambitious objective of maintaining manageable parishes, one would have to admit that it did. In 1910,[57] there were in the area originally covered by Christ Church in the north of the city twelve pastors[58] in four parishes, with an average of 6,850 parishioners per pastor. At St Martin's in Linden, together with its filial parishes, there were ten pastors, with an average of 5,876 parishioners each, and in the filial churches of the Garden Church sixteen pastors cared for an average of 4,576 parishioners each. These figures indicate the efforts of the Hanover church to keep pace with the growth of the parishes, and the ratio of pastors to people was more favourable than in Berlin[59] or Hamburg.[60] Next to the inner-city area, with an average of 4,361 parishioners per pastor, the south side of the city (Garden Church) was best provided for. In the working-class parishes of the north (Christ Church) and in Linden the working conditions of the pastors were clearly worse. However, the pastors were perhaps not so much taken up with the 'new' types of parish work as in the bourgeois south, for the proletarian culture and its institutions caused a greater distance in the workers' districts between church organizations and most of the parishioners.

Equally, the statistics of religious practice would hardly suggest that the programme of 'more churches – more churchgoers' was a long-term success. In the short term the church-building programme did definitely lead to an increase in religious practice, which the pastors gratefully celebrated.[61] Statistically, religious practice was measured in two ways: first, through church attendance and participation in Holy Communion and, second, through the rites of passage.[62] In 1870 average church attendance in the inner city had fallen to 5 per cent of parishioners, and in the suburban churches, still small in number, the figure was only 2.6 per cent.[63] In the following years church attendance went up again, reaching a peak in 1895 of 6.4 per cent in the inner city and over 5 per cent in the new suburban parishes and Linden. Then there was a further decline in attendance, and by 1909 the figure was 4 per cent both for the inner city and for the suburbs, although it was precisely after 1900 that numerous churches were built and pastorates established. By comparison with the long-established metropolitan centres of Berlin and Hamburg these were still favourable figures, but they show that the church-building programme did not lead so clearly to an increase in religious practice as the confessional clergy had hoped and promised. At first the improvement in the church's infrastructure had led to a rise in the number of churchgoers, because the few suburban churches had previously provided insufficient space for those who wished to attend. But once the building programme had answered this need for places in churches, there was no further increase in the number of attenders.

The situation with regard to participation in communion was similar. Around 1825 the number of communions per annum as a proportion of all parishioners stood at 25 per cent, which meant that approximately a quarter of all parishioners were communicants, though the total included some parishioners who took communion several times in the year. The figures dropped in the following years, and in 1870 they reached a low point of approximately 10 per cent. There was an increase in the following years, with a high point of almost 25 per cent being reached in 1900, after which there was again a gradual decline. A more detailed analysis of the communicants in an inner-city church shows that the rise in the number of communions was made possible not so much through the development of the system of churches and pastors as through the mobilization of families. Those family members, mainly women, who were strongly involved in the church persuaded other family members to come along as well. There was little success in attracting new sections of the population to take part in communion. The Linden parishes present a similar picture. These were originally rural in character, but with the rapid growth of new proletarian quarters, the proportion of traditional church members dropped so fast that there were few parishioners who might have brought in family members. Here, too, the ratio of communicants to population continually deteriorated.

Admittedly, church customs remained strong in respect of the central biographical events in family life, which were marked by baptisms, confirmations, weddings and funerals. After a short period of irritation after 1875–6,[64] nearly all children were baptized and confirmed, well over 90 per cent of weddings were celebrated with a religious service and burials normally took place with a pastor present.[65] This latter custom had gone out of fashion in the eighteenth and early nineteenth centuries, and it owed its revival above all to the efforts of the confessional clergy, who on this point, too, urged a return to the requirements of the Reformation church regulations. This coincided with the need for the participation of a pastor at such an important point in the family biography. In this respect the efforts of the clergy to increase religious participation were successful.

A certain success for church work can also be attributed to the clergy of that time in that the number of resignations from the church remained small. Since 1875 it had been possible to leave the church, but until 1900 the proportion of church members doing so in any year remained under 0.02 per cent. From 1906 freethinking organizations began to operate in the Hanover region, but up until 1914 they had not succeeded in persuading more than 0.05 per cent of members to resign from the Protestant church.[66]

So if we ask how 'successful' church work was, two quite different answers are possible. The hopes of the confessional pastors, who thought that attendances at Sunday services might be decisively increased through parish work and church-building, were not fulfilled. However, in other areas of church work, notably with regard to the rites of passage, parishioners very largely fulfilled the duties that the clergy expected of them.

Certainly it is questionable whether 'success' in religious matters can actually be measured. Indeed, the liberal clergy, who kept their distance from organized religion, constantly emphasized that 'real religion' could not be confined within the boundaries of the church.[67] Among most of them this led to an indifference towards church activity,[68] which the confessional clergy in turn denounced as an acceptance of irreligion.[69] The latter also felt that their own efforts were not enough, and that even more undertakings were necessary to make the parishioners 'more churchly'. The dynamic of their programme explains this. Fixated on the ordained clergy and on the participation of parishioners in church services, they tried in the course of the years to take advantage of the various possibilities of realizing the church-building programme. The results of pursuing this objective distinguished the Hanoverian church from other evangelical churches. Since building churches alone was not enough, the Hanoverian church people were also ready to supplement their programme. They opened themselves to the work of the Inner Mission and later carried over the experience gained there into the area of parish work. The 'new' form of parish work was intended also to influence the parishioners' free time. But in comparison with other regions, these groups remained marginal in Hanover, and a stable church milieu could not be built up.[70] So from the clergy's point of view, in spite of all their effort, one could not speak of success.

If one refuses to accept this ambiguity in the question of how 'successful' the work was, one has to look again at the definition of religious practice. If one compares the variability of participation in Sunday services and in the Holy Communion with the high degree of stability of church 'custom' in respect of the rites of passage, it becomes clear that the confessionally determined definition of religious practice is too limited. It would be better to interpret the two types of participation in the rites of the church as two different kinds of religious practice. The first type, which involved regular attendance at services, was much more strongly affected by the changes which the rise of the city brought for organized religion. The second type which, with a different logic, concerned itself with the rites of passage in family life,[71] was little affected by the fact that very different kinds of social milieu were developing in the cities. The upper middle class in the south-east of Hanover made use of these religious facilities in much the same way as the working-class family in Linden. Precisely for this reason, this area of pastoral work seemed unproblematic and uninteresting to the clergy.[72] Thus this work scarcely entered their definition of the church's objectives, and so their feeling of failure was inevitable. At the same time, by turning to God they gained a comfort which was not bad: 'It is not for us to determine the destiny of our church, but it lies in the hand of him who is the Lord of the church.'[73]

NOTES

1 H. Plath, 'Die topographische und bauliche Entwicklung der Stadt Hannover', *Heimatchronik der Hauptstadt Hannover*, Cologne, 1956, pp. 198ff.; H.-W. Niemann, 'Zur Wirtschafts- und Sozialgeschichte der Städte Linden und Hannover im 19.Jahrhundert', *Jahrbuch der Gesellschaft für niedersächsische Kirchengeschichte* (hereafter *JGnKG*), 84, 1986, pp. 75ff.

2 See W. Buschmann, *Linden. Geschichte einer Industriestadt im 19. Jahrhundert*, Hildesheim, 1981, pp. 523f.

3 In 1824 the Old City had been united with the so-called New City, and in social terms there was little difference between the two. Here they will both be described as the inner city. In 1859 large parts of the surrounding fields were brought into the city of Hanover as suburban districts, and in the following years both Hanover and Linden annexed many neighbouring areas.

HANS OTTE

4 See H.-G. Aschoff, *Um des Menschens willen*, Hanover, 1983, p. 56.
5 L. Hölscher and U. Männich-Polenz, 'Die Sozialstruktur der Kirchengemeinden Hannovers im 19.Jahrhundert, Eine statistische Analyse', *JGnKG*, 88, 1990, p. 176.
6 For an overview of the evolution of parish populations, see ibid., pp. 204ff.; and Ph. Meyer, 'Die Kirchengemeinden Hannovers in der werdenden Grosstadt (1830–1890)', *JGnKG*, 38, 1933, pp. 334f., 345f.
7 The restriction of voting rights to income tax-payers continued until 1918, whereas the requirement that voters own property was dropped in most parishes after 1874. The problems caused by these restrictions were indicated in a petition by the orthodox–conservative members of St Egidius parish, following the election of a liberal pastor. They complained that the rich voters who supported the liberal candidate held several pieces of land, and had a corresponding number of votes. It was claimed that one large builder had forty votes. See F. Düsterdick, *Der Portig'sche Handel*, Hanover, 1873, p. 22.
8 Meyer, 'Kirchengemeinden', p. 351.
9 Up to now there has been no study which investigated whether they made a serious attempt to do this elsewhere. For their efforts in a rural area, see W. Marquardt, *Arbeiterbewegung und evangelische Kirchengemeinde im wilhelminischen Deutschland*, Göttingen, 1985.
10 See J. Meyer, 'Die ersten 20 Jahre des Protestantenvereins', *ZGnKG*, 44, 1939, pp. 209ff.; Meyer, 'Kirchengemeinden', pp. 334f., 345f.
11 In the case of celebrations which the authorities organized rather unwillingly, and thus without great display, it was a simple matter for them to ordain that the participation by the church would take the form of special services for schoolchildren. See K. Kreter, 'Bürger, trau nicht dem Fürsten', *Hannoversche Geschichtsblatter*, new series, 46, 1992, p. 55.
12 See E. Petri, *D. Ludwig Adolf Petri, weiland Pastor zu St Crucis in Hannover*, 2 vols, Hanover 1888–96, vol. 1, pp. 153ff., vol. 2, pp. 24ff.
13 Wichern (1849) as cited by G. Brakelmann, *Die soziale Frage des 19. Jahrhunderts*, Witten, 1986, p. 124.
14 See H.-W. Krumwiede, 'Die Gründung der Inneren Mission in Hannover', *JGnKG*, 63, 1965, pp. 213ff.
15 Petri, quoted in ibid., p. 218.
16 Münchmeyer (1849), quoted in ibid., p. 214.
17 See M. Hasselblatt and H. Otte (eds), *Der Liebestätigkeit Raum geben*, Hanover, 1990, pp. 45f.
18 Meyer, 'Kirchengemeinden', pp. 339ff.
19 R. Greve, *Die Christuskirche zu Hannover*, Hanover, 1909, p. 7.
20 *Festschrift zum 200 jährigen Jubiläum der St Martins-Kirche in Hannover–Linden*, Hanover, 1928, p. 21.
21 Buschmann, *Linden*, p. 280.
22 ibid.
23 See M. Greschat, 'Die Berliner Stadtmission', in K. Elm and H.-D. Loock (eds), *Seelsorge und Diakonie in Berlin*, Berlin, 1990, pp. 455ff.
24 For a general discussion, see U. Baumann, *Protestantismus und*

114

Frauenemanzipation in Deutschland 1850 bis 1920, Frankfurt am Main, 1992, pp. 39ff.

25 See Hasselblatt and Otte (eds), *Liebestätigkeit,* p. 69.

26 ibid., p. 70.

27 See J. Freytag, 'Lebenserinnerungen eines 89jährigen', *Hannoversches Sonntagsblatt,* 58, 1925, pp. 96ff.

28 As well as the associations with a charitable purpose there were also those which were directed towards specific age-groups (for example, the Young Men's Association) or occupation, which attracted relatively small numbers (up to 150 members) and were limited to artisanal occupations (for example, bakers and waiters).

29 G. Uhlhorn, *Schriften zur Sozialethik und Diakonie,* Hanover, 1990, pp. 128ff.

30 Hasselblatt and Otte (eds), *Liebestätigkeit,* p. 26.

31 Breakdown of readership by area are only available from 1924, but it is unlikely that there had been dramatic changes. Landeskirchliches Archiv, Hannover (hereafter LkAH), Bestand E2, Nr 536.

32 See K. Mlynek, 'Stadt und Stift', in W. Helbig (ed.), *Neue Wege, alte Ziele. 125 Jahre Henriettenstiftung Hannover,* Hanover, 1985, p. 104. As is shown by the example of the liberal Pastor Bödeker of the Market Church, the liberal bourgeoisie were not fundamentally opposed to social work, but they refused to link it with missionary work, in the way that was characteristic of the confessional clergy.

33 Cited in Hasselblatt and Otte (eds), *Liebestätigkeit,* p. 59.

34 For the figures in Hanover, see Hölscher and Männich-Polenz, 'Sozialstruktur', pp. 168ff.

35 Gerhard Uhlhorn, born 1826, died 1901. *Privatdozent* in Göttingen, 1857 Royal Chaplain and member of the Consistory in Hanover, 1866 Vice-President of the Consistory, 1868–80 Superintendent of the suburban areas of Hanover, 1878 Abbot of the Loccum Monastery.

36 *Protokoll der Bezirkssynode der Inspektion Hannover* (hereafter *BSPH*), 1877, p. 16.

37 Because of the conflict over the financing of church-building and over the rights of patrons continued until the end of the 1880s to hinder the building of new parish churches in Berlin, this solution was tried there until, in the 1890s, Berlin too had a big church-building programme. See W. Ribbe, 'Zur Entwicklung und Funktion der Pfarrgemeinden in der evangelischen Kirche Berlins bis zum Ende der Monarchie', in Elm and Loock (eds), *Seelsorge und Diakonie,* pp. 256ff.

38 This solution was chosen in Hamburg. See G. Daur, *Von Predigern und Bürgern,* Hamburg, 1970, pp. 203ff, 248f.

39 Cited in Meyer, 'Kirchengemeinden', p. 344.

40 ibid.

41 See F. Mahling, *Beiträge zur Geschichte der Inneren Mission mit besonderer Beziehung auf Hamburg,* Hamburg, 1898, pp. 152ff.

42 *BSPH,* 1896, p. 24.

43 Pfarrarchiv Christuskirche, Rep. 511–41: 'Spenden zur Baufinanzierung'.

44 *BSPH*, 1896, p. 25.
45 See *Festschrift zur 100-Jahrfeier der Erlöserkirche Hannover–Linden*, Hanover, 1980, p. 12.
46 *BSPH*, 1898, p. 23.
47 Greve, *Christuskirche*, pp. 38f., 80f., indicates the conflict between pastoral reality and the claims made by confessional pastoral theology.
48 I. Gundermann, *Kaiserin Auguste Victoria und der Evang.-kirchliche Hilfsverein*, Berlin, 1991, p. 13.
49 For the press polemics against the *Hilfsverein*, see V. Frowein-Ziroff, 'Der Berliner Kirchenbau des 19. Jahrhunderts vor seinem historischen und kultur-politischen Hintergrund', in Karl Schwarz (ed.), *Berlin. Von der Reichshauptstadt zur Industriemetropole*, 3 vols, Berlin, 1981, vol. 1, pp. 128–48.
50 Uhlhorn to Kammerherr Mirbach, as quoted in F. Uhlhorn, *Gerhard Uhlhorn. Ein Lebensbild*, Stuttgart, 1903, p. 258.
51 Factory-owner Berding (1882), as quoted in M. von Boetticher, 'Gründerjahre und soziale Herausforderung', in Helbig, *Neue Wege, alte Ziele*, p. 125.
52 ibid., pp. 115ff.
53 For the changing forms of work, see C. Cordes, *Geschichte der Kirchengemeinden der ev.-luth. Landeskirche Hannovers*, Hanover, 1983, pp. 31ff.
54 The most precise figures are found in the short parish bulletins which, from 1900, were being issued by certain pastors.
55 Programme of the Linden Workers' Association, quoted in Buschmann, *Linden*, p. 426.
56 See the overview in M. Schian, *Die evangelische Kirchgemeinde*, Giessen, 1907, pp. 8ff.
57 Figures from *BSPH*, 1911.
58 Including assistants.
59 See Ribbe, 'Zur Entwicklung und Funktion der Pfarrgemeinden', pp. 251ff.
60 See *Kirchlich-statistische Zusammenstellungen über die Stadt- und Land-Gemeinden*, 48, 1912, pp. 28f. Since in Hamburg there was no longer any requirement that people use their own parish church, the workload, as measured in sacramental acts or work for parish organizations, varied from pastor to pastor.
61 Thus in 1907 the chairman of the Hanover District Synod, commenting on a church attendance rate of 4 per cent declared with satisfaction

> that overall an increase in churchgoers is to be recorded, and once again the rule has been proved: the more churches there are, the more churchgoers there will be. By comparison with other cities . . . our church attendance figures can still be rated as good.

62 For the problems and areas of debate in the use of church statistics, see L. Hölscher, 'Möglichkeit und Grenzen der statistischen Erfassung kirchlicher Bindungen', in Elm and Loock (eds), *Seelsorge und Diakonie*, pp. 39ff.

63 For a detailed explanation of these figures, see Hölscher and Männich-Polenz, 'Sozialstruktur', pp. 159ff.
64 This period of irritation was associated with the transition from a church-based to a state system of registration, which took place in 1874, when state officials took over responsibility.
65 For the problems of interpreting burial statistics, see Hölscher and Männich-Polenz, 'Sozialstruktur', p. 176 n. 43.
66 ibid., pp. 176f.
67 See the articles in the journal of the Hanover liberals, *Kirchliche Gegenwart*, 11, 1912, columns 20ff., 82f.
68 *Kirchliche Gegenwart*, 12, 1913, columns 69f.:

> As it [the Inner Mission] came into fashion as the authentic expression of practical Christianity, it spread the idea that those parishes which did not support its efforts were inactive, and were neglecting their duty. As a result of many-sided influences, the parishes were thus under constant pressure to undertake some project or other which would justify their existence. . . . Active parishes are an excellent thing. But what the term usually means is a new cult of works. . . . We hope, however, that the parishes will gradually come to remember again the religious 'Word'. And then too we shall have active parishes.

69 Since there were very few liberal clergy in Hanover, criticisms of this kind were seldom made, though one such attack was made by Pastor Crome at the District Synod in 1902, and was subsequently reported in the local press: see *Hannoversches Tageblatt*, 31 August 1902. In Hamburg, where the liberals formed a large minority in the church, this argument was frequently advanced by the confessional side: see the many examples in *Zeitschrift für die evang.-luth. Kirche in Hamburg*, 10, 1904.
70 Thus, in the wake of the 1918–19 revolution the Workers' Associations completely collapsed, and the organizations for Protestant women workers also lost a large part of their membership. See E. Rolffs, *Evang. Kirchenkunde Niedersachsens*, Göttingen, 1938, p. 167.
71 This logic is described by J. Matthes, 'Volkskirchliche Amtshandlungen, Lebenszyklus und Lebensgeschichte', in J. Matthes (ed.), *Erneuerung der Kirche*, Gelnhausen and Berlin, 1975, pp. 83ff.
72 Worth noting are those cases in which the two meanings of church adherence overlapped. A good example is the astonishingly high participation in church services and prayer meetings at the beginning of the First World War. For representatives of the church this offered the prospect of an effective religious revival, which would eventually ensure the attachment to the church which they wished for and expected. However, for those church members who did not belong to the small group of those who were very strongly involved in the church, these services during the transitional period at the start of the war were meaningful because the departure of the soldiers cut into family life. Those members whose participation in the church related

to biographical events ceased to take part when the war became a taken for granted reality. To the distress of the pastors, the high attendance at these services stopped after the end of 1914.

73 LkAH, Bestand A 12e: Circular Letter by the General Superintendent, Hanover, 18 March 1907.

4

THE ORTHODOX CHURCH AND THE WORKERS OF ST PETERSBURG 1880–1914

Simon Dixon

Commenting on the workers who joined Father Gapon's fateful procession to the Winter Palace on 9 January 1905, Robert Latimer, a British evangelical committed to spreading the Word in Russia, wrote that: 'Their religious aspirations, such of them as had any, were satisfied upon the extremely low level of the ordinary church ceremonial.'[1] Few modern scholars have openly dissented from this doubly disdainful judgement.[2] Indeed, by concentrating almost exclusively on Russian workers' economic and political concerns, they have tacitly confirmed Latimer's condescending opinion not only of the Russian Orthodox Church but also of the degree of religious awareness it managed to inculcate among its urban flock. I use the word 'tacitly' advisedly. In 1910, a contributor to the secular journal *Zhizn' dlia vsekh* remarked that the average Petersburg worker was 'neither for nor against religion. He had somehow expunged the very question of it'.[3] The same could be fairly said of many historians.[4] Yet the prevailing image of a sclerotic, not to say dormant, church ministering to an overwhelmingly apathetic flock surely merits further investigation: if it is accurate, it must be explained; if it is false, or exaggerated to the point of caricature, we may be in danger of neglecting an important dimension of Russian working-class life.

There is certainly no paucity of ecclesiastical evidence to throw light on the subject, however diffracted its beam may be. Since the former Holy Synod building in St Petersburg was appropriated by the Soviet regime as its major nineteenth-century archive, the church's working papers were spared the chaos inflicted on other repositories in transit during the post-revolutionary period. By supplementing the Synodal files with local diocesan archives and the voluminous ecclesiastical press, one gains access to a remarkably rich range of sources.[5] Plainly, to rely solely on establishment evidence is to see the religion of the people through a distorted prism. If it is hazardous, at best, to judge a construction worker's religious cast of mind from a missionary's report upon him, then to extrapolate a collective psychology of working-class religion from scattered episcopal comments about proletarian piety is surely to overburden an already fragile source.[6] Yet 'we make nonsense of popular religion if we take official religion out of it'.[7] The church's teachings may never have been assimilated by its flock to a degree capable of satisfying the clergy, since the people's 'dual faith' (*dvoeverie*) continued to incorporate elements of paganism in the twentieth century.[8] But both ecclesiastical provision and supervision were none the less formative influences on the religion of the people, just as popular reactions in turn helped to reshape the pastoral work of the church. Problematic as they are, therefore, ecclesiastical sources have a wholly legitimate part to play in the reconstruction of working-class religion. Fortunately, however, there is no need to rely solely on them in the case of St Petersburg. Indeed, a central aim of the present chapter will be to test and explore them in the context of conclusions reached by a flourishing recent historiography of the city and its workers.[9] Thus far, Russian secular and ecclesiastical sources have tended to be approached in isolation: this chapter marks a preliminary attempt to combine the two.[10]

Mountainous though the material at his disposal may be, the historian of Russian religion nevertheless operates under certain constraints imposed by a number of distinctive features of Orthodox practice. First, Orthodoxy in late imperial Russia did not depend on regularity of worship. Communion, like confession, was conventionally an annual observance. In part, this was because annual confession was a legal obligation imposed by the state. Yet there was also a more authentic justification for it. So difficult was psychological preparation for the full mystery of the sacraments held to be that it was thought better to prepare well once a year than inadequately more often or habitually.[11] Pious communities of predominantly peasant women, a prominent feature of late nineteenth-century Russian religious life, were the exceptions who proved the rule.[12] In St Petersburg, communion was celebrated every Sunday at the church of the Georgievskaia community on the Vyborg side.[13] But priests who exhorted their flock to follow this fervent female example commented on a marked reluctance on the part of their parishioners to change the worshipping habits of a lifetime.[14]

So, although some evidence points to a remarkably high level of religious observance in pre-revolutionary Petersburg (70 per cent of the male workers and 85 per cent of the females who responded to a Soviet survey in the 1920s said that they had attended church in the years before the October Revolution),[15] and although 'the annual statistics on confession and communion did not give grounds for fear of dechristianization in the city',[16] Russian communicant statistics scarcely constitute the kind of semi-precision tool that more regular information has provided for historians of Christian denominations in the industrialized West.[17]

If it is impossible to measure the alienating impact of urbanization in statistical terms, confessional evidence nevertheless hints at encroaching secular values. As the monk Stefan (Tverdynskii) commented in 1913, confession – designed to allow priests 'to enter the inner world' of their confessants and to investigate 'the most intimate recesses' of their minds – depended for its success on mutual empathy and understanding between confessor and confessant. In the city, he claimed, this relationship no longer existed. Instead, the priest was 'usually confronted' with 'a completely new and entirely distinctive system of moral views, with which there is no sufficient point of contact either in the rite of confession or in the world-view of the priest himself'.[18]

The lateness of the date enhances the plausibility of the observation. One of the most important contributions made by recent historians has been to show that, far from being an intellectually supine and politically anarchic rabble, reeling involuntarily between the rival attractions of underground Marxism, ecclesiastical proselytism and government propaganda, the workers of St Petersburg were increasingly capable of developing their own sense of self-identity and making up their own minds. The ability to read was a crucial weapon in their armoury. As Jeffrey Brooks has written, 'the belief that the printed word is a means to attain power over oneself and one's environment was at the heart of the demand for literacy in Russia'.[19] And St Petersburg boasted the most literate population in the Empire. Whereas national literacy rates rose only from 21 to 40 per cent between 1897 and 1914, 75 per cent of the capital's residents were literate in 1910 (85 per cent of men and 65 per cent of women), an advance of 7 or 8 per cent since the turn of the century. As one would expect, a detailed breakdown of these totals reveals that literacy was differentiated not only by sex, but also by age and skill. There was a world of difference between illiterate female peasant migrants and the articulate, young, male metalworkers, who, alongside artisan tailors, joiners and goldsmiths, formed part of a small, permanently-resident vanguard seeking 'to broaden their intellectual horizons by attending Sunday schools, evening classes, the courses of the St Petersburg Society of Popular Universities, and by taking out a reader's ticket in one of the city's eight public reading rooms'.[20] After 1905, workers could find not only entertainment, but also education in their own legally constituted clubs and societies. By 1909, there were twenty-one of these in St Petersburg, 'with a peak nominal combined membership of 6,830'.[21] But even before 1905, workers had been able to explore, in their treasured leisure time, a range of cultural opportunities organized for them by others.[22] Of the two theatres which opened in St Petersburg in 1886, the melodramatic repertoire at the Vasileostrovskii, a commercial enterprise, proved more attractive than the edificatory productions at the Nevskii, which was sponsored by members of the intelligentsia seeking 'to provide the local working population with moral, temperate, and cheap entertainments'.[23] Yet although incipiently radical workers like Semen Kanatchikov preferred *The Workers' Suburb* to *Othello*,[24] neither the Nevskii Theatre nor the Ligovskii House of the People (*narodnyi dom*), a cultural centre opened in 1903 by the philanthropist Countess S.V. Panina, found it difficult to attract full working-class houses for classical productions.

There were certainly some priests, alarmed by the impiety of the spectacle, who wanted to censor secular public entertainments.[25] But to suppose that the church's reaction was merely negative is to underestimate the resourcefulness of the clergy and to overstate the secularity of workers' interests. Many zealous priests believed that the best way to recapture people for the church was to infuse popular forms of entertainment with an authentically spiritual content, and the evidence of the 1880s and 1890s suggests that they had no little success. From 1887, hundreds of workers gathered in factory refectories to hear peripatetic Orthodox preachers co-ordinated by the Society for the Propagation of Religious and Moral Enlightenment in the Spirit of the Orthodox Church founded in 1881. Among the preachers' most popular performances were lantern-shows illustrating stories of the saints' lives. The same technique was employed by the Alexander Nevsky Temperance Society, which claimed more than 75,000 members by 1905, a year in which it distributed some 10,000 pamphlets on the workers' question alone. When the society's founder and guiding spirit,

Father A.P. Rozhdestvenskii, died later in the year, hundreds of workers and their families flocked to his funeral.[26]

We can only guess at the full complexity of the motives which underlay this lasting popular reverence for the saints. In part, as the church intended, saints' lives no doubt offered 'practical images of holiness and piety' which were echoed in best-selling secular literature. Bandit tales, 'preoccupied with the personal questions of sin, redemption and punishment', were especially reminiscent of stories of saintly suffering and martyrdom.[27] But it also seems certain that one of the most important reasons for the survival of both local and national cults was rather more dubious in the eyes of the church. This was the hope that St Nicholas the Miracle Worker, or any one of a myriad of other popular saints, might be persuaded personally to intervene directly against disease. The chances of survival had never been high in Russia, where overall mortality rates showed no significant decline until the 1890s, more than a century after the corresponding shift in western Europe. They remained disproportionately low in *fin de siècle* Petersburg, whose sewage-infested water supply made it the most insanitary city in Europe. Cholera was not the only menace. At 165 cases per 10,000 head of population, the incidence of typhus in St Petersburg was nearly eight times higher at the turn of the century than in Moscow. In 1908, a year in which 47 per cent of all deaths were caused by infectious diseases, typhus caused more fatalities in the Russian capital than in all German cities with more than 10,000 inhabitants put together.[28] While medical provision remained expensive and insufficient – as indeed it was bound to do provided that the city fathers' approach to unhygienic municipal services remained motivated by profit rather than the 'civic spirit' urged upon them by reformers – popular appeals for saintly intervention could be expected to persist.[29]

Unfortunately for the church, it proved unable to capitalize on the undoubted progress it had made among the workers in the 1880s and 1890s because of the political uproar that was caused when a few younger priests slid imperceptibly over the invisible line dividing philanthropic activity within an existing system from implicit advocacy of far-reaching social and political reform.[30] Incontrovertible evidence that the line had been crossed came with Gapon's involvement with the Assembly of Russian Workers.[31] In the aftermath of Bloody Sunday, overt attempts to woo the workers were politically suspect, and made to seem still more subversive by their association, in the publications of the radical 'Group of Thirty-Two' Petersburg priests, with calls for root-and-branch ecclesiastical reform.[32] The group's most prominent member, the charismatic preacher Father Grigorii Petrov,[33] eventually fell victim to his enemies among influential clerical supporters of the far-right Union of Russian People, who subsequently vented their spleen on the mild-mannered Metropolitan Antonii (Vadkovskii), who had earlier sought to protect Petrov.[34] Since this was scarcely an atmosphere in which moderate opinion could flourish, Father D.I. Bogoliubov, a sensitive and intelligent man who was appointed diocesan missionary to the Old Believers in the following year, was one of very few priests in St Petersburg who publicly questioned the value in 1905 of homilies 'supporting the bosses against the workers, come what may', and openly advocated instead sermons designed to reconcile the two sides.[35]

However, there are grounds for believing that even had the political context in which it operated been more propitious, the church faced too many obstacles for its evangelism to stand much chance of preventing the workers of St Petersburg from being drawn towards its rivals. In the remainder of this chapter, I shall focus on three of these obstacles: the provision of worship, the social isolation of the clergy and the impact of transience on the church's pastoral work.

In a church frequently ill at ease with itself, one of the few points on which churchmen of all persuasions could readily agree was the inadequate provision of worship in St Petersburg. One of the most lamentable consequences of the prevailing practice of annual communion and confession was to require the construction of inordinately large churches, which were not only expensive to build but remained empty for much of the year, constituting a significant drain on ecclesiastical resources, and were still too small to satisfy demand at the peak periods. Father Evgenii Kondrat'ev of the Spasosennovskaia Church wrote in 1904 that 'what happens here ... at Saturday morning services during the Great Fast, beggars description'. Yet he went on to depict an elemental scene:

> As the time for communion draws near, the crowd, which gets more tightly packed by the minute, moves forward in some spontaneous way, those at the back leaning on those at the front so that the crush is so bad that those standing in it

cannot even raise an arm; the front rows are not strong enough
to bear the weight and so people frequently cry out, louder
and ever more frequently, until the noise rings out above the
crowd as it sways from side to side like a solid mass . . . and
all this with women (some of them pregnant) and children in
there.[36]

Since Kondrat'ev's church was in the Haymarket, one of the capital's
most densely populated and least salubrious areas, and since he was
writing partly in order to stress the need for better behaviour in
church, we must allow for a degree of hyperbole here. But there is
abundant evidence to confirm his general point.

Metropolitan Isidor (Nikol'skii) realized that the Smolenskaia
parish church, beyond the Shlisselburg gate, required a second priest
when he discovered that its incumbent had been required to admin-
ister the sacraments to almost 600 children in a single day in 1882.[37]
While the traffic of communicants and confessants remained so
congested, the level of spiritual admonition offered by the clergy
could scarcely be expected to rise above the perfunctory. K.P.
Pobedonostsev, lay Over Procurator of the Holy Synod between
1880 and 1905, was concerned lest sectarians fill the vacuum
created by the Orthodox Church. Not only did he occasionally
intervene to urge the formation of 'a new parish for the worker
population of an outlying part of the city now lacking both clergy
and church',[38] but he also made the general shortfall in provision a
rare admission of failure in his reports to the tsar, acknowledging
that even St Petersburg's 'huge churches' were unable to 'accommodate half the worshippers who appear, especially at the major festivals'.[39] *Tserkovnyi vestnik*, a candid weekly journal published at the
St Petersburg Ecclesiastical Academy, commented in 1906 that since
the capital's churches could hold a maximum congregation of
345,000–350,000, then even assuming that only two-thirds of the
Orthodox population were to choose to worship at the great
festivals, some 200,000 of them would fail to gain access: 'And if we
take into account that at such festivals admission is already restricted
in a number of ways (by ticket, by token, etc.), then the number
of those deprived of the opportunity to enter God's church is even
greater.'[40]

It is not necessary to accept the precision of such figures,
calculated from the appendices to a guidebook to the city's churches,
in order to recognize that the provision of worship in St Petersburg

SIMON DIXON

was simply outpaced by demographic growth, even though the rate of church building increased towards the end of the nineteenth century. Nationwide, it has been calculated on the basis of figures published by the Over Procurator that the number of parish churches increased 1.6 per cent between 1860 and 1880, rising 10.2 per cent in the 1880s and a further 10.1 per cent between 1890 and 1904.[41] Yet by then, as Rogger has written, the same source shows that

> Russia had only about half as many churches for any 100,000 Orthodox inhabitants as there had been two centuries earlier – fifty-two as compared with 106 – and the lack was greatest in areas of greatest population growth, among uprooted peasants and workers in cities and factory towns.[42]

The diocese of St Petersburg exemplifies the point. Between 1881 and 1914, the population of the capital alone rose from 861,000 to some 2.2 million. Yet the diocesan building rate was never more than average and compared highly unfavourably with that of the old capital: for example, between 1876 and 1887, whereas 258 new churches were built in the diocese of Moscow, the diocese of St Petersburg constructed only eighty-five.[43] Even this moderate figure overstates the expansion of provision, since not only was it common to erect temporary wooden churches which could be dismantled once a permanent stone structure had been completed, but, still more importantly, approximately half the newly-built churches were not parish churches but institutional or private chapels designed to serve a limited congregation.

Why was so little done? In the West, McLeod has suggested, it was 'lack of will, or more frequently, the strength of opposing forces that hindered the churches' response to urban growth'.[44] The same was also true to some extent in Russia. Certainly the obstacles facing prospective builders were formidable. In order to justify to the consistory the need to build a new church, applicants had not only to prove that the existing provision of worship was inadequate, but also that they possessed land, a site suitable for a sacred building and enough money to fund both the construction and the subsequent upkeep of buildings and clergy.[45] This was no small undertaking. Between 1883 and 1894, Count A.S. Apraksin and his widow spent a million roubles on the Church of the Resurrection of Christ on the Fontanka Canal and donated a further 130,000 roubles to maintaining the building and its clergy.[46] This, of course, was a

126

show-piece church, and so, to a lesser degree, was the one built for the Society of Religious and Moral Enlightenment between 1904 and 1908 at a total cost of 450,000 roubles.[47] But the capital investment required for even the most modest new church was nevertheless substantial. Even the chapel at the home for impoverished clergy was only maintained thanks to a bequest of 25,000 roubles from its founder, the merchant G.M. Petrov.[48]

For most humble parishioners, such exorbitant costs were obviously prohibitive. In 1910 one of the capital's deans (*blagochinnye*) 'spoke straightforwardly' to the diocesan consistory, predicting that the problem of provision would remain intractable so long as private funds were the mainstay of church construction. For while only the simple people (*prostonarod'e*) – 'a class far from strong in economic terms' – attended parish churches, the wealthy were building their own domestic chapels and becoming 'increasingly indifferent to the interests and needs of the parish'.[49] The consistory admitted that it had no panacea. Acknowledging that 'the construction of new churches and the division of small and outlying parishes would undoubtedly be the most correct resolution of the question of fully satisfying the needs of the people', it nevertheless insisted that

> the shortage of money, both for church building and for subsequent maintenance, and equally the difficulty of supporting the clergy in new parishes, mean that for the time being we must adopt the limited measure of allowing the liturgy to be said in prayer-houses.[50]

One way round the problem was to attempt to harness popular enthusiasm for the kind of cults we have already mentioned. At the glass factory on the road to Schlüsselburg, for example, a building project was launched in 1888 in thanksgiving for the preservation of a local icon during the fire which destroyed the old chapel. Within two years, however, enthusiasm had evaporated. It was revived only when a 14-year-old epileptic, declared by doctors to be incurable, made a miraculous recovery while praying in front of the icon. In 1894, Metropolitan Palladii himself laid the foundation stone, and 20,000 roubles were collected on that day alone. The church was completed in 1898 at a total cost of 200,000 roubles.[51] The drawback with this method, however, was that it led to an irrational distribution of churches which bore little relation to the density of population. An alternative solution, designed to produce churches where they were most needed, was to rely on political lobbying. But Father Filosof Ornatskii's experience as a clerical member of the municipal duma between 1894 and 1904 proved that the city fathers in St Petersburg were no more anxious to subsidize church construction than their western contemporaries. Initially they tried to fob him off with patently unsuitable plots, one of which was within sniffing range of a fish-glue factory, presumably on the grounds that this was the least valuable land at their disposal. Ultimately, Ornatskii appears to have succeeded only by sleight of hand – he astutely named the churches he wanted to build after patriotic and imperial triumphs, to which it would have been awkward for the duma to refuse its assent.[52] It was therefore no mere witticism for a British visitor to observe that 'where we should build a bridge, the Russians raise a house of God; so that their political and social history is brightly written in their sacred piles'.[53]

Ornatskii argued in the aftermath of Bloody Sunday, as he had been arguing for at least the previous decade, that a chapel at every factory would be the best solution to the problem of irrational distribution. Metropolitan Antonii forwarded his report to the Synod, marking it 'extremely useful and highly desirable'.[54] But his tone had not always been so urgent. When one of Ornatskii's building schemes ran into planning difficulties in 1902, Antonii wrote coolly to a suffragan bishop that it was no great 'calamity': 'Let Father Filosof go on pleading. It will be no offence to us if the Economic Administration finds it impossible to satisfy our request.'[55] As Metropolitan of St Petersburg and leading member of the Holy Synod, Antonii had other fish to fry. But his lack of enthusiasm cannot solely be attributed to the fact that he was distracted by great affairs of church and state. He also knew that church-building was a cause of considerable tension among the clergy. The problem, as so often, was financial. In theory, all the income from rites performed by the clergy in any parish was due to the priest of the parish church. But not only was St Petersburg home to a number of famous priests who attracted more than their 'fair share' of business, but there were also, as we have seen, many private or institutional chapels and a growing number of monastic residences, acquired primarily as investments but used to accommo-date visiting bishops. In the eyes of the parish clergy, these merely deflected donations that would otherwise have filled the coffers of the parish church, while providing nothing in return.[56]

The case of the chapel at the Putilov works, authorized in late

1905, provides an acute illustration of the difficulty. The president of its construction committee pleaded that it should be treated as a special case. Although it was to cater only for the needs of the workforce, he wanted it to be granted all the rights of a parish church, and especially the right to keep all fee income 'without entering into any kind of co-operation with the neighbouring parish church'. However, since the chapel was effectively to be self-contained, its clergy being paid from a compulsory 0.25 per cent monthly contribution from the wages of the workforce, the president wanted it to be released from the normal obligations of a parish church to contribute the lion's share of diocesan funding. A local dean sardonically remarked that it would be strange if the consistory were to authorize a parish church with no parish that would not only deprive thousands of local residents who were not employed at the Putilov works of its services but compound the insult by contributing nothing to the diocesan economy. But so anxious was the consistory to have the chapel at the strife-torn factory built, and moreover at the expense of the owners, that the dissenting views of neighbouring clergy were simply overridden.[57]

In the West, statistical evidence of the kind furnished in England by the religious census of 1851 had already begun to throw doubt on the relationship between the provision of worship and the church's influence in society. In London, for example, Bishop Tait was particularly sceptical of the view that 'the sole way to remedy the evils of an overwhelming population, and to propagate true religion, was to multiply churches'.[58] So, the Orthodox Church might have built all the churches they wanted in St Petersburg and still faced problems in ministering to the city's workers. Part of their difficulty lay in the social isolation of the priest.

One might think that the notoriously impoverished status of the Russian clergy could have helped it to avoid the opprobrium, suffered by almost all their western counterparts, of being firmly identified with middle-class interests.[59] It is certainly true that the Orthodox Church never baptized materialistic bourgeois values with anything like the vigour or consistency apparently displayed by the Catholic Church in the nascent Irish Free State.[60] Yet the clergy of St Petersburg surely lost more than they gained from their distinctiveness as a caste-like social estate. Priests in the capital may have been better educated, better housed and generally better off than their rural contemporaries,[61] but while their superior articulacy and security did nothing to ease their assimilation into respectable 'society' (*obshchestvo*), it probably helped to increase their isolation from the majority of their parishioners among the dispossessed '*nizy*'. A senior official in the Ministry of Foreign Affairs, V.N. Lambsdorff, caught their dilemma well in a withering critique of Metropolitan Palladii in 1894. Palladii, he thought, was 'inclined to pose', yet his 'pretensions to secular elegance' clearly exerted 'no influence at all on the people, whose idea of a saint is incompatible with such a kind of person, who is rather a novelty in our church'.[62]

Conflict was particularly evident in the strained relationships between priests and their churchwardens, who in St Petersburg were mostly drawn from the ranks of wealthy merchants. Earlier in his career, while Bishop of Riazan in 1881, Palladii had himself chaired a Synodal commission charged with reasserting clerical control. But the move met with a scornful response.[63] The capital's wardens convened to resist change, and when renewed regulations were finally issued on 12 June 1890, their authority over their churches' financial affairs survived intact.[64] Few bothered to conceal their innate sense of superiority. As one young priest complained in 1904, 'it is noticeable that the richer the churchwarden, the more he feels independent and the less inclined to consult the priest'.[65]

But for all the bickering between priests and wardens, they nevertheless presented a united and sometimes hostile front to their impoverished parishioners. In a move plainly designed to exclude the transient workers who constituted the majority of the city's population, the regulations governing the election of wardens at parish churches enfranchised only residents of the parish aged 25 or over who were already entitled to participate in meetings of local municipal bodies or gentry assemblies.[66] Workers clearly resented their exclusion. As Metropolitan Isidor noted in his diary on 1 April 1891, 'there was uproar at the Smolenskaia church yesterday . . . when the priest announced after prayers that the churchwarden would be elected after evening service and that workers would not be allowed in'.[67]

This isolated incident is indicative of a wider problem: the relatively impotent role of the laity, and especially of workers, in the affairs of their church. As the diocesan consistory admitted in its report to the Synod in 1908, this was one respect in which the Old Believers were at a distinct advantage over Orthodox:

> Every schismatic considers himself a master in his own society. His vote and opinion count for something. Without his direct participation, not one ecclesiastical issue is decided. . . . Not

so an Orthodox. He is no more than a guest in church and takes practically no part in either the service or the business of the church. As a result, our parishioners become uninterested in the affairs of the parish, and as a consequence of their lack of interest, become cold in their relationship with their parish church in general and affairs of the faith in particular.[68]

Much has been written about workers' resentment of affronts to their dignity in the workplace.[69] There is just as much to say about the consequences of their vain search for an established and dignified role in the affairs of their church.

Priests and their parishioners, already separated by social barriers, were driven further apart by the dual pattern of transience which characterized the population of Russian cities after the emancipation of the serfs in 1861. The first type of transience – seasonal migration between city and countryside – resulted from the fact that although the emancipation settlement had tied the peasantry to the rural commune, unexpectedly rampant demographic growth in the second half of the nineteenth century had created a shortage of land which drove peasants to seek temporary employment in the cities. The result was something disturbingly close to the kind of landless proletariat that bureaucrats who drafted the emancipation statutes, with the spectre of 1848 firmly in mind, had been so anxious to avoid. St Petersburg was certainly a 'migrant city'.[70] Throughout the period of population explosion between the 1870s and the First World War, the percentage of migrants (*prishli*) among the population remained almost constant at between 68 and 70 per cent of the total. By 1910, nearly half the city's population had been resident for less than a decade and 13 per cent had arrived that year. But as Bater has shown, even the capital's permanent residents showed a surprisingly low level of 'residential persistence'. Moves within the City therefore constitute our second type of transience. Of the systematic sample of 500 males whom he traced between the municipal directories of 1909 and 1912, approximately 29 per cent changed address at least once during this period. It may, as Bater claims, be 'difficult to recapture, or indeed imagine, what a high level of transience meant in terms of relationships between individuals, classes, or socioeconomic groups', but its impact on the church's relationship with the workers is surely worth exploring, and it seems certain that it was the first type of transience – seasonal migration – that did the greatest damage.[71]

In 1911, Father Antonii Bykov wrote in his student dissertation at the St Petersburg Ecclesiastical Academy, that the church must ensure that 'people, on coming into church, do not feel alienated from each other, but closely linked, just as members of the first Christian community did, united in one body, one soul, one faith and one love'.[72] But reality lay far from his apostolic ideal. Not only were parishioners strangers to each other, but, as the diocesan missionary confessed in 1900, priests were in turn prevented from getting to know their parishioners because 'their flock changes not year by year but depending on the season of the year'.[73] The degree of fluctuation deserves emphasis. Between December 1888 and July 1889, for example, the city's population dropped by over 180,000, more than a fifth of the total, and though the net loss was to some extent compensated by the influx of about 35,000 seasonal workers into outlying suburbs, these aggregate figures nevertheless understate the total volume of flux.[74]

The issue is further complicated by the fact that until 1900, when a diocesan commission published the boundaries of thirty-two parishes (to serve a population then more than a million strong), there had been no clearly defined parishes in St Petersburg.[75] And it would have taken more than an administrative map to resuscitate parochial consciousness in the Russian capital. As a commission of priests under the presidency of Suffragan Bishop Kirill of Gdov was forced to concede in 1901, there may have been parish churches in St Petersburg, but they were hardly at the centre of proper parish communities.[76] The contrast with Moscow is revealing. The geography of St Petersburg, a planned city, was always defined by its linear streets. In Moscow, which grew organically, districts were more important and parishes retained their historical significance as territorial units.[77] Not so in the capital, whose clergy discussed the problem of alienation at their first pastoral assembly in 1897, noting the inability of even a team of several priests to minister properly to as many as 60,000 transient peasant migrants.[78] But in 1904–5 they rejected a potential solution – a scheme to register Petersburg's parishioners, a practice not normally demanded by the Orthodox Church – on the grounds that this would have introduced yet a further level of bureaucracy at a time when priests were striving to cut back rather than multiply the red tape which inhibited their pastoral contacts.[79]

The neo-Slavophile critic, A.A. Papkov, a layman long committed to church reform, unhesitatingly blamed the clergy for the 'deplorable anomaly' that so few parishioners knew each other.[80] Influential members of the government thought along similar lines. In 1913, the Lykoshin Commission, investigating hooliganism (unmotivated, often violent crime, prevalent among seasonal labourers from villages around St Petersburg), was particularly struck by the relationship between religion and crime. Areas with predominantly non-Orthodox populations were found to be significantly less prone to hooliganism than Orthodox areas, a fact which was attributed to the superior moral influence of Catholic, Muslim and Lutheran clergy. By contrast, N.A. Maklakov, the Minister of Internal Affairs, commented on 'a certain isolation' between priest and people in Orthodox parishes.[81] Even some priests joined the critical chorus. Renovationists (*obnovlentsy*) who despised bureaucratic and episcopal control over the church made the restoration of proper pastoral contact a key plank in their programme of ecclesiastical reform and religious regeneration.[82] Yet Professor Freeze surely comes closer to a balanced judgement when he claims that 'the urban parish was so territorially amorphous, so socially heterogeneous, and so numerically overpopulated that even the most conscientious priest had difficulty establishing strong bonds to his flock'.[83]

The debilitating consequences of this fact were many. Not the least was that it became very difficult even to count, still less to counteract sectarian rivals. But even the most basic ecclesiastical functions were obstructed by transience, as we can see by focusing on marriage. Churchmen continued to insist on the sanctity of the marriage vow.[84] But since family life was one of the first casualties of the migrant city, their earnest protestations have subsequently seemed to be nothing more than expressions of 'ostrich-like piety'.[85] Marriage rates among men and women were lower in the capital than in the Empire as a whole and it was common for married couples to live apart. In 1897, for example, 81 per cent of married male workers in St Petersburg lived alone (though the proportion was lower in the case of skilled men, 31 per cent among metal-workers, for example). An investigation of 2,506 married male textile workers in 1900–2 found that 27 per cent had dispatched pregnant wives to their native villages, where their children were subsequently to be reared.[86]

Both married and single men preyed on the vulnerable single women in the city. Some were forced to remain spinsters by their employers. In 1897, in a ban which remained in force until 1913,

St Petersburg's women schoolteachers were formally forbidden to marry by the municipal Commission on Education, which sought to make financial savings by preventing its staff from gaining seniority and experience.[87] Yet the women most at risk were clearly servants and prostitutes. In keeping with his apocalyptic vision of St Petersburg as the symbol of a decadent Empire – a doomed, disintegrating city, 'pagan and corrupt' – Alexander Blok once described the Russian capital as 'a gigantic brothel'.[88] Prostitution was certainly rife. Only around 3,000 whores were registered in 1914, an increase of 50 per cent since 1867, but the total in reality probably exceeded 30,000 and may even have reached 50,000.[89] It was peasants who predominated among prostitutes, most of them having worked as domestic servants before economic pressures forced them to sell their bodies rather than their labour.[90]

Illegitimacy rates are hard to calculate. But Ransel has argued persuasively that an apparent decline in Russian extramarital fertility (parallel to that experienced in western Europe in the late nineteenth century) is the artificial product of changes in the legislation regulating admission to foundling homes. New demands that candidates be declared illegitimate by a parish priest or other responsible authority caused a 34 per cent decline in admissions between 1888 and 1894. Had it not been for this reform, the recorded illegitimacy rate in St Petersburg would have risen in the 1890s, as it did everywhere in Russia but Moscow. Even as it was, St Petersburg province's illegitimacy rate of 15.92 per cent was still the highest in the country. Significantly, the Central Statistical Committee, whose figure this is, noted that it was the Orthodox population which was predominantly responsible for illegitimate births.[91]

In these circumstances, the rekindling of family life was a Utopian prospect: the best the church could hope for was to make marriage available to those who legitimately requested it. Yet even this utilitarian goal lay beyond its reach. While the church continued to preach the sanctity of marriage, the ceremony became surrounded by so much red tape that priests became reluctant to conduct it.

The law demanded that before a couple could marry, the marriage had to be announced in the parish church of both bride and groom.[92] This apparently simple condition proved a major stumbling block in St Petersburg where the priest's difficulty lay in deciding whether a couple were his parishioners. Since the consistory laid down no guidelines to help him select suitable criteria, he was left in doubt whether he should demand evidence of residence in the parish or whether the fact that the couple had confessed in his church should suffice. The only certainty was that he would be punished if the marriage were later proved invalid: charges of irregularities in marriage services were among the most serious that the clergy might face. In the diocese of St Petersburg in 1910, for example, one priest was unfrocked and two were sentenced to three months' imprisonment in a monastery for convictions of this kind.[93]

Apart from the difficulty of establishing their status as his parishioners, priests needed to make sure that parental consent had been given to the marriage, even after the couple had reached the age of majority (18 for men, 16 for women). In a paper discussed by clerical assemblies in February and March 1900, Professor M.I. Gorchakov, himself a priest and a canon lawyer at St Petersburg University, warned clergy to do nothing that might incite parents explicitly to refuse their permission because he took the law to allow the assumption of parental consent in all other cases.[94] There is little evidence that priests shared his confidence. The reluctance of clergy to conduct marriage services became a scandal, gleefully publicized by V.V. Rozanov in *Novoe Vremia*.[95] The church had few arguments with which to refute such criticisms, though it was at least possible to deny Rozanov's wilder claim that clergy were refusing to marry *any* of the city's migrant workers. Father Drozdov published figures which claimed that there had been 319 marriages at his church between 1900 and 1902, of which 211 involved transient peasant-workers. The church had also issued documents to allow a further eighty marriages elsewhere.[96] Information of this sort, however, was not enough to dispel the overwhelming image of a church unable to practise what it preached.

If we now return to the quotations with which we began, it will be plain that Latimer's scepticism about the level of provision afforded by the Orthodox Church in St Petersburg was not wholly unfounded. However, judging from the evidence presented here, it would be misleading to suppose that the church's problems arose simply from inactivity and intellectual inadequacy. Instead, it seems more likely that there were many zealous priests in the Russian capital who struggled hard, if ultimately in vain, against contradictions in the Orthodox pattern of worship, restrictions in the legal framework under which they were obliged to operate and social and political forces beyond their control. It is impossible to tell what would have been their level of religious observance had the Orthodox Church been able to offer workers more of what they wanted. But we have surely said enough to suggest that it may be unwise to take a condescending view of working-class religious feeling. As Latimer himself was to write on returning from Russia in 1910: 'St Petersburg is ripe to be reaped for the Lord Jesus. The precious grain is even falling out of the ears.'[97] Research on this subject is in its infancy. But one thing is already clear: no balanced judgement about the spiritual life of the Russian worker will be reached so long as social historians continue to 'expunge' religious questions from their agenda.

NOTES

1   R.S. Latimer, *Under Three Tsars: Liberty of Conscience in Russia 1856–1909*, London, 1909, p. 209. On the demonstration, see Walter Sablinsky, *The Road to Bloody Sunday: Father Gapon and the St Petersburg Massacre of 1905*, Princeton, NJ, 1976.

2   A rare attempt to explain rather than condemn is Gregory L. Freeze, '"Going to the intelligentsia": The church and its urban mission in post-reform Russia', in Edith W. Clowes, Samuel D. Kassow and James L. West (eds), *Between Tsar and People: Educated Society and the Quest for Public Identity in Late Imperial Russia*, Princeton, NJ, 1991, pp. 215–32. As his title indicates, Freeze's social focus is different from mine.

3   Quoted by I.S. Rozental, 'Dukhovnye zaprosy rabochikh Rossii posle revoliutsii 1905–1907gg.', *Istoricheskie zapiski*, 107, Moscow, 1982, p. 86.

4   Daniel R. Brower, *The Russian City between Tradition and Modernity, 1850–1900*, Berkeley, Calif., 1990, makes a valiant attempt to cover religion, but his expert synthesis merely serves to emphasize the overwhelmingly secular concerns of modern urban historians.

5   Among primary sources, I rely principally upon the archive of the Synodal chancellery at Russkii (formerly Tsentral'nyi) gosudarstvennyi istoricheskii arkhiv, St Petersburg (henceforth TsGIA), fond 796; the archive of the St Petersburg diocesan consistory, at Peterburgskii (formerly Leningradskii) gosudarstvenii istoricheskii arkhiv, St Petersburg (henceforth LGIA), fond 19; *Tserkovnyi vestnik* (*Church Herald*, henceforth *TsV*); *Sankt-Peterburgskii dukhovnyi vestnik* (*St Petersburg Spiritual Herald*, henceforward *SPbDV*); and *Izvestiia Sankt-Peterburgskoi eparkhii* (*St Petersburg Diocesan News*, henceforth *ISPbE*).

6   Compare I.Z. Kadson, 'Otnoshenii rabochikh razlichnykh raionov Rossii k religii i tserkvi (1907– 1916)', in *Rabochie Rossii v epokhu kapitalizma: Sravnitel'nyi poraionnyi analiz*, Rostov on Don, 1972.

7   For some characteristically trenchant remarks on this theme, see John McManners, *'Popular Religion' in 17th and 18th Century France: A*

New Theme in French Historiography, John Coffin Memorial Lecture, University of London, 1982, quoted at p. 8. I owe this reference to Professor Derek Beales.

8 Though Moshe Lewin falls into many of the traps set by McManners, ibid., he acknowledges that the 'Orthodox church in its ruralized version could be called a popular religion in its own right': 'Popular Religion in Twentieth-Century Russia', in his, *The Making of the Soviet System: Essays in the Social History of Interwar Russia*, London, 1985, p. 70.

9 The standard historical geography is James H. Bater, *St Petersburg: Industrialization and Change*, London, 1976. Major studies of the workers include Reginald E. Zelnik, *Labor and Society in Tsarist Russia: The Factory Workers of St Petersburg, 1855–1870*, Stanford, Calif., 1971; Richard Pipes, *Social Democracy and the St Petersburg Labor Movement, 1885–1897*, Cambridge, Mass., 1963; Gerald D. Surh, *1905 in St Petersburg: Labor, Society, and Revolution*, Stanford, Calif., 1989; Robert B. McKean, *St Petersburg Between the Revolutions: Workers and Revolutionaries, June 1907 – February 1917*, New Haven, Conn. and London, 1990; and S.A. Smith, *Red Petrograd*, Cambridge, 1984. For an evocative collection of photographs, *c.* 1900, see Boris Otmetev and John Stuart, *St Petersburg: Portrait of an Imperial City*, London, 1990.

10 Some of the evidence presented here draws on ch. 5 of my unpublished Ph.D. thesis, 'Church, state and society in late imperial Russia: The Diocese of St Petersburg, 1880–1914', University of London, 1993.

11 See S.V. Bulgakov, *Nastol'naia kniga dlia sviashchenno-tserkovno-sluzhitelei: Sbornik svedenii, kasaiushchikhsia preimushchestvenno prakticheskoi deiatel'nosti otechestvennago dukhovenstva*, 2nd ed, Khar'kov, 1900, pp. 961–1040, for a clerical manual setting out the essential features of Orthodox repentance, confession and penance as it was supposed to be practised at the end of the nineteenth century.

12 Brenda Meehan-Waters, 'To save oneself: Russian peasant women and the development of women's religious communities in prerevolutionary Russia', in Beatrice Farnsworth and Lynne Viola (eds), *Russian Peasant Women*, New York, 1992, pp. 121–33, introduces the Trinity–Torozhkovo convent in the diocese of St Petersburg.

13 'Razmyshleniia ob ispovednoi praktike', *TsV*, 3 March 1888, pp. 197–8.

14 *ISPbE*, 1 July 1904, pp. 1–6, Father Evgenii Kondrat'ev.

15 Victoria E. Bonnell (ed.), *The Russian Worker: Life and Labor under the Tsarist Regime*, Berkeley, Calif., 1983, p. 26.

16 Freeze, '"Going to the intelligentsia"', p. 218 n. 13.

17 Compare, for example, Hugh McLeod, 'Protestantism and the working class in imperial Germany', *European Studies Review*, 12, 1982, pp. 324–6.

18 Ieromonakh Stefan (Tverdynskii), 'Velikaia pastyrskaia obiazannost'', *Tserkovno-obshchestvennyi vestnik*, 2 May 1913, pp. 6–8.

19 Jeffrey Brooks, *When Russia Learned to Read: Literacy and Popular Literature, 1861–1917*, Princeton, NJ, 1985, p. 34.

20 ibid., p. 4; McKean, *St Petersburg*, pp. 22–4.
21 Victoria E. Bonnell, *Roots of Rebellion: Workers' Politics and Organizations in St Petersburg and Moscow, 1900–1914*, Berkeley, Calif., 1983, p. 328.
22 Since even the hard-won gains of 1905 had been lost by 1909, factory hours were lengthened again from 8 or 9 to 10 or 11 hours. Bakers and restaurant staff commonly worked a 16- or 18-hour day (see McKean, *St Petersburg*, pp. 9, 179). But because religious holidays (*prazdniki*) accounted for more than a quarter of the year, leisure time was more abundant than such figures might imply.
23 Gary Thurston, 'The impact of Russian popular theatre, 1886–1915', *Journal of Modern History*, 55, 1983, pp. 257–61.
24 *A Radical Worker in Tsarist Russia: The Autobiography of Semen Ivanovich Kanatchikov*, transl. and ed. Reginald E. Zelnik, Stanford, Calif., 1986, p. 103.
25 For an unusually well-balanced Soviet account, see M.I. Chudnovtsev, *Tserkov' i teatr konets XIX-nachalo XXv*, Moscow, 1970, *passim*.
26 This passage draws on my essay 'The church's social role in St Petersburg, 1880–1914', in Geoffrey A. Hosking (ed.), *Church, Nation and State in Russia and Ukraine*, London, 1991, pp. 167–92, which stresses that the church's new-found evangelism was directed as much at sectarian as against secular rivals.
27 Brooks, *When Russia Learned to Read*, pp. 24, 188–9.
28 Bater, *St Petersburg*, pp. 342–53, esp. p. 351.
29 James H. Bater, 'Modernization and municipality: Moscow and St Petersburg on the eve of the Great War', in James H. Bater and R.A. French (eds), *Studies in Russian Historical Geography*, 2 vols, London, 1983, vol. 2, pp. 305–27.
30 Brian Harrison, 'Philanthropy and the Victorians', in his, *Peaceable Kingdom*, Oxford, 1982, pp. 217–59, is particularly good on this point.
31 On which see Surh, *1905 in St Petersburg*, pp. 106–15.
32 *K tserkovnomu soboru: sbornik gruppy peterburgskikh sviashchennikov*, St Petersburg, 1906.
33 Paul R. Valliere, 'Modes of social action in Russian Orthodoxy: The case of Father Petrov's *Zateinik*', *Russian History*, 4, 1977, pp. 142–58.
34 Mikhail Agursky, 'Caught in a cross fire: the Russian church between Holy Synod and radical right', *Orientalia Christiana Periodica*, 50, 1984, pp. 163–96; and John H.M. Geekie, 'The church and politics in Russia, 1905–1917: A study of the political behaviour of the Russian Orthodox clergy in the reign of Nicholas II', Ph.D. thesis, University of East Anglia, 1976.
35 Sv. D.I. Bogoliubov, 'O zhelatel'nom napravlenii tserkovnoi propovedi', *TsV*, 45, 24 November 1905, cols 1484–7.
36 Sv. E. Kondrat'ev, 'K voprosu o poriadkakh v prikhodsksikh khramakh', *ISPbE*, 10 July 1904, pp. 1–6.
37 TsGIA, f. 796, op. 205, d. 450, 1. 102ob, Isidor's diary, 5 April 1882.
38 Pobedonostsev to Palladii, 30 April 1893, TsGIA, f. 684, op. 1, d. 34, 1. 38ob.

39 *Vsepoddanneishii otchet ober-prokurora sviateishago Sinoda K.P. Pobedonostseva po vedomstvu Pravoslavnago Ispovedaniia za 1888 i 1889 gody* (henceforward *VO*), St Petersburg, 1891, pp. 30–4.

40 *TsV*, 40, 1906, cols 1312–13, reviewing N.A. Tikhomirov, *Putevoditel' po tserkvam g. S-Peterburga*, St Petersburg, 1906, from whose appendices the statistics were calculated.

41 Gregory L. Freeze, *The Parish Clergy in Nineteenth-Century Russia*, Princeton, NJ, 1983, p. 453 n. 24.

42 Hans Rogger, *Russia in the Age of Modernisation and Revolution, 1881–1917*, London, 1983, p. 66.

43 *VO za 1888 i 1889 gody*, Vedomost' 5ª.

44 Hugh McLeod, *Religion and the People of Western Europe, 1789–1970*, Oxford, 1981, p. 88.

45 *Ustav dukhovnykh konsistorii*, St Petersburg, 1883, articles 45–53.

46 Dominic Lieven, *The Aristocracy in Europe, 1815–1914*, London, 1992, p. 117.

47 TsGIA, f. 796, op. 442, d. 2290, p. 93.

48 TsGIA, f. 796, op. 205, d. 450, 1. 39ob, Isidor's diary, 18 November 1881.

49 TsGIA, f. 796, op. 442, d. 2407, p. 201.

50 ibid. A proper consideration of the diocesan economy lies beyond the scope of this chapter. It is, in any case, a surprisingly elusive subject: *faute de mieux*, see John S. Curtiss, *Church and State in Russia: The Last Years of the Empire, 1900–1917*, New York, 1940, pp. 87–130.

51 *SPbDV*, 31 July 1898, pp. 525–31.

52 *Izvestiia S-Peterburgskoi gorodskoi (obshchei) dumy*, 102: 17, 1891, pp. 310–17; 114: 8, 1894, pp. 439–46.

53 W.H. Dixon, *Free Russia*, 2 vols, London, 1870, vol. 1, p. 41.

54 TsGIA, f. 797, op. 75, II otdel, 3 stol, d. 102, 1. 1.

55 Letter of 2 July 1902, TsGIA, f 834, op. 4, d. 1196, 1. 2.

56 On monastic *podvor'e*, TsGIA, f. 796, op. 442, d. 1598 (1913g.), 1. 58; on private chapels, *Prikhodskii sviashchennik*, 14 May 1911, pp. 8–9.

57 LGIA, f. 19, op. 97 (1905g.), d. 8, 11. 1–11.

58 Quoted in E.R. Norman, *Church and Society in England, 1770–1970*, Oxford, 1976, p. 124.

59 A distillation of Gregory Freeze's outstanding work on the clergy appears in his 'Between estate and profession: The clergy in imperial Russia', in M.L. Bush (ed.), *Social Orders and Social Classes in Europe since 1500: Studies in Social Stratification*, London, 1992, pp. 47–65.

60 J.J. Lee, *Ireland, 1912–1985: Politics and Society*, Cambridge, 1989, pp. 158–9.

61 See P.N. Zyrianov, *Pravoslavnaia tserkov' v bor'be s revoliutsiei 1905–1907gg.*, Moscow, 1984, pp. 35–6; and my 'Church, state and society', pp. 203–9.

62 V.N. Lamzdorf, *Dnevnik: 1894–1896*, ed. V.I. Bovykin, Moscow, 1991, p. 45, diary for 2 March 1894.

63 A. Bogdanovich, *Tri poslednykh samoderzhtsa*, Moscow, 1990, pp. 63–4, diary for 28 and 30 March 1881. The author's husband,

SIMON DIXON

General Bogdanovich, was then churchwarden of St Isaac's Cathedral.

64 *Instruktsiia tserkovnym starostam*, St Petersburg, 1890. See also K.I. (Ivan Kalaidovich), *Chto takoe tserkovnyi starosta: Opyt istoriko-kritich-eskago izsledovaniia o proiskhozhdeniia i razvitii instituta tserkovnykh starost v Rossii*, St Petersburg, 1902.
65 *TsV*, 27, 1904, cols 846–50.
66 *Instruktsiia*, arts 8–17.
67 TsGIA, f. 796, op. 205, d. 454, 1. 771.
68 ibid., f. 796, op. 442, d. 2290, pp. 207–8.
69 See, in particular, S.A. Smith, 'Workers and supervisors: St Petersburg 1905–17 and Shanghai 1895–1927', *Past and Present*, 139, 1993, pp. 131–77, esp. pp. 138–55.
70 For further references, see Brower, *The Russian City*, pp. 75–91.
71 James H. Bater, 'Transience, residential persistence, and mobility in Moscow and St Petersburg, 1900–1914', *Slavic Review*, 39, 1980, pp. 239–54, quoted at p. 252.
72 Sv. A. Bykov, 'Pastyrskoe bogoslovie', Otdel rukopisei, Gosudarstvennaia publichnaia biblioteka, (Filial: Arkhiv Doma Plekhanova), St Petersburg, f. 574, no. 21, pp. 135–6.
73 TsGIA, f. 796, op. 442, d. 1855, 1. 76 ob.
74 Bater, 'Transience', pp. 240–1.
75 *Raspisanie prikhodov eparkhial'nogo vedomstva v gorode S-Peterburge*, St Petersburg, 1900.
76 TsGIA, f. 796, op. 442, d. 2046 (1904g.), 11. 50ob–51ob.
77 Iu.M. Lotman, *Roman A.S. Pushkina 'Evgenii Onegin': Kommentarii*, Leningrad, 1983, pp. 67–8.
78 'Pervoe pastyrskoe sobranie stolichnago dukhovenstva', *SPbDV*, 14, 4 April 1897, pp. 275–9.
79 M.P. Chel'tsov, *O prikhode i registratsii prikhozhan*, St Petersburg, 1905.
80 A.A. Papkov, 'Chto delat', *Bratskaia zhizn': sbornik statei o vozrozhdenii russkoi zhizni*, issue 1, St Petersburg, 1910, p. 38.
81 Neil B. Weissman, 'Rural crime in tsarist Russia: The question of hooliganism, 1905–1914', *Slavic Review*, 37, 1978, pp. 228–45.
82 A. Iasnev, 'S narodom ili bez naroda', *Tserkovnoe obnovlenie*, 4, 3 December 1906, pp. 49–53.
83 Freeze, '"Going to the intelligentsia"', p. 230.
84 See, for example, A.P. Rain, 'Sv. Ioann Zlatoust i semeinaia zhizn' ego vremeni', *Khristianskoe chtenie*, 1, 1895, pp. 225–48, 465–504.
85 Richard Stites, *The Women's Movement in Russia: Feminism, Nihilism and Bolshevism, 1860–1930*, Princeton, NJ, 1990, p. 189.
86 Surh, *1905 in St Petersburg*, p. 34; McKean, *St Petersburg*, p. 28.
87 Christine Ruane, 'The vestal virgins of St Petersburg: Schoolteachers and the 1897 marriage ban', *Russian Review*, 50, 1991, pp. 163–82.
88 Sergei Hackel, *The Poet and the Revolution*, Oxford, 1975, p. 149.
89 Bater, *St Petersburg*, pp. 202–4; R. Stites, 'Prostitute and society in pre-revolutionary Russia', *Jahrbücher für Geschichte Osteuropas*, 31, 1983, pp. 348–64 .
90 B. Engel, 'St Petersburg prostitutes in the late nineteenth century: A

personal and social profile', *Russian Review*, 48, 1989, pp. 21–44; L. Engelstein, *The Keys to Happiness: Sex and the Search for Modernity in Fin-de-Siècle Russia*, Ithaca, NY, 1992.

91 D.L. Ransel, 'Problems in measuring illegitimacy in prerevolutionary Russia', *Journal of Social History*, 16, 1982, pp. 111–27; and D.L. Ransel, *Mothers of Misery: Child Abandonment in Russia*, Princeton, NJ, 1988, pp. 223–35. The figure for St Petersburg province is from B. Madison, 'Russia's illegitimate children before and after the revolution', *Slavic Review*, 22, 1963, pp. 82–95.

92 Bulgakov, *Nastol'naia kniga*, sets out the bewilderingly complex regulations governing marriage (pp. 1072–1180). For a summary, I.S. Berdnikov, *Kratkii kurs tserkovnago prava*, Kazan', 1888, paras 53–90.

93 TsGIA, f. 796, op. 442, d. 2407, p. 219.

94 *SPbDV*, 17 March 1900, pp. 136–42, 'Proekt pastyrskoi deiatel'nosti v sluchaiakh otkaza detiam vstupat' v zakonnyia supruzhestva'.

95 V.V. Rozanov, *Semeinyi vopros v Rossii*, 2 vols, St Petersburg, 1903, *passim*.

96 *Tserkovnyi golos*, 2 March 1907, pp. 260–4.

97 R.S. Latimer, *With Christ in Russia*, London, 1910, p. 16.

Part II

URBAN RELIGIOUS CULTURES

5

BELFAST: THE UNIQUE CITY?

David Hempton

Belfast at first sight has all the characteristics of a quintessentially British Victorian city.[1] Its population growth, from just under 20,000 to just under 350,000 over the course of the nineteenth century, is not spectacularly at variance with the growth rates of many other industrial cities in the north of England.[2] Its economic development from its early dependence on textiles to its later expansion into ship-building and heavy engineering is typical of many nineteenth-century British cities. Similar also are Belfast's relatively high levels of immigration from the surrounding countryside, its evolution as a major centre of trade and transport and its characteristically industrial occupational and social structure.[3] Even its architecture and public entertainments were classically Victorian in style and content. Belfast's 'red bricked and smoke blackened buildings', wrote the Frenchman Paul Dubois in 1907, 'resembles Liverpool or Glasgow rather than an Irish town'.[4] This early comparison between the great industrial and trading ports of northern Britain has surfaced again and again in the literature, not least because each city was notorious for its ethnic and religious rivalries.[5] Such conflicts, because of their persistence and longevity, have come to be regarded as peculiar to Belfast, but they were by no means untypical of nineteenth-century cities in Britain, Europe and North America as population migrations, challenges to *ancien régime* established churches and economic and social inequalities produced different configurations of ethnic and religious conflict in many western cities.

Belfast's impeccable Victorian façade nevertheless concealed some unusual demographic, economic and social features in its urban development which go some way to explaining its notorious sectarian disturbances. Of chief significance is the remarkable growth in the proportion of Roman Catholics living in the city from its base of around 8 per cent in the late 1780s. This percentage doubled every twenty-five years until the mid-1830s when the proportion of Roman Catholics stood at 32 per cent and continued to climb, possibly to around 40 per cent in the 1840s when the ethnic tide started to turn as a result of the famine, the growth of shipbuilding, engineering and skilled trades in the 1850s and the increased rate of Catholic emigration to Britain and the rest of the world. The proportion of Roman Catholics in Belfast settled to around a third in the mid-Victorian period and had declined to nearer a quarter by the Edwardian period. The absolute numbers of Roman Catholics in Belfast nevertheless continued to grow rapidly. There were, for example, more Roman Catholics in Belfast in 1871 than the total number of inhabitants in 1831.[6]

As with other Victorian cities in the British Isles, population increase was primarily due to immigration from outside. Where exactly the migrants came from, however, is still too unclear for statistical precision, but reliable figures of household heads within street categories from the later nineteenth century show different patterns of Protestant and Catholic migration. Whereas the bulk of Protestant migrants came from the predominantly Protestant counties of Down and Antrim, Catholics were more likely than Protestants to have been born in Belfast – so-called 'ghetto Catholics' were the most likely of all urban groups to be city-born – or to have migrated from other counties in Ulster.[7] What can be said with certainty is that whereas Catholics had migrated in greater numbers than Protestants before and during the famine, the reverse was the case from the 1860s. Moreover, despite popular Protestant rumours to the contrary, more migrants from Britain fetched up in Belfast in the Victorian period than came from Leinster, Munster and Connaught. Whatever else may have injected the poison of sectarianism into religious life in Belfast it had little to do with the migration of either southern Catholics or non-Irish Protestants into the city. Rather, most migrants came from rural Ulster where economic and political competition had dramatically sharpened sectarian conflict in the last two decades of the eighteenth century.[8] Urban religious conflict thus had important rural antecedents and continued to have a symbiotic relationship with rural disorder throughout the nineteenth century.[9] Thus, the problems of Ulster's major city originated largely within the province itself, and nineteenth-century Belfast was not only a divided city, but was also the regional capital of a divided province.

Another feature of Belfast's demographic growth in the nineteenth century was the high degree of religious segregation that characterized its residential geography; but even here there is a need for perspective. Religious segregation in Belfast at the end of the nineteenth century was not as rigid as racial segregation in American cities, and Belfast was by no means unique among British cities in having monochromatic working-class communities of Catholic Irish within its boundaries.[10] What is unusual about Belfast, however, is that whereas by the late Victorian period more than half of the Catholic Irish in Britain's great industrial cities lived in enumeration districts with low or medium concentrations of Irish population, the pattern of residential segregation in Belfast seemed almost immutably fixed. Research on the District Electoral Divisions of the 1901 census, for example, has shown that residential segregation was most advanced in the working-class districts of the west of the city and that 'all predominantly Catholic districts were more or less exclusively Catholic, whereas most Protestant districts outside west Belfast contained Catholic minorities which varied considerably in both size and degree of dispersal amongst the majority'.[11] What is particularly chilling about residential segregation in Belfast, however, is the way in which its boundaries were solidified by recurrent riots in the nineteenth century and the fact that indices measuring segregation have increased, not diminished, in the course of the twentieth century.[12]

The residential segregation of Protestants and Roman Catholics in Belfast was reflected also in the occupational and social structure of the city. In practically all measurable aspects of prosperity Protestants appear more advantaged than their Catholic neighbours. The rateable value of Protestant housing was higher than that of Catholic housing, a higher percentage of Protestant workers were skilled than Catholic workers, Protestant literacy levels were higher than Catholic ones and Catholic households were more likely to be headed by single women than were Protestant households.[13] Similarly, the Catholic middle class was much smaller than its Protestant counterpart, with Catholics being underrepresented in commerce, manufacturing and the professions. Indeed, the Catholic bourgeoisie was so small that it was more likely to be dependent upon its poorer co-religionists than it was to be integrated within Protestant élites. Belfast's social structure and labour force were thus characterized by structural inequalities which if anything became more pronounced in the period 1871 to 1911.

If Belfast's demographic patterns and social structures are less conventional than at first appears, the same is true of its economic and social development. Not only was Belfast Ireland's only industrial city in the nineteenth century, but its economic development was determined more by the industrial regions of Britain than by the internal economy of Ireland.[14] After the great famine in the 1840s, Belfast was the only town or city in Ireland that attracted people in large and continuing numbers, and this was accomplished in a province where the population declined by some 800,000 between 1841 and 1911. In this context, Victorian Belfast's position as the fastest growing city, not only in Ireland, but in the British Isles, is quite remarkable. It was, as Clarkson has suggested, 'the last great urban creation of the Industrial Revolution'.[15] While contemporaries were not averse to attributing Belfast's economic growth to the work discipline of its predominantly Protestant people, economic historians have more judiciously emphasized Belfast's importance in the growing maritime trade in agriculture and linen, the convenient vertical linkages between many Belfast industries, the entrepreneurial talents of some key industrialists in the shipbuilding industry and the availability of an abundant and cheap labour force.[16] Whatever the reasons for Belfast's growth as a centre of manufacturing industry, its consequence was that by the late nineteenth century its continuing prosperity seemed to depend more on its connections with Britain and the Empire than with the island in which it was located.

What this introduction has tried to show is that while on the one hand Belfast in the nineteenth century appeared to be an archetypal Victorian industrial city not too dissimilar from Leeds and Bradford or Newcastle and Hull, it was nevertheless unlike any other city in Ireland. Moreover, a closer look at its demographic, economic and social characteristics reveals a set of unusual features which have to be taken into account when trying to get to the heart of Belfast's distinctive religious and political conflicts in the nineteenth century.

Although the religious history of nineteenth-century Belfast has been dominated by attempts to explain sectarian conflict, the most pressing problems facing Roman Catholic and Protestant churches in Belfast were not in fact too dissimilar from those encountered by other churches in the British Isles and elsewhere when faced by rapid population growth in the nineteenth century. These include the provision of suitable church buildings in the right place at the right time, the supply of sufficient clergy with a commitment to the urban mission, the attempt to wean the working classes away from popular entertainments and dissolute living and the remorseless emphasis on literacy, sobriety and self-discipline as antidotes to the alleged corruptions of urban life.[17] This agenda transcended denominational differences in Belfast as it did in other industrializing cities in the nineteenth century. What is more unusual, though by no means unique, in Belfast is the way in which this shared agenda paradoxically contributed to an increase in religious competition and sectarian stereotyping which had the unfortunate effect of narrowing the gap between the official and the popular manifestations of Protestant and Roman Catholic conflict – between polite theological disagreement and raucous urban rioting. The religious mechanism by which this was accomplished was the infusion of evangelical zeal into Belfast's Protestant denominations and a process of modernization within the Catholic Church to enable it to get to grips with the ramshackle state of ecclesiastical provision in the city.[18]

The response of enthusiastic Protestants to urban vice and infidelity was much the same in Belfast as it was in other Victorian cities: more church building and services, Sunday schools and tract distribution, domestic visitation and charitable societies, temperance movements and city missions, and open-air preaching as part of a remorseless attack on popular sports and amusements. As in other British cities this dose of religious enthusiasm and respectability was better received by the more upwardly mobile sections of the working classes than by the unskilled and the chronically poor.[19] In fact the records of the ubiquitous evangelical societies in nineteenth-century Belfast convey the same impression of the religiosity of the urban poor as is available from similar records in British cities.[20] Church attendance and institutional affiliation were less important to them than were the emotional resonances of religion and its social utility. What was distinctive about evangelicalism in Belfast, however, was the anti-Catholic baggage it carried with it from its early revivalistic growth and land-lord connections in the border counties of Ulster and its very considerable sponsorship from Britain as a vibrant agent of cultural imperialism.[21]

Evangelical no-popery orators were, of course, popular from time to time in British cities experiencing an influx of the Catholic Irish, but only in Belfast were such figures permanently brought within the clerical fellowship of the mainstream denominations and given influential churches in the centre of the city.[22] In the same way as evangelical Protestantism acquired an anti-Catholic cutting edge within the sectarian equilibrium of the frontier counties of Ulster at the end of the eighteenth century, it performed a similar social function in the frontier zones of Belfast's spatially segregated population. But its significance was even greater than that. David Miller has suggested that although anti-Catholicism had been an element in evangelicalism from the start, its role in creating a degree of Protestant solidarity in the Victorian period derived from more than a new way to stigmatize the ancient enemy:

> The two cultures – Episcopal and Presbyterian – into which Ulster Protestants had been divided in the early eighteenth century were both fundamentally unsuited to a modern world in which religious belief and practice would not be a public duty to be enforced upon the populace, but a private choice whose very validity depended upon its being voluntary. Evangelical emphasis on the individual offered these two churches a way out of the adversarial relationship, over which one should enjoy the right to coerce the conscience, in which they had been cast in the seventeenth century.[23]

The degree of animosity that still existed between the Episcopal and Presbyterian Churches in late Victorian Belfast should act as a caution about pressing this explanation too far, but Miller is right to identify the role of evangelicalism in facilitating a pan-Protestant, anti-Catholic and voluntary dimension to religion in Ulster's regional capital. A different kind of modernization, but with similar results, operated within the Roman Catholic Church in Belfast in the same period.

Two problems dominated the Belfast Catholic community from at least the 1820s. The first was to make suitable religious provision for a fast-increasing Catholic population and the second was a feeling that right down the social scale, from wealthy merchants to unskilled labourers, Belfast Catholics were very much second-class citizens by comparison with their Protestant counterparts. Logistical problems of church provision and parochial organization dominated the episcopates of William Crolly, Cornelius Denvir and Patrick Dorrian who were successively Bishops of Down and Connor and parish priests of Belfast from 1825 to 1885. Dorrian's career in particular as curate, coadjutor bishop and bishop is inextricably bound up with the growth and the shape of the Catholic community in Belfast.[24] As a supporter of O'Connell and Parnell, and as a lifelong critic of Fenianism and violence, Dorrian was both a stout-hearted churchman and a vigorous constitutional nationalist who disliked Orangeism and evangelicalism in equal measure. The mission of the Catholic Church under his leadership was neverthe-less in many respects a mirror image of the Protestant evangelicalism it opposed. More churches, more priests, more services, more confessions, more schools, more religious orders, more Sisters of Mercy, more temperance crusades, more self-improvement societies, more dispensaries and orphanages, more city missions, more religious tracts and less craven subservience to government, the Belfast corporation and the Protestant community. Thus in both Roman Catholic and evangelical Protestant communities there was a renewed emphasis on priests and ministers, a self-conscious reliance on female piety, a strong belief in the religious and social utility of education, an admirable commitment to holy charity and a relentless pursuit of religious respectability which almost certainly increased the gap between 'rough' and 'respectable' cultures.[25]

For Protestant contemporaries the growth of the Catholic community served to confirm their stereotypes of the Roman Church. Since there were far fewer Catholic churches than Protestant ones the former were generally larger and more imposing. Moreover, because of the lack of a substantial mercantile community the Catholic Church was unable to rely on middle-class beneficence for church-building and had to depend instead on more assiduous collections to finance building costs. Protestants interpreted the former as triumphalism and the latter as evidence of a ruthless church grinding down its humble adherents. The striking growth in the number of priests and religious orders fuelled the old fears of priestcraft, and the Italianate devotional forms of the later Victorian period further persuaded evangelical puritans of the essentially foreign and superstitious nature of the Roman Church.[26] Protestants thought they saw a growing, grasping, aggressive and intolerant church. Ironically, the correspondence of Catholic leaders in Belfast tells a different and more defensive tale. Preoccupied by high leakage rates, burdened by huge debts, fearful of Orange excesses and often divided among themselves on issues of politics, strategy and aspiration, the Belfast Catholic leadership resembled anything but the aggressive monolith of Protestant imagination.[27]

Belfast's Catholics also held similarly crude views about their Protestant neighbours. Their opinions were moulded by their experiences of open-air harangues, Orange celebrations and riotous behaviour at the centre of which were often to be found a second generation of evangelical preachers with city churches and Orange connections. Roman Catholics were thus persuaded that popular Protestantism teetered uneasily on the brink of unrestrained bigotry and intimidation. As both the frequency and the intensity of sectarian riots increased in the second half of the nineteenth century there was no shortage of evidence to confirm their fears.

That such religious cultures had the capacity for conflict is self-evident, but it is the multi-layered nature of such conflict which made it such a recurring feature of Belfast life in the nineteenth century and so unamenable to the ether of secularization in the twentieth century. Points of conflict were legion. Open-air sermons, Orange parades, election hustings, funeral processions, the great Protestant protest meetings in the city's botanical gardens, Catholic festivals such as the Feast Day of the Assumption, celebrations of historical events and transferred tensions from the surrounding countryside all contributed to riots at one time or another, especially in the years between 1857 and 1886.[28] All came with their processions, effigies, slogans, party tunes, banners and rituals. To a quite remarkable extent clubs and processions became a way of life. There were already thirty-two Orange lodges in Belfast by the 1830s, and parades in a special way marked out territory. Where you could 'walk' you could control. Underpinning episodic outbreaks of riotous behaviour were irreconcilable disputes over government policy and seemingly interminable local wrangles over powers and privileges. Predominantly Protestant Boards of Guardians administered workhouses for predominantly Catholic paupers amidst allegations of proselytism, a predominantly Protestant magistracy administered the law, a predominantly Protestant corporation allocated civic amenities and predominantly Protestant voters elected Protestant Members of Parliament. Even the allocation of graveyards in good soil or bad soil occasioned sectarian animosity. Belfast was as much a divided city in death as it was in life, but the existence of division in itself does not explain the frequency of sectarian riots which distinguished Belfast from other cities in the British Isles.

Over the course of the nineteenth century there were about a dozen major sectarian riots in Belfast and countless other minor affrays, but the most serious disturbances took place in the mid-Victorian period between 1857 and 1886. It is impossible to determine the precise number of casualties in these riots, but it seems likely that there were about 100 deaths and about 1,000 seriously injured, which is considerably less than the death toll in the Gordon Riots in London in 1780, but probably more than those killed in riots in all other Victorian cities put together.[29] Belfast was therefore an exceptionally violent city by the standards of other nineteenth-century British cities, but rather tame by comparison with the death rates from ethnic disturbances in many twentieth-century cities. Belfast was also unusual in the chronological incidence of its riots. The most troubled period in British industrial cities, for example, was the period from 1839 to 1848 after which there was a significant decline in the number of committals for riotous offences.[30] Ironically, the most serious riots in English cities after 1848 were the anti-Catholic disturbances in Stockport in 1852 and those occasioned by the lectures of the ultra-evangelical, no-popery orator, William Murphy, in the late 1860s.[31] In Belfast the incidence of particularly violent riots increased in the second half of the nineteenth century and reached its peak in the 1880s. How then is this pattern to be explained?

The early riots in Belfast were generally sparked off by the post-Reform Bill election contests, but the summer of discontent in 1857 was provoked initially by a ferociously anti-Catholic sermon preached to an Orange gathering by the evangelical incumbent of Christ Church, Dr Thomas Drew. Christ Church stood on the frontier between the Catholic Pound and Protestant Sandy Row districts of Belfast and Drew's sermon on 12 July set off two months of nakedly sectarian rioting in which open-air preaching played an important part in stoking the fires.[32] When the evangelical street preachers were eventually forced off the streets, the *Belfast Newsletter* thundered that

> The Romish mobs have triumphed in our town. The preaching of the Gospel in our streets to the destitute, ragged poor, is put down. Belfast now ranks with Kilkenny, or Cork, or Limerick. In these Romish cities, where priests are regnant and their mobs omnipotent and the authorities bow to their behest, no Protestant minister dare lift his voice in the streets or highways to proclaim the peaceful message of the cross – he would be stoned or murdered.[33]

It is striking in the literature of the period how often Belfast was compared with other Irish cities when the emphasis was on lack of religious freedom and public order, while it was compared with British cities when the emphasis was on industriousness and social progress.

The next serious outbreak of sectarian rioting in Belfast occurred in 1864 when the stimulus was the return by rail of Belfast Catholics after attending a ceremony to lay the foundation stone for a monument to Daniel O'Connell in Dublin. The riots were marked chiefly by vicious attacks on each other's schools and churches and by the partiality of the city's predominantly Protestant police force. The riots of 1872 were provoked by Belfast's first nationalist parade and were characterized by large-scale evictions of Catholics living in Protestant areas and Protestants living in Catholic areas. But by far the most violent and protracted riots of the nineteenth century took place in 1886 in the wake of the first Home Rule crisis. The threat of Home Rule for Ireland, combined with inflammatory rumours of how Protestant factories and property would be redistributed by raffle in the new Ireland, set off four months of vicious conflict that claimed some fifty lives.[34]

It is not hard to find reasons for Belfast's ubiquitous rioting in the nineteenth century. The spatial separation of its ethnic/religious communities was remorselessly staked out by marches and parades. Its clubs and secret organizations, from the Orange Order to the Ribbon societies, marshalled their respective troops and educated them in the significance of old battles in preparation for new ones. Evangelical preachers and zealous priests persuaded their charges that their temporal battles had cosmic significance and that right-eousness was an exclusively sectarian commodity. Policing was inadequate in good times and brutally contentious in bad times as each side coveted the opportunities of official coercion and complained bitterly when they became victims of the power they sought for themselves. The expansion of the franchise and the electoral representation of Belfast merely weakened the old aristo-cratic control mechanisms without dispersing the sectarian poison into less toxic channels.[35] As the political traditions of unionism and nationalism confronted each other after 1886, Belfast in general, and the closely fought constituency of west Belfast in particular, represented a peculiarly concentrated form of a much greater political conflict. Thus the Victorian era closed in Belfast upon two communities that were

> intransigent in their politics, intolerant in their religion;
> . inured to the violent ethic; trusting neither the English

parliament to promote their interests nor the Irish executive to protect their safety. . . . Dominance and not integration was their goal; force and not persuasion their ultimate weapon.[36]

Whereas the citizens in most British cities by the late nineteenth century had found relatively peaceful ways to express their political and religious differences, Belfast discovered that by 1886 an intractable national question had been grafted on to the sectarian feuding of its segregated slums. It was the Home Rule issue that transformed Belfast from the economic capital of Ulster to the citadel of unionism in Ireland and bound together ever more closely the fortunes of Protestants of all social classes. In a remarkable way the Home Rule crisis brought into sharp focus a Protestant mentality, centred on Ulster's major city, which had been forged over a quarter of a millennium of turbulent history. Moreover, the resistance to Home Rule in Ulster cemented a Protestant identity which succeeding years have done nothing to undermine. The inability of either the British state or Irish nationalism to coerce or accommodate this sturdy and peculiar minority has produced one of the most bitter conflicts in the modern world.

A recent survey of some thirty Ulster Unionist speeches against Home Rule in 1886 has shown that in descending order of priority the arguments employed were as follows: the representatives of an ascendant Roman Catholicism would persecute the Protestant community; Ulster Protestants would be deprived of their imperial heritage and would thus have a reduced status in the world; Catholic nationalists had no respect for law and order and would deliver Ulster into social and economic ruin; Home Rule was a betrayal of loyalism and Ulster would be forced to shoulder the fiscal and economic burden of Ireland under Home Rule.[37] What is striking about the Ulster Protestant world-view represented in these speeches is the number of mutually reinforcing explanations it offered for the plight in which Protestants found themselves in 1886. It was a remarkably cohesive ideology, embracing past, present and future as well as religion, politics and society. The only chink in its armour was its perceived inability to sustain itself against an imperialistic Catholic nationalism without the continued support of the rest of the United Kingdom. That was precisely the frailty exposed by Home Rule, and it was made harder to bear by Gladstone's and Parnell's persistent but erroneous belief that the eighteenth-century Patriot tradition remained a stronger force in

Irish Protestantism than Ulster loyalism. The belief persisted, against formidable evidence to the contrary, because both men wished it were so.

Ulster Protestants had an alternative view of Irish history which was relentlessly rehearsed at Orange, church and political meetings in Belfast throughout the second half of the nineteenth century.[38] Many of the speeches were populist history lectures about the struggles and triumphs of Irish Protestants against an unchanging and disloyal Catholicism. The virtues most admired were staunchness and unchanging principles, the evils most railed against were betrayal and accommodation. These appeals to forefathers, faith and the settlement of the land not only foreshortened the past, but helped even the most impious to believe they were part of a covenanting tradition underpinned by divine providence for a quarter of a millennium. Here was a memorial and celebratory culture resonant with providential turning-points and rich in symbols.[39] Protestants believed that having access to the 'Open Bible', being free from priestcraft and superstition and adhering to a progressive and enlightened faith were at the heart of Ulster's cultural and economic superiority over the rest of Ireland, and, equally important, of Protestant Ulster's superiority over Catholic Ulster.[40] The hotter the Protestantism, in terms of its evangelical zeal, the firmer was this belief and the sharper the antagonism against the 'whole system' of Roman Catholicism.

One of the great strengths of Protestant ideology in Ulster was the way in which it could simultaneously narrow the focus to a contest between reformed religion and Catholic superstition in Ireland and widen it to an international conflict of major proportions. This was facilitated by the late Victorian expansion of the British Empire and by the post-famine migrations of Irish Catholics. Here was a clash of two world empires, one of commerce, Christianity and civilization as exported by Great Britain and the other a sordid, embittered and disloyal Irish Catholic migration, particularly to the United States, where it created another culture in its own image.[41] The corruptions of Tammany Hall and the ill-fated invasion of Manitoba merely confirmed the unchanging character of the Catholic Irish even when thousands of miles from home. 'The Home Rule movement', stated the Reverend Gilbert Mahaffy to the YMCA, 'has been, from first to last, a movement hostile to British rule. And fostered as it has been on American soil, and supported by American dollars, it is essentially republican.'[42]

Thus, depending on circumstances, Ulster Protestants could think of themselves as either a faithful remnant of righteousness in a pagan land or as part of a great and civilizing world empire. They were equally comforting and culturally reinforcing ideas. Such a framework was watertight. Ulster's success was due to the blessings of providence and the energy of its people, its failures were attributable to enemies on all sides pressing in on a loyal but vulnerable remnant. Not surprisingly such ideas frequently gave rise to racial notions of the inherent superiority of Ulster Protestants to Irish Celts.

As with race so with religion. The Roman Catholic Church in Ireland was regarded as all pervasive in influence, monolithic in scope, imperialist in intention, persecuting in its essential nature and impoverishing in its social effects. No state in which its representatives were in control could offer any credible safeguards for the rights of religious minorities. Faced with such a possibility Ulster Protestant theology had the capacity to adapt to new circumstances. The view that all Christian citizens had a sacred duty to support lawfully constituted authorities was capable of being transformed into a sacred duty to resist religious tyranny.[43] As with English Puritanism on the eve of the Civil Wars, the anti-Catholicism of Ulster Protestants was a potentially radical force, and was, of course, more capable of mass realization than was self-sacrificial piety. It was propagated by a resurgent Orangeism whose rank-and-file of agricultural labourers and urban workers was led by Ulster landowners and baptized by the churches. Depending upon the seriousness of the crisis, Orange excesses, including pseudo-military drilling, came to be less feared than Protestant apathy. Even the licence of the Belfast Protestant mobs was ambiguously justified by some religious leaders who apparently saw no incongruity between this and their earlier attacks on Fenian agrarian outrages.

Even allowing for the strength of religious divisions in Belfast, however, it was by no means inevitable that Irish politics, Ulster politics and Belfast politics should come to be dominated by the forces of unionism and nationalism, or that this new political division should so closely reflect the old religious division of Protestant and Catholic, but by the late 1880s these are the patterns that had clearly emerged. 'A liberal–conservative, and eventually labour–conservative split', states Brian Walker, 'might have been the basic divide in Ulster and Irish politics, as happened in nineteenth and early twentieth century Scotland and Wales' where nationalism failed to make a decisive breakthrough, but it turned out not to be so.[44] The answer to this conundrum lies in the different configurations of landed power and religious rivalries inherent in the distinctive histories of the three Celtic kingdoms. Whatever the explanation for its creation, the pattern of Catholic/nationalist and Protestant/unionist politics was cemented at the end of the nineteenth century by an extension of the franchise, the rise of modern political parties and the continued threat, or promise, depending on one's views, of Home Rule for Ireland. Once institutionalized into political parties, sectarian divisions have proved inordinately resilient to erosion from within or without.

This tidy portrayal of politics in late Victorian Ulster does not in itself explain why a vibrant industrial city like Belfast did not give rise to a more vigorous labour movement, though it does supply a superficially persuasive answer; that is that religious sectarianism combined with competing nationalisms to squeeze out the narrow ground of socialist politics. As most of the writing on the history of Irish socialism has been produced by those from a nationalist perspective, the assumption has been that the Protestant working-class in Belfast, corrupted by economic privilege and religious hatred, are the real villains in any explanation of the lack of labour consciousness in pre-partition Ulster.[45] The traditional view has been that with many trades unions tied to the Orange Order, workers, foremen, managers and factory-owners were linked in a self-interested combination against Roman Catholic workers who were more likely than Protestants to be female and unskilled. In this scheme, the predominantly Protestant bourgeoisie in Belfast used the respectable social ethics of evangelical Protestantism to nurture work discipline in the same way as early English industrialists, according to E.P. Thompson, used the Methodists.[46] Moreover, it suited Protestant industrialists to employ only their own co-religionists as one sure way of keeping disruptive sectarian animosities out of the workplace. In this way sectarianism reinforced sectarianism.

Some recent writers on the history of the Belfast working class have not found this interpretation altogether persuasive.[47] It has been suggested, for example, that labour consciousness in Belfast looks weaker than in contemporary British cities because historians have exaggerated the progress of labour politics in them before the First World War. Moreover, the point has been made that the reason for the lack of labour solidarity in Ireland was due as much to James Connolly's agenda to fuse the Irish socialist and nationalist traditions as it was to the self-interest of Belfast Protestants who were in any case less homogeneous, less 'privileged' and less opposed to labourist politics than many have supposed. To say, for example, that the great majority of skilled workers in Belfast were Protestant is not the same thing as saying that the majority of Protestants were skilled workers. Moreover, it was from the skilled section of the working class that trades unionism and labour politics received their greatest support. Many of the problems facing organized unionism in Belfast at the end of the nineteenth century had more to do with the inauspicious economic structure of the linen industry and the intense sectionalism of workers in the engineering and shipbuilding industries than with the religious division of the workforce.[48] Demarcation disputes were a far more common cause of strikes than ethnic rivalry and both the number of strikes (174 in Belfast between 1888 and 1913) and their chronological incidence is similar to the pattern of disputes in other British cities.[49] What is not so common is the way in which political, religious and residential rioting in Belfast frequently spilled over into the workplace leading to expulsions and sectarian violence. It nevertheless seems probable that the only explicitly sectarian strike in Belfast took place in the linen industry during the Home Rule debates of 1893.

Whatever one might say about the complexities of the relationship between trades unionism and religious sectarianism, there can be little doubt that Belfast's electoral politics in the Home Rule era show that unionism and nationalism were much more significant divisions than Labour and Conservative. In these years Belfast politics threw up a populist nationalism represented by Joe Devlin, the MP for West Belfast and a working-class militant, and fundamentalist Orangeism represented by Thomas Sloan, the MP for South Belfast, but the nearest the city came to a genuine labour representation was William Walker's electoral campaign in North Belfast between 1905 and 1907.[50] Walker was a Protestant joiner with an impeccable trades union pedigree and good connections with the British labour movement. He was a labour unionist who mounted a serious but unsuccessful challenge to Conservatism in three elections in North Belfast, but his conduct of those elections showed just how difficult it was to appeal simultaneously to the Protestant and Catholic working classes and to build up a tradition of independent working-class politics in a city divided by the national question. Labour was not a negligible force in prewar Belfast politics, but it was never able to deal with the structural inequalities between Protestant or Catholic workers or to overcome the dominant political division in the city between nationalism and unionism.

Thus, whether one looks at the demographic, economic, social, political or religious structure of Belfast in the nineteenth century, it is hard to resist the conclusion that it was both typical of many other Victorian cities, yet profoundly anomalous in some aspects of its development. Unlike some other cities, Belfast has never escaped from the sectarian patterns that became entrenched in the early Victorian period and, unfortunately for its remarkably resilient citizens, it has found it equally difficult to cast aside its reputation as the most violent city in the British Isles over the past 150 years. Even in its modern form Belfast manages to be beguilingly normal and disconcertingly abnormal at the same time.

Although the ethnic and religious divisions of Belfast have come to be thought of as unique because of their persistence and longevity, they were by no means untypical of nineteenth-century cities in Britain, Europe and North America. It was not unusual for religion to be a major component of the residential, occupational and ethnographic divisions of large cities, nor was it unusual for different religious traditions to keep alive separate heritages in their festivals and riots. Even Belfast's notorious 'Orange' and 'Green' disturbances were reproduced in recognizable forms in Glasgow, Liverpool and New York. But if Belfast was not unique in its violent divisions, a variety of circumstances made its problems particularly intractable. Not only was its population divided by ethnicity, religion, politics and national loyalty, but its economic power and social influence were unequally shared between its rival traditions. Moreover, Belfast was but a populous microcosm of the entire province of Ulster, and Ulster was itself a provincial anomaly in the island of Ireland. In addition, population movements in the eighteenth and nineteenth centuries ensured that Irish problems were given a global dimension. In short, not only was Belfast a divided city in the Victorian period, but its divisions were not easily confined to, or solved within, its own city boundaries. In one sense its difficulties were densely concentrated in the slums of its labouring poor, but in another, they were diffused quite beyond manageable proportions. Belfast was not a uniquely divided nineteenth-century city, but the cumulative burdens of its people's histories made it peculiarly susceptible to a long conflict. Since the 1880s the heart of that conflict has been a contest of national loyalties between unionists and nationalists that both arose from and was superimposed upon much older ethnic and religious divisions. It was Belfast's misfortune, therefore, that the sectarian animosities of its early nineteenth-century inhabitants laid the foundations for even more intractable conflicts between competing forms of nationalism at the end of the century. It is the national question, along with the ethnic, cultural and religious loyalties bound up with it, that has made Belfast a more bitter theatre of conflict than any other city in Britain or in Ireland over the past century.

NOTES

1 The best introductions to the development of Belfast in the nineteenth century are E. Jones, *A Social Geography of Belfast*, London, 1960; J.C. Beckett and R.E. Glassock (eds), *Belfast; The Origins and Growth of an Industrial City*, Belfast, 1967; J.C. Beckett (ed.), *Belfast: The Making of the City*, Belfast, 1983; J. Bardon, *Belfast*, Belfast, 1982. See also the collection of documents, *Problems of a Growing City: Belfast 1780–1870*, Belfast, 1973.
2 L.A. Clarkson, 'Population change and urbanisation', in L. Kennedy and P. Ollerenshaw (eds), *An Economic History of Ulster 1820–1939*, Manchester, 1985, pp. 137–56; J.G. Williamson, *Coping with City Growth during the British Industrial Revolution*, Cambridge, 1990.
3 S.A. Royle, 'Industrialization, urbanization and urban society in post-famine Ireland, c.1850–1921', in B.J. Graham and L.J. Proudfoot (eds), *An Historical Geography of Ireland*, London, 1993, pp. 258–92.
4 Bardon, *Belfast*, p. 156.
5 E. Strauss, *Irish Nationalism and British Democracy*, London, 1951, p. 234; J. Butt, 'Belfast and Glasgow: Connections and comparisons, 1790–1850', in T.M. Devine and D. Dickson (eds), *Ireland and Scotland 1600–1850*, Edinburgh, 1983, pp. 193–203.
6 D. Hempton and M. Hill, *Evangelical Protestantism in Ulster Society 1740–1890*, London, 1992, p. 106.
7 A.C. Hepburn and B. Collins, 'Industrial society: The structure of Belfast, 1901', in P. Roebuck (ed.), *Plantation to Partition*, Belfast, 1981, pp. 210–28.
8 D. Miller, 'The Armagh troubles', in S. Clark and J.S. Donnelly (eds), *Irish Peasants: Violence and Political Unrest, 1730–1914*, Manchester, 1983, pp. 155–91; T. Bartlett, 'Religious rivalries in France and Ireland in the age of the French Revolution', *Eighteenth-Century Ireland*, 6, 1991, pp. 57–76.
9 P. Bew, *Land and the National Question in Ireland 1858–82*, Dublin, 1978.
10 B. Collins, 'The Irish in Britain, 1780–1921', in Graham and

DAVID HEMPTON

Proudfoot (eds), *Historical Geography of Ireland*, pp. 366–98; S.W. Gilley, 'Irish Catholicism in Britain', in D. Kerr (ed.), *Religion, State and Ethnic Groups*, Dartmouth, 1992, pp. 229–59.

11 Hepburn and Collins, 'Industrial society', p. 215.

12 J. Whyte, *Interpreting Northern Ireland*, Oxford, 1991, pp. 33–6.

13 Hepburn and Collins, 'Industrial society', pp. 210–28.

14 B.M. Walker, *Ulster Politics: The Formative Years, 1868–86*, Belfast, 1989, p. 12.

15 Clarkson, 'Population change', p. 153.

16 P. Ollerenshaw, 'Industry, 1820–1914', in Kennedy and Ollerenshaw (eds), *Economic History*, pp. 62–108; F. Geary and W. Johnson, 'Shipbuilding in Belfast 1861–1986', *Irish Economic and Social History*, XVI, 1989, pp. 42–64.

17 The best short introduction to these themes is S. Connolly, *Religion and Society in Nineteenth-Century Ireland*, Dundalk, 1985. See also S. Connolly, 'Religion, work discipline and economic attitudes: The case of Ireland', in Devine and Dickson (eds), *Ireland and Scotland*, pp. 235–45. For the impact of a more earnest Protestantism on city life see John Gray, 'Popular entertainment', in Beckett (ed.), *Belfast*, pp. 99–110; and D. Hempton and M. Hill, '"Godliness and good citizenship": Evangelical Protestantism and social control in Ulster, 1790–1850', *Saothar: Journal of the Irish Labour History Society*, 13, 1988, pp. 68–80.

18 A. Macaulay, *Patrick Dorrian: Bishop of Down and Connor 1865–85*, Dublin, 1987.

19 H. McLeod, *Religion and the Working Class in Nineteenth-Century Britain*, London, 1984, pp. 57–66.

20 Compare, for example, R.M. Sibbett, *For Christ and Crown: The Story of a Mission*, Belfast, 1926, and D.M. Lewis, *Lighten their Darkness: The Evangelical Mission to Working-Class London, 1828–1860*, Westport, Conn., 1986.

21 Hempton and Hill, *Evangelical Protestantism*, pp. 47–102.

22 D.G. Paz, *Popular Anti-Catholicism in Mid-Victorian England*, Stanford, Calif., 1992, pp. 225–65.

23 D. Miller, book review in *Irish Economic and Social History*, XIX, 1992, pp. 121–2. See also D. Miller, 'Presbyterianism and "Modernization" in Ulster', *Past and Present*, 80, 1978, pp. 66–90.

24 Macaulay, *Patrick Dorrian*, pp. 113–62.

25 S.J. Connolly, *Priests and People in Pre-Famine Ireland 1780–1845*, Dublin, 1982.

26 E. Larkin, 'The devotional revolution in Ireland 1850–75', *American Historical Review*, 78, 1972, pp. 625–52. The fortunes of Protestantism and Roman Catholicism in Britain and Europe in the nineteenth century were followed avidly in Ireland and contributed to mutual distrust. See Walker, *Ulster Politics*, p. 28.

27 Macaulay, *Patrick Dorrian*, pp. 163–218.

28 The most insightful treatment of sectarian riots in nineteenth-century Belfast is S.E. Baker, 'Orange and green: Belfast, 1832–1912', in H.J.

Dyos and M. Wolff (eds), *The Victorian City: Images and Realities*, 2 vols, London, 1973, vol. 2, pp. 789–814.

29 J. Stevenson, *Popular Disturbances in England 1700–1870*, London, 1979, pp. 312–13.

30 ibid., pp. 296–300.

31 W.L. Arnstein, 'The Murphy riots: A Victorian dilemma', *Victorian Studies*, XIX, 1975–6, pp. 51–71. G.F.A. Best, 'Popular Protestantism in Victorian Britain', in R. Robson (ed.), *Ideas and Institutions of Victorian Britain*, London, 1967, pp. 115–42. P. Millward, 'The Stockport riots of 1852: A study of anti-Catholic and anti-Irish sentiment', in R. Swift and S. Gilley (eds), *The Irish in the Victorian City*, London, 1985, pp. 207–24.

32 Bardon, *Belfast*, pp. 107–9. See also Annals of Christ Church, Belfast, in the Northern Ireland Public Record Office, T2159.

33 Quoted in A. Boyd, *Holy War in Belfast*, Tralee, 1969, p. 39.

34 Bardon, *Belfast*, pp. 144–50.

35 It is important not to underestimate the structural changes in Ulster's politics in the second half of the nineteenth century. See F.A. Wright, 'Developments in Ulster politics 1843–86', Ph.D. thesis, Queen's University Belfast, 1989; Walker, *Ulster Politics*, pp. 179–267. The conflicts between the landed unionist leadership and Belfast's populist Orangeism are skilfully dissected by A. Jackson in his forthcoming book from Oxford University Press, *Colonel Edward Saunderson: Landlordism and the Union in Nineteenth Century Ireland*, Oxford, 1994. I am grateful to Dr Jackson for allowing me to read this book in advance of publication.

36 Baker, 'Orange and green', p. 800.

37 J. Loughlin, *Gladstone, Home Rule and the Irish Question 1882–93*, Dublin, 1986, appendix 2, pp. 295–6.

38 See, for example, Anon, *The Irish Church Bill: The Great Protestant Demonstration in Belfast*, Belfast, 1869.

39 D.H. Akenson, *God's Peoples: Covenant and Land in South Africa, Israel, and Ulster*, Montreal, 1991, pp. 97–150.

40 See, for example, Anon, *The Home Rule 'Nutshell' Examined by an Irish Unionist*, Belfast and Dublin, 1912.

41 This theme was particularly evident in the columns of the Belfast Methodist newspaper, the *Christian Advocate*, 19 March, 9 April, 4 and 11 June 1886.

42 G. Mahaffy, *The Attitude of Irish Churchmen to the Present Political Crisis: Address to Monkstown Y.M.C.A.*, 3rd edn, Dublin, 1886.

43 D. Miller, *Queen's Rebels: Ulster Loyalism in Historical Perspective*, Dublin, 1978.

44 Walker, *Ulster Politics*, p. 265.

45 See, for example, G. Bell, *The Protestants of Ulster*, London, 1976; M. Farrell, *Northern Ireland: The Orange State*, London, 1976; and E. McCann, *War and an Irish Town*, Harmondsworth, 1974.

46 E.P. Thompson, *The Making of the English Working Class*, London, 1963.

47 H. Patterson, *Class Conflict and Sectarianism: The Protestant Working*

Class and the Belfast Labour Movement 1868–1920, Belfast, 1980; and H. Patterson, 'Industrial labour and the labour movement, 1820–1914', in Kennedy and Ollerenshaw (eds), *Economic History*, pp. 158–83.

48 A. Morgan, *Labour and Partition: The Belfast Working Class 1905–23*, London, 1991, pp. 15–18.

49 R. Munck, 'The formation of the working class in Belfast, 1788–1881', *Saothar: Journal of the Irish Labour History Society*, 11, 1986, pp. 75–89.

50 For a recent and insightful treatment of each of these traditions of popular politics in Belfast at the turn of the century see Morgan, *Labour and Partition*, pp. 27–90.

6

THE VARIETIES OF RELIGIOUS EXPERIENCE IN URBAN FRANCE

Thomas Kselman

After eight years of pastoral work in Paris starting in 1863 the abbé François Courtade was deeply pessimistic about the religious state of Paris workers. Writing in 1871, Courtade asserted that 'The labouring population of Paris is on the way to becoming atheistic. ... The people of Paris are without faith and without God. The notion and the feeling of the divine seem to have entirely withdrawn from them.'[1] Courtade's response was typical of the Catholic clergy, who complained of the rising wave of indifference throughout the nineteenth century, an indifference that could on occasion turn into hostility and violence, as in the sacking of the Church of St-Germaine-l'Auxerrois in 1831, and the murder of clerical hostages, including the Archbishop Darboy, during the Commune in 1871.

These last two incidents, situated in Paris and associated with the revolution of 1830 and the Commune of 1871, suggest the linkages that were habitually made by clergymen like Courtade. Cities, particularly Paris, posed a threat to religion because they housed a growing population of workers who were immune to the teachings of Catholicism and attracted to the pleasures of the café and the seductive power of materialist ideologies. Although it has been challenged and qualified, this stereotypical view of the city as a secularizing force continues to shape the judgements of historians. Maurice Crubellier, in his survey of urban culture, concluded that 'from the perspective of the people, the major fact is indeed the disaffection of workers' families from Catholicism'.[2]

The pessimism of Courtade and of urban historians about the status of religion in the city depends in part on two assumptions that deserve some scrutiny. The first identifies the working class with the city, an association that reflects the numerical weight of this group, but pays little attention to other classes that managed to combine urban existence with religious experience. The energy of those who continued to practise, particularly women, may not have been an effective counter to the dechristianization of many working-class neighbourhoods, but it did contribute a religious dimension to urban life.

Many who see nineteenth-century French cities as intrinsically secular make a second assumption that is perhaps more problematic than the equation of city and working class. There is a tendency among studies of urban religion to use measures of declining Catholic practice as evidence of a decline in religion. To move from findings about Catholic practice to conclusions about religion, however, is to ignore current debates among historians, anthropologists and sociologists that extend the domain of religion beyond its traditional institutional expressions. Without entering into this debate, which is far from being resolved, I want to associate myself with scholars such as Clifford Geertz and Peter Berger who see religion as a set of symbols that provide profoundly satisfying explanations of the meaning of both individual and collective life by linking these to a cosmic order.[3] This approach, by allowing the consideration of non-Catholic and non-Christian symbols and beliefs, including some aspects of 'secular' ideologies, as forms of religion, can provide a more nuanced view of urban religion than one which looks at the evidence only from the perspective of the Catholic clergy.

Taking such an expansive view of religion can lead to an amorphous conceptualization in which it becomes difficult to distinguish religious from non-religious experiences. My willingness to take this risk is based in part on the example of Emile Durkheim, one of the most important modern theorists of religion, who worked in late nineteenth- and early twentieth-century France. Durkheim's exploration of totemic cults and other primitive belief systems led him to identify religion with the collective representations of society; regardless of what cults claim about God and the afterlife, their visions of social order and moral behaviour qualify as authentically religious. In *The Elementary Forms of Religious Life* Durkheim was struck with the moral force of religion which aspires always 'to raise man above himself and to make him lead a life superior to that which he would lead, if he followed only his own individual whims'.[4] Like abbé Courtade, Durkheim was anxious about the moral and religious atmosphere of the modern city, but as a loyal republican he did not look to the church as the solution. The state-sponsored moral education he advocated, however, would qualify as religious in the sense he gives the term in *Elementary Forms*.[5] Like abbé Courtade and the Catholic clergy Durkheim observed the erosion of Catholicism in French cities, but he saw also that other institutions were capable of providing symbols that could evoke a sense of collective life and moral responsibility. In this chapter I will explore the role of the Catholic Church in the French cities of the late nineteenth century, as well as the emergence of religious pluralism through new forms of experience mediated by informal relations in neighbourhoods, political parties and the state. As Peter Berger has suggested in his recent work, pluralism rather than secularization may be the most satisfying way to view the religious changes that have emerged in the modern world, and particularly in modern cities.[6]

CATHOLICISM IN THE CITY

French urban growth was rapid in the nineteenth century, with the percentage of the population living in cities (defined by the modest French standard of 2,000 inhabitants) increasing from 24.4 per cent in 1846 to 39.5 per cent in 1896. Growth was particularly impressive in Paris which went from just over 500,000 in 1800 to just over 2.5 million in 1900. The pace and intensity of French urbanization were modest, however, in comparison with the changes occurring in England and the United States. In France, for example, the percentage of people in cities over 10,000 grew from 10.5 to 25.9 per cent between 1800 and 1890, while the percentage for England moved from 21.3 per cent to 61.8 and for the United States from 3.8 per cent to 27.6 per cent.[7]

From the perspective of the French clergy, urbanization, whatever its pace, was a major source of the alienation of the French people from the church. Recent research suggests, however, that cities generally shared the religious character of their regions.[8] The percentage of those who received communion during the Easter season is perhaps the most common index used for measuring attachment to Catholicism, since it indicates those who not only identify themselves as Catholic but who also make the effort to fulfil the minimum canonical requirement established by the church since the Middle Ages. In French cities of the late nineteenth and early twentieth centuries, as Table 6.1 shows, a majority of people living in cities received Easter communion only in the pious areas of

Brittany (Quimper) and Lorraine (Metz).[9] It is worth noting that in the dioceses of Limoges, Sens and Soissons, urban practice, although not extensive, was greater than that in the countryside. The anxiety of the clergy about religious practice in cities may have been justified, but the contrast they sometimes drew between city and country was exaggerated; both experienced a decline in practice which varied significantly according to region.

Table 6.1 Catholicism in town and country

Date	Diocese		Easter communion (%) Urban	Rural
1890–6	Arras		30.1	52.0
1908	Le Mans		29.1	30.9
1902–3	Limoges	Men	4.9	1.1
		Women	24.1	15.1
1906	Metz		72.6	89.2
1901–6	Perigueux		46.3	56.2
1909	Quimper		53.0	92.9
1912	Sens	Men	4.2	2.4
		Women	21.5	15.6
1905	Soissons		19.0	11.3

If a more modest standard of religious practice is applied, such as the commitment to the religious celebration of the great transitional moments of life – birth, marriage and death – Catholicism fares better, for only a minority of urban-dwellers was willing to do without the sacraments of baptism, marriage and extreme unction. In Paris only 17.7 per cent of the population received Easter communion during the period 1903–8, but over 70 per cent insisted on a religious burial.[10] Celebrating death with a religious ceremony was by far the *rite de passage* that Parisians were most attached to, but throughout the early years of the Third Republic a majority also continued to insist on Catholic baptism and marriage. The numbers varied, however, depending on the ritual, and during the second half of the nineteenth century Parisians showed themselves increasingly willing to do without Catholic services at these crucial moments (see Table 6.2). I will return to the significance of these *rites de passage*, particularly funerals, later in this chapter (pp. 181–5). For now the commitment of a majority to Catholic baptism, marriage and burial suggests a more complicated picture of religious life than the one depicted by clergy concerned that their pews were empty on Sundays.

Table 6.2 Baptisms, marriages and funerals in Paris[11]

| | Catholic ceremonies | | | Non-religious ceremonies (or no ceremony) | | |
	Baptisms	Marriages	Funerals	Baptisms	Marriages	Funerals
1865	89.2			7.4		
1875	84.5	84.0		11.9	12.6	21.1
1885	68.7	70.6	74.9	27.9	26.0	
1900	69.4	67.5	76.7	27.1	29.0	18.7
1908	58.6	57.3	70.6	37.9	39.0	25.7

The continuing importance of Catholicism in the life of cities in the late nineteenth century can also be measured by the physical presence of the church. The existence of cathedrals such as Notre-Dame in the heart of Paris established an imposing Catholic atmosphere that linked nineteenth-century cities with their medieval past. The power of the churches as symbols of Catholic authority can be seen in the activity of the Commune of 1871, when many of them were seized for meetings by revolutionary clubs and the National Guard. These occupations were turned into ceremonial occasions; at the Panthéon two battalions of the National Guard were assembled to witness the sawing off of the arms of the cross that surmounted the dome and the attaching of a red flag to the stump. At St-Germaine-l'Auxerrois a National Guardsman excited a crowd by sticking a pipe in the mouth of a statue of the Virgin and then parading around the church with the infant Jesus from the statue extended from the end of his bayonet.[12] Such actions betray not only a resentment of Catholicism, but a sense that the churches remained centres of collective life that needed to be ritually purged.

In addition to the survival of medieval monuments, a number of significant additions to urban religious architecture were initiated or completed during the Third Republic. The basilica of Sacré Coeur on Montmartre, which along with the Eiffel Tower of 1889 dominates the skyline of Paris, was begun in 1876 and completed in 1910, with most of the construction costs of 40 million francs coming from small contributions left by pilgrims in the *chapelle provisoire*.[13] In Marseille the 'Cathédrale de la Major', built in the heart of the old port alongside the remnants of the Romanesque cathedral from the twelfth century, was completed in 1892 after forty years of work. Urban-dwellers had various opinions about Catholicism, ranging from devotion to hostility, but the church continued to be a physical presence they could not ignore, particularly in the older central cities whose streets and buildings had survived from the Middle Ages.

The growth of French cities in the nineteenth century, however, resulted in the creation of new neighbourhoods far from the old central areas and without the imposing presence of cathedrals and churches, and the clergy who staffed them. Mgr Guibert, the Archbishop of Paris, understood the consequences of the church's failure to keep up with this urban spread. In a decree of 1873 he wrote with great anxiety about the

> baptized Christians who had become in large numbers strangers to religious practice because of the distance and insufficiency of parish churches. One can say that they are a people without altars: they take no part in the holy mysteries, they do not hear the word of God, and after several years the idea of Christian and moral truths is almost entirely effaced from their minds.[14]

The population of Belleville, the working-class quarter in eastern Paris incorporated into the city in 1860, illustrates the problem addressed by Guibert. Belleville grew from 96,147 in 1861 to 216,620 in 1911, but during this time the neighbourhood continued to be served by only three parishes.[15] For Paris as a whole the population grew from 1,696,141 in 1861 to 2,888,110 in 1914, while the number of priests increased only from 555 to 603; in 1861 there was one priest for every 3,056 inhabitants, in 1914 there was one priest for every 4,790 Parisians.[16] In Marseille the situation was similar, with one priest for every 2,450 in 1861 and one for every 4,550 in 1921.[17]

The relative scarcity of churches and clergy in the new neighbourhoods is one reason why the working classes of Paris and other cities became alienated from Catholic practice. The same was not true of more affluent neighbourhoods, where levels of practice were significantly higher. For Paris, in the aristocratic seventh *arrondissement* in 1909–14, 45.9 per cent of the population received Easter communion, compared to only 5.8 per cent in the twentieth *arrondissement* of eastern Paris, which included much of Belleville. The twentieth also had the highest percentage of civil funerals; in 1885 only 10.7 per cent of those who died in the seventh *arrondissement* were buried with such a ceremony, compared to 39.5 per cent for the twentieth.[18]

It was not only the absence of the clergy that explains the relatively low levels of Catholic practice in working-class neighbourhoods. Many urban workers resented the clergy for collaborating with the owners in preaching the value of resignation to their fate. In the industrial city of Roubaix in northern France, the Redemptorist priest Bouchage made the following appeal to workers during an 1885 ceremony in which he blessed a crucifix in the weaving room of a textile factory: 'When work is at its most difficult and the sweat burns, instead of blaspheming as so many do; look at the crucifix, for the sight of it will do you good, and will turn your sufferings into coins with which you may purchase the crowns of paradise.'[19] In Limoges, the owner of a corset factory worked closely with the clergy in enforcing strict religious and industrial discipline. Forty-two of the 105 women who worked there struck in 1896, protesting about arbitrary fines, the obligatory prayers they were forced to say on their knees at the start of the workday and the yearly confession, retreat and mass that they were required to attend together.[20]

Not all owners attempted to draw on the church's support in dealing with their workers, and clergy from the Paris region complained about the lack of concern that industrialists felt towards the moral and religious state of their workers.[21] The church may have suffered in some places from an alliance between Catholicism and capitalism, but this association was not universal, and is not sufficient to explain the disaffection of the working class. In the end, it was not only the failure of the church to serve the workers that led to dechristianization. Alternative systems of belief and ritual, which I will explore later in this chapter (pp. 175–85), pulled in workers to complement the push that they received, or at least perceived, from the church.

The dechristianization of the working class was a serious problem from the point of view of the clergy, but despite the significance of this development, it is not the only story that can be told about Catholicism in the cities of France. The data in Table 6.1 suggest that women were much more likely to practise Catholicism than men, and their experiences, particularly those from the middle classes, cast a very different light on the role of Catholicism in the city. The *bourgeoises* from the northern cities described by Bonnie Smith retained a Catholic world-view that shaped every aspect of their lives:

They summoned priests to bless each household as it opened. They adorned their walls with crucifixes and filled niches with statuary, especially of the Virgin Mary; many even erected small chapels in their homes. Each morning they greeted their children with holy words; at meals they asked God's blessing; each evening they gathered servants and family members alike for prayer; and before bed they gave each child a special benediction. . . . The sacred became so connected with family that at times the home seemed sacred of itself, while anything outside its perimeters appeared profane.[22]

The character of urban Catholicism was increasingly shaped by these women, whether they were wives and mothers or members of religious congregations. Theresa Martin, from a pious Catholic family in the Norman city of Lisieux, became an exemplar for this feminized style of Catholicism through her life as described in her autobiography. After receiving special permission to enter the local Carmelite convent at the age of 15, Theresa led a life committed to small sacrifices for the sake of Jesus. She would listen uncomplainingly to an old nun, refuse to criticize the careless work of others in the laundry room and make a special effort to be pleasant towards those she didn't like. This 'little way' of sanctification was recorded in Theresa's autobiography, which the Carmelites of Lisieux published the year after her death at the age of 24 in 1897. By 1925, the year of her canonization, the autobiography had sold 410,000 complete editions and over 2 million abridged versions in France. In the same period the Carmelite convent distributed over 30 million holy cards of the Little Flower, and over 17 million relic sachets.[23]

The commerce in the words and images of the Little Flower was only a small part of the enormous market in pious images, whose centre of production and distribution was in the heart of Paris, in the neighbourhood around the Church of Saint-Sulpice. Following the Franco-Prussian War of 1870–1, and in response also to the assault on Catholicism by the republican governments of the 1880s, publishers such as Bouasse-Lebel produced millions of images full of bleeding hearts and sentimental representations of the sufferings of Christ, Mary and the saints. The Catholic culture of the late nineteenth century emphasized quiet suffering as a way to win redemption for yourself, for your loved ones and for France. The growing appeal of these images and the creation of the cult of Theresa Martin in the late nineteenth and early twentieth centuries reflects a feminized Catholicism which emphasized the importance of women in the salvation of a country increasingly dominated by materialism and atheism. Through prayer, the sacraments and lives of constant self-sacrifice, women could, in collaboration with the clergy, save France.

The mission that Catholic women took on themselves led them out of the domestic sphere and into the urban world of disbelief, poverty and unemployment. At Lille women met monthly as members of the Confraternity of Christian Mothers to pray for the conversion of their husbands and sons and for miraculous healings. Women also founded charitable organizations to assist working-class mothers in childbirth and to provide day care for the children of working women and recreational societies for teenage girls. By the beginning of the twentieth century these activities were being discussed and co-ordinated by national associations, the Ligue des femmes françaises, founded at Lyon by Madame Jean Lestra in 1901, and the Ligue patriotique des françaises, founded at Paris in 1902 by the Baronesses Brigode and Reille. By 1910 the LPDF had founded 124 libraries and 121 recreational societies, as well as numerous other works, and by 1914 it had enlisted over 600,000 members.[24] All of these activities were informed by a deep commitment to Catholicism, which the ladies also strove to communicate to their working-class clients. The *patronages* for the teenagers, for example, directed girls either to a religious marriage or entry into a convent.[25]

The alternative of joining a religious order was attractive to large numbers of women from both the middle and working classes in France throughout the nineteenth century; their numbers grew from 12,300 in 1808 to 135,000 in 1878.[26] Large numbers of these sisters were recruited from rural areas, and they were a common sight in both villages and cities. But the research of Claude Langlois has demonstrated that women's religious congregations were concentrated in urban areas, particularly in middle-sized cities of 30,000 to 50,000, where there were 7.5 nuns for every 1,000 people. In the great cities, including Paris, Lyon and Marseille, their relative numbers were not as great, but they none the less made an impact through their work as nurses and teachers.[27] The secularization of schools that began in the 1880s and the law on associations of 1901 led to a decline in the role of both male and female Catholic orders in French education, though many accepted secularization and were still teaching in private schools on the eve of the First World War. Religious orders resisted anticlerical pressure much more successfully in the areas of health care; the expulsion of nuns from the hospitals of Paris in the 1880s was exceptional, and the numbers of nursing

THOMAS KSELMAN

sisters continued to rise throughout the Third Republic, reaching
a peak of 12,887 in 1912. In cities throughout France their work
in hospitals, old people's homes, lunatic asylums and shelters for
prostitutes provided services that were in demand, and which, as
Ralph Gibson puts it, 'nobody else cared much to satisfy'.[28]

Urbanization posed a threat to Catholicism, and the growth of
cities contributed to a decline in regular practice, especially in the
newly constructed working-class neighbourhoods. The alienation of
these recently arrived city-dwellers did not mean, however, that the
church was eliminated from the urban scene. Women, particularly
middle-class women, created Catholic environments in their homes
that responded to the threats they saw around them, and they and
the nuns who joined congregations moved into the world as social
workers, teachers and nurses. It should be noted that many clergy
were also active in social work, and that Catholic laymen such as
Albert de Mun and Léon Harmel responded to the growth of
the cities by organizing groups of workers into discussion circles
and recreational societies. Although even sympathetic historians
acknowledge the limited results of these initiatives, they note also
that they succeeded in forming the nucleus of Catholic action
groups that were active in the interwar periods.[29] A number of
leaders of the Christian labor movement, for example, emerged
from the association of Saint Benoît Labre, an élite organization
dedicated to spiritual development founded by the Christian
Brothers at Passy in 1882.[30]

The situation of the Catholic Church in urban France was therefore complex, and is not adequately described in the exclusively
negative terms used by abbé Courtade. Clerical concerns were
understandable given the overall erosion of the church's position.
The standard applied by Courtade and the clergy, however, and the
language they used to describe the city were derived from a Catholic
perspective that valued regular attendance at mass and participation
in the sacraments. To judge the religious state of France exclusively
in terms supplied by the Catholic clergy is to miss aspects of urban
life that can be understood as religious, though they have not
generally been interpreted in this sense.

RELIGIOUS ALTERNATIVES

Catholicism was the religion of the majority of urban-dwellers, but,
although their numbers were generally small, Protestants and Jews

174

also lived in French cities. In Paris the two groups together made up less than 5 per cent of the population. Following the Franco-Prussian War of 1870–1, France lost about one-fourth of the nation's Protestants in the transfer of Alsace to Germany, and most of the 650,000 who remained lived in rural areas or small towns.[31] Many of these lived in the southern department of the Gard, where they formed an important element in the capital of Nîmes. Protestant ministers there, however, had similar anxieties about the effects of urbanization and the growth of working-class neighboourhoods. In Nîmes these developments contributed to the erosion of the sense of community that had formerly bound together owners and workers in the silk industry.[32] The Franco-Prussian War also had a substantial effect on the Jewish population of France, reducing the numbers of Jews from 90,000 to 50,000, most of them concentrated in Paris. During the Third Republic many of these practised what Michael Marrus has called 'the politics of assimilation'.[33] Jewish religious practice declined and rituals were redesigned to resemble those of the Catholic majority. However, this older and assimilated population was joined by immigrants from Russia as a result of the pogroms that began in 1881. By the time of the Dreyfus Affair in the 1890s the character of the Parisian Jewish population had changed. The language and customs of the new arrivals were in sharp contrast to their co-religionists, and made them highly visible targets of anti-Semitic propaganda, a movement that had religious overtones.[34]

The city-dwellers who turned away from the regular practice of Catholicism, however, did not convert to either Protestantism or Judaism. The minority who refused contact with the Catholic clergy and sacraments became part of the 'unchurched', but this is not to say they were irreligious. Many of those who rejected Catholicism completely, or who reduced their participation to the *rites de passage*, constructed religious systems from a combination of sources that included Catholicism, the occult, socialist ideology and nationalism. The new forms of religious experiences that were available in cities during the late nineteenth century are difficult to study because they were not generally grounded in traditional institutions. It is also true that urban life during the period after 1870, particularly in Paris, became increasingly preoccupied with leisure activities, with cafés, circuses and nightclubs.[35] In so far as these activities drew the attention of the urban crowds, a process of secularization can be said to have occurred. But there is enough evidence in the language and rituals that were familiar to *citadins* to suggest that they retained an interest in finding justifications for their lives that extended beyond the immediate satisfaction of their material wants, and linked them to a transcendent order.

A revival of interest in the occult constitutes one of the alternative roads to the transcendent that became increasingly and publicly available in the French cities of the late nineteenth century.[36] It is not an easy task to trace the development of interest in the occult, and most who have studied the problem have concentrated on its influence among literary élites.[37] Even this evidence, however, reveals a subculture in which mystical knowledge, secret books, magical practices and the invocation of spirits gave people access to a world of value and mystery beyond this one. The spiritist movement founded in the 1850s by Allan Kardec continued to prosper, especially in Paris and Lyon, in the late nineteenth century. Laymen and women who claimed to be able to contact the dead had been common in French cities at least since the late eighteenth century, when Swedenborgianism and mesmerism both fuelled a taste for such experiences.[38] Spiritism gained an organized doctrine and an acknowledged leader in Kardec, whose many books continued to be published throughout the Third Republic. Respected intellectuals such as the philosopher Henri Bergson, the Nobel prize-winning scientist Charles Richet and the popular science writer Camille Flammarion all lent their reputations to spiritism in the late nineteenth and early twentieth centuries. There were frauds, of course, and in 1875 the spiritist M. Leymarie was convicted by the Parisian police for conspiring with a photographer to provide spirit-photos of dead relatives to the aggrieved who came to his office in Montmartre. But this case also suggests the popular appeal of spiritism, which claimed to provide direct access to the world of the dead through techniques associated with the discoveries and the prestige of modern science.[39]

The careers of Madame Orsat, a medium from the working-class suburb of St Denis, and Mlle Couédon, who had attended the Wednesday seances of Madame Orsat before developing her own practice on the rue du Paradis, indicate the kinds of concerns that Parisians brought to their mediums.[40] Both of these women, who were active in the 1890s, claimed to be loyal Catholics, and Mlle Couédon in particular became a prophet who predicted the restoration of the Bourbon monarchy. But they also counselled people about their daily problems, giving them medical and family advice, reassuring them about their dead relatives, looking into the future and on occasion helping to locate lost treasure.[41] All of these tasks resemble those that were still being carried out by village sorcerers throughout much of the nineteenth century, and it seems likely that both mediums and their clients, many of them newly arrived from the countryside, were drawing on these older traditions.[42]

What distinguishes Madame Orsat and Mlle Couédon from their colleagues and brought them to public attention was the fascination they held for occultist groups of Paris and Lyon, middle-class intellectuals for the most part whose quest for gnosis led them into a range of diverse beliefs and practices. In the late nineteenth century an occultist circle centred in Lyon formed around the defrocked priest abbé Boullan, whose sect claimed to carry on the work of the visionary Vintras, who died in 1875. In Paris Sar Joséphin Peladan and Stanislaus de Guaïta a founded a new rosicrucian sect in 1888.[43] None of the circles around these individuals or others drew large numbers, but their extravagant claims of spiritual conspiracies and their battles against each other made excellent copy for a daily press whose circulation grew rapidly during this period. Boullan, whose sect was infiltrated by a rival occultist, was accused of engaging in sexual orgies as part of his religious services, an accusation which now seems likely to have been accurate. Boullan was defended, however, by the journalist Jules Bois and the novelist Joris-Karl Huysmans, who in turn accused Guaïta of murdering Boullan in 1896 by employing black magic.[44]

The bitter exchanges in this affair were similar to those published about the fraud perpetrated by Léo Taxil, an anticlerical journalist who pretended to convert to Catholicism in 1885. Taxil spent the next decade publishing books and pamphlets that described the satanic practices of the freemasons, who were plotting with the devil to destroy the Catholic Church. These revelations were welcomed by the church, and Taxil's supporters included Pope Leo XIII, who received him in a private audience. After an enormously successful career publishing these tales, Taxil announced the fraud at a raucous and well-attended public meeting at the Geographic Society of Paris in 1897.[45]

There was a theatricality and a concern for publicity in the explosion of interest in satanism and the occult in the latter years of the nineteenth century which can be seen in the cases of Boullan and Taxil. Another prominent popularizer of the occult was Gérard

Encausse, a publisher and writer who gave himself the name 'Papus'. Encausse, who served as secretary of the International Congress of Spiritism held in Paris in 1900, was also a regular customer at the Chat Noir, the café–cabaret of Montmartre that was a centre for contacts between Bohemian culture and the bourgeoisie in the 1880s and 1890s. Encausse and the other clients of the Chat Noir were attracted in part by Maurice Rollinat, one of the most popular entertainers of the day whose songs of suffering, evil and death captivated the audiences. In the same neighbourhood of Montmartre in the 1890s crowds were drawn also to the Cabaret du Ciel (heaven), where they were served by angels and watched burlesque religious rites. Next door they could enter the Cabaret d'Enfer (hell) through an enormous devil's mouth. At the Cabaret du Néant (nothingness) clients were 'served by undertakers amid caskets and skeletons', and in one of the rooms were entertained by the sight of bodies decomposing and skeletons reappearing.[46] The taste for the macabre and the occult that emerged in spiritist and literary circles of the late nineteenth century also can be seen in the emerging world of popular entertainment designed for urban crowds.

No coherent theology or regularly enacted rituals tie together spiritist seances, occult beliefs and practices and popular entertainments that evoked feelings of mystery and horror. All of these experiences, however, share some common themes that deserve to be noticed in an essay on urban religion in the late nineteenth century. Many Parisians, including some who were practising Catholics, believed in a world of disembodied spirits who could help and sometimes harm humans. This world held the answers to life and death, and although the Catholic clergy had some influence on it, lay experts were frequently the only way to gain access to its mysteries. Good and evil were engaged in conflict, both in this world and in the spirit world, and the results could be deadly for those not properly armed. Knowledge of the proper techniques, however, was uncertain, so that spiritism and its cognate practices could be cultivated if useful or consoling, but just as quickly abandoned. As an alternative to traditional Catholicism the occult held out the promise of secret knowledge that would both solve mundane problems and unlock the mysteries of the universe. Bookshops in Paris, like those in American cities, still have well-stocked sections on the occult, continuing a tradition that can be observed emerging in the early decades of the Third Republic.

The occult alternative, although capable of attracting widespread public attention, was never organized in formal institutions that could gain an intense and long-lasting commitment from large numbers of Parisians. Socialism, as it was defined between 1871 and 1914, was a stronger magnet for those city-dwellers who were dissatisfied with Catholicism. During the first half of the century there had been close ties between the origins of spiritism and utopian socialism.[47] Some contacts between the two movements remained, as is evident in the career of Claude-Anthime Corbon, who was trained as a printer and wood-carver in the July Monarchy, worked as an editor for the working-class paper *L'Atelier* and closed his political career as a deputy in the National Assembly of 1871 and a senator in 1875.[48] In a series of books and pamphlets written in the 1860s and 1870s Corbon criticized the Catholic Church for ignoring gospel truths and claimed that the people possessed an intuitive knowledge of the principles of Christianity: 'One God rules the world; men of all races and colours are equal before him. We all must help each other, and consider ourselves brothers.'[49] Corbon combined his form of Christian socialism, however, with a belief in reincarnation, a doctrine that guaranteed the ultimate achievement of both individual and social perfection. Circles of workers dedicated to the ideas of spiritism were reported in Lyon, where the worker–medium Guillaume organized seances in the silk-workers' neighbourhood of 'Les Brotteaux', in Bordeaux and in some of the cities of northern France.[50]

The religious dimension of socialism, however, did not at all depend on an association with spiritism, or with any other form of supernaturalism. For adherents of socialism such as Corbon, it was the commitment to the earthly goals of mutual aid, justice and social harmony that defined the religious character of the movement, which they saw as an explicit alternative to Catholicism. Edouard Berth, writing in *La revue socialiste* of 1900, echoed Corbon when he accepted the charge that socialism was attempting to establish itself as a new religion:

> And if that's how you want it, yes, [socialism] is a new religion! The feelings that it encourages are in a sense religious! But it is a religion that, to use the words of Marx, will no longer be a false sun, moving around mankind, but a religion that will make man into a real sun, around which it will itself move.[51]

Berth's language reveals the influence of Marxism, a doctrine that attracted increasing numbers of socialists in France in the last two decades of the nineteenth century. Even the explicit atheism and materialism derived from Marx, however, could be expressed in language that qualified as religious. Jules Guesde, the founder of the Parti Ouvrier Français in 1880, and one of the leading proponents of French Marxism, declared in 1897 that 'the Messiah, the Redeemer are the workers'.[52] Jean Jaurès, under whose leadership the various Socialist factions united in 1905, was even more inclined to cast socialism as a counter-church, and to link its ideals with those of Christianity, a line that Guesde firmly rejected. Jaurès, when he called on socialism 'to renew and prolong in humanity the person of Christ', was repeating a theme that was announced among many of the utopian socialists of the first half of the nineteenth century, such as Pierre Leroux and Etienne Cabet.[53]

For Jaurès, socialism offered a moral ideal of social justice and harmony that could motivate people to work and sacrifice for human progress. In his view, capitalism had killed religion by creating a system that emphasized individualism, inequality and conflict at the expense of communal ideals. Jaurès's moral aspirations, couched in religious language, were admired even by his political opponents. According to one story retold by the liberal Protestant, Paul Sabatier, a Catholic bishop in Lyon fooled his audience by asking them to guess the name of a preacher whose sermon he had just read aloud to them. After they had run through the names of several prominent Catholic preachers, the bishop announced that the sermon had been delivered in the Chamber of Deputies by 'Father Jaurès'.[54]

Socialist ideology, with its commitment to peace and justice, could serve as an alternative to Catholic theology, and the socialist emphasis on collective salvation and solidarity was presented as a morally superior alternative to the Catholic concern for individual salvation. These ideas, however, would not have constituted a religious alternative had they not been embodied in organizations and rituals. Pierre Pierrard has compared the POF of Guesde, known for its centralization, carefully articulated hierarchy and discipline, to the structures of Roman Catholicism. The POF also elaborated a set of rituals, including a formal oath-taking ceremony following three months of preparation, which could draw on some of the many socialist catechisms published and distributed in the period 1870–1914.[55] The ritual of acceptance into the POF was generally held in a café, institutions which proliferated in urban neighbourhoods during this period, providing outlets for sociability and solidarity, needs that were not being met by the organized churches.[56] The religious dimension of café life, where workers gathered to talk, drink and sing, was noticed by Paul Leroy-Beaulieu, who wrote in 1868 that 'the cabaret . . . holds for the working classes in present day society the same place as the church in past times'.[57] Communal singing in the cafés was another ritual through which workers could express their sense of themselves, and the values that they embraced. The songs that proliferated in the political atmosphere of the Third Republic included harsh criticisms of Catholicism and the clergy, political anthems and reflections on the hardship of workers' lives.[58]

When Socialists began taking over some municipal governments, a move which began in 1892, they won access to another institution which allowed them to articulate an alternative to Catholicism. Civil baptisms at city halls, for example, were encouraged by some Socialist municipalities, with the children of militants being given a taste of 'the wine of fraternity', a ritual that simultaneously recalled the Catholic mass and the café.[59] In a number of these cities, municipal labour exchanges were established, *bourses de travail* where workers from both the traditional crafts and the newer industries would come for information and training, but also for dances, banquets and other socialist celebrations.[60] During the 1890s the success of Socialists in extending their influence in the cities of France contributed to the creation of a working-class culture in which ideology, organization and ritual provided an alternative to orthodox religion as a source of meaning and moral authority.

The civil burial movement suggests, more than any other set of rituals, the religious dimension of militant socialism as it developed in the last decades of the nineteenth century. For the first two-thirds of the century Catholic clergy had attempted to use their control over funeral and burial rituals as a way of enforcing religious discipline.[61] During the 1860s, however, groups of freethinkers, inspired by the socialist theories of Auguste Blanqui, began to organize civil funerals in Paris as a dignified alternative to Catholic services. Following the collapse of the Second Empire, as we have seen, burial outside the Catholic Church became increasingly popular, particularly in the working-class districts of Paris and Lyon. Blanquists responsible for encouraging the movement in Paris, such as Gustave Tridon, believed that civil burials could play a crucial role in testifying to the value of revolutionary commitment. In its more abstract formulation, the atheism of the Blanquists was 'marked by a sense of immortality in the immutability of the natural processes underpinning the visible cycles of growth and decay'.[62] As put into practice in the civil burial movement, however, socialist ideology expressed simpler sentiments of solidarity with the dead and their relations, a devotion to the cause of liberty and equality and a hope that with the inspiration of the dead to guide them these ideals would be realized.[63]

The burial of M. Despierres in 1876 typifies the socialist ritual that was available in Paris to those who rejected Catholic services during the Third Republic. Following his death in the hospital of Bicêtre, the body of Despierres was accompanied to the cemetery by fifty friends and family members, all of whom wore red forget-me-nots on their lapels. The police reports describe the assistants as members of the working class, and include detailed reports of two speeches made at the graveside, one by M. Dehec and the second by M. Habay, who had been a Socialist candidate from the eighteenth *arrondissement*. Both speakers praised the career of Despierres, who had participated in the revolution of 1830 and had fought consistently for 'the principles of '89' and 'the liberty of humanity'. Dehec closed his speech by calling on those in attendance to continue to work for the cause of liberty: 'We will work so that [the freedom] that you could not see in your lifetime will triumph, and if we don't see it, then our children will.' Habay recalled that Despierres had rejected the 'lying words of the priests' and had found instead 'in the simplicity of free thought another altar than the one found in the churches, which look like palaces'. At the conclusion of both speeches those in attendance shouted 'Vive la République!'[64]

During the first three decades of the Third Republic, socialist parties went beyond the celebration of individual deaths and constructed an elaborate calendar of rituals that recalled events and heroes from the past. The most important of these was the pilgrimage to the *mur des fédérés* in Père Lachaise cemetery, where hundreds were shot and buried in a mass grave in the last battle of the Paris Commune in May 1871.[65] In at least one ceremony socialists engaged in practices normally associated with the Catholic cult of the saints. When the friends and relatives of Théophile Ferré, executed during the Commune, wished to honour him, they exhumed his corpse in 1881, displayed his skull, shot away during the execution and distributed pieces of his hair as relics.[66] Regardless of how one defines religion, it would seem that it should include such behaviour, which was designed to keep alive the memory of the dead and of the values for which they lived and died.

Socialists were not the only ones concerned with creating alternative rituals in urban settings in the last decades of the nineteenth century. The republican regime that triumphed in 1877 sought to legitimize itself through rituals that created a civil religion based on devotion to France, and in particular to republulican heroes who embodied service to the nation. The eighty-two state funerals subsidized by the Third Republic between 1877 and 1940 all took place in Paris, which remained the 'sacred centre' of France, even as the government pursued a policy of dechristianization.[67] State funerals combined elements from the civil burials practised by the Socialists of the 1860s and 1870s and the ostentatious Catholic services available at a high cost throughout the nineteenth century; many funerals also linked traditional religious sites such as the Cathedral of Notre-Dame with state institutions and monuments, in particular the Invalides, the Arc de Triomphe and the Panthéon. The ritual use of these monuments, all of which had associations with death and dying and with the history of pre-republican France, established the continuity of the Republic with the past in the historic and cultural centre of the nation.[68] Victor Hugo's death in 1885 was the occasion for the most famous of the state funerals of the Third Republic, which drew over a million people into the streets of Paris. Despite the carping of the Catholic press, which was offended by the absence of any Catholic service and the seizure of the Panthéon as a site for a cult of national heroes, the funeral was a remarkable success and a key event in the establishment of a French civil religion. Those in attendance remembered Hugo's funeral for years after as a redemptive moment in which the unification of the nation had been realized.[69]

The cult of great men honoured in their death was not just a Paris phenomenon, for during the Third Republic cities throughout France raised statues dedicated to local heroes whose monumental presence in central public areas would remind the citizenry of their social obligations.[70] The coming of the Republic was also marked by the raising of statues to Marianne, its female symbol. In Paris monumental statues of Marianne were raised on the quai Conti and at the Place de la République in 1880, while busts were being placed in the city halls of the *arrondissements*, as they were in city halls throughout France. The Minister of the Interior, De Marcére, defined the values of the cult of Marianne in a speech inaugurating a sculpted group on the Arc de Triomphe that was unveiled as part of the universal exposition of 1878:

> She is noble and simple, calm and strong, seated and at ease. . . . [I]t is the soul of France devoured by noble desires, in love with beautiful things, passionate for justice, and generous. There have been times when she has been disturbed and upset by the ideas and passions of the great Revolution of 1789. But today it seems that our Motherland is at peace.[71]

The cult of the nation enacted through the rituals of state funerals and the symbols of the French heroes was expressed in cemeteries as well, where monuments to those who died in the Franco-Prussian War began to appear in the 1870s. As David Troyansky has shown, these war memorials allowed city-dwellers to relate feelings of grief linked to the deaths of their sons to the sentiments of loss associated with the experience of France.[72] Throughout the nineteenth century cemeteries were being removed from their locations next to churches to sites on the outskirts of towns where they were protected by walls and regulated so that an atmosphere of quiet recollection could be maintained there. This physical separation from the church was given legal sanction in 1881, when the republican government passed legislation that gave control over cemeteries and the placement of graves to communes rather than churches.[73]

The 'laicization' of the cemetery was seen by the clergy and devout Catholics as another sign of the loss of religious faith in France. But the people of Paris and of other French cities remained remarkably loyal to their burial grounds. At the turn of the century, in the midst of the church–state crisis that followed the Dreyfus Affair, over 500,000 people were reported to have visited the cemeteries of Paris on All Saints Day.[74] The mur des fédérés was covered with flowers, city officials laid wreaths at the monument to police officers and firemen who died in the course of duty in the cemetery of Montparnasse and thousands visited their family tombs as well. The celebration of All Saints Day by Socialists as well as believers reminds us that Parisians remained associated with the Catholic calendar and the Catholic religion, a relationship that has endured beyond the official separation of church and state that occurred in 1905. When the government planned to construct a new cemetery well outside the city limits of Paris at Méry-sur-Oise in the 1870s both the Catholic archbishop, Monsignor Guibert, and Pierre Laffite, the leader of the positivists, opposed the measure as one that would compromise the religious and moral sensibilities of all Parisians, regardless of their confessional or political affiliation.[75] The cult of the dead was interpreted differently by Catholics, spiritists, socialists and patriots, but all of these groups shared a common devotion to the dead whose memory ensured continuity with the past and inspiration for the future.

The political history of France in the period 1870–1914 was troubled by endemic and sometimes violent conflicts between the church and the state, conflicts which both the clergy and the anticlericals understood as contributing to fundamental changes in the religious life of France. These trends were highly visible in the cities. They were major sites of industrial growth and political polarization, where new religious movements could develop freely, and were most likely to draw the attention of a rapidly expanding mass audience. At the same time cities remained places where Catholics could look with pride on monuments old and new that suggested that France remained 'the eldest daughter of the church'. They were also places that housed working-class populations that were increasingly disaffected with official Catholicism, even as they remained by and large attached to its major rituals to mark their passage from birth through marriage and death. Finally, cities were places where new religions emerged to compete with Catholicism and with each other. Philippe Joutard, in describing the late nineteenth century, has proposed that 'rather than the progress of incredulity, we see a mutation of belief and of visions of the world'.[76] Religious historians have too frequently been willing to abandon the study of these new beliefs and visions to those interested in social and labour movements. In extending their terrain to include more than just the traditional churches, religious historians run the risk, perhaps, of losing the clarity of focus that has been a chief value of their work. But in taking this risk they may also find that the values and meanings expressed in seances, socialist rituals, state funerals and visits to the cemetery are not as far as they might think from those of the sacraments, masses and pilgrimages of believing Catholics.

NOTES

1 Pierre Pierrard, *L'Eglise et les ouvriers en France (1840–1940)*, Paris, 1984, p. 236.
2 'Les citadins et leurs cultures', in Maurice Agulhon (ed.), *La ville de l'âge industriel*, vol. 4 in *Histoire de la France urbaine*, Paris, 1983,

p. 448. Pierrard, *L'Eglise et les ouvriers* shares the conviction that the working classes were by and large alienated from Catholicism. Religion receives virtually no mention in the important collection edited by John Merriman, *French Cities in the Nineteenth Century*, New York, 1981.

3   Clifford Geertz, 'Religion as a cultural system', in his *The Interpretation of Cultures*, New York, 1973, pp. 89–90; Peter Berger, *The Sacred Canopy: Elements of a Sociological Theory of Religion*, Garden City, NY, 1969. For a thoughtful review of the debates on religion see Gavin Langmuir, *History, Religion, and Antisemitism*, Berkeley, Calif., 1990.

4   Emile Durkheim, *The Elementary Forms of Religious Life*, trans. J.W. Swain, New York, 1965, p. 461.

5   Emile Durkheim, *Moral Education*, New York, 1973; Steven Lukes, *Emile Durkheim: His Life and Work*, New York, 1973.

6   Peter Berger, *A Far Glory – The Quest for Faith in an Age of Credulity*, New York, 1992.

7   Michael Hanagan, 'Urbanization, worker settlement patterns and social protest in nineteenth-century France', in Merriman (ed.), *French Cities*, p. 211. For other data on the growth of French cities see John Merriman, 'Introduction: Images of the nineteenth-century French city', in ibid., pp. 11–41.

8   Fernand Boulard and Jean Rémy, *Pratique religieuse urbaine et régions culturelles*, Paris, 1968; Ralph Gibson, *A Social History of French Catholicism, 1789–1914*, New York, 1989, pp. 170–7; Gérard Cholvy and Yves-Marie Hilaire, *Histoire religieuse de la France contemporaine, 1880–1930*, Paris, 1989, pp. 185–219.

9   The table is an amended version of the one produced by Gibson, *Social History of French Catholicism*, p. 179. The data for the table are derived from Fernand Boulard, *Matériaux pour l'histoire religieuse du peuple français, XIXe – XXe siècles*, 2 vols, Paris, 1982–7.

10 Cholvy and Hilaire, *Histoire religieuse*, pp. 197–8.

11 Adopted from Fernand Boulard, 'La "déchristianisation" de Paris. L'évolution du non-conformisme', *Archives de sociologie des religions*, 31, 1971, pp. 78–9.

12 Stewart Edwards, *The Paris Commune, 1871*, New York, 1971, pp. 283–7. P. Fontoulieu, *Les églises de Paris sous la Commune*, Paris, 1873, reports that fifty-seven of the churches in Paris were attacked in some way during the Commune, while only fourteen were left unscathed.

13 Raymond Jonas, 'Constructing moral order: The Sacré Coeur as an exercise in national regeneration', *Proceedings – Western Society for French History*, ed. Norman Ravitch, 19, 1992, pp. 191–9.

14 Yvan Daniel, *L'équipement paroissial d'un diocèse urbain – Paris (1802–1956)*, Paris, 1957, p. 36.

15 Gerard Jacquemet, *Belleville au XIXe siècle – Du faubourg à la ville*, Paris, 1984, pp. 219–20, 352. In Lyon as well no new parishes were created between 1875 and 1906, when the population grew from 342,000 to nearly half a million. See Jacques Gadille, *Le diocèse de Lyon*, Paris, 1983, p. 251.

16 Daniel, *L'équipement paroissial*, p. 104.
17 F. L. Charpin, *Pratique religieuse et formation d'une grande ville: Le geste du baptême et sa signification religieuse*, Paris, 1964, p. 204.
18 Boulard, 'La "déchristianisation" de Paris', p. 87; for religion in Belleville see also Jacquemet, *Belleville au XIXe siècle*, pp. 351–3.
19 Pierrard, *L'Eglise et les ouvriers*, p. 432.
20 John Merriman, *The Red City – Limoges and the French Nineteenth Century*, New York, 1985, p. 219.
21 Cholvy and Hilaire, *Histoire religieuse*, p. 181.
22 Bonnie Smith, *Ladies of the Leisure Class – The Bourgeoises of Northern France in the Nineteenth Century*, Princeton, NJ, 1981, pp. 97–8.
23 Barbara Corrado Pope, 'A heroine without heroics: The Little Flower of Jesus and her times', *Church History*, 57, 1988, pp. 46–60.
24 Cholvy and Hilaire, *Histoire religieuse*, pp. 155–6; Odile Sarti, *The Ligue Patriotique des Françaises – A Feminine Response to the Secularization of French Society*, New York, 1992.
25 Smith, *Ladies of the Leisure Class*, pp. 138–45.
26 Gibson, *Social History of French Catholicism*, p. 105; Claude Langlois, *Le catholicisme au féminin. Les congrégations françaises à supérieure générale au XIXe siècle*, Paris, 1984.
27 ibid., p. 496.
28 Gibson, *Social History of French Catholicism*, pp. 125–6; Pierre Guillaume, *Médecins, église et foi – XIXe–XXe siècles*, Paris, 1990, pp. 82–8. Langlois points out that the nursing orders drew a disproportionate number of their recruits from cities; see his *Le catholicisme au féminin*, pp. 602–7.
29 Cholvy and Hilaire, *Histoire religieuse*, pp. 182–5; Paul Misner covers the major social achievements in France as part of his work, *Social Catholicism in Europe – From the Onset of Industrialization to the First World War*, New York, 1991, pp. 148–68, 175–88, 288–318. The same ground is covered, but in a more pessimistic context, by Pierrard, *L'Eglise et les ouvriers*, pp. 292–307, 342–411; and the older work of Henri Rollet, *L'Action sociale des catholiques en France, 1871–1914*, 2 vols, Paris, 1951–8.
30 Marcel Launay, 'Les "Saint-Labre" à leurs débuts, 1882–1900', in Yves-Marie Hilaire (ed.), *Benoît Labre: Errance et sainteté – histoire d'un culte, 1783–1983*, Paris, 1984, pp. 117–32.
31 Cholvy and Hilaire, *Histoire religieuse*, pp. 36–50.
32 James Deming, 'Social change, religious renewal, and the transformation of Protestant politics in the department of the Gard, 1830–1852', *French Historical Studies*, 18, 1994, pp. 700–21.
33 Michael Marrus, *The Politics of Assimilation: A Study of the French Jewish Community at the Time of the Dreyfus Affair*, New York, 1971; Cholvy and Hilaire, *Histoire religieuse*, pp. 50–7.
34 Stephen Wilson, 'Le Monument Henry: La structure de l'antisémitisme en France, 1898–1899', *Annales – economies, sociétés, civilisations*, 32, 1977, pp. 265–91.
35 Charles Rearick, *Pleasures of the Belle Epoque: Entertainment and Festivity in Turn-of-the-Century France*, New Haven, Conn., 1985.

THOMAS KSELMAN

36 Eugen Weber, *France – fin-de-siècle*, Cambridge, Mass., 1986, pp. 32–4.
37 Richard Griffiths, *The Reactionary Revolution: The Catholic Revival in French Literature, 1870–1914*, New York, 1965, pp. 122–46; Robert Pincus-Witten, *Occult Symbolism in France: Joséphin Peladan and the Salons de la Rose-Croix*, New York, 1976.
38 Thomas Kselman, *Death and the Afterlife in Modern France*, Princeton, NJ, 1993, pp. 148–50.
39 ibid., pp. 143–59; Yvonne Castellan, *Le spiritisme*, Paris, 1974; Jean Vartier, *Allan Kardec – la naissance du spiritisme*, Paris, 1971, pp. 263–75.
40 Gaston Méry, *La voyante de la rue de Paradis*, Paris, 1896. Méry was a journalist whose articles on these mediums originally appeared in Drumont's *La libre parole*. His work on the mediums include numerous citations from the daily press, which gave Couédon extensive coverage in 1896.
41 Méry, *La voyante*, pp. 98–9, 150–1, 158–9. *Le temps*, 12 March 1898, p. 2, 16 March 1898, p. 2.
42 Judith Devlin, *The Superstitious Mind: French Peasants and the Supernatural in the Nineteenth Century*, New Haven, Conn., 1987.
43 James Webb, *The Flight from Reason*, London, 1971, pp. 95–118.
44 J.K. Huysmans, *Là-bas (Down There)*, trans. Keene Wallace, New York, 1972, which first appeared in 1891, provides a great deal of information about the concerns and beliefs of the occultist circles operating in Paris at the end of the nineteenth century.
45 Eugen Weber, *Satan Franc-Maçon – la mystification de Leo Taxil*, Paris, 1964.
46 Rearick, *Pleasures of the Belle Epoque*, p. 64; Jerrold Seigel, *Bohemian Paris: Culture, Politics, and the Boundaries of Bourgeois Life, 1830–1930*, New York, Penguin, 1986, pp. 231–4.
47 Kselman, *Death and the Afterlife*, pp. 143–50.
48 François Isambert, *Christianisme et classe ouvrière*, Paris, 1961, pp. 236–8.
49 Claude-Anthime Corbon, *Le secret du peuple de Paris*, Paris, 1863. For an excellent summary of Corbon's religious ideas see Isambert, *Christianisme et classe ouvrière*, pp. 238–59.
50 Cholvy and Hilaire, *Histoire religieuse*, p. 180; Lynn Sharp, 'Life's just desserts: Merit and reincarnation in nineteenth-century France', paper delivered at meeting of Western Society for French History, October 1992.
51 Cited in Pierrard, *L'Eglise et les ouvriers*, p. 338.
52 *Almanach de la question sociale pour 1897*, cited in Pierrard, *L'Eglise et les ouvriers*, 1897, p. 425.
53 For a selection of texts by Jean Jaurès see the work edited by Michel Launay, *La question religieuse et le socialisme*, Paris, 1959. Jaurès's sensitivity towards religion may have derived in part from his marriage to a devout Catholic. When his wife insisted that their daughter receive her first communion in 1901 Jaurès co-operated, despite the criticism this earned him from anticlericals; see James Kloppenberg, *Uncertain Victory: Social Democracy and Progressivism in European and American*

Thought, 1870–1920, New York, 1986, p. 215. For the relations between Christianity and utopian socialism see Edward Berenson, *Populist Religion and Left-Wing Politics in France*, Princeton, NJ, 1984.

54 Paul Sabatier, *France Today – Its Religious Orientation*, trans. Henry Binns, New York, 1913, pp. 35–6.

55 Pierrard, *L'Eglise et les ouvriers*, pp. 339–41, 436–7.

56 W. Scott Haine, 'Café friend: Friendship and fraternity in Parisian working-class cafés, 1850–1914', *Journal of Contemporary History*, 27, 1992, pp. 607–26. For the importance of cafés in the industrial cities of the department of the Loire see Michael Hanagan, *The Logic of Solidarity: Artisans and Industrial Workers in Three French Towns*, Urbana, Ill., 1980, pp. 103–5, 137–42.

57 Paul Leroy-Beaulieu, *De l'état moral et intellectuel des populations ouvrières*, Paris, 1868, pp. 73–4, cited in Hanagan, *Logic of Solidarity*, p. 137.

58 For an introduction to the themes of working-class songs in the mill towns of northern France see William Reddy, *The Rise of Market Culture: The Textile Trade and French Society, 1750–1900*, Cambridge, 1987, pp. 253–88. Reddy argues at one point that the dialect songs written by labourers were 'adamantly secular, if not to say irreligious' (ibid., p. 266). But towards the end of his treatment he notes that 'the ethical tenor of the literature was partially compatible with Christian moral teaching' (ibid., p. 285). In my view, it is the 'ethical tenor' of the songs that qualifies them as religious. For the political content of the songs of Aristide Bruant, sung at the Chat Noir of Paris, see Seigel, *Bohemian Paris*, pp. 137–9; for selections from a number of songs see Pierrard, *L'Eglise et les ouvriers*, pp. 315–19, 420–6, 432–4.

59 Joan Scott, 'Mayors versus police chiefs: Socialist municipalities confront the French state', in Merriman (ed.), *French Cities*, pp. 241–3.

60 Merriman, *The Red City*, pp. 210–12; Peter Schöttler, *Naissance des bourses du travail*, Paris, 1985.

61 Thomas Kselman, 'Funeral conflicts in nineteenth-century France', *Comparative Studies in Society and History*, 30, 1988, pp. 312–32.

62 Patrick Hutton, *The Cult of the Revolutionary Tradition: The Blanquists in Politics, 1864–1893*, Berkeley, Calif., 1986, p. 47.

63 ibid., pp. 53–5; Jacqueline Lalouette, 'Les enterrements civils dans les premières décennies de la Troisième République', *Ethnologie française*, 13, 1983, pp. 111–28; Kselman, *Death and the Afterlife*, pp. 106–10; Avner Ben-Amos, 'Molding the national memory: The state funerals of the French Third Republic', unpublished Ph.D. dissertation, University of California, 1988, pp. 158–97.

64 Archives de la Préfecture de Police, Paris, BA 495, 1876.

65 Madeleine Rebérioux, 'Le mur des fédérés', in Pierre Nora (ed.), *Les lieux de mémoire*, vol. 1: *La République*, Paris, 1984, pp. 619–49.

66 Hutton, *Cult of the Revolutionary Tradition*, pp. 121–2.

67 Ben-Amos, 'Molding the national memory', p. 602; Avner Ben-Amos, 'The sacred center of power: Paris and republican state funerals', *Journal of Interdisciplinary History*, 22, 1991, pp. 27–48; Avner Ben-Amos, 'The other world of memory: State funerals of the French

Third Republic as rites of commemoration', *History and Memory*, 1, 1989, pp. 85–108.

68 Ben-Amos, 'Sacred center of power'.

69 Avner Ben-Amos, 'Les funérailles de Victor Hugo', in Nora (ed.), *Les lieux de mémoire*, vol. 1: *La République*, pp. 473–522; André Comte-Sponville, Emmanuel Fraise, Jacqueline Lalouette and Philippe Regnier (eds), *Tombeau de Victor Hugo*, Paris, 1985.

70 William Cohen, 'Symbols of power: Statues of nineteenth-century provincial France', *Comparative Studies in Society and History*, 31, 1989, pp. 491–513; Maurice Agulhon, 'La statumanie et l'histoire', *Ethnologie française*, 8, 1978, pp. 145–72.

71 Maurice Agulhon, *Marianne into Battle: Republican Imagery and Symbolism in France, 1789–1880*, trans. Janet Lloyd, Cambridge, 1981, p. 173.

72 David Troyansky, 'Monumental politics: National history and local memory in French *Monuments aux morts* in the Department of the Aisne since 1870', *French Historical Studies*, 15, 1987, pp. 121–41.

73 Kselman, *Death and the Afterlife*, pp. 165–221.

74 *L'Humanité*, 2 November 1904, p. 3.

75 Philippe Ariès, *The Hour of Our Death*, trans. Helen Weaver, New York, 1981, pp. 541–5.

76 Philippe Joutard, 'Une mutation des croyances plus qu'un progrès de l'incrédultié?' in Philippe Joutard (ed.), *Du roi très Chrétien à la laïcité républicaine*, vol. 3 of J. Le Goff and R. Rémond (eds), *Histoire de la France religieuse*, 4 vols, Paris, 1988–92, p. 529.

7

'A CRUCIBLE OF MODEST THOUGH CONCENTRATED EXPERIMENT'

Religion in Sheffield *c.* 1840–1950

Clyde Binfield

A city's religion accents and is accented by the interaction of its topography, its economy, its culture and its politics. Sheffield's topography, economy, culture and politics are distinctive. Here is a place which had been in the second rank of British towns since the early eighteenth century and has been in the first rank of British cities since the mid-nineteenth century and yet it has at no point been a regional capital and it is hard even to see it as a centre. It was incorporated only in 1843 and became a city only in 1893. Until the 1980s it was demonstrably Britain's largest industrial city, unusually dependent on one cluster of trades, the metal trades. Their structure, however, was a strange mix of giant firms in the 'heavy' metal and small firms in the 'light' trades. That mix balanced (or unbalanced) Sheffield's economy from the 1840s to the 1950s. Suggestive correlations can be drawn between human relationships within those trades and a politics whose Liberal, Conservative and Labour aspects have all been distinctive. Similar correlations might be made with the city's culture. Sheffield might not spring to mind for music, art or literature, but it has been locally influential (which is not necessarily the same as parochial) in all three. Sheffield's culture may be qualitatively elusive but it is satisfyingly complex.[1]

Sheffield's religion shares the characteristics of its other faces. In conventional terms it has been an ecclesiastical late developer. It became an Anglican cathedral city in 1913, with a bishop from 1914, and it became a Roman Catholic one in 1980.[2] That defines the public contours of a city whose chief religious features have been consistently evangelical while their complexion has been decidedly

Methodist. Methodism, indeed, has accented the Anglicanism of a city whose Catholicism, whether Roman or Anglican, has been relatively weak, for all that the chief ground landlords have been the Dukes of Norfolk. It has certainly stamped the city's trinitarian Protestant Dissent, not least because Sheffield was strong in non-Wesleyan Methodism.[3]

> The pulpit stood on the inside of the front wall, not as at present, and on three sides of the chapel there was a deep, sloping gallery capable of holding a couple of hundred people. On the basement floor the old worm-eaten pews were rather heterogeneous in shape, some square, some long, and some very short. A kind of large, square communion pew fronted the pulpit. There was no mistaking the dilapidated appearance of all this antiquated pewing. The wood-buttons could hardly hold the old doors upright, and the wooden flooring was so broken to pieces that only boys playing at marbles or rabbits seeking a warren could make any use of it. Consequently the congregation used to ascend to the gallery, leaving downstairs a sort of wilderness of empty old pews. [Thus one visitor to the usual afternoon service who arrived late] of course, seated himself in one of the numerous empty pews below, and found himself almost alone. The parson, however, appeared to have a congregation somewhere, as hymns were loudly sung, and the sermon, judging from the preacher's looks, must have had very attentive listeners. No wonder, after service, that the lonely downstairs worshipper asked. . . . 'Where was your congregation concealed, for I couldn't see one of them?'[4]

This is the first of five quotations which form the spine of this chapter. They are expressive of urban or urbanized religion between 1860 and 1914, broadly representative but also particular to Sheffield. This one represents Old Dissent as it survived into the 1860s reflecting, its heterodoxy notwithstanding, the folk religion of an area which, being neither wholly rural nor wholly urban, had sustained a disproportionate number of Dissenters since 1662.[5] The second quotation, which is also about the 1860s, although as re-created in 1914, represents New Dissent reflecting the folk religion of a rapidly industrialized city:

> The people are all assembled in the gallery – there each can see, as well as hear, all that is going on. Perhaps the Superintendent

Minister is in the pulpit and president at the feast. It may be Thomas Nightingale. Grace has been sung, the 'Mugs' containing the water, and the 'Baskets' containing the bread, have been passed from hand to hand, and each has taken his or her portion, and in solemn silence the symbols of fellowship have been supped and eaten, save when the hush was broken by a half-subdued 'Hallelujah!' or repressed 'Glory!' from Thomas Gregory or Richard Woodcock. This over, thanks sung, and the collections for the poor taken, the minister rises with his thumb in his waistcoat pocket, and 'facing' the people side-ways, he begins seriously to tell of all the way the Lord has brought him, of his anxiety for the souls of men, of how his soul is in travail till men be born again, and as he proceeds his speech sparkles with proverb and adverbial phrases, humorous and sententious, each brilliant flash evoking some interjection from a soul in sympathy. Or it may be that J.S. Workman is the minister, and while he relates his experiences he makes some statement or other, when Brother Gregory cries out 'I believe it!' 'Whether Brother Gregory believes it or not it's true', replies this emotional and dramatic minister. That man's ministry was 'a flame of fire', and his experience would have heat enough in it to warm every soul of that gathering of the saints.

Or it may be the 'ruler' of the feast was the saintly, scholarly, refined and eloquent Thomas M'Cullagh, a man whose charm and grace would melt for a moment the assembly into a mood of subdued feeling, but when he or any other man had sat down all the pent-up and restrained feelings of the company would find vent in some experience of joy and thanksgiving. The meeting would now be fairly warmed up. Then up rose Brother Bowns – now nearing the end of his pilgrimage – from his seat just behind the clock, and round about him sat the young men of his morning class. He told the story of God's love and leading through all the days, and the people knew his fidelity and sincerity to equal his claims to communion with God, and they joined him in praising his Redeemer and Saviour. Perhaps he would be followed by one or other of his young men, if they did not wait for the 'fathers' to have their turn first.

Or, perhaps Brother Depledge was next. This brother, deaf and eccentric, would loudly address his pastor as 'my beloved Minister', and thank God for all His blessings since the last ticket meeting. Before he had finished, his gesticulations and remarks had become extremely interesting; this was one of the 'events' of the Park Love-feast in those days.

Sister Irons might be next, known of all for her self-sacrificing devotion for the weal of womankind in the Park, and she would tell of the secret of her strength and the spring of her devotion, and rally the people to real service for her Lord.

Now that the ladies have begun, others follow, among them, perhaps, Mrs Nightingale, the wife of the Minister, who could hold an audience and help it almost as well as her husband.

George Crowther, whose soul was seen shining through his eyes, Thomas Charlesworth, George Moulson, John Tankard, and many another kept things going either by experience or by song. 'Happy Day' and 'My God, I am Thine' were hymns with which the Experiences were interspersed.

Brother T. Gregory, butcher, class leader, school teacher, and other things all in one, enthusiastic and eager, thanked the Lord that He had given him the best wife in England, and perhaps related on one occasion how that a lady came into his shop to buy meat, and as 'time is fleeting and eternity will soon be upon us', he had, while sharpening his knife that it might better do its work in supplying his customer, asked the good lady, 'Are you prepared to die, madam?' and how, to his surprise, his customer fled.

He had simply been asking whether she had yielded herself to God's claims. He was about his Master's business, but he had made a mess of it.

Another leader told how he had on his class book three kinds of members, Quarterly, Monthly, and Weekly, and liked the last best of all.

Joshua Gregory, not so tempestuous as his brother, spoke with a gentle lisp; 'John Tankard always said words of sense and soberness'; while Jennings's words fell like a torrent upon the assembly, and young and better educated youths sat agape at the wonder of this 'Boanerges' in the parti-coloured suit, who had recently come from Northampton. So with shouts of victory and songs of triumph – the latter sometimes struck too high, it is true – and with testimony following testimony, the time sped happily along, and the clock shewed the hour for bringing this Methodist Agapé to a close.[6]

The third quotation, a biographical recollection of the 1880s, represents Anglican myth in the making, a sacramentalist's view of a town centre parish church:

> The long bare walls of the aisle without any break in them, the poverty and misery of the ornaments, the hideous East Window with its alternate borders of red and blue, the miserable little altar, and above all the stuffy smell of the church through it being opened only twice a week.[7]

The fourth quotation, a journalist's impression of a visit to Sheffield in 1909, represents Liberal evangelicalism and the Social Gospel and it reflects two layers of how Edwardian Sheffield seemed to outsiders:

> Sheffield staggered all the delegates. Its residential districts and its neighbouring hills are good to see. It is a hive of industry. Its name the world over is a warrant for good steel. But its human specimens! The condition of the poor may, perhaps, be worse in other industrial centres in England, but certainly no delegate . . . had ever seen the like in any white country overseas or even imagined it possible within the limits of human nature.
>
> We had been at the great gun works. We had seen the making of armour-plate and of cannon. It was all wonderful. Then our procession of motor-cars wound slowly and with many blockades through the narrow crowded streets to the type foundry whence came the fonts that furnish the printing offices of the world. The finished product of the machines everywhere was perfect. The human product alone was marred.
>
> It was not that the people were poor. It was not even that they were hungry. Poverty and hunger are curable conditions. What struck every observant delegate was the utter blankness of the faces that looked up at us from the pavement or down at us from the windows, with scarcely enough capacity for human interest to wonder who we were or what we wanted. Block after block it was the same. Never a sign of humour. Never even a flush of human envy. Stooped shoulders, hollow chests, ash coloured faces, lightless eyes, and, ghastliest of all, loose-set mouths, with bloodless gums, and only here and there a useful tooth.

195

Literally, hundreds of women between seventeen and seventy crowded close to our motor-cars that day, and the marks were on them all. Those toothless mouths of men and women and children told the story. One touch of disease made that whole crowd kin. 'What do you think of it?' asked a London reporter of a Canadian editor. 'It's Hell', said the Canadian. And his companion from Australia could not suggest any other fitting word.[8]

The fifth quotation, from 1913, suggests the possibility of those points where Sheffield's farthest residential districts met their neighbouring hills:

This new building is now being erected on an excellent site, overlooking the Derbyshire moors. It is designed to serve the purposes of a chapel for the time being, with the idea of eventually becoming the school hall when the future church is erected on the unoccupied portion of the site.

The chapel has seating accommodation for 210 adults, and chairs are proposed to be used instead of pews. At the rear are two large vestries, which can be thrown into one room by folding back the partition which divides them, thus giving a room to serve as church parlour and be used for week-night services, etc.

Ample lavatory and cloak-room accommodation is provided . . . .

The walls are being built of stone obtained from the Derbyshire hills. . . . The building will be thoroughly well lighted throughout, and the stone-mullioned windows are to be glazed with leaded lights. . . .

The style of architecture adopted is a modernised Gothic, with an avoidance of all elaborate detail. . . .[9]

Each of these quotations reflects, and refracts, generalized perceptions as well as nuances of spirituality and of liturgical response, of social attitudes and of citizenship. And each is also peculiar to Sheffield. The first describes Underbank, the Unitarian chapel 4 miles west of Sheffield where, so it was recalled, Foxe's *Book of Martyrs* used to lie on the table for a congregation of craftsmen: Heber Revitt, the razor-blade forger, Gilmans the cutlers, Gillott of Uppergate, Sheffield's last razor scale presser, men whose artisan independence was captured by a local Methodist – 'they believed in liberty; they loved the simplicities of life'.[10] By contrast the second quotation, describing a love-feast in the Wesleyan Park Chapel, conveys at once a volatile society, in visible transition, and a ritual unique to Methodism and close to the heart of its spirituality. Here is a powerful society gripped in prayer, future Master Cutlers, Lord Mayors, Liberal leaders, Presidents of Conference among them. It is Wesleyan, not Primitive Methodist or Free Methodist, in a circuit where, as a sermon-tasting journalist noted of a neighbouring society's large evening congregation a few years later, though the working and poorer classes were in evidence, there was 'more an assembly of the great middle classes than any I had seen'.[11] The third quotation is less a hiccup than the influential exception that none the less proves the general rule. It describes St Matthew's, Carver Street, a small, dignified but jerry-built church, jostled by the premises of little mesters in a constricted central parish endowed by a firmly Protestant snuff manufacturer and awaiting its third incumbent, the sacramentalist G.C. Ommanney (1850–1936). Father Ommanney was a southerner, of naval stock. He was also an Oxford man. He went deeply against the Sheffield grain. Yet he survived rows, riots, obdurate churchwardens, evangelical secessions and thirty years of archiepiscopal discipline to turn St Matthew's into 'one of the famous churches of the Catholic revival in England', with sung mass, confession, the reserved sacrament, incense. With John Sedding, one of the most creative architects of the English Catholic revival, to catholicize the chancel, Ommanney transformed his straight up-and-down essay in Victorian gothic streetscape into a surprising cache for the Arts and Crafts: hammered copper representative of the *Benedicite*, iron screens copied from Pisa, Derbyshire stone and marble in place of linoleum.[12] More than any other man Ommanney brought Catholicism into Sheffield's Anglicanism and made it credible; but he did so on Sheffield's terms. St Matthew's was no more a *parish* church than any other central Sheffield church. It was a congregational church, and although its physical context and Father Ommanney's sense of mission set in train an admirable tradition of social work that could not make it anything else.

The context for the fourth and fifth quotations is avowedly Congregational. In November 1909 the magazine of Highbury Quadrant, a large North London Congregational church, reprinted a piece by J.A. Macdonald, the editor of the *Toronto Globe*. He had returned from the Imperial Press Conference where what for him was 'the background of every reminiscence' – 'the bloodless, mirth-less, hopeless face of the common crowd' – had been intensified by an excursion to Sheffield. The 'social problem everywhere is appalling almost to the point of despair', he sighed:

> How long will a great nation go on breeding weaklings and criminals? How long will such a nation remain great? And how long will it be counted safe for Canada to admit the human output of Britain's drink-cursed slums? But all this may be a matter of politics.

Given the background of the People's Budget and the prospect of old age pensions, Macdonald could see some signs of hope and it was this which encouraged the church magazine to reprint his piece:

> The thing that impressed me most hopefully was the growing recognition on the part of the strong of a real responsibility, personal and national, for those who are weak. With this is joined a growing tendency to go back to the causes of those des-perate results. Original sin and total depravity no longer explain adequately and finally the social problem. Other terms are used. 'Land Laws' and 'liquor laws' are the modern phraseology.[13]

With that the magazine's readers could no doubt return to their traditionary chapel radicalism. Drink was at the bottom of this, as it always had been. Yet could old-fashioned radicalism translated into the language of eugenics, emigration and, for the first real time, democracy, remain old hat for long? Certainly the new language was grist for the mill of chapel suburbia as original sin turned into 'the social problem'. But why Highbury's fascination with Sheffield?

The answer to that lies with Nonconformity's densely meshed networks and connexions. Highbury Quadrant Congregational Church was young, vital and alert, with a minister to match. H.E. Brierley was in his mid-30s, theologically advanced and his first pastorate had been at Queen Street, the most liberal of Sheffield's central Congregational churches. There Brierley's successor, the Londoner William Blackshaw, compounded the theological liberalism with social activism.[14] He created the Croft House Settlement, combining its wardenship with the pastorate of Queen Street. It had been Blackshaw's ambition to convert the moribund Garden Street Chapel into a purpose-built settlement on the lines of London's Toynbee Hall or Mansfield House. Garden Street became Croft Hall, for men and boys, to be followed by Croft

House, 'a Settlement House of Residence, where the Warden could reside and where work among women and girls might be carried on under the roof of a Christian man and woman's home'. In 1908 a 'Citizens' Bazaar' raised £2,500 for this.

Citizenship was the motif for this settlement 'where those who may be wearied of their present surroundings may learn to know a worthier way of living'. It was implicit in its brave rhythm of clubs, classes, camps and easy culture, and signposted in its outdoor services ('The want of a second suit of clothes makes people shy of attending our indoor service'). Blackshaw, brimming over with 'enthusiasm for the poor', left his manse near the Botanical Gardens to live in the Settlement. He used his year as Chairman of Sheffield's Congregational Association to publicize his message:

> Are we keeping the world wholesome? The trade and politics, the domestic and civic life of the world need the purifying influence of the Christian character to keep them clean.
> We live, thank God, in stirring times, we are citizens of a great and progressive city, may God grant that we may help to make our times more definitely Christian, and our City more conspicuously a City of God.[15]

That was in 1908. In 1909 the Imperial Press Conference visited Sheffield and the Congregational Union of England and Wales held its Autumnal Assembly there for the fourth time since 1849. Motions were passed on the Belgian Congo, relations with Germany and education; addresses were given on the Brotherhood Movement, Christian Science, Modernism and Calvin (as theologian and as social reformer); there were demonstrations of teaching methods (the Canadian George Hamilton Archibald had just hit Britain and opened his college for Sunday school teachers at West Hill, near Birmingham) and of preaching; there were testimonies to temperance and to overseas mission. Queen Street housed a conference on 'The Business Side of Church Life' while in the Sunday School Union's Montgomery Hall, J. Wycliffe Wilson, deacon of Nether Chapel, Chairman of the Guardians, former Lord Mayor, uncle of a future Lord Mayor and son-in-law and brother-in-law of past mayors, chaired a Sectional Meeting. Its theme was the Poor Law Report. Its speaker was Sidney Webb.[16]

With this we return to the *Quadrant Magazine*. Sheffield was a crucible for the Nonconformist Conscience and Highbury's bolder spirits were keen to experiment. The church's Young Men's Society ran four Sunday talks in November and December 1909 on 'The Poor Law Commission Reports', following 'more particularly the lines laid down by the Minority [Report], and by Mr Beveridge in his standard work on the question'.[17] They were given by Edward Smallwood and Arnold Freeman.[18] Smallwood was a coal merchant who briefly became Liberal MP for East Islington. Freeman, whose family were cigar and tobacco manufacturers, was an outrageously Oxford young man whose life work lay neither in North London nor Oxford but in Oxford Street, Sheffield, where in 1918 he took charge of a YMCA settlement. There the young man who in August 1909 had assured Highbury's Congregationalists that the Poor Law Commission's Report reflected 'the greatest social campaign ever fought in the history of England',[19] now under YMCA auspices plunged himself into investigating the equipment, education and environment of Sheffield's workers and ran Social Study Schools helped by keen young Christian university men – Donald Wilson, who was a great-nephew of Wycliffe Wilson, Hedley Hodkin, whose father ran a building firm and helped run Sheffield's Wesleyan Methodism, although he himself took Anglican orders, Edwin Barker, who became Education Secretary for the National Council of YMCAs and Social Responsibility Secretary for the Church of England. Although this was too orthodox for Freeman who took the Sheffield Educational Settlement out of the YMCA and himself out of his Baptist and Congregational upbringing, it was of a piece with what was already a firm tradition of Christian radicalism in Sheffield.[20]

For Freeman's settlement was *sui generis* without being unique. Wycliffe Wilson's niece, Dr Helen Wilson, Sheffield's first woman general practitioner, was closely associated with Rutland Hall, a settlement which was later named after her.[21] William Blackshaw's Croft House had its parallel in the work of T.T. Broad, minister at Burngreave Congregational Church from 1893, pioneer of Kingsley House (the North Sheffield Settlement), advocate of district nursing and colonies for epileptics and Liberal MP for Clay Cross from 1918 to 1922.[22] For their part the Wesleyans turned their developing work into one of the city centre's most suggestive architectural statements, and its social context was no less suggestive. At Brunswick, where the city first edged into its suburbs, the minister from 1893 to 1896 was Samuel Edward Keeble. His response to inner-city change led to complaints of politics in the pulpit. 'God bless you', shouted a supporter during one of Keeble's sermons: 'Aye,

Brother Webster, God bless me and you, and God help me to give the right message with all the faces I see around me lined with greed, money-making and sensuality – and they don't know it.' Keeble's experiences as a London draper's boy had made him 'vow that if ever I got into the ministry I would wage ceaseless and uncompromising warfare against such a system'. At Leeds in the late 1880s he read *Das Kapital*, that 'masterly study of the economic development of human society', and in Sheffield he wrote his first book, *Industrial Day-Dreams*, with its description of socialism as 'neither a tendency nor a sentiment, but carefully defined and logically formulated theory' which, in a purified form, was 'simply an industrially applied Christianity'. Like Blackshaw, Keeble remained denominationally credible, for it was his social rather than his theological views that were advanced, and while they were enough to keep him out of connexional office he became a key figure in Methodist social development.[23]

The first Sheffield outworkings of that development were focused from 1905 on the Victoria Hall which replaced Norfolk Street, the mother church of Sheffield Methodism. Here was an exercise in Edwardian superlatives: £46,000 cleared in three years, opening collections of £9,000, a mix of civic drama proclaimed externally by a tower which was Sheffield's best celebration of social religion and evangelistic ingenuity and expressed internally by an arrangement which put all the galleries at street level, with 'hardly a dark corner'. Here from 1905 to 1924 George McNeal proclaimed the full Edwardian social gospel with two deaconesses on his staff, a cinematograph for the hall, a 'Gospel Chariot' for meetings out of doors, a holiday cottage for those who could not afford such things and what later generations would describe as job creation: a wood yard which diversified into cleaning, whitewashing and light industry and in 1908–9 gave 5,903 day's work to 6,000 men.[24]

That style, continued in the 1920s by Percy Medcraft with his nightly Open Conferences on the Christian Approach to Industrial Problems and his unease at the superficiality of the social gospel's charitable ambulance work, had its echoes elsewhere in Sheffield. In 1915 the congregation of Sheffield's second Unitarian church moved uphill and upmarket to Unity Church, Crookesmoor, described as the last Unitarian church to be built on the grand scale. There it appointed J.R. Vint Laughland, fresh from an attempt to turn his Islington church into 'a flourishing worker's centre'. Congregations rose at what now became 'Unity Church and Social

Centre' and Laughland supposedly claimed that 'In what was loosely termed the Labour movement there was more religion than was to be found in all the churches put together.' He certainly told Unity that 'if you are going to be anything other than progressive I can readily foresee this place becoming a warehouse or a cinema, or an up-to-date boarding house. I would urge you to fight shy of respectability'.

Laughland lasted eighteen months at Unity, moving on to two Labour candidatures and a literally riotous ministry at a maverick Liverpool Baptist chapel before returning to the United States where he had trained.[25] Crookes was a restless suburb, for there were more shades of social experiment at its Congregational church built in 1907.

This had Sheffield's first Congregational woman deacon, elected in 1912, and its first woman minister, Wilna Constable, called jointly with her husband in 1918, a year after Constance Coltman, the first in Britain, had been ordained in London. Crookes's 236 members took nervous pride in an experiment 'unique so far as Sheffield is concerned' and the Constables, their departure regretted in 'religious, educational, social and literary circles', left in August 1920 after a brief and bumpy ministry.[26] Crookes's lay preachers included the General Secretary of the Sheffield YMCA responsible for Arnold Freeman's involvement in the Educational Settlement and through whom another YMCA secretary entered the local Congregational ministry to serve the Tabernacle, in an area lately made notorious by the Sheffield gangs. This man, 'the poor man's lawyer of Upperthorpe' (the very district vacated by Unity Church, in its flight to Crookesmoor), also had oversight of Sheffield's first new Congregational church for twenty-five years, planned as an 'artistic utility building' in three stages from 1933 and placed centrally though none too strategically in Shiregreen, a new housing estate for people from the Tabernacle's Upperthorpe hinterland.[27]

Perhaps Laughland and the Constables offered notoriety rather than experiment in the Sheffield of William Blackshaw, T.T. Broad and George McNeal. They went beyond what might be accepted as advanced or incorporated within the local tradition; but the point is that there was an acceptable local tradition rippling out from the city centre to suburbs and council estates alike.

In this context the fifth quotation becomes relevant. Park Wesleyan Chapel, whose love-feasters have already been glimpsed, had begun in 1831 as a suburban cause. In 1901 the love-feasters' children moved uphill to where Park's best houses now were and opened Victoria Church, spired, gothic and expensive, £1,000 of it plus pulpit, font, oriel window and ornamental board bearing the decalogue, given by Bassett, the workmen's overalls manufacturer whose Wesleyan family connections made liquorice allsorts, furniture and machinery and were turning whole ranges of the grander western suburbs into select Methodist reserves.[28] Park's suburban folk of 1831 were thus still suburban seventy years on, but on new sites with new buildings to reshape what were now traditions, while their old buildings, serviced by an obstinate remnant, had become inner city. Those were natural processes, common to all large cities and to all denominations. They were none the less without precedent for the people who experienced them. Consequently they exercised the minds of lay and ministerial leaders.

Some of the responses have been referred to – Croft House, the Victoria Hall, an imaginative range of social gospel work sustained by the still deep-pocketed consciences of still strong central congregations; or the restless attempts of artisan, clerkly and middle-management Burngreave, Crookes and Crookesmoor to retain the best of all worlds in ambitious new causes. Their suburban responses were as urgent, necessary and problematic as any inner-city ones. Hence the significance of Dore and Totley Union Church, subject of the fifth quotation, at Sheffield's outermost south-west suburban rim.[29]

This fifth quotation concerns the announcement in a national denominational yearbook of a seminal stage in a cause's development. What had started in the 1860s as an isolated preaching station for a subrural community of metal trades artisans, serviced by the Wesleyan Reform Union (Sheffield's home-grown Methodist denomination which has consistently stood apart from all other Methodist attempts at union), had become by the 1890s a suburban community of professional and managerial refugees gamely worshipping in a tin tabernacle next to the new railway station which had made their flight possible. These people were Congregationalists, Baptists and Free Methodists, joined by Presbyterians, Plymouth Brethren and some Anglicans, but not by Wesleyans, since they already had their own chapel. The Wesleyan Reform preaching station was now a Union Church although its Baptist members never succeeded in installing a baptistry and bread-and-butter considerations took it steadily into the Congregationalism which best reflected a pragmatically evolving church order, carefully hammered out by the trial-and-error of self-consciously representative and articulate men and women. Theirs was a church on the prosperous side, whose people stood on their own feet, none of them rich, none therefore needing to defer to anyone, a collection of strong personalities balanced more by mutual respect than social position. Class barely came into it because there were very few working-class members. Such a church could only grow: fifty-three members in 1911, sixty-seven in 1913, over eighty in the Sunday school with sixteen teachers by 1912, and all the accessories for homely chapel daily life – the Ladies' Sewing Circle, the Quiet Hour, the League of Young Worshippers, the Literary Society and the Football Club and that perennial theme with variations, the annual fund-raising event. The result was opened by Mrs Wycliffe Wilson, backed by Sir Francis Belsey, doyen of the national Sunday School Union whose family united Baptists and Congregationalists,[30] and by the Sheffield Congregational chairman who hailed it as a Free Church, a Democratic Church and a Union Church. Certainly it was a decent, sensible, gently ecclesiastical building echoing the Derbyshire moors with its stone from the Derbyshire hills. Externally, thanks to its architect's sense of colour and material, it was clearly a church. Internally it was a no-nonsense assembly hall, a space ready to subordinate itself to grander things come the next forward movement.

Yet that is not quite how events turned out. Although the church was cumulatively successful by the standards of an active and extrovert community, and in the next fifty years its architects supervised further significant ancillary extensions, its membership never exceeded 200 and there was no need for the main church as originally planned. So had the cause failed? Here was a natural Sunday meeting place for incomers to a city which was at last developing the infrastructure of a city rather than of an industrial agglomeration, as well as for those who were moving out from that city. Theirs were semi-detached lives, but their consciences alerted them in a variety of practical ways to the needs of housing-estate religion in Sheffield's north-east in the 1930s and in Sheffield's south-east in the 1950s. They were an outworking and not simply an outpost of what had been emerging as Sheffield's response to the Christian imperative.

Which brings us to the historiographical myth which has so powerfully coloured all perceptions of that response: E.R. Wickham's *Church and People in an Industrial City*.[31] The book's motor was the

Anglicanism which has so far played little part in this account. In 1913 Sheffield became a diocese. There had been fears that the impedimenta of cathedral episcopalianism would hinder evangelistic advance in what in Anglican terms, and Father Ommanney notwithstanding, was a famously Low Church city. Those fears were justified in so far as they concerned the emergence of cathedral ideas, with predictable conflicts, which remain unresolved, about the proper role of a cathedral in an industrial city when all the national models were set in the mould of Barset.[32] None the less Sheffield's first two bishops, Leonard Hedley Burrows (1914–39) and Leslie Stannard Hunter (1939–62), were powerful solvents of such fears. Although Bishop Burrows was a southerner whose sympathies were on the high side (so that at the last there was a notable *rapprochement* with Father Ommanney), he was able to channel his manliness as 'defined in the nineteenth-century public school tradition' into an acceptably visible episcopal bearing and authority which he combined with diplomacy, stamina and a determination to get to know his long, thin, disparate diocese. He began with a motor car even if he remained tall-hatted to the end, and his episcopate saw a flurry of necessary administration as well as church extension in new housing estates and rationalization in central areas that no other denomination could match.[33] Bishop Hunter lacked his predecessor's style, he had none of his visible authority and there was nothing traditionary about his Anglicanism: his background was Congregationalist, his wife's was Methodist and each developed within rather than reacted against those backgrounds.[34] He belonged to no ecclesiastical party. He was felt to be an ineffectual preacher and known to be a forbidding pastor. None the less his gifts, liberated by service in that seed-bed of ecclesiastical leadership, the Student Christian Movement, lay in strategic administration on a national stage. What precluded him from success in Congregationalism's still pulpit-bound polity and would have found inadequate scope in Methodist connexionalism or Presbyterian collegiality, discovered its proper level in the English national church. Hunter was beyond peradventure a National Churchman under whose leadership a notoriously counter-national diocese set the pace for national change. Yet he combined experiment with considerable skill in tapping traditional sources. The generously directed Victorian world of local Anglican grandees, whose giving steadily exceeded that of the Methodist cousinhoods of what was popularly and fairly seen as a Methodist city, had its last flowering under Hunter. A case in point is the Sheffield Industrial Mission, which outsiders might regard as Hunter's chief memorial and which was as much an opportunity for employers as for their employees, and would have been inconceivable without their copartnership.

The mission's prehistory began with a creative exploitation of Barsetshire. In February 1944 the Duke of Norfolk appointed a new chaplain, E.R. Wickham, to the Shrewsbury Hospital, an old Sheffield charitable foundation. In April Hunter made him Bishop's Chaplain to Industry and in 1950 he became Industrial Missioner to the diocese in what Hunter later described as 'a long-drawn penetration; a slow breaking down of suspicion and misunderstanding, a combined operation of clergy and laity within industry'.[35]

It will be clear that Hunter experimented in a city already used to religious experiment, but he did so at a watershed point. Traditional ecclesiastical loyalties had been shaken by the inner-city clearances and new estates of the 1930s, and war and the reconstruction which followed intensified the process. The political loyalties, too, which had become part of Sheffield's religious face also disintegrated, or were transformed, or went underground. The Congregational dominance of Sheffield's Liberalism ended with the Liberal Party's disintegration and the scattering of municipally-minded Free Churchmen to the winds. Some became prominent in the Conservative-dominated opposition, others in the swiftly consolidating Labour establishment, but all did so as individuals who happened to be Methodists or Congregationalists or whatever. In such a vacuum Bishop Hunter, the national churchman, shaping citizens for the Kingdom, was the man for the hour. Hunter liberated a political Christianity which addressed the changed situation. It had a model in the Industrial Mission and a core text in Wickham's *Church and People in an Industrial City*.

This book was a pioneer in its contexting of urban religion. Its methods have since been refined, redefined, queried and developed but it remains an important source for any Sheffield historian and a key document in its own right. It is best seen as a Hunterian tract. Wickham worked on two assumptions. First, that the 'weakness and collapse of the churches in the urbanized and industrialized areas of the country should be transparently clear to any who are not wilfully blind', and, second, that 'to-day the religious life of the city is weak, probably weaker than many other industrial cities'.[36] He aimed to explain this by exploring the interrelated history of

Sheffield's churches and their people and then to apply what he found to answering the acute modern missionary problem. He assumed, naturally for a national churchman, that in a Christian nation the Kingdom is accessible to all and the church is its prime agent. He also assumed, more surprisingly for a national churchman although not for one who knew his Sheffield, that the parish was not enough. It no longer projected the totality of community life. To reach that totality an agency was needed which could be 'deployed to cover an industrial area, ... to create that web of personal relationships which is the very heart and foundation of any serious contribution that the Church might make'.[37] This fitted in with the powerful congregational tendencies in Sheffield's Low Church tradition; it drew on Wickham's fascination with that other Sheffield fact, Methodism; it had an ecumenical logic; it predicated a partnership between ministers and laity; and it was an adventure in public Christian citizenship, marking the Catholic Church rather than some shrunken fellowship of 'saints'.[38] If these ideas had an impact far beyond the Industrial Mission's actuality it was because Wickham was only one of a whole generation of able men ensnared into wider usefulness by the Kingdom-directed, citizen-oriented Hunter. Their immediate credibility was certainly buttressed by Wickham's novel and convincing use of statistics of church attendance over the previous 100 years, but perhaps more significant if less arresting was his understanding of the Sheffield context and his shaping of a solution true to that context and, arguably, independent of any apparent statistical message.

With this we return to the context with which this chapter began, the topography, demography and economy of Sheffield, as accented by an aristocratic landownership which was none the less divorced from its defining ecclesiastical jurisdiction.

A population which increases from just over 2,000 in the early seventeenth century to just over 14,000 in the early eighteenth, and from 65,000 in the early nineteenth century to 460,000 100 years later, poses problems for those who believe that a nationally accepted religion embraces all within the community and for those who believe that religion should grip all hearts. For the former the problem is one of provision, for the latter of mission. Here, on the one hand, is a city of such mushroom growth that it has become both Britain's largest proletarian and its largest industrial city which, because it has never been an administrative or commercial capital, has not developed the quality of professional and mercantile leadership which distinguishes other provincial centres. On the other hand, here is a long-established settlement consistently characterized by a specialized economy, its characteristics encouraged and further defined by a topography which fostered clusters of self-contained communities and which also marked the area as the frontier between the North and the Midlands. Here, moreover, is the economic heart of Britain's only surviving dukedom of medieval creation, its holders great officers of state, whose undoubted influence has none the less been doubly deflected by the vagaries of inheritance and the implications of the family's Roman Catholicism.[39] If Sheffield's small Catholic community benefited, its Anglican community benefited even more since, though the larger part of the tithes of Sheffield parish church belonged to the Dukes of Norfolk, the patronage was in the hands of a succession of local families whose churchmanship was generally low. If the advowson and the tithes had not been separated and the Howards had not been Catholic, then, given the size of the original parish of Sheffield, its ecclesiastical history would have been very different.[40] Instead, the temper of Sheffield's Anglicanism has been complemented by that of its Protestant Dissent, and for all their mutual tensions both reflected or adapted to the peculiar rhythms of the town's long-established, specialist economy; as indeed did the immigrant Christian communities, the Irish Catholics, who added numbers to the select local presence fostered by the Norfolk connection, the Midland General Baptists whose church became Yorkshire's largest Baptist congregation, the Scottish and Irish Presbyterians whose prosperous St Andrew's point-edly added Sheffield's first Free Church spire to those of the inner city. This was because a local economy characterized into the early decades of the twentieth century by the persistence and resilience of small metal firms naturally fostered a craft and artisan culture which provided a counterpoint to the national culture and formed particularly grateful ground for Dissenters. It was this community which the Congregational Union tapped for its Autumnal Assembly in 1909, and Alderman Wycliffe Wilson, the precious metal smelter whose firm had started in 1760, was its representative man. People knew their place in this community, and Anglicanism had its place in it as well as Methodism, yet it was not class-ridden. Neither was it the whole community by 1909.

For over and against this artisan world, with its generations of Sheffield names and settled occupations, there was the frontier world of mushroom growth. Politically this new world of heavy industry, with its hierarchies of line management and its proletariat, was where the Liberal city turned into a Labour one, but religiously there was no comparable development save where the new communities managed to develop something of the networks and continuities of the old. Then, perhaps, the proletarian and artisan cultures met in the Co-operative Movement, or the Settlements, or the experiments pioneered by Anglicans, Methodists and Congregationalists, or, indeed, the Catholic parishes laboriously staked out in new housing estates, and 'the bloodless, mirthless, hopeless face of the common crowd', which so haunted the editor of the *Toronto Globe* and the readers of the *Quadrant Magazine*, was, here and there, individualized.

To press the point further: Sheffield's Anglicanism was shaped in one very large parish, 24 miles in circumference. Given its size, the separation of its tithes and patronage and the nature of that patronage, it was never more than an adequate living. Its incumbents, however, were resident; several had long ministries, and from the nineteenth century all were evangelicals and all were energetic. The parochial ideal made least sense in a Low Church climate where good preaching was at a premium as well as good pastoral practice and it left open the problem of those who, it might be argued, were socially and politically unreachable: for could they, even should they, be reached religiously, however the local ecclesiastical unit was structured? Only Christians were bound to answer in the affirmative.

Sheffield's achievement was, at first, against the odds. The relevant surveys of Sheffield's religious attendance are the Census of 1851 and the 'census' undertaken locally in 1881 by the *Sheffield Independent*. In that time Anglican attendances rose from 14,881 to 33,835, their proportion of church attendances increased and there were signs, even within the Low Church economy, of a significant shift in sacramental practice.[41] This was a considerable feat even if the unreached had thickened visibly and were a generation further set in their ways, an inevitable testament of failure.

Inevitably, too, much of that Anglican effort had been reflected in the subdivision of Sheffield's monster parish, the strategic local planting of parishes and the redefinition of boundaries, although none of this ran counter to the essential congregationalism of local Anglican life. This Anglican forward movement is best seen as a complementary response to Methodism rather than as the reaction against Rome or Political Dissent that it might have been in other cities. For Methodism had become the cement of Sheffield's religious experience. By 1851 Sheffield was a Dissenting town. Considerably more of its attendances in March 1851 were in chapel (56.5 per cent) than in church (34.3 per cent) and the balance lay in Methodist chapel. Wesleyan attendances (24 per cent) were second only to Anglican ones and the Methodist totality (36 per cent) exceeded Anglican attendances.[42] Wesleyan Methodism was thus Sheffield's likeliest alternative to the Established Church, and given the Methodist temper not just of South Yorkshire but of the adjoining counties and the rest of the West Riding, born (disruption notwithstanding) of over eighty years of connexional discipline and localized flexibility, it was a powerful alternative. It was also a young alternative, for the peak decade of Sheffield's Methodist chapel-building had been 1830–40.[43]

Now the heart of this chapel worship lay not in attendance but in commitment: the privileged believer's membership, with its consequent duties. The congregational polity of Baptists and Congregationalists no doubt bred a different dynamic from the connexional polity of Methodism but believers' membership characterized each. In E.R. Wickham's phrase: 'To the church one "went", the chapel one "joined".'[44] Church embraced the whole community; it had catholicity. Chapel was all-inclusive – for those who joined. That need for commitment kept down numbers, but the equal need to make believers presupposed a missionary approach. The fellowship of believers was thus apart from the world and yet constantly engaging with it; and then there were the inescapable social and political implications for any who dissented from the national church which had somehow to be compensated for within Dissent. Hence the networks characteristic of all Dissenting communities, including Quakers and Unitarians, the two least marked by *believers'* membership in 1851. It might seem, therefore, that the religious temper and polities likeliest to succeed in a society fashioning its own structures were those least likely to benefit from any crude numbers game; but their dynamic was bound to have a profound affect across the denominational board.

The resolution of that paradox, and the impact of the dynamic which it bred, can be seen in the five quotations which have formed the spine of this chapter. They have illuminated a tradition of experiment at least as old as Sheffield's municipal incorporation. They have not exhausted that tradition. There has been no mention in this chapter, for example, of the People's College, founded in the

1840s by the Congregational minister, R.S. Bayley, or of the Church of England Educational Institute, in its prime in the 1860s, or of the initiatives pursued after 1886 by the Sunday School Union from its powerhouse in the Montgomery Hall or after 1891 by the YMCA from its complex a stone's throw away in Fargate.[45] These straddled the accessible artisan and working classes as well as the lower middle classes, all of them consolidating in the 'unimaginative but well-built' brick terraces encouraged by the ninety-nine year leases granted to small-time speculative builders thanks to the relaxed policies of successive Dukes of Norfolk and their local agents.[46]

What can be made of this, granted that conclusions cannot properly be drawn from a story which obstinately refuses to end? Two broad points might be adduced. The first is that Sheffield's Christian strategies have been notably fertile in releasing energy and talent. They have steadily issued in new directions, they have left their imprint on the city and they continue to do so. They have also, as must happen to any living organism, contributed to their own decline: nineteenth-century competition, twentieth-century rationalization, parochialism and extra-parochialism have all 'failed'. The statistics prove it. Churchgoing in Sheffield, which in 1881 was put at 29 per cent of the population, in 1965 was estimated to range from 4 to 15 per cent, according to areas of housing type, but one-third of Sheffielders lived in those areas where only 4 per cent worshipped.[47] In 1989, 5.8 per cent of South Yorkshire's adults attended church, compared with a national average of 9.5 per cent.[48] There was little statistical comfort here for any of the mainstream Christian traditions. The importance of all the effort, none the less, lies more in what it has generated than whom it has brought in.

This brings us both to the second broad, though more complex, generalization and to where this chapter began. If a city's religion accents and is accented by the interaction of its topography, its economy, its culture and its politics, so the interactions of its church life will be marked by a periodic, perhaps a constant, redefinition of boundaries. This has certainly been a feature of Sheffield's church life at any point since the 1840s. Organizationally there can be no doubt of it: the development, for example, of two twentieth-century dioceses and the parochial ebb and flow of their nineteenth-century prehistory, or the shaping between 1932 and 1972 of Methodist and United Reformed districts from the pooled resources of separated Methodists and of Congregationalists and Presbyterians respectively, testify to an intelligent corporate determination to adapt, consolidate and survive. While a similar point might be made about Sheffield's political establishments, understanding them to include such bodies as the Cutlers' Company or the Town Trustees, there is no other local organizational complex so broadly, so continuously, yet so flexibly rooted as Sheffield's churches. Is their tenacity, then, tribute to an organizational mastery that has been underestimated by analysts who have understandably focused on the inescapable statistics of numerical decline? Or is there, literally, another genius at work? For if a city's religion accents and is accented by its culture, politics and topography, the historian, in catching the nuances of accent must never mistake them for the language itself. The organizational aspect of church life is a matter of accent. It is ignored at the historian's peril since accents tell a great deal about origins and assumptions; but it is not the language. Neither is the redefinition of boundaries a purely administrative matter, for convincing boundaries must define concepts as well as areas or populations. In the case of religion the concepts have somewhere to do with revelation, its apprehension, its interpretation and its consequent communication as truth. Those boundaries can never be immutable. Their significance is constantly changing, for although the truth can never be relative its interpretation can never be anything else; and the ecclesiastical charting of this means that a theological understanding must be added to all the historian's other skills. Indeed, a theological understanding should be foundational for a church historian.[49] Church history is easily reduced to a series of organizational responses to a presumed fall from grace: it becomes one long heroic pessimism. That is not unreasonable provided always that a host of counterpoints are also brought duly into play, chief among them that of a constant, and therefore hope-full, response to call. E.R. Wickham's seminal *Church and People*, too often seen and perhaps largely written as a contribution to the organizational debate, might now best be seen as a contribution to the theological debate and striking testimony to what he himself described, but none the less understated, as 'a crucible of modest though concentrated experiment'.[50]

NOTES

1 The complexity might be deduced from a select bibliography: S. Pollard, *A History of Labour in Sheffield*, Liverpool, 1959; D. Smith,

Conflict and Compromise: Class Formation in English Society 1830–1914: A Comparative Study of Birmingham and Sheffield, London, 1982; S. Pollard and C. Holmes (eds), *Essays in the Economic and Social History of South Yorkshire*, Barnsley,1976; E.D. Mackerness, *Somewhere Further North: A History of Music in Sheffield*, Sheffield, 1974; M. Tooby, *Our Home and Native Land: Sheffield's Canadian Artists*, Sheffield, 1991; and, of course, Ruskin's *Fors Clavigera: Letters to the Workmen and Labourers of Great Britain*, London, 1871–84, were Sheffield focused. These aspects are brought together in J.C.G. Binfield, R. Childs, R. Harper, D. Hey, D. Martin and G. Tweedale (eds), *The History of the City of Sheffield*, 3 vols, Sheffield, 1993.

2   In both cases the way to a diocese was paved by a suffragan or auxiliary bishop: in the case of the Anglicans there was a resident suffragan bishop of Sheffield from 1901; for the Catholics there was a resident bishop of Tinisa from 1968.

3   Sheffield's Quakerism and Unitarianism have been more distinguished in individuals than numbers. For religion in Sheffield see the chapter of that name by C. Binfield, in Binfield *et al.*, *History of the City of Sheffield*, vol. 2. What follows is a shortened and reshaped version of that chapter.

4   W. Blazeby, recalling the 1860s, quoted in F.T. Wood, *A History of Underbank Chapel Stannington*, Sheffield, 1944, p. 116. This compares with the account of a comparable, if orthodox, local cause, under the same minister for forty-six years, with Dr Watts's hymns pitched to a tuning-fork, sermon texts painstakingly translated from the Greek, Squire Woodcroft in his large square corner pew each Sunday evening (he was at Church each Sunday morning) and Dissenting funerals, preferably on a Saturday, solemnized by the minister at the deceased's house before the vicar conducted the statutory Anglican rite in the parish graveyard: H. Garside Rhodes, 'Reminiscences of Fulwood Chapel', *Sheffield Congregational Year Book*, 1906, pp. 42–4.

5   This is explored in D.G. Hey, 'The changing pattern of Nonconformity, 1660–1851', in Pollard and Holmes (eds), *Essays*, pp. 204–17.

6   J.J. Graham, *A History of Wesleyan Methodism in Sheffield Park, Sheffield*, Sheffield, 1914, pp. 159–61.

7   F.G. Belton, *Ommanney of Sheffield*, London, 1936, pp. 43–4.

8   J.A. Macdonald in *Public Opinion*, quoted in *Quadrant Magazine*, 12: 11, November 1909, pp. 225–7.

9   *Congregational Year Book* (hereafter *CYB*), 1914, p. 140.

10   Wood, *History of Underbank Chapel*, p. 115, 123–8.

11   'Criticus', who between 1869 and 1874 wrote for the Sheffield *Post*, quoted in E.R. Wickham, *Church and People in an Industrial City*, London, 1957, p. 139.

12   Belton, *Ommanney of Sheffield*; [J.D. Preece], *St Matthew's Sheffield*, 2nd edn, Sheffield, 1976.

13   Macdonald, *Public Opinion*.

14   The church was formed in 1878 and had 602 members by 1909 (*CYB*, 1910, p. 278). For Harold Eustace Brierley (1873–1954), see

CYB, 1955, p. 507; for William Blackshaw (1866–1953), see *CYB*, 1954, pp. 505–6.

15 *Sheffield Congregational Year Book*, 1908, pp. 3, 19–21, 1909, p. 14.

16 *CYB*, 1910, pp. 26–32.

17 *Quadrant Magazine*, 12: 11, November 1909, pp. 222, 229: 12: 12, December 1909, pp. 238–9.

18 For Edward Smallwood (1861–1939), see M. Stenton and S. Lees (eds), *Who's Who of British Members of Parliament*, vol. 2, 1886–1918, Hassocks, 1978, p. 330; for Arnold Freeman (1886–1972), see J. Bellamy and J. Saville (eds), *Dictionary of Labour Biography*, vol. 9, 1993, pp. 91–5.

19 *Quadrant Magazine*, 12: 8, August 1909, pp. 162–3.

20 Freeman's spiritual future lay with Anthroposophy and his settlement was now quite definitely *sui generis*, or rather *Freemanii generis*. I am indebted to the late Edwin Barker, Dr Sylvia Dunkley, Miss Grace Hoy, Dr David Martin and Professor Jonathan Rose for further information about Arnold Freeman.

21 Dr Helen Wilson (1864–1951) practised in Sheffield from 1892. See C.L. Dickins, *In Memoriam Helen Wilson 1864–1951*, London, 1952.

22 Thomas Tucker Broad (1863–1935), *Sheffield and District Who's Who*, Sheffield, 1905, pp. 155–6; Stenton and Lees (eds), *Who's Who of British Members of Parliament*, vol. 3, 1919–1945, Hassocks, 1979, p. 42.

23 For S.E. Keeble (1853–1946), see M.G. Edwards, *The Rejected Prophet*, Chester, 1977, pp. 7, 12–13; S.E. Keeble, *Industrial Day-Dreams: Studies in Industrial Ethics and Economics*, London, 1896, pp. 33, 105.

24 N. Farr, *At the Heart of the City: A Methodist Mission in the Twentieth Century*, Sheffield, 1991, esp. pp. 17–26.

25 He was right about Unity: just as its predecessor became a cinema so Unity is now a university hall of residence. For James Robert Vint Laughland (1885–1957), see D. Steers, '"The bare headed minister" – The radical career of James Vint Laughland', *Transactions Unitarian Historical Society*, 20: 2, April 1992, pp. 114–23 .

26 *Sheffield Congregational Year Book*, 1919, p. 62; 1921, p. 81.

27 For Stephen Tredinnick (1885–1970), minister at the Tabernacle, see *Yorkshire Congregational Year Book*, 1972–3, p. 38; I am also indebted for information to Mrs N. Aizlewood. The church at Shiregreen is contexted in an unpublished paper by C. Binfield, part of which has appeared as 'A climate for art's encouragement: A provincial architect and his contacts, John Mansell Jenkinson 1883–1964', *Sheffield Art Review*, 1992, pp. 2–11.

28 Graham, *History of Wesleyan Methodism in Sheffield Past*, p. 244.

29 This section is based on the Executive, Deacons' and Church Meeting Minute Books in the possession of Dore and Totley United Reformed Church Sheffield.

30 For Sir Francis Flint Belsey (1837–1914), see *Who Was Who, 1897–1916*, London, 1920.

31 Wickham, *Church and People*. The historiography of the Wickhamite

myth has been very helpfully traced in H. McLeod, *Religion and Irreligion in Victorian England: How Secular was the Working Class?* Bangor, 1993.

32 See D. Lunn, *Chapters Toward a History of the Parish and Cathedral Church of St Peter and St Paul*, Sheffield, 1987.

33 For L.H. Burrows (1857–1940) see Mary Walton, *A History of the Diocese of Sheffield 1914–1979*, Sheffield, 1981, pp. 17–59.

34 For L.S. Hunter (1890–1983), see Walton, ibid., pp. 59–119. The most accessible treatment is G. Hewitt (ed.), *Strategist of the Spirit*, Oxford, 1985; the fullest account is J.D. Preece, 'Leslie Stannard Hunter (1890–1983): Bishop of Sheffield (1939–62)', M.Phil. thesis, University of Sheffield, 1986.

35 For an appraisal of the mission, see D.L. Jeremy, *Capitalists and Christians: Business Leaders and the Churches in Britain 1900–1960*, Oxford, 1990, pp. 313–20; P. Bagshaw, *The Church Beyond the Church: Sheffield Industrial Mission 1944–1994*, Sheffield, 1994.

36 Wickham, *Church and People*, pp. 11, 13.

37 ibid., p. 245.

38 ibid., p. 271.

39 See J.M. Robinson, *The Dukes of Norfolk: A Quincentennial History*, Oxford, 1982.

40 See Lunn, *Chapters Toward a History*, passim.

41 Wickham, *Church and People*, p. 141.

42 H. Mann, *Census of Great Britain, 1851: Religious Worship in England and Wales. Abridged from the Official Reports*, London, 1854, p. 129.

43 Hey, 'Changing pattern of Nonconformity', p. 217.

44 Wickham, *Church and People*, p. 141.

45 For R.S. Bayley (1801–59), see *Dictionary of National Biography*, 22 vols, Oxford, 1885–1900; *CYB*, 1860, p. 175; for the Institute, see W. Odom, *Fifty Years of Sheffield Church Life 1866–1916*, Sheffield, 1917, pp. 10–13; for the Montgomery Hall, see M. Bamfield, *Sheffield Christian Education Council: Montgomery Hall. A Centenary of Christian Education 1886-1986*, Sheffield, 1986; for Sheffield YMCA, see D. Thompson, 'Sheffield Young Men's Christian Association. A short centennial history', typescript, Sheffield, 1955.

46 Robinson, *The Dukes of Norfolk*, pp. 177, 194, 199.

47 McLeod, *Religion and Irreligion*, p. 57; M. Reardon, *Christian Unity in Sheffield: A Report Presented to the Sheffield Council of Churches, September 1967*, Sheffield, 1967.

48 P. Brierley, *'Christian' England: What the 1989 English Church Census Reveals*, London, 1991; P. Brierley, *Prospects for the Nineties: Yorkshire and Humberside Region*, London, 1991.

49 This is a theme explored by P. Catterall, 'Church decline, secularisation and ecumenism', *Contemporary Record: The Journal of Contemporary British History*, 5: 2, autumn 1991, esp. p. 283.

50 Wickham, *Church and People*, p. 243.

8

URBAN POPULAR RELIGION AND THE RITES OF PASSAGE

Sarah Williams

Descriptions of urban religion in the late nineteenth and early twentieth centuries reveal a high level of participation among working-class populations in religious rites of passage.[1] The involvement of these groups with the church at strategic moments in family and community life is frequently regarded as anomalous in the light of the failure of the majority of the working class to attend church on a regular basis. Historians have, in general, followed the avenues carved out by contemporary middle-class observers and have assumed a correlation between an absence of regular church practice and the supposed prevalence of religious indifference among the people. Consequently, the anomaly presented by the pattern of occasional church practice in the form of the rites of passage is generally explained in relation to factors external to the beliefs of the participants and ascribed to motives other than religious persuasion, such as a desire for social status, recognition and respectability.

However, a reliance on the perspectives of contemporary middle-class observers, many of whom were professionally identified with the church has led to the assessment of religious phenomena on the basis of ecclesiastical, institutional and orthodox criteria and to a tendency to overlook the meaning which the actors themselves ascribed to the pattern of occasional conformity and to the concerns and goals of which the enactment of these rituals was a part.

In recent years, the use of oral and autobiographical material has offered an effective medium by which to escape from some of the dilemmas of this approach. It has presented the historian with a means through which to counterbalance and cross-verify the external observations of contemporary commentators with the perspectives provided by the actors themselves. In so doing it has suggested a way in which to appreciate in more detail the inner life of popular culture and to consider the complex and multifarious character of urban popular religion. Despite these developments the value of this wider approach has, as yet, to be fully appreciated. Where oral and auto-biographical material has been used in studies of late nineteenth-century urban religion it has been employed primarily to shed light on the relationship between working-class culture and institutional Christianity.[2] Yet Christian elements of belief, such as the occasional observance of the rites of passage, were simply one part of a more complex and wide-ranging pattern of urban popular belief which, if it is to be appreciated fully, must he considered within the wider repertoire of popular values and presuppositions, which extended beyond the parameters of both the church and orthodoxy

During a study of the south London borough of Southwark between c.1880 and 1939 an attempt was made to expand the ways in which these kinds of material can be used in order to reconstruct the character and content of the beliefs of infrequent church attenders.[3] Southwark was at this time an area notorious not only for its concentration of working-class life but for low levels of working-class church attendance and for what was regarded as lamentable irreligion. In addition, the period roughly from 1880 to 1939 was marked by the consolidation and stabilization of a distinct urban popular culture within the area. The metropolitan borough thus provides an ideal context in which to consider religious sentiment outside the parameters of formal church practice as an integral facet of culture. A series of interviews was carried out with former inhabitants of the borough, the majority of whom attended church simply for marriages, baptisms, churchings or funerals The oral recollections of these individuals were considered alongside working-class autobiographies, written reminiscences and folklore material. These, in turn, were examined in the light of the perspectives provided by churchmen such as those interviewed by Charles Booth's team in 1898–9. The religious values of these groups were examined from the perspective of popular culture while the institutional church and its attendant practices and teachings were considered only in so far as they emerged within the actor's frame of reference.

This study challenged a straightforward association between infrequent church attendance and religious indifference. It suggested that the occasional participation of working-class groups in the rites of passage was part of a system of popular belief which, although it embraced certain aspects of church-based religion, remained independent of the full arbitration of both the church and orthodoxy.

This popular expression of religiosity was based upon different definitions of religious duty, belief and association and it arose from distinctive ideals and images of goodness and morality.

The characteristic feature of this kind of religious response was its defiance of institutional categories and definitions and its combination of various types of religious expression. The inhabitants of south London were exposed to a range of religious idioms which interacted with one another and were combined within popular culture to form a distinct repertoire of popular belief. Popular religion was neither church-based religion nor folk religion but nor was it divorced from either type of religious discourse. The inhabitants of Southwark both talked about the world and saw the world through a combination of theoretically competing discursive worlds. On occasions such as the watch-night service and the baptism different discourses overlapped within a single understanding of religious meaning. The two narratives could operate in conjunction with one another, not merely in terms of a crude opposition between the vicar and the participant but within a range of beliefs held by the single actor. For the participants the two discourses were intermeshed. They may well have been able to employ an orthodox narrative to explain their motives in bringing a child forward for baptism. This was not merely adopted to placate or appeal to the vicar or the lady visitor on the doorstep, nor was it solely an instrument of *embourgeoisement*. The participant may have believed sincerely in the efficacy, the validity and the importance of the content of that narrative, and yet at the same time they may also have acted and justified their behaviour as part of a folk discourse in which other expectations and assumptions were operating to constrain them to act in a certain way.

The dual operation of these dimensions or languages of belief did not, however, necessarily diminish the depth of each component part. The vigour and persistence of the various elements which composed the religious repertoire should not be underestimated. Orthodox rites and symbols, for example, continued to hold an evocative power within popular culture, while, on the other hand, elements of folk belief had not been fully depersonalized nor had they degenerate into mere luck as some suggest.[4] They retained many of the characteristics which historians are more ready to ascribe to them in the mid-nineteenth-century rural context.

The present chapter will consider briefly this characteristic feature of urban religion by examining some of the meanings, values and explanations ascribed by the participants to their involvement in church ceremonies at major transitional points in life. Individuals such as Ivy Sutton, born in 1910, the daughter of a compositor from Peckham, and Ivy Philimore, born in 1904, the daughter of a clerk in Dulwich, were among a substantial number of former inhabitants of Southwark who held strong and clearly articulated folk beliefs and who, at the same time, insisted vehemently on the necessity of observing various orthodox rites. For them participation in the rites of passage formed one part of a response to the superempirical realm which embraced and extended beyond orthodox images and ideals. These rituals were facets of a belief in an overarching supernatural realm in which the affairs of men were bound up in a cycle of fortune, fate and good and ill luck. This realm was not seen as removed or far off but as an immanent presence through which the fortunes of individuals were mediated as ill luck or good fortune affected their daily lives. Furthermore, the superempirical realm was not seen as above the manipulation of individuals. The mediation of one's fortunes could be effected, for example, through certain actions, practices or rituals. These included seemingly 'trivial' practices, but they also extended on occasions to the weaving of spells and to more elaborate rituals. In addition, they involved the employment of specific charms, mascots and amulets and the use of a body of folk wisdom in the form of medical lore. The latter involved a strategy for controlling, allaying or transferring the adverse effects of illness through the enactment of rituals or the use of charmed objects. On occasions, the charms used for this purpose drew on overtly Christian symbolism and imagery to increase their power or efficacy, and for some south Londoners the church-based rituals of churching, baptism, marriage and watch-night services to celebrate New Year were associated with these responses to the superempirical sphere. Ivy Sutton, for example, recalled during one oral interview how her mother ensured that her daughters were churched after giving birth, that her children and her grandchildren were baptized and that members of her family were married in church:

> She wasn't [a churchgoer] and nor was my Dad, they never punched that in to 'y, the church, church, church . . . but say when you had a child, oh before you went out to have that baby christened you had to go to church, oh yes and she wouldn't let you in her house if you hadn't been churched . . .

no, she believed all that, but . . . no we were all been married
in a church, because she didn't hold in with registry office. If
you, anybody said . . . in her mind you wasn't married and ur
. . . you only had to mention going up to town hall and she'd
do her nut.[5]

Ivy Sutton's oral testimony does not explicitly state that her mother's
refusal to admit an unchurched person to her house was connected
to specific superstitions but the connection is strongly implied: 'She
was very superstitious. I don't know what she thought you was if you
didn't go to be churched'.[6]

The description of churching was given in the context of a description of folk practices and it was a prelude to Ivy Sutton's description
of her mother's other superstitions. These included the prescription
of behaviour within the household in order to ensure that various
kinds of ill luck would not befall the family and that specific forms
of good fortune would be attracted in their place. Incidental habits
and actions, such as avoiding the spilling of salt, the crossing of
knives, the opening of umbrellas indoors and the placing of shoes on
the table, were caught up in a more extensive expression of folk belief.
This included a belief in portents and foreknowledge, the enactment
of spells and rituals and the employment of charms for particular
purposes including the cure of diseases. In much the same way that
certain household practices were limited on the basis of a fear of
invoking ill luck or from a desire to attract good luck, so the behaviour and actions of a woman who had just given birth were restricted
until such time as she underwent the churching ceremony. Ivy Sutton
gave a vivid account of the implications of this:

I know one of my sisters, it was November, thick fog, that was
her second child. We started out early . . . well where we'd
been all the churches were closed and she said, 'Ivy we'll come
this way round'. We walked everywhere to be churched and
um . . . (never knew it, you don't never have a church shut
really), no every one we tried . . . closed. . . . 'We'll go over
Surrey Square . . .'. Where we walked . . . all closed but I knew
I couldn't take her back home and she knew we daren't go to
my mum's house but we ended up at St George' Church (thick
fog), 'Oh look', I said, 'there's a light on in the church.' I had
her other little girl with me, up the steps we went. They used
to have a kind of nurse there. I spoke to her, she said, 'Oh yes
straight away, Come in where is she?' I stood for that babe

as well 'cos in them days you had to get another witness
and anyway . . . I stood outside the church I could hear . . .
(the fog was so thick), I could hear this little kid and I could
hear the mother speaking so I said 'Excuse me' (you couldn't
see a hand before 'y). 'What's the matter love?' the woman
said, 'don't be offended by what I am going to ask but could
you come in the church and stand by my sister? the baby's
being christened and we've got to get somebody else where
we've been.' 'Oh yeah', but whoever that woman was I don't
know. . . . My mum once you'd had a baby if you hadn't been
to be churched she wouldn't have 'y in her house and we knew
it.[7]

It is striking that in this case the ceremonies of churching and
baptism were held together. The dramatic structuring of the narrative of the memory underlines the meaning of the experience. David
Clark has highlighted a similar pattern of the social 'liminality' of
the mother after childbirth in his study of a late nineteenth- and
twentieth-century Yorkshire fishing village. Here, a mother's actions
were also limited and she was prevented from engaging in normal
day-to-day activity until she had been churched.[8] These kinds
of restriction were associated with the belief that bad luck would
follow the appearance of an unchurched woman in the community.
They form a common theme in the writings of folklorists describing rural communities of the late nineteenth century. William
Henderson, for example, when describing the folklore of the
northern counties of England described how

As to the mother's churching, it is very uncanny for her to
enter any house before she goes to church and she carries ill
luck with her. It is believed also that if she appears out-of-
doors under these circumstances and receiving any insult or
blow from her neighbours she has no remedy at law.[9]

Such associations were also made in early twentieth-century
Southwark. The Reverend T. P. Stevens, the rector of Southwark
Cathedral from 1917 to 1924 and the vicar of St Matthew's, New
Kent Road from then until 1930, described in his memoirs of cler-
ical life in London how

In the poorer parishes churching is a matter of very great
importance. The mother must be churched at the earliest
possible moment. There is superstition that something will

happen if there is delay. I discovered a poor woman waiting for the church door to open one bitterly cold night. She told me she had been there half an hour, having made a mistake in the hour, she said she did not like to return home because she might meet an acquaintance on the stairs and that was unlucky.[10]

Similarly, in Southwark getting married in church was, in some cases, associated with a range of folk beliefs and practices. Certain churches were believed to be particularly lucky. St Paul's Church in Kipling Street, Bermondsey, for example, was a very popular church for weddings as it was considered to be highly efficacious in this respect. The marriage ceremony itself was surrounded by a number of superstitions. *Cassell's Saturday Journal* for 1906 for instance described how

> Superstition played its part at another wedding solemnised at the same church [St George-the-Martyr, Southwark]. It is a belief with many people, not exceeding the coster and the labouring element of the London community, that an interrupted marriage ceremony is a bad omen. The crowd rushing into the church could not be kept back whereupon the clergyman left his place at the altar and gave orders for a padlock to be put on the door. The married couple and their friends felt sure that bad luck would follow this interruption and made smothered protests in the church. The next day the sister of the bride lost a baby girl and shortly afterwards the father of the bridegroom died.[11]

The *Journal* claimed that in a certain part of the borough this marriage was talked about for months afterwards. In addition, whenever a member of Ivy Sutton's family was married, her mother would take a bit of salt and a bit of bread and a few 'odd coppers' and a bit of coal and place them in a box to ensure the lasting prosperity and good fortune of the new family,[12] just as her rural counterparts had done and were still doing at this date:[13]

> Yeah, take a bit of salt (any of us got married), bit of salt bit of bread a few odd coppers and a bit of coal and it's all be covered up. You don't touch that box . . . you'll never be without money, course you wouldn't, 'cos that couple of coppers would be up there.[14]

The watch-night service was also associated with the prevention of bad luck and the ensuring of good fortune. For many individuals, their absence from a religious service on New Year's Eve was sufficient to generate anxiety about their fortunes in the new year. Henry Bradley, the son of a carman from Cromer Road, London, born in 1903, described in his interview with the Essex Oral History Project how his parents would only ever attend church for the watch-night,[15] and Rose Embleton of Bonner Street, Elephant and Castle, insisted that she attended the midnight service each year without fail.[16] Similarly, F.A. Kent, the son of a crane-slinger from Canning Town, born in 1901, when asked if his parents attended church replied 'Oh yes – they were inclined to be that way; they would go on – nearly always go on – nearly always go on – Old Year's Night.'[17] Kent went on to describe his own attendance at these services.[18] Descriptions highlight the crowded nature of these services. They were often filled to overflowing with those who had left a nearby pub just before the stroke of midnight in order to see the new year in inside the church, chapel or mission hall: 'In many cases they rush out of the public house to get into the watchnight service just before the stroke of midnight.'[19] Some would even bring their fish and chips in with them,[20] while others were clearly the worse for drink. Yet it was none the less important to 'spend the closing minutes of the old year in a religious service',[21] whatever may have preceded those moments. The desire of participants to 'start the year right', by undergoing a public act of worship, was associated with a belief that to do otherwise was unlucky.[22] The notion of spiritual cleansing which formed a prominent part of these services may have closely paralleled the practice of cleaning and tidying the house, washing the crockery and cleaning the hearth before the new year as a symbol implying starting time over again at its beginning, or, as David Clark puts it, 'scourging the passing year's accumulated dirt'.[23] Clark describes such cleansing rituals in the North Yorkshire fishing village as both a physical and a moral act whereby past actions, misdemeanours and failings were ritually expelled: 'The slate thus wiped clean is prepared once more for the imprint of "New Year's resolutions".'[24]

In much the same way, during the First World War, an extensive survey carried out by a committee of churchmen attributed a super-stitious attachment to the ritual of communion. It noted that for a number of people participation in the communion service before going into combat was sufficient to ensure divine protection, just

as the enactment of a folk ritual or carrying a lucky charm
was believed to enhance one's chances of safety in battle. One
respondent noted that 'They believe that having taken communion
they will be safe.'[25]

Such evidence might appear to support the claim made by A.W.
Jephson, the vicar of St John's Parish Church, Walworth from 1893
to 1908, that the enactment of orthodox rituals was associated with
folk superstitions and luck:

> At present the people come to church to this extent; for
> marriage, churchings and baptism, for the last night of the old
> year and for Harvest thanksgiving but all this is mainly from
> superstition, they do it to keep or change their luck.[26]

Yet the range of evidence considered in Southwark, while superficially supporting Jephson's observations, goes further than them by
suggesting that the association of orthodox rituals with luck did not
necessarily prevent other types of meaning being ascribed to the
ritual. Jephson's comments implied that church rituals were carried
out mainly, or merely, from superstition. The comparable evidence,
however, suggests that to state the connection between the
enactment of a ritual and the maintenance of good fortune did not
necessarily diminish the sincerity attached to the orthodox meaning
of that ritual. In his study of the south London borough of
Lambeth, Jeffrey Cox has argued that 'In the popular mind the
Christian sacraments were associated with luck more than anything
resembling Christian devotion.'[27] But in many cases what the actor
saw as the Christian Deity was not excluded from the ritual; rather,
attributing thanks to Him or receiving His blessing through the
enactment of the ritual, became the agent by which bad luck was
averted. Thus 'luck' and 'Christian devotion' were too intimately
associated with one another to be distinguished in these terms.

At the watch-night service, for example, a belief in the importance
of 'starting the year right' in order to ensure good luck, did not
preclude a sincere belief in the importance of repentance and
reaffirming a commitment to a church-based ideal of Christian
living. Those who performed the ritual of attending church in the
closing minutes of the old year were exposed to what was often
a highly-charged emotional atmosphere into which many of them
appear to have entered with reverence and sincerity, even
when they were, in some cases, the worse for drink. The service
consisted of prayer, hymn-singing and a short address and it was not

infrequently accompanied by great shows of emotion on the part of the congregation. A watch-night service held at the Surrey Gardens Memorial Hall in Penrose Street, Walworth, in 1913 included a rousing address illustrated by limelight slides. On such occasions it was common for a large number of the congregation to stand and testify to a dramatic conversion experience or to go forward at the close of a meeting and sign the pledge. Mr Rounsfell, a local south London missioner noted that at a similar service in the Old Vic a large number of the audience rose to their feet in order to express their desire to lead a new life in the new year and specifically to sign the pledge.[28] Similarly, John Harper, the minister at Walworth Road Baptist Church from 1910 claimed that 'We have never held a watchnight service at which less than half a dozen people accepted Christ as saviour'.[29]

Participation in the service could include a reaffirmation of an ideal of 'right living' drawn from church-based culture. It aroused a wave of nostalgia which was signified in the response to prayer, preaching and hymn-singing and it involved an emotional link with the church which formed a powerful, if intangible bond with church-based culture even among those who only attended very infrequently. Participating in these services cannot simply be dismissed as a desire for good luck in the new year when the vehicle by which this good luck was obtained involved a complex interweaving of various kinds of religious language and experience, much of which drew on overtly Christian symbolism and sentiment.

Similarly, getting married in church was not only considered lucky, it was often inseparable from a belief in the importance of securing the divine blessing on the couple. Ivy Sutton's mother could make a deliberate effort to ensure the luck of the couple by making a package of bread and coppers, but at the same time she believed that if they failed to get married in church they were also not blessed. The church emerges in a number of the interviews carried out in Southwark as a special and holy place which was believed to be endowed with particular efficacy as the correct arena in which to ask for and to receive the divine blessing. Ivy Sutton recalled the alarm and contempt with which her mother viewed any couple who had not been married in church: 'and if you got married not in a church you might as well not be married – didn't hold with it. For one thing you're not blessed and you're not gone to God Almighty'.[30] To go to church to enact these rituals was not only considered lucky but it was also associated specifically with 'going to the Almighty', both to thank Him and to receive His blessing.

In the same way, at the churching service the desire for good luck was inseparable from the belief that it was inappropriate to omit one's visit to the church where one ritually thanked the Almighty for a safe delivery. Ethel Saunders, the daughter of a costermonger, born in Decimer Street, Bermondsey, in 1919, described in her oral interview how 'after you'd been in bed for ten days you had to go to church . . . you went to church to thank the Almighty for getting you over it'.[31] She re-emphasized this point later in her interview by repeating it. She insisted that to be churched was to thank God: 'we all went to church to thank the Almighty for getting us over our delivery'.[32] Indeed, in the case of churching, the act of going to church to thank the Almighty was in itself considered a vital responsibility as well as a morally or religiously appropriate act. It is described in a number of cases as one's duty after a safe delivery. Emily Clayton, for example, described churching along with baptism as an imperative: 'You had to be christened and to thank God for getting you over your confinement in those days, you know'.[33] Moreover, Ivy Sutton's mother considered it wholly inappropriate, even immoral, to leave the Almighty unthanked for a safe delivery:

> She'd say if you haven't been to thank God see, for the pain of hell you've gone through, oh no don't know what she wouldn't call'y. But she let you go in then, as soon as we got home after all that, 'oh' she said, 'aint'y been a long time out in all this fog?'. Then she said, 'Was she churched', and I said 'Oh yes' but otherwise. . . .[34]

Going to church in order to enact such rituals had, in this way, to be carried out not only to ensure good fortune but also to discharge a responsibility towards the Deity.

In much the same way that the church was endowed with a sacred quality as the place in which to go to the Almighty, so the vicar, the priest or the Nonconformist minister who conducted these ceremonies was believed to have particular powers of prayer and benediction. By the end of the century, churches were not chosen randomly as places in which to enact these rituals, but individual families and communities had formed strong links with certain local churches and through them with the representative religious figure. The rites of passage were generally carried out in a local church which the inhabitants of surrounding courts and alleys viewed as 'our church'. For instance, Lilian Monger, the daughter of a printer, born in 1918, described how her family considered St Mary Magdalene Church which lay at the end of a small court by the name of Massinger Street, Southwark, as 'our church':

> We had a church, St Mary Magdalene, that was our church, we was all christened there, my Mum was married there, we was all christened and we all went to church I was in the Brownies, then in the Guides and my brothers in the Band of Hope.[35]

Similarly, Emily Clayton's family who lived in South Street, Walworth, were all married at St Peter's Parish Church; as she recalled, 'I was married in 1935 in St Peter's church on the Walworth Road and all my family's been married there, me nieces, sisters and all relatives, at that church'.[36]

In both these cases, the maintenance of such loyalty was from one generation of women to the next, just as women were the primary agents whereby this pattern of participation was integrated with popular folk culture and tradition.[37] The association of these families with the local church, chapel or mission extended to an identification with the representative religious figure of these institutions. Mrs Duckes, the daughter of a chimney-sweep from King Street, born in 1892, specifically identified the mission chapel in which all her family were christened and married with the person of the clergyman: 'We was all christened in a chapel at Wolfendale down in Somers Town, the Rev . . . yes and he was a lovely man. I had him afterwards when I got married he lived to a good old age'.[38] Her narrative concerning the local church continued with an extended description of the local vicar who visited and cared for the community. In her mind the place of ritual benediction was connected with the person who gave the benediction. The religious figure was considered part of the fabric of communal life and in some senses as 'belonging' to the community. The Reverend James Mackrell, for example, the vicar of the parish of St Alphege, Southwark, at the turn of the century, described an argument which broke out among a group of local children over the identification of a former parish vicar, the Reverend A.B. Goulden, with their respective communities:

I shall never forget the battle royal which raged one day between the kiddies of St Alphege and those of the neighbouring parish of All Hallows. Both laid claim to the present vicar of St Alphege who was previously assistant priest at All Hallows, "e's our father' cried the All Hallowites 'no 'e ain't', volleyed back the Alphegians, "e's our father'.[39]

It was expected that the community could lay a special claim upon the representative of the local religious establishment by virtue of its identification with that church. This special claim consisted not merely in the demand for references for jobs or clothing and food for the distressed, though it could and often did involve these things as well, but it was also associated with his representative role as a holy man.[40] His prayers were believed to have particular potency at these times of benediction as well as in times of sickness and distress. Similarly, in a number of cases the presence of the vicar or the missioner in a street was sufficient to quell bad language and to stop a fight. As well as providing prayer and relief for the suffering, the religious man was also believed by some to provide an extra degree of divine protection. The son of a missioner, who was interviewed by Alan Bartlett during a series of interviews in Bermondsey, recorded how during the Zeppelin raids on London during the First World War, the people of the area believed that they would be safer in his father's house than in their own houses due to his association with God: 'So we had a long passage and a staircase and we used to have about twenty to thirty people in there you see, because it was with Dad you see and I suppose something to do with God.'[41]

Much of the evidence considered in Southwark goes so far as to suggest that it was this image of the priest or vicar as the 'holy man' which provided the crucial determinant in the relationship between a community and the religious figure. Alan Bartlett, however, articulated a widespread view among historians when he argued in his thesis on Bermondsey that the Oxbridge associations which clung to the majority of clergymen working in the Bermondsey area before 1935 erected a clear and often insurmountable barrier between the minister and his working-class flock.[42] Yet the results of oral interviewing, in particular, suggest that vicars were accepted or rejected as desirable mediums for the conferment of blessing in the community not primarily on the basis of their social class but in relation to their success or failure in upholding a definition of goodness, morality and holiness which both included and extended beyond social criteria. An individual churchman, for example, was designated a 'good man', and may even have been described as 'one of us', if he provided prayer, healing and protection in a neighbourly and friendly manner within the community, irrespective of his social background or status.

Such glimpses of the attitudes of the community towards the religious man strengthen the suggestion that the enactment of the rites of passage involved a notion of the holy and a desire for specific benediction and blessing within the context of the church and under the auspices of the local religious figure whose position was related to particular ideals and definitions of morality and spirituality. The desire for this kind of ritual benediction did not, however, preclude a desire to ensure good luck for the participant. Receiving the protection afforded by taking shelter in the missioner's house, for example, did not preclude the use of a lucky charm to effect the same purpose, nor did getting married in certain churches preclude the belief that they were, like St Paul's Church, Bermondsey, in some sense lucky. The notion of blessing and the notion of luck were bound up with one another in a way which did not necessarily nullify, preclude or diminish the sincerity attached to either dimension of belief.

In addition to stressing the variety of sentiments attached to the context in which these rituals were enacted, the oral evidence also highlights the importance attached to the orthodox content of the ritual itself. It suggests that orthodox elements should not be played down as a motivating factor in participation in these rituals. Baptism, for example, was believed to have efficacy from a clearly Christian point of view. Undergoing the ritual was believed to make a child a 'Christian' while it allowed him or her to enter both the earthly fold of the church and the eternal fold of Heaven. Helen Wetherall, of Camberwell, asserted confidently that she had always believed that 'if you're not christened you're not in the fold'.[43] The view was widely held that an association with the church in infancy was sufficient to entitle an individual to claim the various privileges of that community without fulfilling what the church itself saw as the obligations. The nominal membership of the church which was conferred through the baptismal ritual was believed to be sufficient to ensure that an individual would be 'alright' when it came to the final judgement: their identification with the sacred community was ensured.

A number of the interviews also suggest that an individual's insistence on the importance of participating in church rituals was interpreted and seen within popular culture as an indication of genuine religious belief. When asked if her mother went to church, Miriam Wright, for example, replied, 'no but . . . ' and provided the qualification that her mother none the less believed (by implication in the teaching and values which that institution was seen to represent) because she participated in various church rituals:

> Q: Did your mother go to church?
> A: She believed and I mean when any of us children were born she'd go to the church before she went out anywhere to be blessed and she'd make sure we was all christened.[44]

Ivy Sutton also considered that the act of having her children baptized provided evidence of her commitment to both the Deity and the church. She even criticized the local vicar when he failed to recognize this action as sufficient evidence of the sincerity of her belief. She went into considerable detail when describing Mr Riddle, their local vicar at All Saints Church, Dulwich, in order to point out that his predecessor was, by contrast to him, a 'good vicar'. He was good, she argued, because he understood and accepted that, for the infrequent church attender, to have a child baptized and churched was proof enough of both their commitment to and belief in the Deity and their support of the church:

> Cornelius was our vicar round All Saints. Cornelius was a good man but the other man wasn't . . . Mr Riddle . . . 'Cos he knew that we was all working-class people and he knew that there was all families and he knew what the families was like didn't he? They'd go there round there straight away up out of confinement to be churched. Had their children christened.[45]

Unlike his successor Mr Riddle, Mr Cornelius did not seek to impose an additional standard of regular attendance on his parishioners, but would continue to visit them in their homes when they were sick and would happily baptize their children.

The examples considered so far also suggest a further strand in the meaning which these rituals held within the community. Participation was seen as fulfilling one's duty not only to the Deity but also to the wider community. As such it could be employed as evidence not only of the sincerity of religious commitment but also of a concern for social respectability. Speaking of Limehouse in the 1910s and 1920s, Annie Foley recalled that,

> When I had my Billy I got out of bed to change his napkins they came and caught me and said I was flying in the face of the Lord. You couldn't come out of the door into the open air unless you went straight to the church after you had children and the child wasn't allowed out until it was christened. If you did not you was treated like dirt.[46]

Her description suggests that to omit the religious ritual was to displease the Deity; it was 'to fly in the face of the Lord'; to do so was, at the same time, to make oneself socially unacceptable. These two emphases exist together within a range of meanings associated with the enactment of the ritual. To be churched and to have one's baby christened was to be socially as well as spiritually cleansed. Thus, as Alan Smith has argued,

> Such was the fear of ritual uncleanliness that to undergo the 'churching' ceremony – for all its official name the thanksgiving of women after childbirth – was a social necessity for a new mother wishing to resume her place, however humble, in the community.[47]

It should be noted that this kind of social necessity along with the other expressions of belief found in the desire to ritually acknowledge the birth of a child were characteristic both of Catholic and Protestant elements of Southwark's local commmunity. The services of churching and baptism formed part of a general expression of popular religion which was characterized by a marked undenominational flavour.

The social dimension of the ritual, just like the superstitious elements encompassed by it, did not necessarily preclude a desire to please the Deity. One cannot explain participation in the rituals simply as a desire for social status without reference to the wider range of meanings which were combined in the motivation to act in this way. A concern with social propriety and even conformity as a result of pure habit or communal pressure did not necessarily exclude a respect for the orthodox meaning of the ritual. The christenings and weddings of south London street traders or costermongers, pearlies, as they were locally known (due to the habit of adorning their attire with tiny pearl buttons), were occasions during which the church ceremony was used as a stage on which to display the grandeur of the local costermonger leaders, or pearly king and queen, and thus to celebrate the lifestyle and status of the London street trader. Alfred Ireson, the London City Missioner for the New Cut area of Lambeth between 1882 and 1911, described the show made by pearlies at public events: 'They generally made a great show at public events: When a babe was christened its dress would be covered with pearl buttons. Weddings produced a gorgeous display. Their funerals were made splendid with flowers and pearls.'[48]

It would be easy to focus solely upon the social function of such ceremonies within the pearly community, but when a wider range of material is considered it is clear that the social meaning attached to life cycle rituals by the pearlies did not nullify the sincerity with which the participants sought to identify their community and lifestyle with God, the church and the representative religious figure in the area. The ritual was carefully associated with specific churches in Southwark. St Mary Magdalene's, for example, was known as the 'pearly cathedral' from the turn of the century, because of the frequency with which the coster community sought ecclesiastical benediction there on their familial and communal events. Even the business meetings of the pearly association were held in St Mary's church hall with the curate presiding as chairman over the gathering. Each meeting was solemnly closed by the entire gathering joining in the Lord's Prayer before adjourning to a public house on the Old Kent Road known as the World Turned Upside Down.[49]

A commitment to the Christian efficacy of an orthodox ritual was often inseparable from a web of folk superstition, from the customary expectations of communal society and from an assertion of communal identity. Apparently incompatible narratives of religious belief thus formed one rationale for action in which many dimensions of belief were present. The eclectic character of popular attitudes tends to be overlooked when the actions of participants are interpreted with reference to factors external to the meanings and interpretations which the actors themselves brought to bear upon their practices. The incorporation of oral and autobiographical material into an examination of urban popular religion, however, has suggested that while orthodox rituals were enacted by south Londoners as part of a wide range of belief which sought to induce good luck or remove ill luck by manipulating the super-empirical realm, they were at the same time part of a desire to seek

and gain the blessing of a personal God via the medium of the representative religious figure within the community. They were in this
way bound up with a sense of communal or familial heritage, memory
and nostalgia which included a belief in the Christian efficacy of the
ritual, a sense of its social propriety as well as a belief in the attendant
benefits it bestowed in terms of securing good luck. Orthodox
elements of belief were not excluded by the diffusion of folk beliefs
and neither of these elements of the popular religious repertoire were
excluded by the presence of social pressures. Consequently, good luck
could be secured by reaffirming one's commitment to a church-based
ideal at the watch-night service and through the blessing received or
the gratitude given to God at the churching, baptism or wedding
without any apparent incongruity from the perspective of the
observer.

The coalescence of these kinds of religious discourse in popular
attitudes to the rites of passage constituted a characteristic feature
of late nineteenth-century urban popular religion. This pattern of
belief cannot merely be described as a residue of Christian teaching
or practice, or, as Cox suggests, as the most that a 'millennium of
indoctrination had achieved in implanting Christian ideas in the
popular mind'.[50] It was a dynamic and vibrant system of belief which
retained its own autonomous existence within the urban context.
There is a relation between patterns of popular belief in London
and those which have been recognized in rural areas. John Rule
highlighted a similar pattern of mixing between religious idioms
in Cornwall between 1800 and 1850.[51] He has described the
convergence of popular Methodism with the indigenous superstitions of the common people. Popular religion included a conception
of Christian doctrine which, as he argues, was 'adapted and transformed as it moved from the church to the cottage'.[52] Village people
possessed a background of beliefs which were partly Christian and
partly magic against which they sought to understand the realities of
the human situation. David Clark identified a similar pattern of
interaction in Staithes during the latter half of the nineteenth century and during the early decades of the twentieth century.[53] He
argued that the religion through which the villagers made sense of
their lives, and created a sense of communal identity, consisted of a
combination of 'official' and 'folk' religion. He highlighted the diver-
gent traditions from which these two kinds of religiosity sprang but
argued for their complex interconnection in the social setting into
which the ordinary villager was born.

The similar pattern of duality found in Southwark not only links this study to contrasting geographical areas during the nineteenth century, but it also links the modern with the early modern period in this respect. Barry Reay's study of seventeenth-century England, for example, demonstrates a similar pattern of amalgamation. He identified the prominence of a popular religious tradition for which he considers the term 'folklorised Christianity'[54] to be the most apt description: 'In many cases the two conditions, Christian and non-Christian were inextricably fused. Indeed some of the pagan examples given were found in combination with the symbolism, theology and language of Christianity.'[55]

This basic continuity in patterns of popular belief argues in favour of its consideration as a distinct religious expression which should not simply be equated with the premodern and rural world. The specific content of popular religious belief was, of course, adapted within different situations, but the basic coalescence of types of belief continued to form the central feature of its expression with a remarkable degree of resilience over time.

NOTES

1 J. Cox, *The English Churches in a Secular Society: Lambeth 1870–1930*, Oxford, 1982, p. 99; A.B. Bartlett, 'The churches in Bermondsey 1880–1939', Ph.D. thesis, University of Birmingham, 1987; O. Chadwick, *The Victorian Church*, 2 vols, London, 1970, vol. 2, pp. 221–2; J. Kent, 'Feelings and festivals', in H.J. Dyos and M. Wolff (eds), *The Victorian City*, 2 vols, London, 1973, vol. 2, pp. 855–72.
2 See, for example, Bartlett, 'The churches in Bermondsey'.
3 S.C. Williams, 'Religious belief and popular culture: A study of the south London borough of Southwark, c1880–1939', D.Phil. thesis, Oxford University, 1993.
4 Cox, *English Churches in a Secular Society*, p. 94.
5 Williams, 'Religious belief and popular culture', p. 169.
6 ibid., p. 170.
7 ibid., p. 170.
8 D. Clark, *Between Pulpit and Pew*, London, 1982, p. 115.
9 W. Henderson, *Notes on the Folklore of the Northern Counties of England and the Borders*, London, 1866, p. 8. Cf. R. Blakeborough, *Wit, Character, Folklore and Customs of North Yorkshire*, London, 1898, p. 115.
10 T.P. Stevens, *Cassock and Surplice*, London, 1947, p. 49; cf. the comments of Barbara Domany (born in Peckham in 1921, the daughter of a ladies' tailor): see Williams, 'Religious belief and popular culture', p. 172.
11 *Cassell's Saturday Journal*, 11 April 1906, p. 725.

12 Williams, 'Religious belief and popular culture', p. 173.
13 J. Harland and T.T. Wilkinson, *Lancashire Legends*, London, 1873, p. 236.
14 Williams, 'Religious belief and popular culture', p. 173.
15 Essex University, Department of Sociology, Essex Oral History Archive Interview 214, p. 27.
16 Essex Oral History Archive Interview 299, p. 71.
17 Essex Oral History Archive Interview 334, p. 46.
18 ibid.
19 *Christian World*, 4 January 1900.
20 Southwark Local Studies Library, Alan Bartlett Interview 7.
21 *Christian World*, 4 January 1900.
22 ibid.
23 Clark, *Between Pulpit and Pew*, p. 92.
24 ibid., pp. 92–3.
25 D.S. Cairns (ed.), *The Army and Religion*, London, 1919, p. 172.
26 London School of Economics, Booth Collection, B270, p. 27.
27 Cox, *English Churches in a Secular Society*, p. 97.
28 *Christian World*, 4 January 1990.
29 From the manuscript notes donated to the Southwark Local Studies Library by Miss Doris Worthy, 1980, p. 2.
30 Williams, 'Religious belief and popular culture', p. 178.
31 ibid., p. 179.
32 ibid.
33 ibid.
34 ibid., pp. 179–80.
35 ibid., pp. 181–2.
36 ibid., p. 182.
37 For further discussion of the role of women in religious life and popular culture in Southwark, see ibid., pp. 160–2, 261–8.
38 Essex Oral History Archive Interview 3, p. 16.
39 *St Alphege Mission, Annual Report*, London, 1897, p. 35.
40 Cf. G.P. Connolly, 'Little brother be at peace; the priest as the holy man in the nineteenth century ghetto', in W.J. Sheils (ed.), *The Church and Healing*, Studies in Church History, vol. 19, Oxford, 1982, pp. 191–206.
41 Bartlett Interview 7.
42 Bartlett, 'The churches in Bermondsey', pp. 116–29.
43 Williams, 'Religious belief and popular culture', p. 189.
44 ibid., p. 190.
45 ibid., p. 191.
46 Age Exchange, *On the River*, London, 1989, p. 34.
47 A. Smith, *The Established Church and Popular Religion*, London, 1971, p. 19.
48 Brunel University Library, Burnett Collection, A. Ireson, 'Written reminiscence', n.p., 1930.
49 P.F. Brooks, *The Pearly Kings and Queens of England*, London, 1975, p. 42.
50 Cox, *English Churches in a Secular Society*, p. 95.

51 J. Rule 'Methodism, popular beliefs and village culture in Cornwall', in R.D. Storch (ed.), *Popular Culture and Custom in Nineteenth-Century England*, New York, 1982, pp. 48–70.
52 ibid., p. 62.
53 Clark, *Between Pulpit and Pew*.
54 B. Reay, 'Popular religion', in B. Reay (ed.), *Popular Culture in Seventeenth-Century England*, Worcester, 1985, p. 121.
55 ibid., p. 112.

Part III

THE RELIGIOUS CONSEQUENCES OF URBANIZATION

9

THE MECHANISM OF RELIGIOUS GROWTH IN URBAN SOCIETIES

British cities since the eighteenth century[1]

Callum G. Brown

Historians and sociologists think of religion as environmentally temperamental. In certain types of society – according to established academic thinking – religion tends to flourish, while in others it languishes and decays. The 'flourishing' environment is almost always thought of as the countryside, especially the countryside of pre-industrial times, where people are thinly scattered, united under the authority of one state-run parish church and dependent through lack of education upon other-worldly explanations of the soil, weather and crop yields. By contrast, the modern industrial or metropolitan city is viewed as the main form of hostile environment for religion. The pluralism of the urban economy, the breakdown of social consensus and the disintegration of religious monopoly in leisure and thought spell disaster for the churches. In the traditional explanation, urbanization leads to the decline of religion.

This simple dichotomy between rural and urban provides the orthodox outline history of modern religion. Few historians or sociologists have seriously doubted that modern cities represent the ultimate environmental challenge to popular religious adherence and faith. Yet, recent decades have seen the slow but steady collection of evidence which, at the minimum, engenders niggling doubts about urbanization's inexorable capacity to secularize, and which, at the maximum, suggest that modern cities have been and remain venues for rapid growth in religion. This chapter is devoted to exploring the maximum strand – a strand not merely unfashionable in social history, but until recently almost unthinkable.

239

THE PROBLEMS WITH THEORY

If the Enlightenment and the French Revolution instigated the secularization of the European *mind*[2] around 1800, it was the contemporary growth of cities which nursed religious uncertainties into civil realities of class-riven churches, secularized social policy and a godless machine age. Ideas may have been just as powerful as economics in this. But whether cities were consumed by cotton, coal or *sans-culottes*, it has long been said that the European people lost their faith and the churches their flocks.

In contrast to France and imperial Germany, where revolutionary ideologies played a leading role in secularization of both state and people,[3] secularism has played a comparatively small part in the way historians have understood religious decline in Britain. Emphasis here has been placed on the impact of urban-based social change: on the 'birth of class' and the growth of religious Dissent to which it gave rise; the intensity of deprivation for the majority in even comparatively small cities; and the emerging religious alienation of the world's first industrial proletariat. For a working class which embraced Methodism temporarily but Marxism never, the British experience of religious decline has been understood mainly in terms of social rather than intellectual forces.

Few academics baulked in 1973 when John Kent wrote that 'it seemed that Victorian working class religion would vanish'.[4] However, the decline of religion in Britain is no longer seen in the crude way it was twenty years ago. There is now an increasingly sophisticated literature of case-study and statistics which reveals the significant strength of religious ideas, church-influenced social and civil institutions and popular adherence until the end of the nineteenth century. Part of the explanation offered has been that much of Britain remained small town and village, and rural religion displayed a stamina of a kind similar to other village customs and rituals. In this way, the watchword in recent academic approaches to British religion has been 'survival'. Despite evidence of dynamic church growth during much of the nineteenth century,[5] it tends to be seen as peculiar, temporary or aberrant – the product or emerging class conflict, party-political necessity or ethnic antagonisms.[6] Decline is taken as the long-term norm, 'revival' as the short-term aberration.

One way of understanding the reason for this is to think of the story of British religious decline since 1800 as the product of the script-writing talents of a predominantly bourgeois intellectual triumvirate: the cleric, the intellectual and the historian. The industrial worker, as often as not, is the silent player whose story of alienation from religion the cleric berates, the intellectual applauds and the historian sympathetically chronicles. While the churchman has feared the secularizing city, and the intellectual has wished it, the historian has merely recorded it. Secularization the reality, as faced by the cleric in the urbanizing maelstrom of the nineteenth-century city, became transmogrified through Marx, Durkheim and Weber into the intellectual's sociological theory of secularization. These three may have not *liked* what each other stood for, but their often frictional interaction is the source of today's social history of religion.

It is through the historian's treatment of the working classes during the process of urban growth and change that we need to approach the revision of the social history of modern British religion. Much research since the mid-1970s has given cause for such a revision. Advances in statistical analysis have shown the growth of formal church adherence during the fast urban development between the 1840s and 1900,[7] the weakness of city population size and city growth rate as predictors of church attendance at the British state census of religion in 1851,[8] and the strength of working-class membership of church congregations in the nineteenth century and the relatively small shrinkage in the proletarian proportion of churchgoers in the twentieth century.[9] Studies of 'history from the bottom up', notably oral history and studies of popular culture, have been indicating the strength of religious habits and values in the working-class neighbourhoods of cities from the 1870s to the 1940s.[10] While these studies have been conducted in varying forms and with different aims and intentions, and few revisionist overviews have been produced,[11] a most important net consequence has been to weaken the empirical argument of British religious decline as a result of urbanization.

The extent to which this new revisionist research – statistical, social composition and oral – changes or undermines the concept of secularization in modern urban society is open to dispute. At a minimum, three traditional *images* of urban–industrial religion have been, and continue to be, upset. First, the image of 'religious decline' is appearing inconsistent with the evidence on Britain between *c.* 1750 and *c.* 1880, and arguably up to the first decade of the twentieth century. Second, the image of *steep* decline – starting during early industrialization in the late eighteenth or early nineteenth centuries as a sharp discontinuity with the pre-industrial period, and continuing apace until sharply accelerated in the first half of the twentieth century – is being displaced with an image of much slower change. And, third, the image of some great haemorrhage of the working classes from the churches occurring at some point – early Industrial Revolution, late Victorian and Edwardian period or in the interwar or postwar periods – is upset by the evidence of only a marginal lowering of the working-class element in the churchgoing population during the twentieth century.

In interpreting the new evidence, that should be taken as the *minimum* extent to which historical understanding of the social history of modern British religion has changed. But there is also a maximum position, composed of three main elements. First, over the course of the nineteenth century, and certainly from the 1830s until the 1880s (and possibly till the 1900s), there was a very significant *growth* in formal church adherence, and the decline in adherence which then ensued was mild until the 1950s. Second, from the early Industrial Revolution period until the 1880s there was a significant *growth* in churchgoing per capita. And, third, as the British working class evolved in the nineteenth century, religion became a major element in its culture and values, and this involvement was sustained at a similarly high level through until at least the middle of the twentieth century.

Taken together, this maximum position amounts to an hypothesis that religion has grown during the main period of industrialization and urbanization of Britain. Such a turnaround in accepted historical orthodoxies may not be easy to accomplish, but it is something that requires exploration.

THE MECHANISM OF RELIGIOUS GROWTH

To envision religious growth in industrial and urban society, there is a need to place religion within the whole gamut of popular culture (rather than institutional church or political history). The basis of the model to be outlined below is an emphasis upon cultural continuity between agriculture and industry and between rural and urban, and the location of fundamental change in popular religiosity alongside general change in popular culture at the end, not the beginning, of rapid urbanization.

The discussion that follows divides the movement towards modern urban society into five major phases and types: rural change (*c.* 1700–*c.* 1850, but with an emphasis on the eighteenth century), proto-urbanization (characteristically industrial villages of the 1770–1840 period), urbanization (the formation of large towns and cities, predominantly of *c.* 1780–1910); suburbanization (a process of considerable duration for London, but assigned especially to the period *c.* 1880–*c.* 1940 for other cities); and planned overspill (incorporating new town and peripheral development, essentially of the post-1945 period).

Rural change *c.* 1700–*c.* 1850

The emphasis of recent studies of popular culture has been the continuity in forms between pre-industrial and industrial, with the survival and redevelopment of rural patterns until the mid-Victorian period, roughly 1850–80. Within that continuity, as several historians have observed, popular culture adapted and changed remarkably slowly, with the 'invention of tradition' a vital ingredient in resisting and negotiating change.[12] Examples here include the survival and spread of 'Saint Monday', the survival of 'traditional' fairs and the maintenance of folk sports. In part, such activities formed a complex pattern of resistance to economic change, in which claims to 'custom' operated as negotiating positions in relation to new work practices. In part, also, they served to maintain plebeian recreations as 'tradition', defiant in the face of the authorities' desire to reorder recreation and culture for the urban capitalist age.

Popular religion went through very similar changes. The characteristic evangelical culture which emerged in the second half of the eighteenth century incorporated family piety, community chiliasm, individual aspiration and, above all, the claim to class independence through 'democratic' church government. E.P. Thompson and Alan Gilbert have offered opposing though equally valid interpretations for early industrial workers' religious enthusiasm – respectively the 'chiliasm of the defeated and hopeless' under capitalist oppression, and 'the *aspirations* rather than the *despair* of the working classes'.[13] The establishment of working-class-run chapels and Sunday schools was, in the words of one Welsh historian, the claim to 'ecclesiastical republics' where the common people could be 'free of the inhibiting influence of the landlord or parson'.[14]

The crucial issue here is that the emergence of this new religious culture was initiated in rural society. Popular confrontation with modern economic conditions and class relations was predominantly agricultural not industrial, and rural not urban. It was in the countryside that the capitalist system impacted upon the working people, and it was there that the ecclesiastical changes of modernization were born and nurtured.

For the eighteenth-century small farmer, labourer or farm servant, the breaching of relations with the landowner meant not merely an economic break but also a social and cultural one. The parish church stood as a symbol of consensual class relations, the paternalism of the gentry and aristocratic landowner(s) and the deference of the common people. The system was a flexible one that contained conflict by a *mixture* of oppression and concession, and sufficient peasants (and landowners or their agents) would go to church so as to confirm the social order. The priest/parson/minister was the embodiment of the social bonding – the appointee of the religious–secular establishment.

The breaching of that bond occurred in the countryside. The agricultural changes of the eighteenth and nineteenth centuries fuelled population growth and migration to industrial and urban areas. These changes – completing the shift from subsistence to capitalist farming, the widespread introduction of domestic-based manufacturing (especially textiles) in some farming districts and the disintegration of consensual class relations – produced a number of manifestations in the religious sphere. The principal one was to turn a latent class resistance into mounting defection from the state churches, to be replaced by adherence to Dissenting chapels and churches, self-help sects and denominations. In these, as the Hammonds observed, the common people (both tenant farmer and labourer) gained social identity and self-affirmation: 'As a mere exercise in self-government and social life, the Chapel occupied a central place in the affections and the thoughts of people who had very little to do with the government of anything else.'[15] Popular faith became disjoined from the state or established church, and became much more *of* the people than *for* them. As Obelkevich has observed, 'a capitalist class structure . . . was established more firmly in the villages than in the towns', and his exploration of this process in the truly agricultural area of South Lindsey in Lincolnshire during 1825–75 convincingly shows how religion emerged from the process 'more adaptable to the parts of society, less expressive of the whole'.[16]

With population growth, Dissent grew more rapidly (possibly in part because of a higher birth rate among Dissenters).[17] Parish churches of the establishment, especially in Scotland and some northern parts of England,[18] often could not accommodate all those requiring worship. The reservation of seats in many churches for the rising numbers of élites meant increasing exclusion of the common people and the poor from collective worship.[19] Manufacturing became increasingly important to an agricultural population. The home weaver and spinner became a characteristic supporter of Dissent – the self-educating and improving worker who read and prayed at the loom. Finally, the insecurity of livelihood for the plebeian going through such changes led to periodic unemployment and underemployment, a cathartic disruption which reinforced the feeling of alienation from the establishment and encouraged sect and denominational development.

The English agricultural labourer and the Scottish farm servant were in a common predicament of alienation from the increasingly status-conscious farmers; they decreasingly dined at the same table, and were decreasingly urged or indeed welcomed to the same churches. They turned to Dissent for protest, self-respect and entertainment.[20] With overpopulation and increasing efficiency in farming, the outmigrant was in many cases already a Dissenter in one form or other.

The migration in search of work led increasingly in the eighteenth and nineteenth centuries from farm labouring to urban work. The move was not one performed in ignorance. The worker would characteristically follow a 'chain of migration' from his community, following where temporary migrants from his family or community had gone before, with news sent home either in person or by letter. News of urban life was becoming available through newspapers and journals, through increasing and improving levels of basic education and literacy. Moreover, the city might be a surprise for its scale and density of habitation, for its diversity of livelihood and cultural diversions, but – and this is crucial to the model – the essence of its class system would already be familiar in its rudiments to most migrants.

Proto-urbanization 1770–1840

The migrant as religious Dissenter is an important key to what followed in urban–industrial society. The evangelical piety of rural populations increasingly overcome with manufacturing was easily

CALLUM G. BROWN

translated into evangelical urban-dwellers. But anyone reading in
the field of urban religion in Britain between 1750 and 1850 must
be struck by the sense of increasing religious interest and concern
coming upon new village-dwellers. Where cotton-spinning towns,
large-scale bleach and print works, pit villages or large quarry operations were being formed in rural locations, there were frequently
reports of 'evangelizing opportunities', religious enthusiasm and
'craving for sermon and superintendence'.[21] While most of these villages never became towns or cities, they contained the kernel of
industrial urban society and of urban–industrial religion.

The characteristic industrial or mining village of 2,000 to 20,000
people often was, or became, dominated by one large enterprise
or firm. In such places, factory paternalism was often present, with
the family-owned factory providing chapels, pastors, Sunday
schools, day schools, canteens and other recreational facilities and
activities.[22] The religious facilities provided were not necessarily
those of the state church; factory owners often provided the financial support and the allocation of land on which to build a church
for the denomination of the workers' choice. In some instances
where the new workers were mixed, the provision was of more than
one denomination – both Catholic and Protestant chapels, for
instance. None the less, alienation from the state church could
lead to self-provision in religious affairs for industrial workers in
small communities. The self-help ethos which started in rural
communities became extended to industrial ones. The Dissenting
religion that followed was often forged by the anguish, the pain and
the chiliasm of the disinherited. As Colls has said of the northern
coalfields, 'Methodism did not "come" to save anybody trailing
clouds of glory; rather, it was made by people.'[23]

The religiosity of the industrial villages in the early Industrial
Revolution is acknowledged by most historians – even those most
convinced of the secularizing of urban society.[24] But in describing
a model of religious growth in urban society, two opposing interpretations arise of small-town religiosity. First, was this religiosity
a 'survival' and only a temporary transitional stage in the creation
of a largely secular urban society? Alternatively, was it something
new to, or an enhancement of, rural religion, and something which
found its parallel in large towns and cities of the nineteenth century?
In short, did the village religiosity of early industrialism relate more
to the agrarian past or to the urban future? Scholars as diverse as
Eric Hobsbawm and E.R. Norman[25] would argue for the past; the

246

argument here is that it was fundamentally the marker to the immediate urban future – for three main reasons.

First, the tremendous growth of Dissent among the indigenous
population of Britain after 1750 was in itself partly a sign of, and
reaction to, the extent to which the state churches (and, in England,
Old Dissent) were failing to resonate with popular religious desires
before 1750.

Second, before 1750 'religion' meant 'the system'; it meant
supporting it, being heretic to it or ignoring it. Whichever 'party'
was in power – be it Anglican or puritan in England, presbyterian
or episcopal in Scotland – the vast majority of the people, the
'common people', ignored it (or at least tried to). After 1750, things
changed. Religion was no longer 'the system' but a fragmenting and
class-challenged power bloc – the established churches of England
and Wales and of Scotland running before the storm of Dissent,
anti-tithes agitation[26] and internal divisions. The growth of Dissent
meant 'religion' had a new meaning. It emerged as an arena, a very
large and varied arena, for class conflict. It developed for different
social, occupational and interest groups as a part of life which
generated new values underpinning status in capitalist society. It was
religion that underpinned respectability, the ethos of hard work,
sobriety, temperance, thrift and providence, and which gave rise
to hundreds of voluntary organizations to promote these various
values.

Third, the parish church of the pre-industrial period was a
community symbol, and around it revolved many of the recreational
activities of the people. Religion celebrated harmonious work,
especially in agricultural life. But if before 1750 it defined the
community at work, religion thereafter defined escape from work
– the Dissenting chapel representing the safe haven from the slavery
of loom and overseer, the venue for outpouring democratic inclina-
tions, a statement of independence – Davies's 'ecclesiastical republics'.
Industrial religion promoted individualism – spiritual, social,
economic – of individuals within a capitalist class system. Religion
became apart from the work *system*, yet a glorification of the values
and aspirations which the people invested in their own labour.

So, the new urbanism of the manufacturing and mining villages
represented a culture of continuity within a new ecclesiastical shell.
Dissent was the defining characteristic of them, even if far from all
the inhabitants or industrial workers adhered to Dissenting chapels.
Clearly, if Dissent had not existed before the mill town, it would

have to have been invented. But the fact is that Dissent was already there, the product of rural and agricultural change.

If we accept, at least for the sake of argument, that proto-urbanization represented a sharpening and an awakening of popular religiosity, did a parallel development take place in larger towns and in cities, to be sustained there throughout urban growth? The growth of large cities represents the crux of the issue, and the case must ultimately rest or fall on them.

Urbanization *c.* 1780–1910

The story of British urban growth can be expressed in two main periods, *c.* 1910 marking the division between the two. The importance of this divide comes in three demographic ways. First, nearly all the main industrial towns and cities forged by the Industrial Revolution experienced their main periods of rapid growth between the late eighteenth century and 1900. There was a notable slowing down of growth for most cities between *c.* 1890 and *c.* 1910, after which they remained at roughly the same size during the next forty to fifty years. In short, the main period of rural–urban migration-driven growth of cities lay before 1880. Second, urban development in Britain was characterized down to *c.* 1910 by the greatest growth being of the larger-sized cities, while after that date the trend was for increasing numbers of small and medium cities with actual *contraction* in the number of large and giant cities. Third, the proportion of the population living in urban areas (with a population of over 10,000) grew rapidly and continuously down to 1911, after which date the proportion remained almost unchanged (at around 75–80 per cent) for the rest of the century.[27]

The social and demographic nature of the nineteenth-century city was thus very different from that which followed it in the next century. In our century we have for the most part been born in cities (and might subsequently move between them, within them or out of them); in the last century, people *came* to cities, whether from industrial villages or the countryside. Short-term urban population growth could be staggering – Liverpool grew by 116 per cent between 1821 and 1841, Bradford by 158 per cent. Over longer periods, growth transformed the scale of most towns: between 1801 and 1851 Leeds grew by 224 per cent, Merthyr Tydfil by 301 per cent, while the non-industrial communities of Brighton and Cheltenham grew by 849 per cent and 1,039 per cent respectively.

In 1851, 53 per cent of the population of Glasgow was born elsewhere. In the twentieth century, urban growth has been much less spectacular. A small number of towns, mostly in the south of England, have experienced high growth, while nearly all of the larger cities over a quarter of million people have *lost* population since 1950. In any event, migrants to the high-growth cities of the twentieth century were invariably coming from other towns and cities, many as overspill. By contrast, the new cities of the nineteenth century were cities of migrants, bringing from the countryside country customs and country religion.[28]

Even where the migrants of the last century were strangers to cities, city life, including its religious life, was less likely to be unfamiliar to them. Much of what has been said above about the transition from rural to industrial village also can be said for the transition from country (including industrial villages) to towns and cities. When the rural–urban migrant saw urban churches divided by social class, and perceived the churchgoer and non-churchgoer also divided by level of wealth, he or she was not in essence seeing something new. He/she was not being confronted with a new agenda of issues upon which to make his/her own decisions about religious affiliation. The rural environment he/she had just left not only replicated those divisions, but had in essence *created* them. Pluralization of denominations started in the countryside and then spread to the cities, not vice versa.

Familiar religious things started with the decaying authority of the established churches, and the strength of Dissent. There was in many places a tendency for those who migrated to be Dissenters. Urdank has shown in his study of the industrialization of the agricultural village of Nailsworth in Gloucestershire that Non-conformists were more likely than Anglicans to enter industrial employment, were more likely to be outmigrants during periods of trade stagnation, and may have been more important to rising birth rate which promoted total population increase in (and outflow from) that locality.[29]

From another perspective, much of the material culture of the new city-dwellers had been brought with them. In a sense, until the replenishing of migrant culture diminished in British industrial cities in the late nineteenth century, and until the urban authorities managed to suppress rural patterns of behaviour, the cultural environment remained strongly 'rural'. The new in-migrating inhabitants often brought some of their livestock with them, notably cows, creating one of the characteristic sanitary problems for civic improvers to tackle in the middle decades of the nineteenth century. The popular culture of these towns retained a strong rural quality – fairs, seasonal games and non-rules sport – long into the period of mass production and urban-style class relations. Indeed, the suppression of such fairs and games, like the reformation of sanitary habits, was a main effort of civic leaders and social reformers in the eighteenth and nineteenth centuries, and it was not until the 1860s and 1870s that it can be said that any significant measure of success was achieved across the board. Rules sports emerged with a flurry in the 1860s (soccer, rugby, boxing) to displace folk sports, commercial music hall and allied pursuits emerged to displace fairs, the police became more efficient at suppressing 'traditional' culture and more generally traditional popular culture became confined and regulated in the way which we as urban-dwellers would recognize as 'modern'.[30]

In the same way, many aspects of the religious life of cities down to the 1860–80 period should be viewed – like the rest of popular culture – as imports from rural society. Religious revivalism of the pre-industrial mould – disorganized, spontaneous, emotional and, to the authorities, often frightening – was only displaced from the 1860s and 1870s with the controlled revival of the Moody and Sankey variety. Indeed, this change in the nature of revivalism marked a much more profound transformation in the character of plebeian religion, especially of Dissent. It was in the last three decades of the nineteenth century that urban Dissenting churches witnessed the real decay of the puritan tradition which had characterized all of Dissent for a century and more: the spread of 'high church' practices, of ritual and, in Scotland, of instrumental music and stained glass. Characteristically in rural and urban life, the physical release of the conversion experience of the early nineteenth century was generally displaced by the 1880s by the 'respectability' of taking the pledge.[31]

Until those changes of the late Victorian period, cities contained a religious culture which resonated with that of the countryside from where migrants had been coming. The cultural environment of pre-1880 cities was thus not as unpropitious for religion as some historians (and nineteenth-century churchmen) have felt. Cities contained large numbers of new arrivals, often poor, isolated, homeless, eager for work, sometimes linguistically alienated (through accent or language). As institutions, churches were an obvious point of introduction, a focus for initial 'networking'. The minister, priest or preacher was a contact and a comfort, possibly a translator and invariably a migrant himself. In Scotland as late as 1910, when half of Scotland's population lived in towns of more than 20,000 people, nearly three-quarters of *new* Church of Scotland ministers were born in rural areas (a half in the Highlands); it was only by 1950 that the proportion had fallen to a half (with a fifth from the Highlands).[32] The implication of such figures is that many, if not most, city congregations were in the hands of rural-born pastors during rapid urbanization.

In addition migrants were the target for much of the urban mission work of the nineteenth century. In many cities, perhaps in virtually all, the early nineteenth century was difficult in terms of channelling clergy and financial resources to erect churches to service the swelling population. Certainly, statistical and qualitative evidence from a number of sources suggests a testing time for organized religion and for the people who sought to fund their own Dissenting chapels or new churches of the establishment.[33] The Catholic Church was in serious difficulties in many places – notably Liverpool and Glasgow, with large-scale immigration from Ireland and a poor constituency unable to provide the resources needed. As a result, evidence from Glasgow suggests that in the mid-1830s, when provision of Catholic churches and priests was poor, mass attendance and communion rates were significantly lower than in areas of Ireland from which many of the migrants came. For them, religiosity had to be *learned*.[34]

But if initial rapid urbanization in the early nineteenth century was not matched quickly enough by ecclesiastical response, many historians have pointed to the growth of provision and, thus, of participation after *c.* 1850. For some groups of migrants, initial poverty and social disdain among existing city inhabitants was displaced quite quickly by economic and cultural assimilation, including ecclesiastical assimilation. In Scotland, Gaelic-speaking Presbyterian Highlanders were so successfully assimilated that special churches for them in cities had difficulty in surviving after peak-migration decades had passed.[35] The city of Glasgow had a church attendance rate in 1851 higher than in a quarter of Scotland's rural counties, and in nearly all cases major Scottish towns had higher rates than their immediate hinterlands.[36] In industrial northern England, the second half of the nineteenth century constituted 'the years of religious boom' in Sheffield and Halifax.[37] This interpretation also arises from studies of Oldham and the Lancashire mill towns.[38] Further south, in the London region, studies of Reading, Lambeth and Croydon all suggest, by implication, the strength of religious organizations until a common crisis for religion in the last ten or twenty years of the century.[39]

If rural–urban migration was instrumental in forging the religious characteristics of city populations during industrialization, we should expect to find an individual city showing some reflection of the religious character of the areas from which its migrants were drawn, and perhaps some relationship between rapidly growing and slower growing cities.

To take first of all towns and cities characterized by high levels of population growth, and thus of in-migration, at some point in their development. This afflicted London, the giant industrial cities and the majority of large, medium and small cities. Major variations in churchgoing rates were evident in these places at the time of the state census of religion in 1851, but thus far research has not produced clear guidelines as to the factors determining even this simplest of characteristics. For instance, size and rate of growth of cities up to 1851 were poor predictors of level of church attendance in that year.[40] The economic base of a town – broadly industrial, metropolitan or 'traditional' market/county town – may have had some effect. Among the towns with the lowest rates of gross church attendances per capita, industrial communities and the metropolis dominated: in ascending order Gateshead, Preston, Oldham, Sheffield, Carlisle, Manchester, Birmingham, Bolton, Salford and London. Yet among the ten towns with the highest gross church attendances per capita, two were industrial (Merthyr Tydfil and Wakefield), though the other eight were broadly 'non-industrial' and/or of some antiquity (Colchester, Exeter, Bath, Ipswich, Reading, Cambridge, Cheltenham and Worcester).[41]

Before accepting too quickly that industrialism may have been the key determinant, it is as well to make some qualifications. First, though the overall geography of churchgoing in England in 1851 suggests that the industrial counties were zones of low attendance, there were notable examples of agricultural counties with low rates: Cumberland, Northumberland, Surrey and Herefordshire.[42] Further, the urban evidence from Scotland suggests some different conclusions. Of the twelve largest towns (which equate to the size definition used in England and Wales), the lists of the four highest churchgoing towns (Perth, Aberdeen, Greenock and Edinburgh) and the four lowest churchgoing towns (Airdrie, Glasgow, Arbroath and Ayr) each contain a virtually equal mix of industrial/non-industrial character. Moreover, in both Scotland and Wales the geography of high churchgoing in 1851 appears to be relatively unaffected by the location of major industrial zones.[43] Taking mainland Britain as a whole, the degree to which industry contributed to a city's economy is probably a poor predictor of church participation.

More interesting to the model would be relationships between migration patterns and the religious characteristics of a city. The in-migration patterns of British cities varied considerably between 1770 and 1910. Certain obvious points can be made initially.

First, cities with high immigration from Ireland during this period tended to experience two similar consequences: a heritage of relative high church participation rates, both in the nineteenth century and more spectacularly in the twentieth century, and high levels of sectarian tension between Catholics and Protestants. Cities falling into this category include Liverpool and Glasgow, and towns in their vicinity.[44] Indeed, it may be the case that the level of Catholics per capita could be a significant predictor of the level of church participation rate in British cities from 1850 to the present.

Second, cities which experienced a relatively high inflow of long-distance and 'alien' linguistic/ethnic migrants tended to have a greater degree of in-migrant ghettoization in which churches played a heightened role. Apart from the Irish Catholic example, this phenomenon is particularly noticeable in cities like London, Manchester and Glasgow where Jewish 'quarters' were established. However, it may also apply to groups like Welsh migrants to Liverpool and Highland migrants to Glasgow. But it is important to stress that the longevity of the effect varied according to the ethnic group concerned; while Jewish and Irish ghettos tended to break up although a strong church role in migrant identity remained, native migrant groups tended to be assimilated in both spatial and ecclesiastical terms relatively quickly.[45]

Third, the effect of rural migrants upon urban religion was dependent upon the pace and timing of cultural change in the locality that they had left. At one extreme, the durability of Irish Catholic culture in British cities has been heightened by family, political and church connections with 'the old country'. For other groups, the distinctiveness of the migrants' urban culture has been weakened, often fatally, by the disintegration of the original cultural milieu. Where no revitalization in terms of personnel and cultural interchange from an 'old country' takes place, a migrant religious culture becomes weakened.

The recruitment of what, for want of a better phrase, might be described as 'non-ethnic' migrant groups from within Britain to urban populations is clearly of enormous importance in any model on church growth (or decline, for that matter). Sadly, it is not a topic upon which historians have focused much research, rendering it difficult to extend generalizations. Even if it were possible to do so at this stage, precise correlations between, on the one hand, types of migrants – peasants, dispossessed small farmers, farm labourers/ servants or proto-industrial workers (such as handloom weavers) – and, on the other hand, religious characteristics of urban religion, could be highly problematic. The interactions *among* ethnic and 'non-ethnic' migrants clearly have an impact upon the religious character of a city; not only did the relations between native Protestant and Irish Catholic affect the character of Liverpool and Glasgow, but so too did relations between Irish Protestant and Irish Catholic. The level of migrant homogeneity, which related to a great extent to the size of a community, was probably also of importance.

This list of variables is by no means exhaustive; the workings of the urban religious mix were complex. Yet, the cultural and religious heritage of migrants *could* have lasting effects upon the British cities to which they moved (as with both Irish religious camps and with the Jews), while with other groups the effects may have lasted only a generation or two (as in the case of Highland Gaels and most 'non-ethnic' migrants). For as long as replenishing migration of any group, ethnic or 'non-ethnic', was maintained, urban religion was attached to and revitalized by its rural roots. While this lasted, the circumstances which had made class formation in the changing agricultural economy of 1750–1840 a venue for religious growth were also preserved in growing towns. When that process was all but exhausted for *most* migrant sectors in the later nineteenth century, the real potential for a truly 'urban' form of religion, and for secularization, emerged.

Suburbanization c. 1870–c. 1940

The suggestion that is developing here is that, in the life of any industrial city, there are at least two major stages: the initial period of rapid immigration which produces a religious life strongly influenced by a rural mode, and the subsequent period when a different, more modern urban mode appears. The next suggestion is that the religious history of early industrial cities is dichotomized by this divide – a divide which hit most British industrial cities in the period *c.* 1870–*c.* 1914. The first was a period of religious growth, the second a period of religious stagnation and accelerating decline.

The changes to urban religion in Britain at the turn of the century are arguably the best chronicled of all in the modern period. Parts of the description which follows draw on the key texts on this change by McLeod, Cox, Yeo and Morris.[46]

First, the exact point in the life cycle of an industrial city that a migrant arrives from the countryside will greatly affect the future of his or her religious life. For, moving during the city's 'religious growth century' will take the migrant into a rural style of religion with which he or she will to a great extent feel accustomed. But to arrive when the city's churches are entering or have entered a truly urban mode will greatly increase possible culture shock and alienation. More profoundly, there is a greater likelihood that the operation of the urban church to meet and welcome newcomers will be breaking down; there will be fewer lay helpers in voluntary organizations, perhaps even fewer clergy. In addition, the churches in those parts of cities where migrants tended first to arrive and settle may even be in a state of collapse.

The second point is the effect of suburbanization in the industrial city, the product of the growth of the middle classes. The increasingly subtle distinctions of class produced as British industrial cities matured in the late nineteenth and early twentieth centuries did not immediately *level* social distinction, but, rather, polarized classes. The industrial city started to spawn the great spatial division of social groups, heightening the effects of recreational and ideological divisions. The working classes became further out of the reach, sight and bothersomeness of the middle classes, the slums of the lumpen proletariat became more distant from the apartments of the clerks, and their apartments in turn more distant from the palaces of the managing directors. It is at this juncture, when cities were socially fracturing as a result of spatial and technological change (tramways, railway and metro railway commuting), that the churches were most vulnerable to the very same process.

At the same time the nature of industry was changing. The late nineteenth and early twentieth centuries witnessed the decline of the

CALLUM G. BROWN

family-owned and managed firm and the rise of the shareholding large-scale business, sometimes veering towards branch factory operation, though elsewhere tending towards very high levels of concentration in areas of rich factor endowment. Giantism in the urban–industrial scale was matched by giantism in industrial organization. Employer and trades union organization increased, labour political movements gathered pace and the divide between factory office and factory floor became as large as that between worker housing and suburban retreat.

The churches could not adapt so readily to these new circumstances as they had a century or even fifty years before. Church congregations in the industrial cities in the early phase of urban growth were attracting socially mixed congregations reflective of the low level of spatial social segregation. But as cities grew in size, the tendency was for church congregations to become more restricted in their social composition, even when located within the same denomination. In addition, the role of the churches as cross-class definers of social respectability, as sources of social redemption and hope, diminished. The middle-class mission to the workers decayed, working-class acquiescence to proselytism decreased.

The effects of urban–industrial scale and organization upon the operation of the churches may be perceived at another level. The industrial worker, both the old hand and the new arrival, found that the hope that religion would shape their social change diminished with the transformations of 1870–1914. During the early stages of industrialization, expansion of production was achieved with small levels of mechanization which extended the work process through longer working hours; during it the resilience of traditional skills and artisan culture and pride was remarkable. But in the late nineteenth century, the introduction of scientific management, moving production lines and new forms of worker supervision decreased worker control over the work process. Even if hours of work diminished, and the quality of life improved, the loss of control over time, pace and quality of work (heightened where deskilling accompanied mechanization) increased the worker's sense of alienation: a workplace that was no longer 'his', tools that were no longer 'his', a house that was often no longer 'his' but the company's, living in a city or (as often) a conurbation so large that it could no longer be perceived as 'his'. It is at this point that the urban worker felt the alienation of urban and industrial life. It is at this point that ideological and social functions of the church became less meaningful.

256

One of the major side-effects of this change was the secularization of government, especially local government and social policy.
Town halls were by the late nineteenth century an important venue
for the implementation of evangelical policies on social redemption,
but the period from 1880 to 1914 was one in which the churches
and the religious agenda of collective action lost nearly all their
influence in local government. Religion was past its period of
enforcement in cities; it became diffusive, and by that process
perceptibly irrelevant as a *public* or *community* phenomenon.

The effects are to be seen in the British statistics of churchgoing,
church adherence, religious marriage, religious voluntary organizations (especially Sunday schools and home missions) and religious
influence in social policy and civic government – all of which
experienced a sharp downturn between 1890 and 1910. The
maturation of urban society turned the period of rapid suburbanization in cities in the late nineteenth and early twentieth centuries
into the instigator of real religious crisis and decline. Though
evidence from Scotland suggests that the rate of decline that ensued
in the period down to 1950 should not be exaggerated,[47] the character
change upon organized and popular religion was so profound as to
undermine the mechanism for long-term religious growth in British
cities.

Planned overspill *c.* 1945–90

The place of religion in postwar Britain has still to be examined
seriously by social historians. Cities changed again with the advent
of large-scale planning, with a variety of effects and consequences
which centred on the philosophy that existing large cities should be
prevented from growing in population any further and should have
growth reversed by decanting people to peripheral housing estates,
new towns or retirement homes by the sea.

The period has certainly been perceived as one of 'urban crisis'
– for the churches as for other aspects of social life. In reality,
the level of church adherence in Britain does not appear to have
fallen catastrophically until the late 1950s and early 1960s, and
perhaps should be associated with sweeping changes in popular
culture, especially among the young. Certainly, the crisis of falling
church participation – a very major crisis of the later 1960s and
1970s – was, and continues to be, caused by the religious alienation
of the young.

One key development of the overspill period that may have accelerated urban secularization was the destruction of the community. The notion of the community was relatively successfully transplanted from rural to urban life in the nineteenth century; the 'neighbourhood', especially in working-class terms, was a powerful and cohesive force well into the twentieth century. But it was destroyed by the advent of comprehensive urban planning in the period after 1945. For the churches, a double-edged problem developed. First, blighted inner-city congregations lost their numbers, their social leaders and their financial resources – the 'inner-city' emerged as a deep ecclesiastical problem. Second, the mass movement of population to new peripheral, satellite or dormitory communities inferred not merely a logistical need which exceeded the means of many denominations, but a destruction of the congregation as an entity. Church authorities had neither the apparatus of evangelization nor the will-power to follow the people. The 'new migrants', unlike their predecessors at the start of urbanization in the late eighteenth and early nineteenth centuries, did not take or need religion to be the 'chiliasm' or the 'aspiration' of their condition.

The story of how urban religion faced its final frontier in the 1950s, 1960s and 1970s has yet to be related by historical researchers. But the haemorrhage of the British people from organized religion occurred then – the statistical evidence is convincing – and the state-organized great migration seems to have been a vital demographic ingredient in that process.

CONCLUSION

The early industrial cities of Britain should perhaps be seen in part like the early industrial cities of today's developing world – cities stocked by inhabitants of the countryside. But, like the developing world, the new urban citizens were already experienced in class society through agricultural or proto-industrial capitalism. For some migrants the change was straight from furrow to factory, but for others there were transitional stages where the loom in the home, shed or the mill were steps in the long rather than short transition from rural to urban society.

They were cities which grew so fast that they were full of the culture of the countryside, with the church of the countryside and with the pastors of the countryside. The cities were replenished by contact with the people and ways of the countryside, with a traffic back and forth (with important effects on the countryside). They remained for many decades places where religion was a rock in a sea of change, where the church of the country village was transplanted to the urban village. The sea change for British urban religion came, then, not when the cities were born or shaped, but when they matured at the end of the nineteenth century. The final crisis ensued fifty years later in the redesign of cities.

The mechanism for religious growth which existed in Britain between 1750 and 1900 was not the product of urbanization *per se*. It was the experiences of the people in the face of a developing class society in both country and town. Religious Dissent was the barometer of this mechanism, though by no means the sole beneficiary of growth, nor the sole victim of decay. What happened in British religion during urbanization is unlikely to have been unique. It was just the first.

NOTES

1 The author is indebted to the editor for his crucial suggestions for improvement to an earlier version of this chapter.
2 O. Chadwick, *The Secularisation of the European Mind in the Nineteenth Century*, Cambridge, 1975.
3 H. McLeod, *Religion and the People of Western Europe 1789–1970*, Oxford, 1981.
4 J. Kent, 'Feelings and festivals: An interpretation of some working-class religious attitudes', in H. Dyos and M. Wolff (eds), *The Victorian City*, 2 vols, Leicester, 1973, vol. 2, p. 866.
5 R. Currie, A. Gilbert and L. Horsley, *Churches and Churchgoers: Church Growth in the British Isles since 1700*, Oxford, 1977.
6 Notably in the influential work of Alan Gilbert. See A.D. Gilbert, *The Making of Post-Christian Britain*, London, 1980, pp. 74, 78–9; A.D. Gilbert, *Religion and Society in Industrial England: Church, Chapel and Social Change 1740–1914*, London, 1976, pp. 113–14.
7 Currie, Gilbert and Horsley, *Churches and Churchgoers*; C.G. Brown, 'A revisionist approach to religious change', in S. Bruce (ed.), *Religion and Modernization: Sociologists and Historians Debate the Secularization Thesis*, Oxford, 1992, pp. 40–9.
8 C.G. Brown, 'Did urbanisation secularise Britain?', *Urban History Yearbook*, 1988, pp. 6–8; S. Bruce, 'Pluralism and religious vitality', in Bruce (ed.), *Religion and Modernization*, pp. 182–5.
9 For example, C.D. Field, 'The social structure of English Methodism, eighteenth–twentieth centuries', *British Journal of Sociology*, xxviii, 1977.
10 H. McLeod, 'New perspectives on Victorian working-class religion: The oral evidence', *Oral History Journal*, 14, 1986; C.G. Brown and

CALLUM G. BROWN

J. Stephenson '"Sprouting wings"? Working-class women and religion in Scotland, 1890–1950', in E. Gordon and E. Breitenbach (eds), *Out of Bounds: Women in Scottish Society 1800–1945*, Edinburgh, 1992.

11 Though see J. Cox, *English Churches in a Secular Society: Lambeth 1870–1930*, Oxford, 1982; and R. Gill, *Competing Convictions*, London, 1989.

12 H. Cunningham, *Leisure in the Industrial Revolution c. 1780–c. 1880*, London, 1980; D.A. Reid, 'The decline of Saint Monday 1766–1876', *Past and Present*, 71, 1976; M. Judd, 'The oddest combination of town and country: Popular culture and the London fairs 1780–1860', in J. Walton and J. Walvin (eds), *Leisure in Britain 1780–1939*, Manchester, 1983.

13 E.P. Thompson, *The Making of the English Working Class*, Harmondsworth,1968 edn, pp. 386, 393, 419; Gilbert, *Religion and Society*, p. 83.

14 E.T. Davies, *A New History of Wales: Religion and Society in the Nineteenth Century*, Llandybie, Dyfed, 1981, p. 39.

15 J.L. Hammond and B. Hammond, *The Town Labourer 1760–1832: The New Civilisation*, London, 1917, p. 71.

16 J. Obelkevich, *Religion and Rural Society: South Lindsey 1825–1875*, Oxford, 1976, pp. ix, 320.

17 A.M. Urdank, *Religion and Society in a Cotswold Vale: Nailsworth, Gloucestershire, 1780–1865*, Berkeley, Calif., 1990, pp. 138–54.

18 Gilbert, *Religion and Society*, pp. 98–103; C.G. Brown, *The Social History of Religion in Scotland since 1730*, London, 1987, pp. 101, 106–7.

19 C.G. Brown, 'The costs of pew rents: Church management, churchgoing and social class in nineteenth-century Glasgow', *Journal of Ecclesiastical History*, 38, 1987; but see the critique of this view in S.J.D. Green, 'The death of pew rents, the rise of bazaars, and the end of the traditional political economy of voluntary organisations: The case of the West Riding of Yorkshire, c. 1870–1914', *Northern History*, xxvii, 1991.

20 Obelkevich, *Religion and Rural Society*, pp. 318–19; Brown, *Social History of Religion in Scotland*, pp. 101–15.

21 See for example Urdank, *Religion and Society in a Cotswold Vale*, pp. 84–101; J. Baxter, 'The great Yorkshire revival, 1792–6', in M. Hill (ed.), *A Sociological Yearbook of Religion in Britain*, vol. 7, London, 1974; Brown, *Social History of Religion in Scotland*, p. 112.

22 P. Joyce, *Work, Society and Politics: The Culture of the Factory in Later Victorian England*, London, 1980; A.B. Campbell, *The Lanarkshire Miners 1775–1874*, Edinburgh, 1979.

23 R. Colls, 'Primitive Methodists in the northern coalfields', in J. Obelkevich, L. Rope and R. Samuels (eds), *Disciplines of Faith: Studies in Religion, Politics and Patriarchy*, London, 1987, p. 327.

24 E. Hobsbawm, 'Religion and the rise of socialism', *Marxist Perspectives*, 1, 1978, pp. 14, 18; Gilbert, *Religion and Society*, pp. 113–14.

25 Hobsbawm, 'Religion and the rise of socialism'; E.R. Norman, *Church and Society in England 1770–1970*, Oxford, 1976, p. 7.

26 E.J. Evans, *The Contentious Tithe: The Tithe Problem and English Agriculture 1750–1850*, London, 1976.
27 C.G. Brown, 'Urbanisation and social change', in R. Pope (ed.), *Atlas of British Social and Economic History*, London, 1988.
28 ibid.
29 Urdank, *Religion and Society in a Cotswold Vale*, pp. 131–69.
30 On leisure developments of this period, see Cunningham, *Leisure in the Industrial Revolution*.
31 H. McLeod, *Religion and the Working Class in Nineteenth-Century Britain*, London, 1984, pp. 34–5.
32 M. Maxwell-Arnot, 'Social change and the Church of Scotland', in Hill (ed.), *A Sociological Yearbook of Religion in Britain*, vol. 7.
33 See, for instance, E.R. Wickham, *Church and People in an Industrial City*, London, 1969 edn, pp. 70–81.
34 W. Sloan, 'Religious affiliation and the immigrant experience: Catholic Irish and Protestant Highlanders in Glasgow, 1830–1850', in T.M. Devine (ed.), *Irish Immigrants and Scottish Society in the Nineteenth and Twentieth Centuries*, Edinburgh, 1991, pp. 70–3.
35 ibid., pp. 79–83.
36 R.J. Morris, 'Urbanisation in Scotland', in W.H. Fraser and R.J. Morris (eds), *People and Society in Scotland*, vol. 2, *1830–1914*, Edinburgh, 1990, p. 92.
37 Wickham, *Church and People*, pp. 107–65; S. Green, 'Secularisation by default? Urbanisation, suburbanisation and the strains of voluntary religious organisation in Victorian and Edwardian England', paper delivered to Commission Internationale d'Histoire Ecclésiastique Comparée, Madrid, August 1990.
38 J. Foster, *Class Struggle and the Industrial Revolution*, London 1974; Joyce, *Work, Society and Politics*; A. Ainsworth, 'Religion in the working class community and the evolution of socialism in later nineteenth-century Lancashire', *Histoire Sociale*, 10, 1977.
39 Cox, *English Churches in a Secular Society*; S. Yeo, *Religion and Voluntary Organisations in Crisis*, London, 1976; J.N. Morris, *Religion and Urban Change: Croydon, 1840–1914*, Woodbridge, Suffolk, 1992.
40 See note 8.
41 Data compiled from Census of Great Britain, 1851: Religious Worship, England and Wales, *Parliamentary Papers*, lxxxix, 1852–3.
42 Brown, 'Urbanisation and social change', pp. 212–13.
43 ibid. Data calculated from Census of Great Britain, 1851: Report of Religious Worship and Education, Scotland, *Parliamentary Papers*, lix, 1854.
44 Brown, 'Urbanisation and social change', pp. 216–22; T. Gallagher, *Glasgow: The Uneasy Peace: Religious Tension in Modern Scotland*, Manchester, 1985; P. Waller, *Democracy and Sectarianism: A Political and Social History of Liverpool, 1868–1939*, Liverpool, 1981.
45 This point is made for Glasgow by Sloan, 'Religious affiliation'.
46 H. McLeod, *Class and Religion in the Late Victorian City*, London, 1974; Cox, *English Churches in a Secular Society*; Yeo, *Religion and Voluntary Organisations in Crisis*; Morris, *Religion and Urban Change*.

47 C.G. Brown, 'Religion and secularisation', in T. Dickson and J.H. Treble (eds), *People and Society in Scotland*, vol. 3, *1914–1990*, Edinburgh, 1992.

10

SECULARIZATION AND URBANIZATION IN THE NINETEENTH CENTURY
An interpretative model
Lucian Hölscher

Between secularization and urbanization, between changes in religious life and changes in urban life, there is in modern societies a complex relationship, which is not easy to explain, even to an audience of specialists. Things would be easier for the historian if he could accept one of the pragmatic models in terms of which this relationship is usually described in the historical literature: historians generally accept certain forms of religious and church life – for instance, regular attendance at church and communion, baptism, religious marriage and burial, or participation in church organizations and campaigns – as recognized expressions of Christian piety, and through their rise or decline they measure the social meaning of 'religion' in modern society. Normally they find that in the course of the nineteenth century, church and religious life underwent a sharp decline, first in the cities, and later also in remote country areas, and they attribute this basically to the 'modernization' of the economy, social structure and educational system, associated with industrialization, and having its origins in the cities.[1] Only a few historians realize that the relationship between religious and urban life was shaped not only by structural change in secular society but, equally, by a change in the understanding of 'religion'. Not only were there changes in religious behaviour in modern society, but also changes in the way that this behaviour was perceived. There have also been changes across time in what is defined as religious behaviour, and, indeed, at any one time there has often been no consensus as to what should be defined as religious.[2]

This analysis can be made more concrete by taking three

imaginary examples of how contemporary observers might have analysed the situation at half-century intervals between the end of the eighteenth and the end of the nineteenth centuries.[3] If around 1790 one had asked a typical educated clergyman, whether Protestant or Catholic, in almost any German city, about the current level of religiosity in his parish, he would probably have answered something like this:

> As at all times, there are many people who do not observe the Christian commandments, but the cultural level of society is improving. Certainly all sorts of superstitious religious ideas are still widely held, yet in general, and especially among the educated, religious thinking is more enlightened than fifty years ago. There is thus good reason to hope that the time is now close when even those who up to now have had little education will in the same measure be freed from gloomy religious obsessions, and from the external control of the religious police imposed by the authorities. In these future times people will no longer be forced publicly to confess unbelievable dogmas, or to take part in religious ceremonies which their inner being rejects; on the contrary, they will be free to draw up their own confessions of belief, to choose their own community of faith, and to worship in the ways they want.[4]

Only half a century later, not only in Germany but also in many other parts of Europe, the religious situation had fundamentally altered, both in religious and also in social terms. A city clergyman questioned in the same way would have emphasized the severe shortage of church provision in the parishes and the rapid decline of church and religious life in modern society:

> Fewer and fewer people are attending church or receiving communion, and open contempt for the church and for religious commandments is spreading ever more widely. If this continues, Christianity and the church will be, within a few decades, completely destroyed. In particular it is the upper middle classes in the big cities who are increasingly escaping from their religious duties and setting a bad example to other sections of society. At the same time the social misery of the lower social classes and the tensions between different classes are ever increasing, and these problems can only be alleviated

by the ties formed through active neighbourly love. Only if society undergoes a rapid and fundamental change of heart can it avert the impending social revolution and the complete anarchy which would follow.[5]

Fifty years later, the position of religion and the church in urban society had again fundamentally changed. The conditions had become more complex and more contradictory. On the one hand, the decline of church life which once had been largely an urban phenomenon, now affected large areas of the countryside. On the other, in the cities there had been a certain stabilization of the situation, which encouraged many church observers to think in terms of a possible revival of religious and church life. Meanwhile, growing sections of the clergy were understanding religiosity and piety in terms not only of fidelity to old and traditional church teachings and forms of worship, but also in terms of modern restatements of the old confessions of faith and practical involvement in the church's numerous charitable organizations and communities. One city clergyman of the time might have linked this with the claim that it was the church's task to bring the Christian message to each of the many different sections of society, in terms relevant to the social and religious needs of each group. Another might perhaps even have claimed to be substantially independent of traditional Christian creeds, and to recognize the essence of Christian faith within the many new communities of belief which had recently established themselves within in modern society. In every case, however, the demand at this time was for active Christians, with a sense of social responsibility, whether exercised through church organizations or in the workplace, who would act as a Christian 'leaven in the lump' of a largely secularized society.

It is obvious that by now this analysis, too, has for long been out of date, and that once again the relationship between religion and urban society is evaluated in completely different terms. Precisely in Germany, first the First World War and then the Second World War broke up the culturally optimistic concept of a society that was secularized and yet in its spiritual foundations Christian. However, the culturally pessimistic concept of a continuous decline of religion and the church in modern European societies can hardly be sustained in view of the repeated periods of church growth and the important increases in the political–social prestige of all the major churches in recent decades. When we take an overview of the changes over the last two centuries just described, we see a change not only in people's religious behaviour, not only in the political and social framework of church and religious life, but also in the religious parameters in terms of which this change was perceived. What an enlightened Christian of 1800 understood as religious worship had hardly anything in common with what was understood by this term two generations later, and by 1900 Christian convictions were expressed in ways that were qualitatively different from half a century earlier.

This has serious consequences for the social history of religion. For as historians we cannot limit ourselves to tracing the social factors which were responsible for the decline of traditional forms of church and religious life since the eighteenth century, and for their partial replacement by new forms; we also must take account of the changes in what was understood by contemporaries as church life or religious life. It is thus no longer possible to describe the change in church and religious life in the nineteenth century as 'secularization' in the sense of an objective historical process, as is still generally done in the sociology of religion.

Certainly, there is no lack of contemporary testimonies and indicators which point to a decline of traditional forms of religiosity and of church authority since the eighteenth century. But the difficulty lies in the historical evaluation of this evidence. For the historiographical synthesis of these data in terms of the theoretical concept of 'secularization' suffers, however circumspect the systematic formulation, from two fundamental difficulties. First, there is no consensus today as to what can be described as secularization. The current concepts contradict one another to the extent that many theologians and sociologists of religion understand it to mean the loss of religious concepts to understand and order the world, while others see it as secularization when these concepts are realized by transforming them into new inner-worldly concepts.[6]

But a second, more serious point is that sociological theories of secularization generally ignore contemporary perceptions of the secularization process, in that they have no concern with how the relationship between church and society, the sacred and the profane, God and the world, was understood by people at the time. Because secularization is misunderstood as an historically objective process of the shifting of frontiers, of the supersession or substitution of religious functions and systems of meaning by those that are secular, no consideration is given to where contemporaries themselves drew the frontier between 'religious' and 'secular', between 'church' and 'world'. That, however, is a crucial point: for it is precisely this frontier, and with it the relationship which was established in any period between religious and secular, church and world, that had a decisive effect on the lines of political–religious conflict which were fundamental to the struggle over the secularization of society.

Accordingly, my initial hypothesis runs like this: religion and the church, world and society are, considered as historical quantities, not to be systematically defined in a metahistorical way, but only to be evaluated within a specific contemporary theological and social context. It cannot be denied that from an overall viewpoint church and religious life in the nineteenth century was exposed to a secularization process. However, this process presents itself as much more complex when one takes account of the various changes in contemporary perceptions, rather than contenting oneself, as all too many modern sociologists of religion do, with a systematically designed concept of secularization as an adequate heuristic model for the conditions current in earlier times.

PIETY IN THE FACE OF THE IMMINENT END OF THE WORLD IN EARLY MODERN TIMES (UP TO 1750)

Up to now we have no clear and, from a social–historical viewpoint, satisfactory picture of church and religious life in the urban society of the early modern period. Especially in German historiography, the highly distorted idea became current in the nineteenth century that before the Enlightenment the church customs of regular atttendance at services and participation in communion were still general and undiminished in all sections of the population, but were especially observed among the common people.[7] The basis for this view was found partly in the rapid decline of religious practice in the second half of the eighteenth century, and partly in the fact that at the beginning of the eighteenth century church life does seem to have been particularly active in many places.

Only recently has this idyllic picture of church customs begun to be more differentiated. When we look at other countries, we find that already in the early modern period the observance of church and religious duties in Catholic countries, like France, Spain and Italy, was sometimes very deficient, and that there were also regional differences which clearly went back a very long way.[8] In Germany, too, we need to take account of similar differences between regions and across time, though the evidence from the church visitations of the sixteenth and seventeenth centuries has not yet been adequately collated. Church life in the early modern period seems to have been particularly weakly developed in the Baltic territories, such as Mecklenburg, Pomerania, Schleswig and Holstein. It seems to me that the relatively high level of religious practice in Germany around 1700 should be seen not so much as a reflection of a general and traditionally high level in early modern society, but more as a consequence of the Thirty Years' War, which led to a general, but temporary, intensification of church life.[9]

It is certain that the pressure applied by the church authorities and the clergy to induce parishioners to take part in church life was not only much stronger than in modern society, but also in social terms very unevenly distributed. In the first instance it had its greatest effect on the middle ranks both of urban and of peasant society – those who took an active part in the affairs of their civil parish, and similarly Sunday by Sunday came together to take part in the common worship of the Christian parish. On the other hand, servants, lying below the level of the urban citizenry or of the peasantry did not have special places assigned to them in church, and largely escaped the controlling eye of the clergy: whether or not they took part in church services or in other religious ceremonies depended mainly on how strongly their employer insisted upon it.[10] The church authorities generally took notice of them only when they committed a punishable offence, such as giving birth to an illegitimate child or committing suicide. Thus it is no more possible to speak of any general pastoral supervision of the lower classes in early modern society than it is in modern society.

But the ruling classes – the nobility and the urban patriciate – also to a large extent escaped the control of the clergy and of Christian parish life: for instance, by the appointment of private chaplains, or through the celebration of baptisms and weddings at home, and private funerals, which they were able to organize in their own way. Even within the church they seldom mixed with the populace, being separated during services by sitting in special pews or galleries. All these social differences carried over into the nineteenth century, and right up to the present day they have had an influence on the socially differentiated patterns of religious practice in modern society.

There is, as yet, no evidence of a lower level of religious practice in urban than in rural areas in the early modern period – rather the contrary. At least in the period of the Reformation and Counter-Reformation, church life in the towns was as a rule both qualitatively and quantitatively superior to that in the countryside. In the towns there were more religious foundations and places of piety, also more clergy and members of religious orders, more church services, processions and other religious ceremonies. Thus urban piety was more highly organized, even if we still have no reliable statistical data concerning the level of popular participation. In the early modern period the main centres of Christian piety unquestionably lay in the towns. Rural areas much more frequently escaped the influence of Christian culture.[11]

In the nineteenth century there were still certain regions of Europe, for instance, Lower Saxony, Mecklenburg and the French Mediterranean coast, where there were powerful remnants of pre-Christian forms of religion.[12] In the rest of Europe, too, right into modern times, there was a latent opposition among the rural lower classes to religion and the church, which were seen as instruments of social discipline in the hands of the authorities.[13] This followed from the fact that Christian missionary efforts had their base in the courts of princes and, after the Reformation, in the towns and universities. Spiritual and secular authority, religion and the law, were tightly intermeshed, and spiritual authority concerned itself as much with people's lives as citizens as with their souls. This had a direct effect on the intensity of church life: right up to the beginnings of the Enlightenment, participation in church services and in communion was seen as an important sign of social peaceability. Even a temporary absence from church called into question not only the person's individual peace with God, but also the social peace in the parish. For that reason, and certainly not only because of the religious impatience of the clergy, absentees quickly found themselves exposed to all sorts of inquisitorial questioning. The clergy had to make sure that the threatened peace of the parish was restored as soon as possible. In the early modern parish participation in the affairs of the religious community was thus compulsory for every full member. Both religious and civil offences were frequently punished by compulsory exclusion from communion, from godparenthood, from church offices, etc. Thus, to be excluded from the church community had serious consequences, not only in a religious but also in a civil sense. For instance, those excluded were denied entry to public offices or to membership of a guild, and if they were poor they ranked as outlaws.[14]

From the point of view of salvation history, non-participation in church life, and impiety generally, were understood in relation to the expectation of an imminent apocalypse. Christian mythology held, on the basis of Second Thessalonians, II, 3, that the time before Christ's final return ('Christ's future', as Germans called it) would be marked by a general falling away from Christian belief by the greater part of humanity. So the more signs there were of such a falling away, the closer seemed to be the end of the world and the last judgement. Therefore, manifestations of unbelief could always be interpreted as proofs of the final victory of belief and of the church. In turning away from God, the world became subject to his justice.

THE WORDLY PIETY OF THE AGE OF ENLIGHTENMENT (1750–1810)

In the course of the eighteenth century, this intermeshing of religion and civil life broke up – not suddenly, through revolutionary pressure, but gradually, step by step. This happened very clearly in Protestant Germany, but the same fundamental processes were at work in the Catholic part of Germany too. As church penalties were dropped, so compulsion to take part in the rites of the church disappeared. The church authorities were no longer able to mete out civil penalties, but only spiritual sanctions. Instead of official control, the weight of public opinion now watched over people's practice of their religious duties. And even public opinion gradually, but continuously, lost interest in people's religious practice. In the end, in fact, it turned out itself to be a declining force in questions of religious behaviour, as urban communities became more amorphous and urban populations more mobile.

This was not caused by any atheistic tendency, but by a new understanding of church and religion. In Protestant regions of Germany, these ideas very much took the form of a new Reformation, at first shaped by pietism. Among the educated bourgeoisie, the church was seen less as an official institution, and more as a religious society of those sharing a common faith. They would meet together in small groups where the inner voice of God would be heard, and where the individual's free confession of faith would be given priority over the church's doctrinal tradition.[15] Admittedly this tendency was furthered by the state's interest (especially at first, in the eighteenth century, in Prussia and Austria) in a friendly coexistence between the major Christian confessions within their respective spheres of dominance. Since the Peace of Westphalia in 1648 guaranteed in principle the right to existence of these confessions, the rulers of the larger German states increasingly pursued a policy of toleration and of religious individualism. In the long run this must actually endanger the organizational coherence and dogmatic traditions of the churches.[16]

Naturally the old church rites suffered as a result, and at first this happened to a much greater degree in the towns than in the countryside. Wherever we have data concerning participation in communion in German Protestant urban parishes at the end of the eighteenth century, the figures were much lower than in the surrounding rural areas:[17] in Dresden, for example, in 1795 the ratio of communions to population was 100 per cent, as against 160 per cent in the whole of the Kingdom of Saxony; in Hamburg it was 45 per cent, but in the neighbouring rural parish of Mittels-kirchen 150 per cent; in Breslau it was only 31 per cent in 1800, but it was 110 per cent in the surrounding province of Silesia. Somewhere around the middle of the eighteenth century a gap opened up between urban and rural religious practice, which only began slowly to close again in the second half of the nineteenth century.

But when these statistics of church life are taken as indicators of piety in the age of Enlightenment, they give a false picture of the real situation. For those townspeople who still took part in church services and communion no longer did so as a result of external compulsion, but predominantly as a result of habit and free conviction. For them churchgoing was no longer a matter of legal duty, but a free religious practice. It was possible to give it up without the fear of facing penalties, and the higher bourgeoisie, especially the men, increasingly took advantage of this freedom. Conversely, there were those, notably many women from the upper and educated bourgeoisie, whose churchgoing was very much a matter of free choice, and was the expression of a more individual and personal piety. Because they were seen as an expression of a free and joyful turning to God, pious practices, such as prayer and participation in church services, even if they became less common, had a higher moral worth in the eyes of contemporaries than the compulsory piety of earlier times.

A Protestant country pastor, living to the west of Hamburg at the end of the eighteenth century, actually saw the long-term decline of churchgoing in his parish as a good omen for the gradual disappearance of superstitious ideas. His reasoning was as follows: at the beginning of the century, people still rushed to church in a sheep-like way because they feared personal misfortunes, the sufferings of war, storms, bad harvests and other natural disasters as signs of God's revenge; the decline of such superstitions, and of the forced churchgoing associated with it, should therefore be recognized as a sign of a truer and freer religiosity.[18]

It also happened that the neglect of traditional forms of religious practice corresponded with an enormous religious loading of the whole of bourgeois life: nature and art, science and bourgeois morality, the past and the present, were all loaded with religious significance.[19] What religion as dogmatic tradition and church practice lost, it won back many times over through its incorporation into bourgeois life. And, finally, by means of bourgeois education in catechetical teaching and in church services, in elementary schools and institutions set up by educational reformers, religious norms and ways of interpreting the world were now gradually brought to the lower social classes, where religion had for long been mainly understood as part of the system of authority and control.

If there is anything that corresponds to the liberal theological concept of a 'worldly piety' in the sense of the penetration of the world with religious ideas and norms, it is this process of the reinterpretation and social extension of religion in the age of Enlightenment. Contemporaries had no idea of the less favourable aspects of this metamorphosis, which we define as 'secularization'. Before the beginning of the French Revolution, church life in Germany was not seen as being in decline – quite the contrary. Where middle-class people belonging to different confessions lived in the towns together – Reformed, Lutherans and even Catholics – they often attended the same church services, and confessionally mixed marriages were seen by them as signs of religious enlightenment, reason and love, and as focal points in a new all-embracing, confessionally neutral religion of humanity. In the middle of the eighteenth century, Berlin and Hamburg were already important centres for this kind of religion, and later they were joined by Frankfurt-am-Main, Bremen and many other north and east German cities.[20]

Even church life in the narrower sense was supported by an optimistic spirit of innovation – that is indicated by the numerous reforms in liturgy and hymn-books from the 1770s onwards. Supporters of the Enlightenment saw in the hymns and sermons of the time striking evidence of the progress made since the preceding century.[21]

The lower social classes, both in the countryside and in the towns, were clearly less susceptible to the enlightened religion of the educated: the latter attributed this to the well-known traditionalism of these classes, and relied on the long-term effect of the religious education programme. All this applied equally to Catholic and to Protestant regions. According to the way that people of that time saw things (a few pietistic outsiders excepted) there could be no question of a 'decay' of church life, or of Christian piety dissolving into 'shallow rationalism' – to use the critical terminology of a later generation.

The age of Enlightenment marks a decisive turning-point in modern church and religious history, though its fundamental and irreversible significance for modern society is substantially ignored by the churches right up to the present day.[22] There has been insufficient recognition of the scale of the religious 'conquests' which have been achieved since the later eighteenth century, both in qualitative terms through the engagement of religion with the secular world, and also quantitatively as a result of the wider social coverage of religious education. So, even today, the religiosity and the church of the Enlightenment still has to wait for complete rehabilitation, and for the recognition that the period saw an heroic breakthrough in the development of modern piety.

THE SEPARATION OF STATE AND SOCIETY FROM THE INFLUENCE OF THE CHURCH IN THE NINETEENTH CENTURY

The current conception of the course of secularization in Germany continues up to the present day to be influenced by a simple model.[23] According to this model the churches increasingly lost their influence on state policy and on courtly society from the time of the introduction of absolutism in the seventeenth century. From around the middle of the eighteenth century, the Christian view of the world, Christian moral norms and, with them, the forms of religious practice, which up until then had been strictly adhered to, gradually lost their binding force, first among the middle class in the towns, and then later in the countryside.

From the early nineteenth century onwards, the most important indicator of this decline was taken to be the statistical decline of church life, as defined by regular participation by parishioners in the rites of the church. The long-term re-evaluation of religious practice was a consequence of the persecution of the Catholic Church in France at the time of the Revolution. In Germany, too, it led to a change of mood, first among a section of the clergy and later in the so-called *Erweckungsbewegung* (revival movement). In contrast to the situation in the preceding decades, people once again began to measure piety in terms of regularity of participation in church ceremonies. In particular, regular church attendance, from whatever motive it was undertaken, together with regular prayer and charitable gifts were taken as pre-eminent signs of piety. The redefinition of church festivals as focal points of Christian piety was also supported by the conviction that, in view of the present threatened position of the church, believers could no longer, as formerly happened, leave the strengthening of the church to the authorities – instead they had to do the job themselves by regular participation in church ceremonies.[24]

Political, religious and social positions and ideas of this kind bunched together around 1800 to form the new concept of *'Kirchlichkeit'* (church adherence). By about 1820 this term had advanced to become the fundamental concept of church–political discourse in Protestant Germany, and denoted in equal degree an individual attitude and a collective condition, whereby the church was respected as the spiritual centre of civic life. The term also expressed a certain expectation which now began to preoccupy orthodox and confessional Christians of all denominations: the fear that the church as a public institution and centre of Christian piety could gradually lose importance in the future.[25] The significance and the prevalence of the concept of *'Kirchlichkeit'* can thus be taken as an indication of the changed position of the church in early nineteenth-century society. Two structural changes, in particular, ought to be emphasized:

1 After 1800 a new concept of Christian 'piety' prevailed, which was more narrowly concentrated on the religious sphere, and equally there was a new concentration of church life on its real religious content and tasks.[26] This had two sides. Externally, the church's preaching was freed from civil tasks, such as the announcement of secular laws and regulations, or instruction in all kinds of business and civic matters, such as the use of lightning conductors, the rotation of crops, etc. Internally, the main focus of preaching became the Christian 'facts of salvation': repentance and forgiveness, justification and divine grace. Often

as a result of polemical encounters with the shallow rationalism of the 'world', the mysteries of the faith won in importance and religious depth. The fight against superstition (in contemporary terminology, the 'enlightenment of religious concepts') had been the main theme of the church's preaching and religious education, but it was superseded by the spiritualization of piety.

In Germany this development occurred simultaneously from about 1820 onwards in the Protestant and in the Catholic Churches. In the latter, its chief exponents were the ultramontane clergy, and in the former the Lutheran confessionalists and orthodox clergy who, from the 1830s on, were increasingly driving their rationalist predecessors from the pulpits.[27] Under this regime, church culture separated itself consciously, comprehensively and lastingly from secular culture, which was denounced as being worldly. Even the so-called cultural Protestantism of the late nineteenth century depended on this distinction in its attempt to mediate between culture and religion. Thus church and religion developed at first into an alternative world-view, and then into a subculture within modern pluralistic society.

2 The spiritual change was accompanied by a change of social emphasis: the rural population and the petty bourgeoisie, which the clergy had for long seen as being generally outstandingly superstitious and in need of enlightenment, were now discovered as stable carriers of traditional forms of religious practice and thus as a reliable social basis for church life. This arose not merely from an ideological re-evaluation of the religion of the 'people', but beyond that there was also a genuine turning by the church towards the lower social classes. For through intensive missionary and social work it was now possible to win for the church and Christianity larger sections of this population which had in earlier centuries been largely neglected by the church's pastoral efforts. The main force behind these church initiatives were middle class and aristocratic lay people, who held no church office: on the Protestant side this meant the Bible and tract societies and the many charitable organizations which came together after 1848 in the 'Inner Mission'; on the Catholic side, since the mid-1840s, there were the Borromeus, Vincent de Paul, Boniface, Pius and Kolping societies.[28]

On the other hand, the enlightened bourgeoisie now fell very much into the background as leading representatives of church life.

Their attachment to the church, when measured by regular participation in the church's rites, fell well behind that of the petty bourgeoisie. The reason for this lay in the greatly increased mobility of the professional and business classes since the later eighteenth century; merchants and entrepreneurs, state officials and army officers, artists and members of all kinds of free professions, whenever they changed their place of residence, also changed their religious milieu. For the most part the confessional parish could no longer provide them with a spiritual home, so that in religion, as in cultural matters generally, they turned to relationships on a much wider scale or else to the culture of domestic piety.[29]

Already in the early nineteenth century this had led to a sharply differentiated middle-class religiosity in urban societies. Certainly it is not possible to co-ordinate religious mentalities in an empirically precise way, but only in the form of verifiable stereotypes of particular social groups. Thus it is possible to say, while granting many exceptions, that the academically trained bourgeoisie, and, in particular, doctors and scientists of all kinds, tended towards an enlightened and liberal religiosity, while the lower middle class was generally conventional in church and religious matters, and according to region were orthodox or Lutheran confessionalist.

State officials generally considered religion primarily from the point of view of the needs of the state, and church matters from the point of view of middle-class respectability. Lawyers, officers and other members of the nobility were already in the eighteenth century, and especially in north Germany, widely known, because of their matter-of-fact approach to religion, as critics of all religious mysticism and all claims of the church to power. In the later nineteenth century, many of them certainly made peace externally with the church and religion, but retained an inner scepticism which has remained up to the present day.[30] The social differentiation of church and religious life was visible earlier and more strongly in the towns than in the countryside. For here old regional traditions remained right through the nineteenth century, and the rural bourgeoisie, doctors, teachers and the rural aristocracy were to a large extent integrated into local church life in their capacity as local notables.

There was also a new perspective on the future arising from this experience of the increasing differentiation of Protestant religiosity. While orthodox and confessional Protestants saw in this a clear sign of the progressive decline of church influence, and indeed Christian influence, on society, liberal Protestants were more afraid of the possibility that the church might break up into several religious parties. While the former aimed to mobilize all available forces for a return to the old church of the Reformation, and consciously accepted that wide sections society might be estranged in the process, the latter fought for the unity of the church. As allies in this cause they could count on the state, and especially on the territorial ruler. However, this perspective fell apart with the end of the union of church and state after the First World War.

SECULARIZATION AND SACRALIZATION OF CHURCH LIFE SINCE THE LATER NINETEENTH CENTURY

In the course of the nineteenth century the decisive factor in the relationship between church and society increasingly lay in the socio-economic development of the great industrial centres of population. In Germany from the 1840s, as earlier in England and France, industrialization led to an accelerating process of decline in the urban parish structures. With the breaking-up of the 'house' as integrated living and working space, it became increasingly uncommon for servants and their employers, masters and journeymen, to attend communion together. Thus traditional patriarchal relationships were disappearing, and so, with the increasing mobility of the urban population, were the old parochial neighbourhood ties and the developed social relationships within each quarter.[31]

This situation was produced by the interaction of two demographic processes:[32] the rapid growth and the increasing mobility of the urban population. New social groups were moving from the country to the town, and at first they found only unsatisfactory accommodation. Often it took several years and many moves for newcomers to establish a settled home in the town. The average period of residence in a particular quarter was short – often only a few months or years, so that, even when they wanted to, it was seldom possible to establish firm ties with the parish to which they belonged.

Even the pastor only knew in exceptional cases who had recently entered or left his parish. Because of the size of the parishes, it was no longer possible even to have a clear view of who was participating in church life and who was giving up religious duties. For, with the growth of the towns, social relations within most parishes had loosened so far that, at times, the pastor could only maintain personal contact with a small circle of parishioners who were closely involved in the church through frequent attendance at services or participation in parish organizations.

In the second half of the nineteenth century, church life in Germany was marked by a massive deficiency of religious provision in city parishes, and a structural overloading of the clergy with the administration of church rites.[33] Parishes of 10,000–30,000 souls, with thousands of communions and hundreds of baptisms, weddings, funerals and confirmations per pastor within each year were no longer a rarity. Between 1870 and 1880 Protestant church-going and communion rates reached their lowest point of the century, with weekly rates of 1–5 per cent for the former and annual rates of 5–20 per cent for the latter. (In some places, like Hanover, the lowest point had already been reached in the 1850s and 1860s.) In Catholic parishes the figures were probably higher (how much higher, we do not know exactly), but here, too, by comparison with the decades preceding and following, this period marks a low point for religious practice.

The quantitative level of church life was certainly even lower than it would have been if the religious needs of the urban population had been more satisfactorily met. The reason for this was a structural crisis in parish finance which affected the Protestant population of the cities particularly severely. For, according to premodern church law, the erection of new churches and the creation of new pastorates was the responsibility of the patron, who might be a local landowner, or might be the ruler of the territory. In the course of the nineteenth century, and especially during the decades after 1848, responsibility fell to the now autonomous urban parish.[34] However, it was precisely the population of the poor suburban parishes in the cities who found themselves unable to raise the funds to build a new church or establish a new pastorate. In any case the population of these areas often had no interest in doing these things, because they felt few ties either to the place or to the church.

In Catholic regions the structural deficiency of church provision could at least partly be met through the many religious brotherhoods, congregations and other centres of church piety. The hierarchical centralism of the Catholic Church also facilitated financial assistance to poor parishes in the building of new churches. Protestant cities, on the other hand, paid the penalty for the idealistic concept of parish autonomy which had been developing since the 1820s, and which completely failed to take account of the social structure of modern city parishes.[35] Over several decades the shortage of provision could only be dealt with in individual cases, as a result of assistance in the building of new churches by patrons from the aristocracy or the upper bourgeoisie. More effective help came only with the establishment of state-supported church-building funds in the 1890s and the introduction of financial equalization between the parishes of a region around 1900.

The cumulative elimination of religious underprovision led now to a brief (and illusory) boom in Protestant church life in the cities: from about 1880, wherever new churches and pastorates were established, additional church services provided and welfare services extended, the level of participation in church life stabilized for about two decades. This tendency was assisted by the gradual stabilization of bourgeois conditions of life after the troubles associated with the war of 1870–1 and the economic crisis that followed soon after. Admittedly, contemporaries connected this trend more with Bismarck's church struggle and the swing to conservatism in national politics at the end of the 1870s, which had the effect of bringing both the Catholic and the Protestant middle classes nearer to their churches. By about 1900, at least in Protestant city parishes, this short phase of revitalized church life was already at an end, giving way to another period of declining involvement in the church.[36]

Meanwhile, the century-long contrast between rural church adherence and urban distance from the church gradually began to be blurred. Certainly the towns, and especially large north German cities like Berlin and Hamburg, continued to be regarded as strongholds of irreligion. But increasingly the countryside followed in the same direction: in the first half of the nineteenth century the decline in church life initially mainly involved those rural areas which were closer to the towns, but after 1850 it increasingly affected remoter regions too. The gradual assimilation of rural church culture to that of the towns was caused by the growing influence of urban culture, especially as a result of the extension of tourism in rural areas and of the industrialization of the countryside, which led to the introduction of anti-church liberal and socialist ideas.[37]

Up to now it has only been possible in the case of Protestantism to trace the changes in German church life in precise quantitative terms. In general, however, it is possible to say that the tendencies towards the secularization of social life were more or less balanced by tendencies towards sacralization. A few facts and figures may make this clearer. While in most Protestant city parishes the communion rate more or less stabilized at around 10–20 per cent, the regional average declined between 1862 and 1910 by between a quarter and a half, to reach levels close to those found in the cities.[38] Admittedly, other indicators of church life remained largely stable before the First World War: with the introduction of civil registration in 1876, baptisms and church weddings changed from having a legal function to being voluntary acts relating only to the church, but they continued not only in the countryside, but almost to an equal degree in the town, to be taken for granted traditions, which very few people refused to accept – apart from some radical Social Democrats. Similarly with the right to resign from one's church, which was legally regulated and made freely available from the beginning of the 1870s: for a long time this was mainly used by those wishing to change denomination, which most frequently took the form of Catholics (and Jews) becoming Protestants, and to a lesser extent of Protestants moving from the *Landeskirche* to one of the Protestant sects. Until the beginnings in 1906 of the movement of mass resignations from the church, those adhering to no confession at all remained a marginal phenomenon. Even then, the number of those leaving the churches was never much more than 10,000 in a year, of whom by far the greatest number (well over half) were in Berlin, referred to by McLeod as 'the most irreligious city in the world'.[39]

Some other religious rites were actually attracting increasing numbers of participants. For instance, the custom of religious burial had in many places fallen into disuse in the later eighteenth and early nineteenth centuries, but now again it was increasingly popular; equally with the Protestant confirmation, which, after first being introduced in pietist circles in the early eighteenth century, in the course of the nineteenth century became more and more the general custom. An entirely new institution, which was first introduced during the later decades of the nineteenth century and spread rapidly, was the church service for children. Its purpose was to draw children into church life before the age of confirmation, and it thus had a similar function to the Catholic confirmation which took place at an earlier age.

However, in the Protestant church too, religiosity, the religious mentality and loyalty to the church could no longer be defined only in terms of participation in church rites. Apart from this an ever

greater part of church life was being taken up by church organizations, and, on the periphery of the church, by religious associations,
lectures and evangelistic missions. In the Catholic Church, an
extensive network of church organizations had already been
developing since the 1840s; in Protestantism, after early examples
in the 1830s and 1840s, it was only from about 1880 that an
imposing network of organizations was developed under the aegis of
the Inner Mission. An important aspect of this was the emergence
of such mass organizations as the Protestant League (1887) and
the People's Association for Catholic Germany (1890), which aimed
to provide an aggressive defence of Protestant and Catholic interests
in state and society. In contrast to the devotional and charitable
associations sponsored by the churches, these organizations were
able to mobilize a large section of those middle-class people who
were on the periphery of the churches and were otherwise relatively
uninvolved in church life.

Major shifts in the social formation of the churches were thus
taking place. What they lost in direct political influence as a result of
the formal disengagement of government bodies, they partly won
back through their social network of associations, newspapers
and personal representatives in many social organizations (like
schools, hospitals, etc.). What they lost in terms of traditional
religious practice they partly made good through new religious and
social activities.

At the same time the concept of 'Kirchlichkeit' shifted: in the
Protestant church regular participation in church rites was no longer
a characteristic expression of Christian sentiments. By 1850 at the
latest, the core of loyal church people in German cities made up less
than 10 per cent of nominal parishioners. Admittedly, the members
of this core parish involved themselves more intensively in work for
the church, making many material sacrifices. As well as regular
participation in church life, work for the numerous Bible-reading
and prayer-groups, tract societies and charitable organizations led
in these circles of faithful church people to a growing sacralization of
life, which increasingly separated them from the way of life of secular
society.

The overwhelming majority of Protestant city-dwellers kept their
distance from church life in the traditional meaning of the term, in
that they attended church only at major festivals, such as Christmas
and Easter, and only occasionally participated in communion
– often at intervals of several years.[40] As a rule, however, those

urbanites who lived on the margins of the church sought its blessing at the times of baptism, marriage and burial, gave their children a church upbringing, and at home preserved at least certain religious customs, such as saying grace at meals, prayers at night or private reading of the Bible. So, at the end of the nineteenth century church adherence in the sense of regular participation in church rites had become the concern of a religious subculture embracing a shrinking minority of (urban) society. However, church adherence might also be reflected in participation in a wide range of new charitable and associational forms of church organization, pursued in a Christian spirit.

Only a relatively small minority, estimated at about 10–20 per cent of the urban population, was so estranged from the church that it took no part at all in church life, and also no longer kept up any of the familiar traditions of private piety.[41] They included large sections of the urban lower classes, especially the Social Democratic industrial proletariat, but also parts of the new middle classes of white-collar workers, shopkeepers and minor officials, and finally also small sections of the intelligentsia, members of the free professions and artists. Before the First World War this section of the population certainly was still smaller than it is today, but politically it made more noise, in that it was sharply separated from the churches through membership of atheistic freethought organizations and other ideological associations and movements.

As widely separated as the different attitudes of the urban population towards the church were their different expectations concerning the future fate of the church and of religion. While there were many people who feared (or hoped for) a progressive collapse of church life, there were also wide sections of the city population who expected a progressive Christianization of modern society. Both of these expectations influenced the mentality of the urban population at the beginning of the First World War. This was also reflected in the concepts with which this society sought to make sense of past and future changes in their religious culture.

SECULARIZATION OR RELIGIOUS DIFFERENTIATION IN THE TWENTIETH CENTURY

Since the turn of the twentieth century 'secularization' has been the prevalent term used to describe the change in religious culture in modern society.[42] Max Weber, Ernst Troeltsch and other sociologists of religion used this term to denote a long-term process of social change, which since the Reformation, and more especially since the eighteenth century, had laid hold of all parts of society. Linked with this decline of religious practice, the progressive separation of church and state, the rejection of Christian customs and norms and 'the disenchantment of the world' (Max Weber) in general, would continue without a break into the future. Sadness at the associated loss of old religious values and traditions was mixed with the recognition that this social change was inevitable and indeed rational.

However, the concept of secularization always suffered from a double weakness. On the one hand, in recent decades the expectations associated with this concept have only been very partially fulfilled. We see in many modern societies not only tendencies towards a further dissolution of old Christian ideas and norms, but also evidence of the revitalization of old religious models of understanding and behaviour and the emergence of new ones. These societies appear to be shaped neither by a linear decline in religious life, nor by a general 'rationalization' of people's view of the world. On the other hand, up to now, neither the Christian churches nor the historical and social sciences have been able to agree on a common concept of 'secularization'. Beside the predominant pessimistic concept of a progressive falling away of modern society from 'religion' and 'church', there is also (reflecting the spectrum, outlined above, of varying expectations of the future) the cautiously optimistic concept of a constant springing forth of new religious ideas and norms in society. In terms of historical research into secularization, the most important consequence of this stalemate lies in the fact that there are no longer any unambiguous indicators of the state of religious values and practices, or of their decline. Description of the secularization process thus lacks an objective basis.

What are the implications of this for historical research into religious change in modern urbanized society? Do we have to content ourselves with a resigned acceptance of the fact that all knowledge is conditioned by one's social situation and indeed by one's party allegiances? Do we therefore have to accept that the description of the relationship between church and world, religion and society, always depends on which subjectively selected criteria we apply to the 'religious' quality of social behaviour? As I have tried to show, these criteria have already changed substantially in the course of the last two centuries, and are now less subject to agreement than ever before. How, in this situation, can the historian and the sociologist of religion provide a generally acceptable account of the historical changes in religious ideas and ways of behaving without lapsing into an historical positivism which defines as 'religious' everything which describes itself in this way?

My suggestion is that we should historicize the concepts with which we try to make sense of religious change in modern society. This means that concepts like 'secularization', 'religious pluralism' or 'religious differentiation' must themselves be regarded as historical phenomena. It seems then that the experiences and expectations, the historical models of the past and the future, encapsulated in these concepts, were also a part of the religious culture which they were used to describe. To give some concrete examples it was an essential part of the religious culture of the early modern period that people saw themselves as living in the last days, and equally essential to the religious Enlightenment that the hope of a powerful deepening and internalization of individual religiosity more than compensated for the loss of old religious ideas and norms.

Also, for the religious history of the nineteenth century it is not so crucial whether we think it objectively more accurate to describe it in terms of 'church decline', or 'secularization', or a simultaneous 'secularization' and 'sacralization', or as 'religious differentiation'. The most important question is how contemporaries themselves – apart from such 'objective' descriptive models – used such concepts to understand their own history. Certainly, the historian also has the task of determining how realistic contemporary visions of the future were, by considering how far their expectations were fulfilled, and how far the course of historical development disappointed them. A religious history which refuses to 'sweep under the carpet' the existing conceptual differences concerning the nature of 'the religious' must in this sense be based on reflective research.

Similarly the study of history cannot take place 'outside history', but remains conditioned by time and place. Instead of appealing to 'ultimate religious values', which cannot be scientifically rationalized, history tries to operate in terms of its own discipline, which means that it interprets the past in the light of the possible visions of the future that were available. All depends on how we envisage the future development of religious life in modern society. This applies as much to the present as to any past society. Thus the concepts change as people's religious expectations change. It is a mistake for sociologists of religion and theologians to think that theoretical models, such as 'secularization', provide neutral tools for the analysis of social relationships. It would be much more to the point to see these models as part of what they are describing, and to use them as building blocks in the construction of a religious history which is more sensitive to the history of concepts.

NOTES

1 For Germany, see for instance, R. Marbach, *Säkularisierung und sozialer Wandel im 19. Jahrhundert. Die Stellung von Geistlichen zu Entkirchlichung und Entchristlichung in einem Bezirk der hannoverschen Landeskirche*, Göttingen, 1978; W.K. Blessing, *Staat und Kirche in der Gesellschaft. Institutionelle Autorität und mentaler Wandel in Bayern während des 19. Jahrhunderts*, Göttingen, 1982; L. Hölscher, *Weltgericht oder Revolution. Protestantische und sozialistische Zukunftsvorstellungen im Kaiserreich*, Stuttgart, 1989; T. Nipperdey, *Deutsche Geschichte 1866–1918*, 2 vols, Munich, 1990, vol. 1. For France see the synthesis by G. Cholvy and Y.-M. Hilaire, *Histoire religieuse de la France contemporaine*, 3 vols; vol. 1, 1800–80, Toulouse, 1988. For Britain see. H. McLeod, *Religion and the People of Western Europe 1789–1970*, Oxford, 1981; and his article on 'Religion', in J. Langton and R.J. Morris (eds), *Atlas of Industrialising Britain 1780–1914*, London, 1986, pp. 212–17.

2 See, for instance, F. Schnabel, *Deutsche Geschichte im 19. Jahrhundert*, 4 vols, vol. 4: *Die religiösen Kräfte*, Freiburg im Breisgau, 1936.

3 These sketches are mainly based on the situation in Protestant Germany, but, with slight modifications, they are applicable to many other regions of Europe.

4 See Hans Erich Bodeker, 'Die Religion der Gebildeten', *Wolfenbüttler Studien zur Aufklärung*, XI, 'Religionskritik und Religiosität in der deutschen Aufklärung, Heidelberg, 1989, pp. 145ff.; see also B.H. Bergst, 'Versuch zur Bestimmung der Zu- und Abnahme der äussern Religiosität in der Gemeine zu Mittelskirchen im Alten Land des Herzogtums Bremen innerhalb der 90 Jahre von 1704 bis 1793', *Annalen Braunschweig-Luneburgischen Churlande*, IX, 1795, pp. 423–55.

5 K.G. Bretschneider, *Über die Unkirchlichkeit dieser Zeit im protestantischen Deutschland. Den Gebildeten der protestantischen Kirche gewidmet*, Gotha, 1820; J.H. Wichern, *Die innere Mission der deutschen evangelischen Kirche. Eine Denkschrift an die deutsche Nation*, Hamburg, 1849.

6 See H. Lübbe, *Säkularisierung. Geschichte eines ideenpolitischen Begriffs*, Freiburg, 1965; P.L. Berger, 'Soziologische Betrachtungen über die Zukunft der Religion', in O. Schatz (ed.), *Hat die Religion Zukunft?*, Graz, 1971, pp. 69ff.; H. Blumenberg, *Säkularisierung und*

LUCIAN HÖLSCHER

Selbstbehauptung, Frankfurt-am-Main, 1974; N. Luhmann, *Funktion der Religion,* Frankfurt-am-Main, 1976.

7 See, for instance, Bretschneider, *Über die Unkirchlichkeit;* P. Drews, *Das kirchliche Leben der evangelisch-lutherischen Landeskirche des Königreichs Sachsen,* Tübingen, 1902, pp. 82f.

8 See M. Vovelle, *Piété baroque et déchristianisation en Provence au XVIIIe siècle,* Paris, 1969; K. Thomas, *Religion and the Decline of Magic,* London, 1971; F. Boulard, *Matériaux pour l'histoire religieuse du peuple français,* Paris, 1987.

9 P. Drews, 'Der Ruckgang der Kommunikanten in Sachsen', *Zeitschrift fur Theologie und Kirche,* 10, 1900, pp. 148ff.; L. Hölscher, 'Die Religion des Bürgers. Bürgerliche Frömmigkeit und protestantische Kirche im 19. Jahrhundert', *Historische Zeitschrift,* 250, 1990, pp. 595–630.

10 This is indicated especially by the fact that the parochial communicant registers only record the regular participation of heads of households and their wives, whereas their servants and children are normally counted as a body and treated as their dependants.

11 In 1700 the communicant ratio in Breslau's Eleven Thousand Maidens parish (just under 70 per cent) was still higher than in many rural parishes: M. Schian, *Das kirchliche Leben der evangelischen Kirche der Provinz Schlesien,* Tübingen, 1903, p. 105.

12 R. Wuttke, *Sächsische Volkskunde,* Leipzig, 1901; G. Holtz, article on Mecklenburg in *Die Religion in Geschichte und Gegenwart,* vol. 4, 1960, pp. 820f.; Cholvy and Hilaire, *Histoire religieuse,* vol. 1, pp. 291ff.

13 Cf. D.W. Sabean, *Power in the Blood: Popular Culture and Village Discourse in Early Modern Germany,* Cambridge, 1984.

14 ibid., pp. 37ff.

15 See A. Ritschl, *Geschichte des Pietismus in Deutschland,* 3 vols, Bonn, 1880–6.

16 See E. Förster, *Die Entstehung der preussischen Landeskirche,* 2 vols, 1905.

17 See Hölscher, 'Religion des Bürgers'.

18 Bergst, 'Versuch zur Bestimmung'. See also H.-D. Kittsteiner, *Die Entstehung des modernen Gewissens,* Frankfurt, 1991.

19 W. Lütgert, *Die Religion des deutschen Idealismus und ihr Ende,* 4 vols, Gütersloh, 1923; T. Nipperdey, *Wie das Bürgertum die Moderne fand,* Munich, 1988.

20 For Berlin, see G. Bregulla (ed.), *Die Huguenotten in Berlin,* Berlin, 1988, pp. 78ff.

21 See A. Niebergall, 'Agende', *Theologische Realenzyklopädie,* 1, 1977, pp. 755ff.

22 See K. Barth, *Die protestantische Theologie im 19. Jahrhundert. Ihre Vorgeschichte und ihre Geschichte,* Zurich, 1947; E. Hirsch, *Geschichte der neueren protestantischen Theologie im Zusammenhang mit den allgemeinen Bewegungen des europäischen Denkens,* 5 vols, Gütersloh, 1949–54.

23 Representative examples include H. Hermelink, *Das Christentum in*

der Menschheitsgeschichte, 2 vols, Tübingen, 1951–3; O. Chadwick, *The Secularization of the European Mind in the Nineteenth Century*, London, 1975; Hölscher, 'Religion des Bürgers'.

24 See F.W. Katzenbach, 'Zur Entfaltung der Problematik von "Kirchlichkeit" und "Unkirchlichkeit" in der 1. Hälfte des 19. Jahrhunderts', *Hospitium Ecclesiae*, 11, 1978, pp. 93–128.

25 See Bretschneider, *Unkirchlichkeit*.

26 See Hölscher, 'Religion des Bürgers', pp. 615ff.

27 See R.M. Bigler, *The Politics of German Protestantism: The Rise of the Protestant Church Elite in Prussia 1815–1848*, Los Angeles, Calif., 1972; O. Janz, 'Bürger besonderer Art: Protestantische Pfarrer in Westfalen 1850–1914', dissertation, Berlin Free University, Berlin, 1991; I. Gotz von Olenhusen, *Katholische Pfarrer und Sozialmoral im 19. Jahrhundert am Beispiel der Erzdiozese Freiburg*, Göttingen, 1994; T. Mergel, *Zwischen Klasse und Konfession. Katholisches Bürgertum im Rheinland im 19. Jahrhundert*, Göttingen, 1994.

28 See. Nipperdey, *Deutsche Geschichte*, vol. 1, pp. 411ff., 423ff.

29 See L. Hölscher, 'Bürgerliche Religiosität im protestantischen Deutschland des 19. Jahrhunderts', in W. Schieder (ed.), *Religion und Gesellschaft im 19. Jahrhundert*, Stuttgart, 1993; also Hölscher, 'Religion des Bürgers', pp. 607ff.

30 The evidence on this subject has not yet been systematically collected. But see the series edited by P. Drews, 'Das kirchliche Leben der evangelischen Landeskirchen in Deutschland', Tübingen, 1902–19.

31 For Barmen see W. Köllmann, *Sozialgeschichte der Stadt Barmen im 19. Jahrhundert*, Tübingen, 1960; for Hanover, C. Cordes, *Geschichte der Kirchengemeinden der evangelisch-lutherischen Landeskirche Hannovers 1848–1980*, Hanover, 1983; for the social consequences of industrialization generally see M. Greschat, *Das Zeitalter der industriellen Revolution. Das Christentum vor der Moderne*, Stuttgart, 1982.

32 For the following, see Hölscher, 'Religion des Bürgers', pp. 605ff.

33 Statistical sources: G. Zeller, *Zur kirchlichen Statistik des evangelischen Deutschlands im Jahre 1862*, Stuttgart, 1865; P. Pieper, *Kirchliche Statistik Deutschlands*, Freiburg im Breisgau, 1899; more precise details are available in the series edited by P. Drews, 'Das kirchliche Leben der evangelischen Landeskirchen in Deutschland'; for the extreme example of Berlin see Hölscher, *Weltgericht oder Revolution*; and Hugh McLeod, *Poverty and Piety: Working Class Religion in Berlin, London and New York 1870–1914*, New York, 1994.

34 For Hanover, see Cordes, *Geshichte der Kirchengemeinden*; more generally, see the article by Friedrich, 'Gemindeverfassung, rechtlich', in *Religion in Geschichte und Gegenwart*, 1st edn, vol. 2, 1910, pp. 1257ff.

35 See E. Sulze, *Die evangelische Gemeinde*, Gotha, 1891; M. Schian, *Der gegenwartige Stand der Gemeinderogranisation in den grosseren Orten Deutschlands*, Leipzig, 1913.

36 Hölscher, *Weltgericht oder Revolution*, pp. 141ff.

37 For the Kingdom of Saxony this point was already made in Drews, *Das kirchliche Leben*, pp. 84ff.

38 For details, see Hölscher, *Weltgericht oder Revolution*, pp. 141ff.
39 See H.D. Ermel, *Die Kirchenaustrittsbewegung im Deutschen Reich
    1906–1914*, Cologne, 1971; J.C. Kaiser, 'Sozialdemokratie und
    "praktische" Religionskritik. Das Beispiel der Kirchenaustritts-
    bewegung 1878–1914', *Archiv für Sozialgeschichte*, 22, 1982, pp.
    263–98; Hugh McLeod, 'Is God dead? Irreligion and the masses',
    History Today, 42, October 1992, p. 23.
40 Cf. L. Hölscher and U. Männich-Polenz, 'Die Sozialstruktur der
    Kirchengemeinden Hannovers im 19. Jahrhundert. Eine statistische
    Analyse', *Jahrbuch der Gesellschaft für niedersächsische Kirchengeschichte*,
    88, 1990, pp. 159ff.
41 ibid., pp. 182ff.
42 See Lübbe, *Säkularisierung*; Hölscher, *Weltgericht oder Revolution*.

GUIDE TO FURTHER READING

BELGIUM

Art, Jan, *Kerkelijke Structuur en Pastorale Werking in het Bisdom Gent tussen 1830 en 1914*, Standen en Landen LXXI, Kortrijk-Heule, 1977. Very extensive study of the Catholic Church in a diocese which contained both one of Belgium's largest industrial cities and a large rural population. With Houtart and Saint Moulin, provides the best statistical analysis of religious organization and practice for nineteenth-century Belgium.

Aubert, Roger, 'L'Eglise et l'état en Belgique au XIXe siècle', *Res Publica*, X, 1968. Helpful introduction to the complicated constitutional position of the Catholic Church: autonomous, but in certain ways legally protected and privileged at the same time.

Barnich, Georges, *Le régime clérical en Belgique. L'organisation du parti catholique. La législation sociale et les oeuvres*, Brussels, 1911. Contemporary attack on Belgian Catholics' successful creation of a network of government-subsidized charitable and educational institutions. Useful both for the Liberal perspective and the rich information on Catholic social action.

Gerard, Emmanuel, (ed.) *De Christelijke arbeidersbeweging in België 1891–1991*, KADOC-Jaarboeken en Studies 11, 2 vols, Leuven, 1991. Useful chapters on most aspects of the early Catholic workers' movement.

Gerard, Emmanuel and Mampuys, Jozef (eds), *Voor Kerk en Werk. Opstellen over de geschiedenis van de christelijke arbeidersbeweging, 1886–1986*, KADOC-Jaarboeken en Studies 4, Leuven, 1986. Covers the origins and early growth of the Christian Democratic movement.

Gérin, Paul, *Les débuts de la démocratie chrétienne à Liège*, Liège, 1959. An innovative urban Catholic movement, Liégeois Christian Democrats unfortunately had little success.

Houtart, François, 'Les paroisses de Bruxelles, 1803–1951', *Bulletin de l'institut des recherches économiques et sociales*, 19: 7, 1953. Excellent study of religious practice and social change in the capital.

Jadoulle, Jean-Louis, *La pensée de l'abbé Pottier (1849–1923)*, Brussels,

289

1991. A study of the leader of the 'Liège school' which had great intellectual influence but was largely repressed by conservatives on its home territory.

Joye, Pierre and Lewin, Rosine, *L'Eglise et le mouvement ouvrier en Belgique*, Brussels, 1967. Although written from a critical perspective, provides a good overview of the church's social action.

Kittell, Allan, 'Socialist vs. Catholic in Belgium. The role of anticlericalism in the development of the Belgian left', *Historian*, XXIII, 1961. Describes how radical Liberals used anti-Catholicism to pave the way for early socialism.

Kossmann, E.H, *The Low Countries, 1780–1940*, Oxford, 1978. Provides the best overview of nineteenth-century Belgium in English.

Lamberts, Emiel (ed.), *De Kruistocht Tegen het Liberalisme. Facetten van het Ultramontanisme in België in de 19e eeuw*, KADOC-Jaarboeken en Studies 2, Leuven, 1984. Uncovers the power of ultramontanists who helped transform the established Catholic Party.

Lis, Catharina, *Social Change and the Labouring Poor: Antwerp, 1770–1860*, New Haven, Conn., 1986. Thorough study of poverty and charity in Belgium's leading port in the early Industrial Revolution.

Mallinson, Vernon, *Power and Politics in Belgian Education, 1815 to 1961*, London, 1963. Secular versus religious control over primary and secondary education was the single most divisive issue between Catholics and their Liberal and Socialist opponents.

Mercier, Cardinal Désiré-Joseph, *Modernism*, London, 1910. Provides a good introduction to the flexible defence of orthodoxy provided by a leading Thomistic scholar and, in his role as Archbishop of Mechelen, the primate of the Belgian church.

Rezsohazy, Rudolf, *Origines et formation du catholicisme social en Belgique, 1842–1909*, Leuven, 1959. Especially good on how centrist Christian Democrats fended off the attacks of conservatives and jettisoned radicals such as the abbés Daens and Pottier.

Saint Moulin, Léon de, 'Contribution à l'histoire de la déchristianisation. La pratique religieuse à Seraing depuis 1830', *Annuaire d'histoire liégeoise*, 10, 1967. This sensitive study of religious life in the premier heavy industrial city in Belgium suggests that secularization came relatively late and that, by itself, expanding the number of parishes and priests did not stop dechristianization.

Simon, Alois, *Le Parti catholique belge, 1830–1945*, Brussels, 1958. Solid history of the Catholic Party's institutional development.

Strikwerda, Carl, 'The divided class: Catholics vs. Socialists in Belgium, 1801–1914', *Comparative Studies in Society and History*, 30: 2, 1988. A comparison of Ghent and Brussels which shows how Catholic workers reacted against Socialist anticlericalism and how their leaders were able to take advantage of Socialist mistakes to create a populist movement.

Van Isacker, Karel, *Averrechtse Democratie: Gilden en de Christelijke democratie in België, 1875–1914*, Antwerp, 1959. Careful argument demonstrating how the ultramontanists' failure to revive the guilds provided a stepping stone towards a genuine Christian Democratic movement under Arthur Verhaegen.

FRANCE

Agulhon, Maurice, 'La statumanie et l'histoire', *Ethnologie française*, 8, 1978, pp. 145–72.

—- *Marianne into Battle: Republican Imagery and Symbolism in France, 1789–1880*, trans. by Janet Lloyd, Cambridge, 1981. Explores the development of civil religion in France.

Ben-Amos, Avner, 'Molding the national memory: The state funerals of the French Third Republic', Ph.D. dissertation, University of California, Berkeley, 1988.

—- 'The other world of memory: State funerals of the French Third Republic as rites of commemoration', *History and Memory*, 1, 1989, pp. 85–108.

—- 'The sacred center of power: Paris and republican state funerals', *Journal of Interdisciplinary History*, 22, 1991, pp. 27–48. The role of Paris in the development of French civil religion starting in the 1870s.

Boulard, Fernand and Rémy, Jean, *Pratique religieuse urbaine et régions culturelles*, Paris, 1968. Maps the variations in religious practice in France in the mid-twentieth century.

Charpin, Fernand, *Pratique religieuse et formation d'une grande ville. La geste du baptême et sa signification en sociologie religieuse (Marseille, 1806–1958)*, Paris, 1964. Detailed statistical analysis, but with some interpretive material as well.

Cholvy, Gérard, and Hilaire, Yves-Marie, *Histoire religieuse de la France contemporaine, 1880–1930*, Paris, 1986. Volume 2 of a series that synthesizes recent work in religious history; excellent bibliography.

Cohen, William, 'Symbols of power: Statues in nineteenth-century provincial France', *Comparative Studies in Society and History*, 31, 1989, pp. 491–513.

Daniel, Yvan, *L'équipement paroissial d'un diocèse urbain – Paris (1802–1956)*, Paris, 1957. Statistical analysis concentrating on churches and clergy.

Gadille, Jacques (ed.), *Le diocèse de Lyon*, Paris, 1983. Part of the series 'Histoire de diocèses de France'; material on the city of Lyon.

Gibson, Ralph, *A Social History of French Catholicism, 1789–1914*, New York, 1989. Comprehensive synthesis covering clergy, popular religion and the effects of modern developments, including urbanization, on Catholicism.

Hilaire, Yves-Marie, *Une chrétienté au XIXe siècle? La vie religieuse des populations du diocèse d'Arras (1840–1914)*, Villeneuve-d'Ascq, 1977. French thesis that provides a nuanced account of how social changes, including urbanization, affect religious life.

Hutton, Patrick, *The Cult of the Revolutionary Tradition: The Blanquists in Politics, 1864–1893*, Berkeley, Calif., 1986. Argues that the Blanquists were crucial in developing rituals that embodied socialist values.

Isambert, François, *Christianisme et classe ouvrière*, Paris, 1961. Fundamental work that challenges the common assumption about the irreligion of the working class.

Le Goff, Jacques and Rémond, René (eds), *Du roi très chrétien à la laïcité républicaine (XVIIIe–XIXe siècle)*, vol. 3 of *Histoire de la France religieuse*, Paris, 1991. Includes essays by Philippe Boutry, Claude Langlois and Michel Vovelle that cover developments in urban France.

Palanque, Jean-Rémy (ed.), *Le diocèse de Marseille*, Paris, 1967. Part of the series 'Histoire de diocèses de France'; includes the entire diocese, but has extensive material on the city of Marseille.

Pierrard, Pierre, *L'Eglise et les ouvriers en France (1840–1940)*, Paris, 1984. A survey generally critical of the church and pessimistic about the religious state of the urban working class.

Rosenbaum-Dondaine, Catherine, *L'Image de piété en France, 1814–1914*, Paris, 1984. Traces the development of holy cards; excellent selection of illustrations.

Smith, Bonnie, *Ladies of the Leisure Class – The Bourgeoises of Northern France in the Nineteenth Century*, Princeton, NJ, 1981. Includes chapter on religion that relates Catholicism to the family and social values of middle-class women.

GERMANY

Social-historical research on the relationship between religion and urbanisation has still not developed very far in Germany. The following works, listed in order of publication, offer some initial suggestions:

Oettingen, A. von, *Die Moralstatistik in ihrer Bedeutung für eine christliche Sozialethik*, 3rd edition, Erlangen, 1882. A fundamental statistical study of the changes in church life as evaluated by the orthodox wing of the church.

Drews, P. (ed.), 'Das kirchliche Leben der evangelischen Landeskirchen in Deutschland', Tübingen, 1902–19. A series of seven studies of the major German territorial churches outside Prussia. A pioneering work that has not yet been superseded.

Heitmann, J., *Grosstadt und Religion*, 3 vols, Hamburg, 1913–20. Lively documentation of the religious variety in German cities before the First World War.

Meyer, P., 'Die Kirchengemeinden Hannovers in der werdenden Grosstadt, 1830–1890', Stadtkirchenausschuss Hannover (ed.), *Studien zur Kirchengeschichte der Stadt Hannover*, Hanover, 1933, pp. 283–367. Detailed account of the changes in church life in a north German city.

Hübner, J., *Geschichte der evangelisch-lutherischen Gemeinde Barmen-Elberfeld, 1777–1952*, Wuppertal, 1952. Account of the changes in church life in a religiously turbulent industrial region.

Köllmann, W., *Sozialgeschichte der Stadt Barmen im 19. Jahrhundert*, Tübingen, 1960. An early social-historical account.

Kleinstuck, E., 'Geist und Kirche in Frankfurt von der Aufklärung und Erweckung bis zum Historismus, 1750–1850', *Jahrbuch der hessischen kirchengeschichtlichen Vereinigung*, 12, 1961, pp. 35–70. An account in terms of intellectual history of the religious crisis following the Enlightenment.

Vorländer, H., *Evangelische Kirche und soziale Frage in der werdenden Industriegrosstadt Elberfeld*, Düsseldorf, 1963. Early study of the relationship between church, Social Democracy and urbanization in a religiously turbulent region.

Marbach, R., *Säkularisierung und sozialer Wandel im 19. Jahrhundert. Die Stellung von Geistlichen zu Entkirchlichung und Entchristlichung in einem Bezirk der hannoverschen Landeskirche*, Göttingen, 1978. A detailed study with limited perspectives.

Greschat, M., *Das Zeitalter der industriellen Revolution. Das Christentum vor der Moderne*, Stuttgart, 1980. Heavy emphasis on social–political factors.

Groh, J., *Nineteenth Century German Protestantism. The Church as Social Model*, Washington, DC, 1982. A good overview.

Cordes, C., *Geschichte der Kirchengemeinden der evangelisch-lutherischen Landeskirche Hannovers, 1848–1980*, Hanover, 1983. A good positive account.

Nipperdey, T., *Deutsche Geschichte, 1806–1918*, 2 vols, Munich, 1983–90. Includes the best overview of German Protestantism and Catholicism in this period.

Söldner, L., 'Die evangelischen Kirchengemeinden Essens in den sozialen Spannungen der Zeit von 1870 bis 1914', *Monatshefte für evangelische Kirchengeschichte des Rheinlands*, 33, 1984, pp. 137–75. An account of the characteristic socially-conservative standpoint of the church in the miners' strikes of 1889 and 1905.

Brakelmann, G., *Ruhrgebiets-Protestantismus*, Bielefeld, 1987.

Hölscher, L., *Weltgericht oder Revolution. Protestantische und sozialistische Zukunftsvorstellungen im Kaiserreich*, Stuttgart, 1989. Includes a statistical and social–political analysis of alienation from the church in the *Kaiserreich* period, with the emphasis on the labour movement.

—— 'Die Religion des Bürgers. Bürgerliche Frömmigkeit und protestantische Kirche im 19. Jahrhundert', *Historische Zeitschrift*, 250, 1990, pp. 595–630. Fundamental. Uses a lot of new material.

Hölscher, L. and Männich-Polenz, U., 'Die Sozialstruktur der Kirchengemeinden Hannovers im 19. Jahrhundert. Eine statistische Analyse', *Jahrbuch der Gesellschaft für niedersächsische Kirchengeschichte*, 88, 1990, pp. 159ff. The most intensive analysis yet made of religious statistics relating to alienation from the church in a German Protestant city of the nineteenth century.

Elm, K. and Loock, H.-D. (eds.), *Seelsorge und Diakonie in Berlin. Beiträge zum Verhältnis von Kirche und Grosstadt im 19. und beginnenden 20. Jahrhundert*, Berlin, 1990.

McLeod, H., 'Secular cities? Berlin, London and New York in the later nineteenth and early twentieth centuries', in S. Bruce (ed.), *Religion and Modernization: Sociologists and Historians debate the Secularization Thesis*, Oxford, 1992, pp. 61–88.

Holscher, L., 'Bürgerliche Religiosität im protestantischen Deutschland des 19. Jahrhunderts', in W. Schieder (ed.), *Religion und Gesellschaft im 19. Jahrhundert*, Stuttgart, 1994. An overview.

GREAT BRITAIN

Wickham, E.R., *Church and People in an Industrial City*, London, 1957.
Still valuable pioneering study of Sheffield.

Inglis, K.S., 'Patterns of religious worship in 1851', *Journal of Ecclesiastical
History*, 11, 1960, pp. 74–86. Emphasizes low church attendance in
industrial towns.

——*Churches and the Working Classes in Victorian England*, London, 1963.
Highly influential. Stronger on 'churches' than 'working classes'.

Davies, E.T., *Religion in the Industrial Revolution in South Wales*, Cardiff,
1965. Pioneering study of a still underresearched topic.

Meacham, Standish, 'The church in the Victorian City', *Victorian Studies*,
11, 1968, pp. 359–78. A pessimistic assessment, typical of the historical orthodoxy of that time.

Coleman, B.I., 'Church extension movement in London c. 1800–1860',
Ph.D. thesis, University of Cambridge, 1968. Good discussion of
Anglican debate over, and response to, urban religious crisis.

Kent, J.H.S., 'The role of religion in the cultural structure of the later
Victorian city', *Transactions of the Royal Historical Society*, 5th series, 23,
1973, pp. 153–73. Good synthesis of early work in this area.

Dyos, H.J. and Wolff, M. (eds), *The Victorian City*, 2 vols, London, 1973,
vol, 2. An authoritative and lavishly illustrated compendium, with four
chapters on religion.

McLeod, Hugh, 'Class, community and region: The religious geography of
nineteenth-century England', in Michael Hill (ed.), *A Sociological
Yearbook of Religion in Britain*, vol. 6, London, 1973, pp. 29–72. Argues
that Inglis overstated urban–rural differences and understated regional
differences.

McLaren, A.A., *Religion and Social Class: The Disruption Years in Aberdeen*,
London, 1974. A classic of Marxist-inclined social history.

McLeod, Hugh, *Class and Religion in the late Victorian City*, London,
1974. Emphasizes class differences in religious participation and mentality in London.

Yeo, Stephen, *Religion and Voluntary Organisations in Crisis*, London,
1976. Focuses mainly on Reading c. 1890–1914. The best attempt to
relate religious change to changes in the economy.

Gilbert, A.D., *Religion and Society in Industrial Society: Church, Chapel and
Social Change 1740–1914*, London, 1976. A major synthesis. Argues
that in the short term industrialization favoured religious growth, but
in the longer term it led to secularization.

Williams, Bill, *The Making of Manchester Jewry 1740–1875*, Manchester,
1976. The most thorough study of a Jewish community in an English
city.

Crossick, Geoffrey (ed.), *The Lower Middle Class in Britain 1870–1914*,
London, 1977. Includes two chapters on religion.

Hillis, Peter, 'Presbyterianism and social class in mid-nineteenth-century
Glasgow: A study of nine churches', *Journal of Ecclesiastical History*, 32,
1981, pp. 47–64. A critique of MacLaren.

Cox, Jeffrey, *English Churches in a Secular Society: Lambeth 1870–1930*,

Oxford, 1982. Excellent study of south London, which has strongly influenced recent 'revisionist' research.

Phillips, Paul T., *The Sectarian Spirit*, Toronto, 1982. Church v. chapel in Lancashire towns.

Swift, Roger and Gilley, Sheridan (eds), *The Irish in the Victorian City*, London, 1985. Lively discussion of Catholicism.

Endelman, Todd, 'Communal solidarity among the Jewish elite of Victorian London', *Victorian Studies*, 28, 1985, pp. 491–526. One of several fine studies by Endelman of middle- and upper-class Jews in English cities.

Lewis, Donald M., *Lighten their Darkness: The Evangelical Mission to Working Class London 1828–1860*, New York, 1986. Thorough study of door-to-door evangelism.

Feldman, David, 'Immigrants and workers, Englishmen and Jews: Jewish immigrants to the East End of London c. 1880–1906', Ph.D. thesis, University of Cambridge, 1986. Best study of working-class Jews.

Brown, Callum G., *The Social History of Religion in Scotland since 1730*, London, 1987. Emphasizes the urban dimension.

Smith, Mark, 'Religion in industrial society: Oldham and Saddleworth 1780–1865', D.Phil. thesis, University of Oxford, 1987. Strongly 'revisionist'. (in press)

Bartlett, Alan, 'The churches in Bermondsey 1880–1939', Ph.D. thesis, University of Birmingham, 1987. Comprehensive study of organized religion in a working-class district of London.

Davidoff, Leonore and Hall, Catherine, *Family Fortunes: Men and Women of the English Middle Class 1780–1850*, London, 1987. Good discussion of gender and religion.

Burman, Rickie, 'Women in Jewish religious life: Manchester 1880–1930', in Jim Obelkevich, Lyndal Roper and Raphael Samuel (eds), *Disciplines of Faith*, London, 1987. An important contribution to an outstanding collection of papers on the social history of religion.

Jones, I.G., *Communities: Essays on the Social History of Victorian Wales*, Llandysil, 1987. Considerable emphasis on religion.

Brown, Callum G., 'Did urbanization secularize Britain?', *Urban History Yearbook*, 1988, pp. 1–14. Clearest statement of the 'revisionist' interpretation.

Jeremy, David (ed.), *Business and Religion*, Aldershot, 1988. Essays on the religious role of nineteenth-century businessmen.

McCalman, Iain, *Radical Underworld: Prophets, Revolutionaries and Pornographers in London 1795–1840*, Cambridge, 1988. A vivid portrait of 'alternative' London, including considerable discussion of freethought.

Green, Simon, 'Religion and the industrial town with special reference to the West Riding of Yorkshire c. 1870–1920', D.Phil. thesis, University of Oxford, 1989. One of the best discussions of the organizational and financial aspects of Victorian church life.

Koditschek, Theodore, *Class Formation in Urban–Industrial Society: Bradford 1750–1850*, Cambridge, 1990. Includes good discussion of religious divisions in the town's élite.

Morris, J.N., *Religion and Urban Change: Croydon 1840–1914*, Woodbridge, 1992. Emphasizes key role of local middle-class élite.

GUIDE TO FURTHER READING

Fielding, Steven, *Class and Ethnicity: Irish Catholics in England 1880–1939*, Buckingham, 1993. A good synthesis, illustrated by local material from Manchester.

Williams, Sarah, 'Religious belief and popular culture: A study of the south London borough of Southwark 1880–1939', D.Phil. thesis, University of Oxford, 1993. A pioneering study, drawing heavily on oral history.

McLeod, Hugh, *Poverty and Piety: Working Class Religion in Berlin, London and New York 1870–1914*, New York, 1994.

IRELAND

There is no general history of religion and urbanization in nineteenth-century Ireland nor are there any extensive surveys of religion in any Irish town or city in this period. The best place to start, therefore, is with S. Connolly's superb pamphlet *Religion and Society in Nineteenth-Century Ireland*, Dundalk, 1985, which supplies both a shrewd historiographical analysis and an extensive bibliography.

For more recent interpretations of urbanization and religious change see the articles by L.J. Proudfoot ('Regionalism and localism: Religious change and social protest, c. 1700 to c. 1900') and S.A. Royle ('Industrialization, urbanization and urban society in post-famine Ireland c. 1850–1921') in B.J. Graham and L.J. Proudfoot (eds), *An Historical Geography of Ireland*, London, 1993. The two largest cities in Ireland, Dublin and Belfast, are well served by good social histories (including religion) of the Victorian era. They are M.E. Daly, *Dublin – the Deposed Capital*, Cork, 1984; and E. Jones, *A Social Geography of Belfast*, London, 1960.

D. Keenan, *The Catholic Church in Nineteenth-Century Ireland: A Sociological Study*, Dublin, 1983, is a controversial reappraisal of the Roman Catholic devotional revolution based chiefly on evidence from the city and diocese of Dublin. The best account of Roman Catholicism in Belfast in the Victorian period, from an admittedly sympathetic perspective, is to be found in A. Macauley's biography of *Patrick Dorrian, Bishop of Down and Connor 1865–1885*, Dublin, 1987. Protestantism in Belfast is best followed through the pages of D. Hempton and M. Hill, *Evangelical Protestantism in Ulster Society 1740–1890*, London, 1992. Belfast also has the advantage of several excellent collections of essays which are listed in n. 1, p. 161 and of an authoritative treatment of religious sectarianism by S.E. Baker, 'Orange and Green', in H.J. Dyos and M. Wolff (eds), *The Victorian City*, 2 vols, London, 1973, vol. 2.

For information on the economic, social and religious structures of other Irish towns and cities, including Cork and Armagh, see D. Harkness and M. O'Dowd (eds), *The Town in Ireland*, Belfast, 1981. For a suggestive treatment of the wider themes of tradition and identity in nineteenth-century Ireland see L.M. Cullen, *The Emergence of Modern Ireland 1600–1900*, London, 1981. Finally, A.C. Hepburn and B. Collins, 'Industrial society: The structure of Belfast, 1901', in P. Roebuck (ed.), *Plantation to Partition*, Belfast, 1981, is a good example of what can be achieved by the rigorous application of statistical methods on census data.

RUSSIA

Since the pre-revolutionary intelligentsia was predominantly hostile to the Orthodox Church, and the Soviet authorities subsequently relegated study of religious history to the ideologically predetermined category of 'scientific atheism', imperial Russia is regrettably unique among European *ancien régimes* in the feebleness of its ecclesiastical scholarship. Nineteenth-century churchmen were prolific writers, but neither their literary output nor their pastoral work has been subject to much critical scrutiny, even in the west, where Orthodoxy retains its partially misleading reputation for mystical other-worldliness. If studies of popular belief are uncommon, works concentrating on urban religion are even rarer (an imbalance which partly reflects the natural priorities of the church in what was a predominantly peasant society). There is some important doctoral work in progress, most notably by Page Herrlinger at the University of California, Berkeley, who is writing on workers and religion in St Petersburg and Moscow. But the published literature remains fragmentary, save for the venerable John S. Curtiss, *Church and State in Russia: The Last Years of the Empire, 1900–1917*, New York, 1940, which is little concerned with urban affairs and beginning to show its age. The best place to start is therefore with Gregory L. Freeze, who surveys Orthodox efforts to establish a dialogue with secular intellectuals in '"Going to the intelligentsia": The church and its urban mission in post-reform Russia', in Edith W. Clowes, Samuel D. Kassow and James L. West (eds), *Between Tsar and People: Educated Society and the Quest for Public Identity in Late Imperial Russia*, Princeton, NJ, 1991, pp. 215–32. For a detailed account of the most important forum, see the magnificent monograph by Jutta Scherrer, 'Die Petersburger religiös-philosophischen Vereinigungen', *Forschungen zur Osteuropäischen Geschichte*, vol. 19, Berlin, 1973, which has more to say about the intelligentsia than about the churchmen who participated in these assemblies. Daniel R. Brower, *The Russian City between Tradition and Modernity, 1850–1900*, Berkeley, Calif., 1990, emphasizes the challenges the urban environment posed for Orthodox religion; while Simon Dixon, 'The church's social role in St Petersburg, 1880–1914', in Geoffrey A. Hosking (ed.), *Church, Nation and State in Russia and Ukraine*, London, 1991, pp. 167–92, pays more attention to the church's response. P.N. Zyrianov, *Pravoslavnaia tserkov' v bor'be s revoliutsiei 1905–1907gg.*, Moscow, 1984, touches on urban affairs in the context of a rather unsophisticated study of the church's counter-revolutionary commitment. For a more nuanced account, see John H.M. Geekie, 'The church and politics in Russia, 1905–1917: A study of the political behaviour of the Russian Orthodox clergy in the reign of Nicholas II', Ph.D. dissertation, University of East Anglia, 1976. Recent articles include Reginald E. Zelnik, 'To the unaccustomed eye: religion and irreligion in the experience of St. Petersburg workers in the 1870s', in Robert P. Hughes and Irina Paperno (eds), *Christianity and the Eastern Slavs, vol. II: Russian Culture in Modern Times (California Slavic Studies, vol. XVII)*, Berkeley, CA, 1994, pp. 49–82; and Mark Steinberg, 'Workers on the cross: religious imagination in the writings of Russian workers, 1910–1924', *Russian Review*, 53(2), 1994, pp. 213–39.

SPAIN

Andrés-Gallego, J., *Pensamiento y acción social de la Iglesia en España*, Madrid, 1984. A comprehensive and fundamental study of the ideas and organizational initiatives of Spanish Social Catholicism between the mid-nineteenth and early twentieth centuries. It provides useful information, both statistical and sociological, on the urban distribution of Catholic labour organizations as well as a balanced assessment of the reasons behind their failure.

Arbeola, V.M., *Aquella España católica*, Salamanca, 1975. A series of general essays dealing with the intractable problems confronting the late nineteenth- and early twentieth-century church. Of particular interest are those focusing on dechristianization, the church and the working-class and the development of popular anticlericalism.

Benavides Gómez, D. *Democracia y cristianismo en la España de la Restauración, 1875–1931*, Madrid, 1978. An overview of the church's attempt to come to terms with the political system created by the Restoration state and to devise a new strategy to confront the alienation of urban workers through Catholic labour organizations. Strongly critical of those responsible for the failure of Social Catholicism, the study provides a clear summary of its stormy history.

Callahan, W.J., *Church, Politics and Society in Spain, 1750–1874*, Cambridge, Mass., 1984. Although a general study of the transition experienced by the church during the transition from the absolute monarchy of the eighteenth century to the liberalism of the nineteenth, there is some discussion of the first signs of religious slippage in urban areas.

——'Was Spain Catholic?', *Revista Canadiense de Estudios Hispánicos*, 8: 22, 1984, pp. 159–82. Focuses on the beginnings and later development of both urban and rural dechristianization from 1850 to 1931.

——'The Spanish parish clergy, 1874–1930', *Catholic Historical Review*, 75: 3, 1989, pp. 405–22. A study of the obstacles to effective pastoral work in town and country created by the inflexible organizational structure of the parochial clergy.

Carballo, F. and Magariños, A., *La Iglesia en la Galicia contemporánea: Análisis histórico y teológico del periodo 1931–36*, Madrid, 1978. Although concentrating on the period of the Second Republic, this study provides a wealth of information on how well or badly the church fulfilled its religious mission in the largely rural dioceses of this region during the early twentieth century. In many respects, the monograph stands alone in the literature for its description of religiosity and its sociological background at the grass roots. It is regrettable that similar studies have not been done for the country's large cities.

Cárcel Ortí, V., *Historia de la Iglesia de Valencia*, 2 vols, Valencia, 1986. A good example of a superior diocesan history which provides useful information on the institutional development of the church in a region in which the church found itself embroiled in a constant round of anticlerical battles during the late nineteenth and early twentieth centuries.

Castillo, J.J., *El sindicalismo amarillo en España: Aportación al estudio del catolicismo social español, 1912–1923*, Madrid, 1977. A study of the Catholic labour movement in the period when it took on an increasingly militant role in its opposition towards socialist unions.

Christian, W.A., *Moving Crucifixes in Modern Spain*, Princeton, NJ, 1992. A monograph which focuses on the emergence of a new cult, the moving crucifix of Limpias, in 1919. The cult developed with distinct, conservative overtones during a period of intense social tension. Although largely a rural phenomenon, the cult provides a good example of the politicized devotion which often aroused the hostility of working-class populations.

Jiménez Duque, B., *La espiritualidad en el siglo XIX español*, Madrid, 1974. Although written from a clerical perspective and with little attention paid to the sociological origins of religious alienation, this study is one of the few providing detailed information for the nineteenth century on the elaborate devotional world of the time.

Lannon, F., *Privilege, Persecution and Prophecy: The Catholic Church in Spain, 1875–1975*, Oxford, 1987. An excellent general history providing a valuable discussion of the complex world of religious practice and the church's identification with the bourgeoise élites dominating state and society until 1931. The author's description of the church's involvement in education and charitable assistance is particularly useful for the church's role in urban areas.

Martí, C., *L'Església de Barcelona, 1850–1857*, Barcelona, 1984. One of the few well-documented studies providing a detailed analysis of a local church with special attention given to its organization and religious strategy. There is a brief discussion of the beginnings of religious alienation, although a major study of the progress of dechristianization in the country's industrial centre remains to be written.

Massot i Muntaner, J., *L'Església catalana al segle XX*, Barcelona, 1975. A useful study of the so-called Catholic revival in Catalonia during the twentieth century. Emphasis is placed on a variety of clerical and lay initiatives. The author does not address, however, the fundamental problem of why liturgical, organizational and intellectual renewal failed to reverse the advance of anticlericalism and dechristianization in the region.

Montero Garcia, F., *El primer catolicismo social y la 'Rerum Novarum' en España, 1889–1902*, Madrid, 1983. A well-documented monograph which provides a detailed account of the church's tentative and often uncertain attempt to deal with the problem of the urban workers provoked by Leo XIII's encyclical.

Payne, S.G., *Spanish Catholicism: An Historical Review*, Madison, Wisc., 1984. A concise and useful survey of Catholicism from the Middle Ages to the twentieth century with some consideration given to the problem of religious alienation and the church's efforts to deal with it.

Reig, Ramiro, *Blasquistas y clericales: la lucha por la ciudad en la Valencia de 1900*, Valencia, 1986. Primarily a study of the political struggle between the Catholic right and the populist republicanism of Vicente Blasco Ibáñez. It does, however, give some attention to the appeal of this strongly anticlerical party among the city's workers.

Ullman, J.C., *The Tragic Week: A Study of Anticlericalism in Spain, 1875–1912*, Cambridge, Mass., 1968. Although primarily a study of the events surrounding the incendiary attacks on churches and religious institutions in Barcelona during August 1909, the monograph describes the growth of anticlericalism and its connection to the populist republicanism of Alejandro Lerroux among the city's urban workers in the years preceding the worst example of violence directed against the church between 1834–5 and 1930.

Winston, C.M., *Workers and the Right in Spain, 1900–1936*, Princeton, NJ, 1985. A well-documented monograph which provides the best treatment of the work of Gabriel Palau and the ASP available in either English or Spanish.

INDEX

Denmark 5
Denvir, Bishop C. 150
Despierres 182
DeWinne, A. 79
DeWitte, P. 67
Dissent *see* free churches
Dominicans 54, 56, 85
Dorrian, Bishop P. 150–1
Doutreloux, Bishop V. 72–3
Dresden 271
Drew, T. 153
Dreyfus Affair 175
drinking places 180–1, 232
Dronke, E. 8–9, 23
Drozdov, Fr 135
Dublin 2, 27
Dubois, P. 145
Düsseldorf 28

Edinburgh 252
education 60–1, 66, 68, 173, 272, 280
Ehrenfeuchter, F. 97
employers and church 10, 55–6, 58, 72, 98–9, 108, 124, 129, 158, 171, 203, 246, 268
Encausse, G. 177–8
Engels, F. 8
England 2, 6, 9, 25, 63, 129, 157, 167, 191–212, 216–34, 245, 247, 249, 252
Enlightenment 3, 26, 94, 240, 264, 266–7, 270–3, 284
epidemics 23, 123
Espartero, General 45
Essen 5
Evangelical Social Congress 13
Exeter 252
extreme unction 51, 168

Ferré, T. 182
Flammarion, C. 176
Flanders 62–5, 70, 73, 78–80, 83, 87
France 3–7, 17, 20–1, 26–7, 30, 34–6, 54, 62–3, 65–7, 69, 82–4, 165–85, 240, 267
Francotte, H. 73, 75
Frankfurt am Main 96, 272

Frederick I 11
Frederick II 13
Frederick William I 11
Frederick William III 11
Frederick William IV 11
free churches: in Britain 2, 5–6, 8, 18, 21, 25, 30, 192–212, 244–7; in Germany 280; in Netherlands 2, 25; in Russia 25–6; in Sweden 18
Freeman, A. 200
Freeze, G. 133
French Revolution 4, 6–7, 21, 184, 240, 274
funerals 14, 18, 95, 97, 106, 109, 112, 168–70, 181–3, 213, 224, 263, 278, 280–1

Gafo, J. 57
Galicia 20
Gapon, Fr 119, 123
Gateshead 252
Geertz, C. 166
Geneva 24
George V of Hanover 91, 93–4, 97–9
Gerard, P. 56–7
German Catholics 25
Germany 2, 6, 16–17, 19–20, 23, 25, 27, 30, 56, 62, 69, 72, 84, 90–113, 175, 198, 240, 263–85
Ghent 62, 65–8, 70–82, 87
Gibson, R. 174
Gilbert, A.D. 243
Gladstone, W.E. 155
Glasgow 5, 8, 145, 160, 249, 251, 253–4
Goethe, J.W. 13
Gorchakov, M.I. 135
Gothenberg 29
Göttingen University 97
Goulden, Rev. A.B. 227–8
Greenock 252
Guesde, J. 180
Guiaita, S. de 177
Guibert, Archbishop 170, 184
Guillaume 179
Guisasola, Archbishop 53

Habay 182
Hainault 77
Halifax 251
Hamburg 3, 16, 19, 23, 95, 97,
 99, 101, 103–4, 111, 116–17,
 271–2, 279
Hammond, J.L. and B. 244
Hanover 5, 6, 90–113, 278
Harmel, L. 174
Harper, Rev. J. 225
Harvest Festival 224
Hay, Rev W.R. 7
Heine, H. 13
Helleputte, G. 70
Henderson, W. 221
Herranz Establés, Fr H. 50, 52
historiography of urban religion
 9–10, 15, 18, 119–20, 136,
 165–6, 216–17, 239–42
Hobsbawm, E.J. 246
Horta, V. 82
Hugo, V. 183
Hull 148
Hungary 22
Hunter, Bishop L. 205–7
Huysmans, J.K. 177

icons 127
Iglesias, P. 53
illegitimacy 134, 268
Ipswich 252
Ireland 19, 63, 129, 145–61
Irish migrants 251, 253–4
irreligion 3, 9, 18, 50–1, 270;
 freethought organisations 281;
 growth of unbelief 10, 13, 26,
 96, 264–5; ignorance of religion
 51–2; resignation from church
 12, 23, 112, 280; secular rites
 of passage 181–3
Isidor, Metropolitan 125, 130
Italian migrants 24
Italy 5, 6, 82, 267

Jaurès, J. 180, 188
Jephson, Rev A. 224
Jesuits 3, 28, 44, 54, 58, 65
Jews 2, 6, 10, 14, 21–2, 24–6, 30,
 61, 92, 174–5, 253, 280

Joseph II 67, 84
Joutard, P. 185

Kanatchikoff, S. 122
Kardec, A. 175
Keeble, Rev. S.E. 200–1
Kent, J. 240
Kilkenny 153
Kirill, Bishop 132
Kondrat'ev, Fr E. 124–5
Kurth, G. 72, 78

Labre, St Benoît 174
Labour Party (UK) 206, 209
Laffitte, P. 184
Lambsdorff, V.N. 130
Lamennais, F. 66, 84
Langlois, C. 173
Lantsherre, C. de 76
Latimer, R. 119, 135–6
Laughland, Rev J. 201–2
Le Mans 168
Leeds 3, 148
Leicester 20
Leiden 39
Leo XIII 45, 72
Leopold II 73
Leroux, P. 180
Leroy-Beaulieu, P. 181
Lerroux, A. 53
Lestra, Mme 173
Leymarie 176
Liberal Party (Belgium) 64, 66,
 68–79, 85
Liberal Party (Spain) 47
Liberal Party (UK) 200, 206, 209
Liberal-Conservative party (Spain)
 47
Liberalism and church 5–7, 11,
 13, 15, 25, 28, 45, 48, 61, 279
Liège 62, 67, 69–83, 86, 88
Lille 173
Limburg 77
Limerick 153
Limoges 18, 168
Linden 91–2, 97–9, 104–5,
 108–11, 113
linguistic division: in Belgium
 62–4, 79–80; in Scotland 251

Obelkevich, J. 244
occult 176–8
O'Connell, D. 151, 154
Odessa 30
Old Believers 2, 124, 130
Old Castile 51, 54, 60
Oldham 252
Ommanney, Rev. G.C. 197, 205
Oporto 59
Orange Order 151–4, 156–9
Ornatskii, Fr 128
Orsat, Mme 176–7
Orthodoxy 1, 6, 25, 119–36
Oviedo 56, 58

Paladii, Metropolitan 127, 130
Palau, Bishop A. 43, 50
Palau, F. 44
Palau, G. 55–7
Panina, Countess 122
Papkov, A.A. 132–3
Paris 1, 5, 16–19, 26, 30, 59, 165, 168–70, 172–8, 181–6, 189
Paris Commune 165, 169, 182
parish system: in Belgium 67, 73; in Germany 92–5, 97–9, 278–9; in Russia 127–9, 132; in Spain 49, 59; parish elections 92–3, 130
Parnell, C. 151, 155
Peladan, J. 177
Périgueux 168
Perth 252
Peterloo massacre 7
Petrov, Fr G. 124
Petrov, G.M. 127
Pierrard, P. 180
Pirenne, H. 72
Plymouth 20
Plymouth Brethren 203
Pobedonostsev, K.P. 125
Poland 22
popular religion 22, 120, 123, 127, 216–34
Portugal 1, 6, 36
Pottier, A. 72–5, 78
Práxedes Sagasta 47
Presbyterians 27, 150, 203, 205, 207, 211

Preston 252
Progressives (Spain) 45–6
prostitution 134
Protestantism: anti-Catholicism 149–50, 153, 156; conservative 94, 112; evangelical 150, 153, 156, 192, 195, 209, 245–6; liberal 25, 93–5, 112, 115, 117, 195–6, 198, 275–6; revival movements 95, 149, 250, 274; social gospel 195–6, 198–203; see also entries for specific denominations
Prussia 9–10, 13, 28, 91, 93, 96, 99, 107, 270

Quebec 83
Quimper 168

Reading 252
Reay, B. 233
Reformed churches 17, 21, 92; see also Church of Scotland, Congregationalists, Presbyterians
Renkin, J. 76
Rerum Novarum 45, 48, 72
Rhine/Ruhr industrial region 19–20, 22, 83, 97
Richet, C. 176
rites of passage 14, 17–18, 22, 51, 112–13, 175, 181–2; see also baptism, confirmation, funerals, irreligion, weddings
Rollinat, M. 178
Roman Catholicism: in Belgium 61–83; in France 165–85; in Hanover 92; in Ireland 145–61; in London 231; in Spain 43–58; in early modern period 1–3, 64–5; Christian Democrats 68–83, 85, 88; conservative 6–7, 28, 47–8, 52–3, 77–8; forms of devotion 1–2, 51–2, 68, 151, 171–2; liberal 25; organisations 67–83, 174, 275, 280; religious orders 1, 20, 28, 44, 48–9, 54, 60, 65, 151, 172, 269, 278; ultramontane 30, 51, 68, 73–4, 275